SOVIET AIRMEN IN THE SPANISH CIVIL WAR

1936-1939

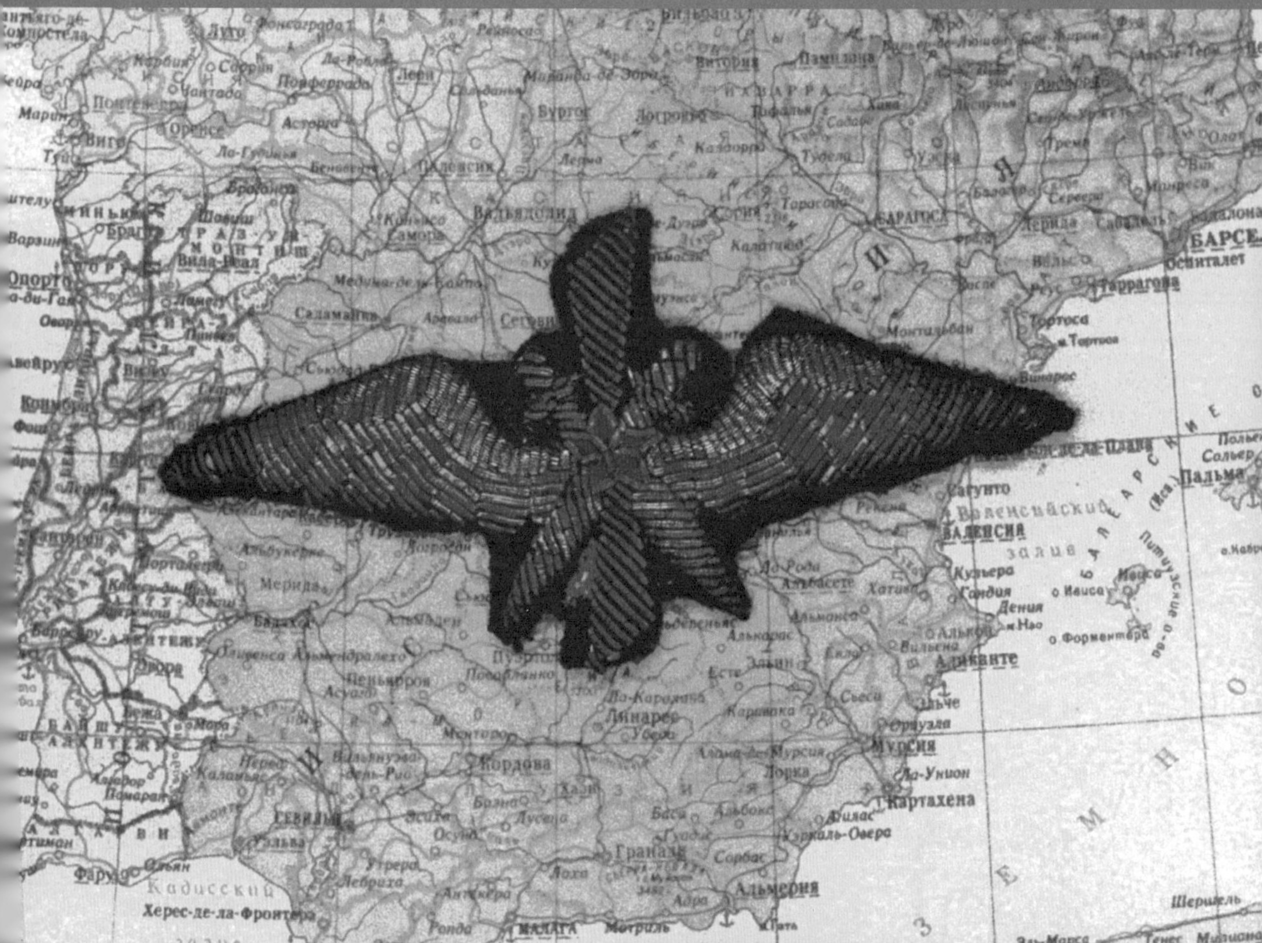

PAUL WHELAN

Schiffer Publishing Ltd®
4880 Lower Valley Road • Atglen, PA 19310

Library of Congress Control Number: 2014943109

Designed by Justin Watkinson
Type set in Zurich BT/Minion Pro

ISBN: 978-0-7643-4633-0
Printed in China

Published by Schiffer Publishing, Ltd.
4880 Lower Valley Road
Atglen, PA 19310
Phone: (610) 593-1777; Fax: (610) 593-2002
E-mail: Info@schifferbooks.com

Note on pronunciation

Those beginning with the letter E are pronounced with a Ye sound like yeh. So the name written as Evgeni would sound like Yevgeni or the name Evsev'ev would pronounce like Yesev'yev. But if there is Ë in the name, then it is pronounced as Yo as in york. So a name like Erëmenko would sound like Yeryomenko or Semen would be Semyon. Those names written with the Kh are sounded with an almost silent K, so Khovanskii would pronounce like Hovanskii.

CONTENTS

INTRODUCTION

In the afternoon of 17 July 1936, in Spanish Morocco, the Tercio or Foreign Legion rose in revolt against the Spanish Government of the Popular Front. They seized all the airports, town halls, government buildings and union halls. They executed all military officers and civilian leaders who opposed them. By the next day the fighting had spread to mainland Spain, where the Rebels took control of Sevilla, Granada and Cordoba. The Army, together with several right wing groups such as the Falange, also tried to take control of Madrid and Barcelona, but were beaten back by Troops and Guarda Civil still loyal to the Government along with workers from the trade Unions. The war then proceeded on somewhat slowly, with both sides requesting military supplies from other Countries. The rebels or nationalists sent emissaries to Germany and Italy asking for aircraft and weapons while the Republic asked France. But fear of a widening war caused France and Britain to come up with a plan called "non intervention," which most of the European countries joined. This was to limit the war to Spain and not sell either side war material. Had this plan been strictly adhered to, it may well have caused the two sides to come to some kind of agreement. Unfortunately, both Germany and Italy sent the rebels aircraft, weapons and personnel within weeks of the outbreak. By the end of the first week in August German and Italian aircraft had arrived in Spain and were ferrying troops from Morocco to the mainland. On the other side, the Republicans, after first receiving some aircraft from France, were basically cut off and had to try buying the things they needed on the black market, for which they paid heavy prices and for the most part only received old junk. They even had to search for new supplies of oil and gasoline. Texaco, Spain's major supplier, refused to sell to the Republic, but supplied the Rebels on credit. The Republic asked the Soviet Union for help on 25 July, to which the Soviets initially offered to supply nonmilitary supplies plus oil and gasoline. As time went by, with no ending of the supplies sent by Germany and Italy to the rebels, the Soviets told the Non Intervention Committee that they could no longer feel constrained from aiding the Republic.

On the 29th of September 1936 the Soviet Union finally made the decision to aid the Spanish Republic.[1] Soon they began sending not only arms and material, but also military personnel, who would then generally serve for a six-month period.[2] These men initially traveled in large groups, as is the case of those who arrived in October-November 1936. These SB, I-16, I-15 and SSS crews and their support teams were dispatched along with their aircraft. Upon arrival, everyone pitched in to assemble the aircraft and the groups into a complete fighting force. Subsequent replacements arrived in smaller groups or even singly. Most came by sea, from the Black Sea ports, and traveled across the Mediterranean, or from northern ports in the Soviet Union like Leningrad or Murmansk. To avoid detection, the ships used were altered or camouflaged to resemble completely different vessels.[3] These were the same routes used to deliver military supplies and the southern route through the Med. eventually had to be closed due to problems with Italian submarines. They then came on the northern route arriving at the French ports of La Havre and Bordeaux, and then went by train across France to Spain. Some of the replacements in 1937 also traveled by train from Moscow to Paris, and then by either train or plane went into Spain. This mode of travel was also somewhat dangerous since the Authorities in the countries they crossed through were very vigilant in their watch for men going to Spain. All of these Soviet military traveled with false identities and passports. Still some were caught and made to return to the USSR, or try again to get to Spain.[4]

Beginning in late October, with the introduction of the SB bombers, and early November 1936, with the I-15 and I-16 fighters, the Soviet airmen made up a large percentage of the Republican Air Force. These proportions remained steady until summer 1937, when the first group of Spanish airmen trained in the USSR returned to Spain. As more trained Spaniards returned, the percentage of Soviets continued to shrink. By August 1938, there were only two Soviet commanded I-16 fighter and one SB bomber Escuadrillas operating in Spain. These were all withdrawn by late October 1938, with the SB Escuadrilla the last to go. They had initially come in November 1936 at a very critical time for the Republic: the Nationalist forces were on the outskirts of Madrid and poised to take the city. The Soviets flyers were able to give the Republicans a short

period of air superiority until late spring 1937. After that the massive aid given to Franco by Germany and Italy coupled with a slowing down of Soviet aid, eventually reduced the Republican Air Force, even though they fought heroically, to basically nothing.

Of the 2,000 Soviet volunteers who saw service in Spain from 1936 till 1939, 772 were air force personnel. Of these thirty-five were awarded the title of "Hero of the Soviet Union" or H.S.U. Six of these were to be awarded posthumously. Soviet losses in Spain were said to total 157 dead, most of which were Air force and Armored personnel.[5] During the battle of Madrid (November 1936 – March 1937) alone, twenty-one pilots were lost.[6] Today outside of Russia, the Ukraine, Belarus or other areas of what used to be called the Soviet Union, very little is known about these men. But even in the Russian-speaking world, the emphasis is on the fighter pilots with very little on the others. In English there is almost nothing on them. For this reason I feel it is important to try and record the names and whatever information is available for as many of them as possible.[7] The sources I used will be found at the end of each biography written as – Abrosov, Kaminskii, Pravda, etc. and the details will be found in the bibliography.

This present list is an extension of one originally begun in the 1970s by the late Mr. Richard S. Allen (listed in the bibliography as RSA), who was unstinting in his help. I also thank Mr. Victor A. Berch, archivist of the Abraham Lincoln Brigade Archives. Mr. Berch has helped researchers on the S.C.W. for many years, translating information on many of the Soviet airmen. He has also found many hard to locate books that had been published in the USSR, contributing quite a bit, which enabled this list to expand. Fortunately in the past few years there have appeared several important books on the subject – S. Abrosov, V. Nebe, *Ispanii 1936-1939 goda*, Moscow, 2003; O. Kaminskii, *Ikh Nazyvali "Ispantsami,"* Odessa, 2008; *Los Rusos en La Guerra de España*, Madrid, 2009; and the two volume set by J. Salas, *Caza Rusa en España segun su "Diario de Operaciones,"* Madrid, 2007-2009 – plus the excellent Russian website http://airaces.narod.ru/spane/spane.htm. Also, due thanks for their help and contributions are Carlos Lazaro Avila, Tom Sarbaugh, Jim Haycraft, Sergei Abrosov, Alfredo Logoluso, Svatopluk Matyas, Allen Herr, Igor Gordelainov, Petr Lukes, Mikhail Zhirokhov, Clemente Ros, C. Ibañez, Mr. François Rude Editor of Icare, and Mr. Ralph Gibson of RIA Novosti and ADAR La Asociacion de Aviadores de la Republica for the many photos they have allowed me to use. I would also like to offer my apology to any copyright holder whose rights I may have unwittingly infringed.

One final thought, is that even with all this new information there are still found many inconsistences in the various memoirs that are hard to explain. Some of this confusion I attribute to the fact that after leaving Spain, many of these men went on to other wars and battles in China, Lake Khasan, Khalkhin-Gol., Finland and all fought in defense of their homeland.

Any comments, corrections, or additions would be greatly appreciated.

Paul Whelan

Notes

[1] Rybalkin, Y. Stalin y España p.51.

[2] The start date actually means the date they departed for Spain, while the end date indicates the date of their return to the USSR. Generally, each individual would serve six months and then return home.

[3] For information on this aspect, see the works of Botin, or Smirnov.

[4] For example see listings for Karpov, I. and Urus, V. Boris SMIRNOV experienced this close examination on his return leg from Spain.

[5] International Solidarity with the Spanish Republic, Progress Pub., Moscow 1975 pgs.328-330, But a Letter from A.S. Osipenko to A. Prago published in The Volunteer December 1989 p.10 gives the following numbers, total Soviet volunteers were 3,002, and more than 200 were killed in combat. Pritsker lists 101 pilots, fifty-one armored, and thirty advisors, Army and Navy personnel lost, while a list of Soviet losses with 218 names appears in Salas, J., Guerra Aerea 1936-39 Tomo 1 p.393. There is also a list from September that I listed at the end of the bibliography with 185 dead.

[6] Solidarity p.317.

[7] In putting this listing together, I have included all the names found in the various sources used. In some cases this consisted solely of a first, last name or codename as in the case of Albert Baumler's Flight Book (see Illustrations section).

BIOGRAPHIES

ABRAMOV, Nikolai Nikolaevich

Navigator SB. Arrived in December 1937. Member of LISOV's Esc., one of the two Escuadrillas under Soviet Command in 1938. His aircraft was one of the eighteen SBs, which attacked Salamanca on 28 January 1938. This striking force was made up of both Spanish and Soviet flown aircraft, the Soviets lifting off from their base at San Clemente. According to Semenov, possible due to a lack of oxygen, ABRAMOV, and his pilot SEREBRYAKOV became very disoriented on their return leg. They apparently flew past their base and found themselves over the Bay of Valencia. They tried to find one of the airfields there, but ran out of fuel and had to ditch the plane in the Mediterranean. The aircraft capsized and the crew was badly banged up and lucky to escape, especially ABRAMOV who suffered a broken collar bone and a contusion on the right side of his body, which required forty-eight stitches. But according to Abrosov p.201 they made a forced landing in Republican territory and that ABRAMOV was slightly injured. There is no return date indicated for his service, so either mid July 1938, like others in his group, or possibly earlier, due to his injuries. (Semenov "*Parol*," Berch, Gagin, Abrosov)

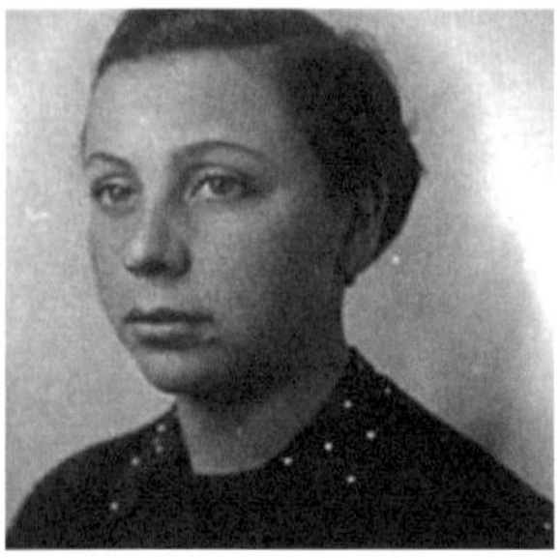

ABRAMSON, Adelina, born 1917

Female translator with the Air Force in 1937. She was born in Buenos Aires; her parents had emigrated from Tsarist Russia. In 1932 the Family returned to what was now the Soviet Union. In January 1937, after the Soviets began helping the Republic, she was sent to Spain. There she became a translator for the Air Force units, working with General Douglas (SMUCHKEVICH) and finally became the translator for General Jose (PTUKHIN). She returned home in 1938. Served in WWII where she was used to interrogate captured Spanish and Italian soldiers. In 1951 her father was arrested on anti-Soviet charges and Adelina was also detained. They were released five years later, after the death of Stalin. In her later years, she traveled extensively, meeting with various International Brigade groups and helping Spanish orginizations to preserve the documentation from the civil war. She passed away on 14 December 2012. (Abramson, www.nodo50.org/age/adelina/adelina.htm)

ADRIASHENKO, Viktor Ivanovich, born 1901

In 1936 he was with the 56th IAB and then the 83rd IAB. He was awarded the Badge of Honor 25 May 1936. In Spain he became Aviation Advisor to Antonio Martin-Luna on the Northern Front, replacing ARZHENUKIN in August 1937. Served from 31 July 1937 to 6 January 1938. In his memoirs he says that at Carreño Field (Gijon) on 1 October 1937,[1] there were only six I-16s and three I-15s left. Only three Soviet pilots were still there: EVSEV'EV, DEMIDOV, and Sergei KUZNETSOV plus ADRIASHENKO. He also claims that in the late evening of the 12th Abel GUIDEZ[2] arrived in a small aircraft, which was only able to carry two passengers, but as there were still three (DEMIDOV had left) the French pilot agreed to try to get off with all three, which he did. They left nothing in the Gijon pocket even taking their pistols, which they threw, into the sea just before landing at Biarritz. Awarded the Red Banner on 2 March, 1938 and in 1938 he became CO of the 84th IAB. During the Great Patriotic War he commanded the 21st IAK. Died August 1985. (Salas, *Modelismo y Hist., G. y Rev. 3* p.160, Shingarev, *Pravda*, Logoluso, Memoir in *MY, Vmeste*, Kaminskii. [1]ADRIASHENKO seems to be confused about this as Abrosov p.175 states that between 2-7 September all the Soviets were evacuated from the North.[2] He is similarly wrong about Abel Guidez, who had been shot down and killed on 7 September 1937, see letter to Guidez's father from J. Dary, in *Revue Andre Malraux Review, Vol. 19/20* p.188. One other thing he seems to have forgotten, is that it was B. SMIRNOV who had brought the group of Spanish I-16 pilots North to join EVSEV'EV and not S. KUZNETSOV.)

AGAFONOV, Pavel Eliseevich, Lt., born 1907

Before Spain, he was CO of a Zvena in the 109th IAE 36th IAB Kiev Mil. Dist. Pilot I-15 in RYCHAGOV Escuadrilla. Served from 20 October 1936 to 7 April 1937. Used the nom de guerre Pedro Jimenez. Listed as having eight aircraft to his credit, five personal and three in patrulla. Awarded the Red Banner twice, 2 January and 4 July 1937. Later fought in China and during WWII he was CO of the 97th SAD. From 9 August to 3 September 1945, he fought against the Japanese in Manchuria/Northern

China, receiving the Victory over Japan award at the end of September According to Berch AGAFONOV was the Russian name used by Ac(h)med AMBA, whereas Kaminskii lists Acmed AMBA as one of his alias'. (Meroño, Shingarev, Zakharov, *Vmeste*, Pritsker, Salas, Abrosov, Gagin, Kaminskii, Amba, *Pravda*)

AGAL'TSOV, Filipp Aleksandrovich, born 20 January 1900
Joined the Red Army in 1919. Served in the Russian Civil War. In 1932 attended the Kachin. Mil. Flying School. Was Assistant Chief of the Political Dept. 114th ShAB Byelorussian Mil. Dist. He was the Air Force Political Commissar under "Douglas," LOPATIN, and PTUKHIN etc. Called "Comrade Martin." In Spain from 30 April 1937 until 27 November 1938. During the Brunete operations, he, together with KOTOV, LOPATIN and PTUKHIN, decided to form a Night Fighter unit inside EREMENKO's 1st Escuadrilla de Chatos. This unit successfully scored the first night kills in Spain. He remained in Spain until the final Soviet pullout in November 1938 (the last SB crews left Spain in November 1938). Awarded the Order of Lenin on 22 October 1937 and the Red Star 2 March 1938. Returned home and was made Head of the VVS Political Directorate, as Deputy Head of GU-VVS a post he occupied until early 1940 when he was removed. In 1943, he was the Commander of the 9th Guards Shturmovik Division (ShAD), and later in 1944 he organized the formation and subsequently commanded the 1st Polish Mixed Air Corps. He served in the post-war years as Chief Inspector and Deputy C. in C. VVS, before becoming Commander of the Long Range Air Force in 1962. Made Marshall of Aviation in 1963. Retiring in August 1969, he died on 29 June 1980. Awarded title of H.S.U. on 21 February 1978. (*Bajo la B.*, Salas, Gusev, *Flieg. Rev.,* R.Allen (RSA), Semenov"*Parol*," Berch, Semenov/*Tov.* 177, *Vmeste*, Boyd, *Pravda*, Abellan on other hand claims first name was Fedor and that he was in the 1st Esc.!)

AGUREEV, Vasilii A., NCO later Lt., born 1911
Pilot in 1st Escuadrilla Internacional in September/October 1936 say Demenchuk in *MY*, also Logoluso, and Berch. But BIBIKOV, V.N. in *Vmeste* etc., Gorilovskii Editor, (*Vmeste* in further listings) says he was a gunner with the SB group, as does Los Rusos who give his service time as December 1936 to 30 June 1937. Awarded Red Banner twice, on 2 January and 11 November 1937. (*Vmeste, Pravda*, Los Rusos who spell it Aguriev.)

AKULENKO, Prokopii Semenovich, Lt., born 1913
Joined Army in 1931. Before going to Spain was a Lt. in the 107th IAE 83rd IAB Byelorussian Mil. Dist. In Spain 13 October 1936 – 26 July 1937, he was a Patrulla commander in the 1st I-16 Escuadrilla under KOLESNIKOV. Participated in the early fighting around Madrid, including the battle of Guadalajara. Credited with six victories plus seven in-group. Awarded the Red Banner twice, 2 January and 4 July 1937. Fought in the Russo Finnish war as CO of the 145th IAP. Awarded the Red Banner again on 21 May 1940. During WWII he was CO of the 164th IAP. Died in 1982. (Gusev, Smirnov, *Vmeste*, Pritsker, Kaminskii, *Pravda*)

AKULENKO, Vasilii Sidorovich, Lt., born 1909
Gunner/Navigator, arrived in November 1936. Flew in the SSS version of the R-5 with VOLKOV. KIA when their aircraft was shot down on 2 December 1936 during an attack on the airfield at Talavera de la Reina. Awarded the Red Banner 2 January 1937. (*Vmeste*, Masse, *Pravda*)

ALEKSANDROVSKAIA, Sof'ia Mikhailovna "Sonia," born 1909
She was interpreter for PTUKHIN from May 1937 until February 1938. (RSA, Berch)

ALEKSANDROVSKAIA, Valentina "Valia," Interpreter (Semenov)

ALEKSEEV, Fedor Stepanovich, NCO, born 1911
Radio/Gunner SB, arrived 14 December 1937 and returned 31 July 1938. Member of the Escuadrilla that attacked and helped sink the Nationalist Cruiser Baleares on 6 March 1938. Awarded the Red Banner on 14 November 1938. (Berch, Semenov "*Parol*," *Los Rusos* list first initial as A.)

ALEKSEEV, Pavel Aleksandrovich, born 1888
Brigade Commander of the Technicians Group. Gagin says from October to December 1936. Arrived in Cartagena in October 1936, where his personnel began assembly of the newly delivered Soviet SBs, I-16s and 15s. *Los Rusos* list as "Jefe de Estado Mayor "Douglas," from November 1936 to 2 February 1937 and then again from 7 May to July 1937. Awarded the Order of Lenin 2 January 1937. *Pravda* lists as "Kombrig," later when awarded the Red Star on 22 February 1939, *Pravda* lists as Komdiv. (*MY*, Berch. Gagin, *Pravda*)

ALFEROV, Maksim Antonovich, Sr.Lt., born 1910
Before going to Spain he was CO of a Zvena in 41st IAE 83rd IAB Belorussian Mil. Dist. I-16 pilot in the 1st Esc. under UKHOV/LAKEEV 14 June – 27 August 1937. Due to health problems, he returned home early. Awarded the Red Star 2 March 1938. At the start of WWII he was CO of the 23rd IAP. Died 18 May 1942. (Pritsker 145, Abrosov, Kaminskii, *Pravda*)

ALIKHNOVICH
Although *Bajo la B* claims he was a SB Radio/Gunner in the 1st Esc., KONDRAT says this was the Serb name written on his documents in Spain. (*Bajo la B*, Kondrat)

ALISIUK, Aleksandr K., NCO, born 1912
Radio/Gunner SB 1st Esc., arrived October 1936 and returned on 27 May 1937. Awarded the Red Banner 2 January 1937. (*Bajo la B., Pravda, Los Rusos* list as ALEKSIUK and say he was a pilot, but there is no listing under this name in *Pravda*)

ALTUSOV, Sergei
A.F. Pol. Commissar at Albacete, w/Douglas. Undoubtedly this is the same person as AGAL'TSOV. (Martinez)

AMBA, Achmed, born 1912
According to his book, he was a Turkish-born pilot in Soviet service, listed as having eight kills and honored by Generals Miaja and Pozas. Note the controversy over his Russian name, in listing for AGAFONOV. There are many problems with AMBA's account in his book. First the year of birth is different. He then states that he along with other pilots, their aircraft and equipment departed for Spain on 23 July 1936. He claims "I was put in charge of assembling, and had forty planes under my command." Also that "On October 17 SEROV,[1] the commander of our group." He then goes on to say that he returned to Moscow on 21 October 1936, and that he was arrested that same day. He tells of his Trial(s) and that after being released in June 1939 rejoined his Squadron at Khalkhin-Gol. He further states that he was shot down by AAA over Finland 14 June 1942 and captured, eventually being sent to Mauthausen and later freed by the Americans. But comparing this to the information in the AGAFONOV listing, there are no similarities other than being in Spain. If indeed this was writtin by AGAFONOV, he was really trying to cover his true identity, yet the author did indeed know a lot of information regarding the shipments of war material to Spain saying "Actually the Soviet transports were so splendidly organized that more than forty vessels reached their destination unharmed." (Amba p.28, Ha 24. [1]SEROV did not arrive in Spain until June 1937.)

ANASHCHENKO, Ivan Semenovich, born 29 August 1905
Before Spain he was a Captain and CO of a Detachment in 57th IAE 142nd IAB Byelorussian Mil. Dist. Served as an I-15 pilot from 26 March to 5 August 1938 as a member of OSIPENKO's 1st Escuadrilla. On 23 May 1938 his Chato was shot down by AAA, but he was able to bail out. He was awarded the Red Banner on 22 February 1939. In April 1940, he became CO of the 133rd IAP, and from June 1942 until January 1943 he was CO of 774th IAP. After that until August 1944 he was CO of the 9th GIAP. Later he was wounded and in February 1945 after his rehabilitation, he was made CO of the 8th GIAD. Died 17 August 1991. (Semenov 169, Gagin wrongly says name was spelled ANISHCHENKO and that he was a member of RODIN's Esc. (I-16s), Lukes, Kaminskii, *Pravda*)

ANDREEV, Aleksandr Petrovich, born 1901

Before going to Spain he was CO of the 51st SAB (Mixed Aviation Brigade) OKDVA (Separate Red Banner Far East Army). In Spanish service 28 June 1938 – 27 February 1939. Traveled on the Soviet ship "Andrei Zhdanov" along with GRITSEVETS and other fighter pilots and bomber crews. They landed at La Havre France, then went by rail to Port Bou in Spain. He replaced ARZHENUKHIN as Soviet Chief of Staff for the Republican Air Force. He filed reports with Moscow about the problems with the M-25A andV(B) engines, some of them failing after only 8-12 hours running time. (*Solidarity*, Semenov"*Parol*," *Vmeste*, Abrosov)

ANDREEV, Vasilii Dmitrievich, Lt. Born 1909

In Red Army 1933. Flew with the 72nd IAE 65th IAB Kiev Mil. Dist. I-16 pilot, served in Spain from 28 April until 5 August 1938. Flew forty missions and fought in eight air battles. On 14 June 1938, after running out of fuel, he crashlanded his aircraft near the airfield. He was only slightly injured in the crash. Awarded the Red Banner 22 February 1939. He fought in the Russo Finnish war, and in September 1941 became CO of an Eskadril'ya in the 526th IAP (In December 1941 this was renamed as the 2nd GIAP flying LaGG-3 and MiG-3s.) He was KIA 12 December 1941 and posthumously awarded the Order of Lenin on 27 December 1941. (Abrosov, airaces.narod.ru, Kaminskii, *Pravda*)

ANDRIUSHIN, Mikhail M., born 1892

Worker from Aircraft Factory #1 assembling I-15 and SSS models. In Spain October 1936 to 26 July 1937. Awarded the Red Star 2 January 1937. (*Pravda, Los Rusos*)

ANDRONOV, Viktor A., born 1907

Aviation Technician, served from 25 October 1936 until 2 August 1937. Awarded the Red Star 2 January 1937. (*Los Rusos, Pravda*)

ANDROSOV, Boris A., Lt., born 1908

Bomber pilot in Spain from October 1936 to 26 July 1937. Awarded the Red Banner 2 January 1937. (*Pravda, Los Rusos* spells it ANDRONOV)

ANISIMOV, Viktor Alekseevich, Lt., born 1909

SB Pilot arrived 26 March and returned 3 September 1938. Awarded the Red Banner on 22 February 1939. (Berch, Semenov"*Parol*," *Los Rusos, Pravda*)

ANTONENKO, Pavel, Lt., born 1910

Pilot, in Spain from October 1936 to 30 January 1937. Awarded the Red Banner according to *Los Rusos*. But cannot find this name in *Pravda* 3 January 1937, and think they are confused with ANTONETS below.

ANTONETS, Pavel Andreevich, Lt., born 1910

Flew with the 71st IAO, awarded the Badge of Honor on 25 May 1936. Then went to the 118th IAE. In Spain he was in TURZHANSKII Esc. and served from October 1936 to 30 January 1937 on the Basque front. Sent home early due to illness. Awarded the Order of the Red Banner 2 January 1937. In the spring of 1938 he became CO of the 2nd IAE of the 16th IAP MVO. Later he served in the 34th IAP, and in 1940 became an IAE CO in the 148th IAP during the Russo-Finnish war. From 1941 until the end of the war, he was CO of the 236th IAP 201st IAD. (Lukes, Abrosov, Kaminskii, *Pravda*)

ANTONOV, Arkadi M., born 1911

Aviation Technician, served from October 1936 until 27 August 1937. Awarded the Red Star 2 January 1937. (*Los Rusos, Pravda*)

ANTONOV, Evgeni Sergeevich, Capt., born 2 March 1910

Before Spain he was CO of a Zvena in 35th IAE 56 IAB Kiev Mil. Dist. In Spain, he was known as "Zhenei" to

Soviets, but used nom de guerre "Antonio." Departed for Spain on 31 May 1937, CO of an I-15 Patrulla in EREMENKO's 1st Escuadrilla where he downed an RO 37 on 26 or 27 August 1937 He was appointed to the Night Fighter Detachment in late July 1937. Later became CO of the 1st Escuadrilla de Chatos on the Aragon front 15 October 1937. Returned home on 28 January 1938 with four aircraft to his credit. Awarded the Order of Lenin 2 March 1938 and Red Banner on 3 November 1937. Arias claims (wrongly) on p.436 that he died in Spain. Fought in the Russo-Finnish war and was later killed in an aviation accident while flying a Yak-1 on 28 June 1942. Laureau claims his first name was Anatoli, as does Abellan who attributes it to Shingarev. But see Shingarev p.93 where he gives correct name. (*Bajo la B.*, Smirnov, Laureau 232, Salas, Pritsker, Arias, Kaminskii, *Pravda*, Meroño claims he downed an Aircraft at night over Madrid in December 1936, but see his dates of service.)

ANTONOV, S.
Fighter pilot July 1937 (*Bajo la B.*, Logoluso, Confusion with above?)

APLESNIN, Grigorii Alekseevich, born 1909
Aircraft Engineer, was in Spain from 14 January 1937. He was with the 1st Moscas according to Tinker who called him Gregoric. He was killed in a Nationalist bombing of Campo Real airfield on 28 July 1937. While going for cover, he was hit in the stomach by a bomb fragment. Tinker adds that after he was hit he realized how bad the damage was and shot himself. Awarded the Red Star 21 June 1937 and the Red Banner 11 November 1937. (Pritsker, *Los Rusos, Pravda*, Tinker)

ARADY, Bela Ignat'evich, Sr.Lt., born 14 June 1905
Joined the Red army in 1930. Before going to Spain, he was an Instructor in the 70th OIAO Military Brigade at the Zhukovskii Flying School. Served in Spain from 14 November 1937 to 25 April 1938. (Airaces site lists as 14 January 1937, while Abrosov says arrived in December 1937) as I-15 Fighter pilot where he flew forty combat missions and fought in eleven air combats. On 18 January, while flying CA-014, he crashedlanded at Sarrión. Later on 12 March 1938, during operations near Alcañiz, his aircraft CA-057 was shot down by a CR 32. He was able to bail out, but was badly burned. Awarded the Red Banner 14 November 1938. *Kto ectb Kto* states that during 1939-1940 he was a test pilot at Factory #1 and died in an accident on 9 April 1940 while test flying an I-153. (Semenov "*Parol*," Abrosov, airforce.ru/staff/who_is_who/index.htm, Kaminskii, *Los Rusos*)

ARAKCHEEV, Nikolai V., Lt., born 1913
Radio/Gunner on SB, served from October 1936 to 8 March 1937. On 10 February 1937, the SB he was in was shot up and had to make an emergency landing near Motril, but he was not injured. Awarded the Red Banner 2 January 1937. (Abrosov, *Los Rusos* claims he was a pilot, *Pravda*)

ARKHANGEL'SKII, Petr Petrovich, Lt., born 1910
SB Bomber pilot, in Spain from 31 May 1937 to 28 January 1938. Awarded the Red Banner twice, 22 October 1937 and 2 March 1938. In WWII, he commanded the IV Bomber Corps with the rank of General. (*Solidarnost*, Semenov'*Parol*," *Vmeste*, Shingarev, Boyd, *Los Rusos* spells name ARJANHULSKI)

ARKHIPOV, Gavrill Ilich, born 1908
Flew in the 40th IAE 83rd IAB Byelorussian Mil. Dist. In Spain was an I-16 Pilot from 31 May – 18 October 1937. Fought in the Winter War in Finland, awarded the Red Banner 7 April 1940. (Abrosov, Kaminskii)

ARONOV, Aleksandr V., NCO, born 1913
Radio/Gunner on SB, in Spain from May to 27 August 1937. He is said to have shot down a Bf 109 on 21 July 1937, while attacking Avila Airfield. He was wounded during that mission, when his aircraft flown by GALIN was shot down and had to make a force landing just behind the frontlines. Awarded the Red Banner 21 June 1937. (Abrosov, *Los Rusos, Pravda*)

ARTAMONOV, Ivan Mikhailovich, Lt., born 1912

Flew in the 121st IAE 95th IAB Transcaucasian Mil. Dist. In Spain he flew an I-15 serving from 14 January to 26 July 1937. Shot down two aircraft. Awarded the Red Banner 17 July 1937. In 1940 he was CO of an Eskadril'ya in the 67th IAP, which at the beginning of WWII was still flying I-16s. From July 1943 to March 1944 he was CO of the 651st IAP NVO flying P-40s. Awarded the Order of Lenin on 31 May 1945. (*Bajo la B*, Lukes, Kaminskii, *Pravda*)

ARTEM'EV, Nikolai Sergeevich, Lt., born 1909

He was CO of a Zvena in the 109th IAE 36th IAB Kiev Mil. Dist. He was in the first group of I-15 pilots to go to Spain on 20 October 1936. ZAKHAROV says he was in a Detachment of RYCHAGOV's Escuadrilla at Malaga under KOVALEVSKII. He and the others of this detachment were in mid-February absorbed into the KAZAKOV (OSADCHII) Esc. where he was known to Baumler as "Artimio." Had three aircraft to his credit. Returned home on 26 March 1937. Awarded Red Banner twice, on 2 January 1937 and 4 July 1937. In 1940 he was CO of the 196th IAP and in 1942 was on staff of 147th IAP. Died in 1942. (Berch, Zakharov, *Vmeste*, Pritsker, Lukes, Kaminskii, *Pravda*, Baumler, Gagin claims he was in TURZHANSKII's Esc. on the Madrid front September to December 1936. But this is not possible as that escuadrilla was fighting on the Northern or Basque front.)

ARZHENUKHIN, Fedor Konstantinovich, Col., born 15 July 1902

Attended the Borisoglebsk Military Flying School 1923-1927. From 1927-28 he was Assistant Chief of Staff of the 3rd BAB and then became CO until 1930. From 1930-31 he was CO of the 21st Independent BAE and in 1931-32 he was CO of the 57th BAE. From 1932 to 1936 he held various positions in the VVS and then, until he departed for Spain in early 1937, he was chief of staff of the 4th TBAK. Left for Spain on 2 February 1937 and returned on 13 August 1938. He was appointed advisor to Antonio Martin-Luna in the North. "General Fedorio," as he was known, turned over his duties in the North to ADRIASHENKO on the morning of 22 August 1937 and departed for Valencia. He was then made Chief of Staff of Soviet Volunteers and Soviet Chief of Staff for the Republican Air Force replacing PTUKHIN who was moved up. Later he replaced PTUKHIN as Soviet Commander of Republican Aviation, when the latter left Spain in January 1938. In July/August 1938 he was replaced in this capacity by ANDREEV. On his return he was made Chief of Air Staff RKKA (Red Army). In 1941, as a Lt. General he was appointed head of the Air Academy, a post he held for a brief five months before being arrested on 28 June 1941 at age thirty-four. He was shot 28 October 1941 without being given a trial. Later after Stalin's death, he was rehabilitated on 23 November 1954. Awarded the Order of Lenin 3 November 1937, also the Red Banner on 2 March 1938. (*Solidarity*, Semenov"*Parol*," Lario, Meroño, Smirnov, Zugazagoitia, Logoluso, *Vmeste*, Shingarev, Shukman, Boyd, *Pravda*, Pritsker lists as ARZHANUKHIN, V.F., *Los Rusos* list start date as 15 February 1937)

ASAULOV, Sergei Pavlovich, Lt., born 1914

SB Pilot arrived 26 March and returned 5 August 1938. He was a member of KRASNOGLAZOV's Escuadrilla. Wounded when his aircraft was hit by AAA fire during an attack on Zaragoza on 22 May 1938, according to GUDOVICH in *My* (1986). Awarded the Red Banner 22 February 1939. (Berch, Semenov "*Parol*," *My 2*, *Pravda*, Abrosov, *Los Rusos* says first name Afanseev)

ASTAKHOV, Sergei Fedorovich, born 1913

He was CO of a Zvena in the 33rd IAE 142 IAB Byelorussian Mil. Dist. Was an I-16 Fighter pilot, in Spain from 31 May until 26 July 1937 when while testing an I-16, it went into a spin and could not recover. He crashed on the airfield and was killed. Awarded the Red Banner on 2 March 1938 (Abrosov, airaces.narod.ru, Kaminski, *Pravda*)

BABIN, Viktor. A., Lt., born 1908

Arrived October 1936, Gagin lists as flying in one of K.M. GUSEV's SSS Escuadrillas. Awarded the Red Banner on 2 January 1937. (*Los Rusos, Pravda*, Gagin)

BAGROV, Vasilii Vasil'evich, born 1915

On staff of the 3rd IAE VVS KBF Red Banner Baltic Fleet. In Spain he was an I-16 pilot from 14 December 1937 to 15 June 1938. First he was in DEVOTCHENKO's Esc. and later became CO of the 5th Escuadrilla. Two aircraft to his credit in group. Awarded the Red Banner twice, on 14 November 1938 and 22 February 1939. Fought in the Russo Finnish war and was awarded the order of Lenin on 21 April 1940. From December 1942 to July 1943 he was CO of 62nd SAP VVS ChF (Black Sea Fleet), then became CO of the 25th IAP. Died 10 January 1944, when his aircraft was hit by shrapnel from an exploding AAA shell in the Eltigen region Crimea. (Semenov "*Parol*," Pritsker, Kaminskii, *Pravda*)

BALANOV, Nikifor Fedotovich, Lt., born 10 July 1909.

Joined the Army in 1931. Attended the Orenburg Mil. Flying School in 1933. Before going to Spain, he was in the 107th IAE 83rd IAB Byelorussian Mil. Dist. He arrived in Spain in November 1936, returning home on 27 May 1937, used name "Luis." Flew an I-16 in TARKHOV's Esc. Later was a Patrulla commander in the Escuadrilla under KOLESNIKOV. Claimed a Ju 52 in November 1936 (19th-22nd pw). Had at least two aerial victories. Awarded the Red Banner 2 January 1937. Wounded on 23 January 1937 in a raid on Getafe. Awarded the H.S.U. on 27 June 1937 (Abrosov claims it was 27 July 1937) and Order of Lenin. After returning from Spain, he became a zvena CO in the 107th IAE. In 1938 was CO of the 31st IAP and from January 1941 to April 1942 he was CO of the 71st SAD, then the 295th IAD in August 1942 until August 1943. After August 1943 he was CO of the 317th IAD PVO. He retired in 1946 and lived in Bryansk. Died 3 June 1981. (RSA, Berch, Ha 24, *Vmeste*, Pritsker, Rumyantsev *"Antonio,"* *Geroi*, Kaminskii, *Pravda*)

BALIN, Aleksei M., Lt., born 1918

SB pilot according to POLUSHKO in (Vmeste). In Spain from 31 May to 23 December 1937. Awarded the Red Banner 3 November 1937. (*Pravda, Los Rusos, Vmeste*)

BALKIN, Andrei

Salas says I-15 pilot, Conforti in "*Guadalajara*" says I-16 pilot. Lukes says Esc. OSADCHII (Very doubtful, as no mention in either Abrosov or Kaminskii.)

BAL'TSEV, Boris Ivanovich, Lt., born 8 January 1908

Was in the 121st IAE 95th IAB Transcaucasian Mil. Dist. In Spain he was an I-16 pilot from 14 January to 26 July 1937. Awarded the Red Banner 27 June 1937. After his return home he became CO of a Detachment in the 121st IAE and in March 1938 he went to the 45th IAP 60th IAB. In June 1938 he became CO of the 50th IAP and in February 1940 he was appointed as CO of the 116th IAP. Awarded the Medal of Courage 14 November 1938. On 29 August 1940 he was killed when his I-16 crashed. (Abrosov, Kaminskii, *Pravda*)

BAL'TSEV, Ilya, Sgt., born 1908

Pilot in Spain 20 August 1937 to 24 March 1938, according to *Los Rusos*. I wonder if they are confused with the man above, as the date would indicate a fighter pilot, but there is no support in Abrosov

BARANCHUK, Konstantin Gavrilovich, Lt., born 8 March 1907

He was CO of a Zvena in the 118th IAE 92nd IAB Moscow Mil. Dist. Served in Spain from October 1936 to 26 June 1937. Initially he was an I-15 Detachment CO but after TURZHANSKII was shot down and badly injured. In December 1936, he took over command of the Escuadrilla. The Spanish pilot Leopoldo Morquillas flew in his Esc. on the northern front. Awarded the Red Banner twice, on 2 January and 4 July 1937. On returning home, he became CO of the 117th IAE. Later in July 1938 he was made CO of the 40th IAP and fought in the battles at Lake Khasan. From February 1939 to August 1940 he was CO of the 63rd IAB and in August 1940 became CO of the 34th SAD. In June 1941 he was made CO of the 16th Air Army. During WWII in May 1942 he was CO of the 203 IAD (This was later renamed the 12th GIAD in February 1944). Awarded the Order of Lenin on 29 May 1945 and the Red Banner 23 August 1943. Died on 29 September 1971. Salas lists as WARANCHUK. (*Vmeste* 98, Salas/*Mod. and His.*, Shingarev, Fernandez, Kaminskii, *Pravda.* See also listing for Varanchuk. I believe his codename was "Ramon.")

BARANNIKOV, Nikolai P., Lt., born 1911

Pilot, CO of an SSS patrulla, served from November 1936 to 8 May 1937. Awarded the Red Banner 2 January 1937. (Abrosov p.376, *Los Rusos, Pravda*)

BARKHATOV, Nikolai V., born 1910

Aviation Technician, served from October 1936 to 9 July 1937. Awarded the Red Star 2 January 1937. (*Los Rusos, Pravda*)

BARKOV, Vasilii I., born 1898

Mechanic from Aircraft Factory #1 assembling I-15 and SSS aircraft, in Spain from 20 October 1936 to 7 April 1937. Awarded the Red Star on 2 January 1937 (*Los Rusos, Pravda*)

BARYSHPOL, Vasilii P., Sr.Lt., born 1904

SB Navigator in SENATOROV's Esc., served from 31 May 1937 to 28 January 1938 (the Russian edition of the book *Solidarnost* lists his name as BARYSHNIKOV, but this was corrected in the English Edition of *Solidarity*). *Los Rusos* p.265 lists as BARISHNOV, Vasilii. SB navigator. These are undoubtedly all one in the same person. *Pravda* lists it as BARYSHPOL, Awarded the Red Banner 11 November 1937 and 2 March 1938.

BASHMAKOV, Petr Dmitrievich, born 1913

Lt. CO of a detachment in the 107th IAE 83rd IAB Byelorussian Mil. Dist. In Spain from 26 March to 23 August 1938, he was CO of an I-16 Patrulla. Claimed four aircraft; one personal, one with a Spanish pilot, and two others in group. Some list as having seven victories. Wounded in air combat on 13 May 1938, he was able bring his aircraft back and land at Villar Field. Order of Lenin 22 February 1939. From the beginning of WWII he was CO of the 34th IAP. Died 26 January 1942 of an illness. (Semenov"*Parol,*" *Vmeste*, Kaminskii, *Pravda*)

BASKOVI

Howson says was an instructor on RZs, while Salas in his history of the "Natacha" (RZ) says he was a member of the initial Grupo. (Howson 265, Salas in R de A #458. Not listed in *Pravda*.)

BATALIN, Aleksandr I., born 1909

Mechanic from Aircraft Factory #1 assembling I-15 and SSS models. In Spain from October 1936 to 7 April 1937. Awarded the Red Star 2 January 1937. (*Los Rusos, Pravda*)

BAZAROV, Il'ia Aleksandrovich, born 18 July 1913, but according to other sources 1909

Flew in the 17th IAE 142nd IAB Byelorussian Mil. Dist. In Spain he was an I-16 Pilot and CO of a Patrulla in the 6th Moscas under GUSEV, from 20 August 1937 to 24 March 1938.[1] In May 1941 he was CO of an Eskadril'ya in the 241st IAP, then in September 1941 became CO of an Eskadril'ya in the 573rd IAP. Later in April 1942 became CO of an Eskadril'ya in the 116th IAP, and in September 1943 was made CO of an Eskadril'ya in the 263rd IAP. In December 1944 he was CO of a zvena in the 484th IAP. Awarded the Red Banner in September 1944. [1]Abrosov in his biography says 24 March but in a chart indicates 25 April 1938. (Gusev 76, Abrosov, Kaminskii)

BAZHENOV, Valerii Vasil'evich, Lt., born 1905

SB Pilot on Madrid front October 1936 in the 1st Esc. under SCHACHT. Killed in a midair collision with another SB flown by FEDOROV on 12 November 1936 after an attack on the airfield at Avila. Also killed were the two navigators ROSHCHIN and SEROV plus both unnamed gunners. Awarded the Red Banner on 2 January 1937. Laureau and Howson say name was BAKHENOV. (*Bajo la B*, Laureau, Howson 278, Salas, Abrosov, *Los Rusos, Pravda*)

BELIKOV, Dmitri N., born 1908

Was a Technician on SBs, served from October 1936 to 27 March 1937. Awarded the Red Star on 2 January 1937. (*Vmeste* BIBIKOV p.17, *Los Rusos, Pravda*)

BELIKOV, Fedor F., born 1903

Fitter from aircraft factory #1 assembling I-15 and SSS models. In Spain from October 1936 to 27 March 1937. Awarded the Red Star 2 January 1937. (*Los Rusos, Pravda*)

BELITSKII, Andrei Vasil'evich, Lt., born 1911

Navigator on SB, arrived 20 March, was wounded when his aircraft flown by MURAV'EV was shot down by Bf 109s on 10 January 1938. All three crewmembers including the gunner PARAKHIN were able to bail

out. Returned home 27 August 1938. Awarded the Red Banner 22 February 1939. (Berch, Semenov"*Parol*," Kotelnikov, *Los Rusos, Pravda*)

BELOUSOV, Nikolai Vasil'evich, Lt., born 1906
SB Navigator, served from 29 June to 11 July 1938 – most likely this should read November as that is when these SB crewmembers returned home. Awarded the Red Banner 22 February 1939. (Semenov "*Parol*," *Pravda, Los Rusos* spells name BELOUS)

BELOV, Aleksandr Vasil'evich, born 1906, died 1983
Served from October 1936 to 27 August 1937 as an aviation technician. He along with other technicians helped off load fifteen I-16s at Alicante in October 1936 from the Soviet ship "Kursk." He also helped assemble thirty-one aircraft in eight days. Awarded the Red Star on 2 January 1937. (*Vmeste, Pravda, Los Rusos* list as Instrument Technician)

BELOV, Andrei Ivanovich, born 25 August 1913
Flew in the 13th IAP[1] VVS KBF (Red Banner Baltic Fleet). An I-16 pilot, he arrived in Spain on 14 December 1937 and returned 13 July 1938. Flew in DEVOTCHENKO's 2nd Escuadrilla. He and SHUBIKOV, A. were in the Patrulla led by ZHURAVLEV, N. P. In his Memoirs published in "*Leningradtsy v Ispanii*" he said that at the time he joined this Escuadrilla, "it was composed of only nine pilots who had originally arrived in August," it was then operating out of La Cenia airfield. Wounded, on 21 February 1938 in a battle with Messerschmitts and Fiats over Teruel. DENISOV and TAKHTAROV were also wounded plus TROSHKIN was KIA. But they claimed eighteen enemy aircraft downed. Awarded the Red Banner 14 November 1938. After Spain he flew in the 13th IAP VVS KBF. Fought in the Russo-Finnish War, and was awarded the Order of Lenin on 21 April 1940. He was named Eskadril'ya CO of the 62nd IAP VVS Black Sea Fleet in December 1941. But from March until July 1942 he was an Eskadril'ya CO in the 20th IAP on the Leningrad Front with the OMAG, then later with the 1st GIAD VVS KBF. Died 3 May 1982. [1]Abrosov lists as the 3rd IAP. (Pritsker, Semenov"*Parol*," Kaminskii, *Pravda*, Abrosov)

BELYAKOV, Konstantin Dmitrievich, born 28 May 1909
From December 1935 to December 1936, he was a zvena CO in 11th IAE 111st IAB Leningrad Mil. Dist. Served in Spain from 1 January until 7 September 1937, he was an I-16 pilot in UKHOV's 1st Esc. along with YAMANOV. Wounded over the Madrid frontlines by AAA fire on 8 July 1937. Tinker spelled his name as BELIEKOV. Abellan claims he was shot down during a battle with a He 111, but Tinker says he landed wounded with a piece of shrapnel in his shoulder. Awarded the Red Banner on 17 July 1937. After Spain in 1937 he became a Detachment CO in the 47th IAE 2nd TBAB (Heavy Bomber Aviation Brigade). From April 1938 to September 1939, was CO of an IAE in the 7th TBAP. In June 1940 he became CO of an IAE of the 80th SAP. Fought in the Russo-Finnish War for which he was awarded the Order of Lenin on 21 May 1940. In August 1941 he was named CO of the 348th IAP (in January 1942 this became the 743rd IAP.) From 17 December 1944 to 11 May 1945 was CO of the 104th IAD PVO, then the 122nd IAD. Major Gen. Deputy CO of the VVS 1956-58. Died 19 May 1986. (Baumler, Tinker p.271, Berch, Pritsker, Gagin claims initial was P, Kaminskii, *Pravda*, allaces.ru, *Los Rusos* claim dates were November 1937 to 7 September 1937 (?))

BEN'KOVSKI, Kiril Stanoev (real name: KIRILOV, Kiril Aleksandrov.), born 1907
In Sofia, Bulgaria. SB pilot, he came to Spain from the USSR, served from October 1936 to 23 January 1937. Awarded the Red Banner 2 January 1937. (RSA, Berch, *Pravda, Los Rusos*)

BEREZHNOI, Stepan Ivanovich, Maj., born 1910
Pilot SB, CO of a Patrulla. In Spain 14 December 1937 to 13 July 1938. His unit was involved in the attack on the Nationalist Cruiser Baleares on 6 March 1938. Awarded the Red Banner on 14 November 1938 and the Red Star on 22 February 1939. (Berch, Semenov "*Parol*," *Los Rusos, Pravda*)

BEREZKIN, A.K.
Worker sent from Aircraft Factory #1 to assemble I-15 and SSS aircraft. In Spain from October to at least the end of December 1936. Awarded the Red Star 2 January 1937. (*Pravda*)

BERGOL'TS, Avgust Ivanovich "Rinaldo," born June 1897
Born in Libau, Latvia, he joined the Russian Army 1915 and fought in WWI. After the October Revolution he joined the Red Army and fought on the western front against the Poles as a pilot/observer. In 1920, he commanded a Eskadril'ya on the western front. After the civil war, he became Chief of technicians of the 1st independent IAE. In 1923 he graduated from Sevastopol flying school and in 1925 he graduated from Frunze Military Academy. He then became CO of the 7th IAE and 30th independent IAE. In November 1926 he became CO of the 20th IAE and then in December 1928 CO of the 7th AB. In 1932 he commanded the 15th TBAB and later in December 1933 he was appointed as head of the faculty at the Military Air Academy RKKA. In April 1935 he was made deputy Commander of aviation MVO. In Spain he acted as First Head counselor attached to the staff of I. Hidalgo de Cisneros, Commander of Aviation for Republican Spain. He arrived in October 1936 and served until 18 January 1937. He was replaced by SMUSCHKEVICH. As to his conduct while in Spain, see Radosh et al. pgs.69-70. On his return he became a senior leader of the Joint Staffs Academy RKKA. He was arrested in the purge of the military on 13 December 1937, tried, and executed on 29 July 1938. He had been awarded the Order of Lenin in 1936. (Semenov"*Parol*," *Solidarity*, Boyd, Abrosov, Suvenirov, ru.wikipedia.org)

BERSHAK, Ivan A., NCO, born 1914
Radio/gunner SB arrived 12 January and returned home on 1 May 1938 due to his being wounded. Awarded the Red Banner 14 November 1938. (Berch, Semenov"*Parol*," *Los Rusos, Pravda*)

BIBIKOV, Vasilii Nikolaevich, Sr.Lt., born 1910
Before going to Spain he served with the 114th ShAB Byelorussian Mil. Dist. based at Gomel. In Spain from September (October) 1936 to 8 May 1937. He was at first a member of the 1st Escuadrilla Internacional under Capt. Martin Luna based at Albacete in September 1936. He then became an SB pilot in the 2nd Escuadrilla at the beginning of 1937, later he became a Patrulla leader. In his memoirs he states that in November 1936 three Soviet ships, the *Staryi Bolshevik*, *Volgoles* and *Kim*, arrived carrying ten SB bombers each. He participated in an SB attack on Salamanca in an effort to kill General Franco. In December 1937 he was CO of a BAE and then in February 1938 CO of a BAP. In August 1939 he was appointed CO of VVS forces in the 2nd Independent Red Banner Army Far East, and in June 1940 as CO VVS forces on the Far East Front. In July 1942 he became CO of the 11th Air Army. In December 1944 this was reformed into the 18th ShAK and became part of the 10th Air Army Far East Front. BIBIKOV remained with the 18th ShAK, which, under his command, participated in the war against Japan in August 1945. *Vmeste* (1986) says he was a retired Lt. General. Passed away in 1989. Awarded the Red Banner twice, on 2 January 1937 and 22 October 1937. (Salas, *Bajo la B*, *Vmeste, MY, Pravda*, OnAirpower.org., *Los Rusos* spell name BABIKOV)

BISEROV, Vasilii F., born 1913
Fitter from aircraft Factory #22 assembling SBs. Served in Spain from October to 12 December 1936. Awarded the Red Star 2 January 1937. (*Los Rusos, Pravda*)

BLYAKHER, Danil Moiseevich, born 1912
Aviation Technician, arrived in Spain November 1936. *Los Rusos* list as killed 28 November 1937(?), the 1991 Soviet list of dead gives the date of death as 28 February 1937. Awarded the Red Star 2 January 1937. (*Los Rusos, Pravda*)

BOBROV, Ivan Fedorovich
I-16 pilot. (RSA, Semenov doubtful, but see below.)

BOBROV, Vladimir Ivanovich, Lt., born 11 July 1915
In November 1936 he attended the Lugansk Military Aviation School. In November 1936, he was in the 57th IAE 142nd IAB Byelorussian Mil. Dist. An I-16 Fighter pilot, called "Camarada Vol'demar," Vladimir had gone to Spain in the spring of 1938, serving there from 26 March until he returned home on 13 August 1938. He first flew in the 2nd Escuadrilla commanded by F. RODIN, and later under S. GRITSEVETS where he was a Patrulla leader. His rank at time of volunteering for Spanish duty was Starshina (Master Sergeant). During his tour in Spain, he flew 100 sorties and claimed thirteen victories plus four others in-group. Most of his missions were in the Aragon and Catalonia sectors. He was awarded the Red Banner on 22 February 1939. Returning from Spain, he was promoted to the rank of Lieutenant and became a Zvena CO in the 4th IAP. He

then went to the 10th IAP from October to December 1940 where he was an Eskadril'ya CO. Fought in the Russo-Finnish War, then later became Eskadril'ya CO in the 238th IAP. From June 1941 when the Germans attacked the Soviet Union until February 1942, he commanded an Eskadril'ya in the 237th IAP. He was then tranferred to the 521st IAP, next he became CO of the 21st. IAP. From November 1942 to February 1943 he commanded the 161st IAP. He was shot down and wounded on 23 January 1943. In February 1943 he took command of the 27th IAP, which later in October became the 129th GIAP flying P-39 Bell Aircobras. Later he took over command of the 104th GIAP also using Aircobras. His rank at that time was Polkovnik (Colonel). He finished the war, having added thirty more victories to his score for a total of forty-three. He retired from the VVS in 1954, lived in Moscow and passed away in 1970 (Abrosov says date was 28 March 1970 while Kaminskii says 28 February). There is some misinformation, in regards to awards he was given during the course of his military service, with Polak saying he was only given one ORB and both Polak and Seidl saying he was never given the H.S.U. But Gagin, Abrosov, Bodrikhin and Kaminskii all say that he was awarded the title of H.S.U. on 20 March 1991, twenty-one years after his death. Also, the photo above taken from Golubev shows him as a Colonel in command of the 104th wearing two ORB, one Order of Lenin, plus three other medals, one of which looks like the Order of Aleksandr Nevskii. *Let. Kosm.* #23 1971 has a photo of him with a chest full of medals. Bodrikhin, N. gives his awards as H.S.U. 20 March 1991, Order of Lenin twice, Order of the Red Banner four times, Order of Suvorov 3rd Cl., Aleksandr Nevskii, Great Patriotic War 1st Cl., Order of the Red Star twice. (*Flieger Revue* 3/1972, *Let. Kosm.*, Semenov "*Parol*," Gusev, *Vmeste*, Gagin, Seidl, Polak, Ha 24, Bodrikhin, Abrosov, Kaminskii, *Pravda*)

BOCHAROV, Vladimir Mikhailovich, "Jose Galarza," born 1910

Finished school and in 1928 entered the Vol'sk United School of Flying for Pilots and Aviation Technicians. In 1931, completed Orenburg Military Pilots School. Before Spain. He was a Detachment CO in the 40th IAE 83rd IAB Byelorussian Mil. Dist. Awarded the Red Star on 25 May 1936. When he went to Spain in October 1936, he was a Sr.Lt. and was appointed as leader of a Detachment in TARKHOV's I-16 Escuadrilla. He is listed as having two aircraft to his credit. He was involved in combat on 13 November 1936 with a group of five Heinkel He 51s, he downed one but his aircraft was then hit and went down. It was seen to crashland in enemy territory near Segovia. The next day (14th) an enemy aircraft dropped a parachute with a wooden box attached. When opened, it was found to contain the mutilated corpse of BOCHAROV. This is mentioned by Koltsov, who confirms that it was one of "Antonio's" flyers. (A booklet on the life of Primo GIBELLI claims it was GIBELLI's body in the box.) KRAVCHENKO in *Vmeste* p.45 lists the 13th as the date of that combat and says that both BOCHAROV and TARKHOV were lost that same day. Geroi, the book of Heroes of the Soviet Union, says he was badly wounded when captured and then subjected to torture before being killed. Named H.S.U. on 31 December 1936. Other awards received were Order of Lenin, and the Red Star. (RSA, Logoluso, *Vmeste*, Pritsker, Rumyantsev "*Antonio*," Hidalgo de Cisneros part 2 p.187, Abrosov, Kaminskii, *Pravda, Geroi,* Koltsov)

BOCHESHIN, Ivan, born 1907

Mechanic with the Bomb Group from October 1936 to 29 September 1937. Awarded the Red Banner and Red Star. (*Los Rusos*, but not found on the 2 January 1937 *Pravda* list of awards, so may have come after the end of 1936.)

BOGACHEV, Nikita G., Lt., born 1906

Pilot, leader of an SSS Patrulla, in Spain from October 1936 until 23 January 1937. During a mission against Navalmora de la Mata on 4 December, his SSS was hit by fragments from an exploding bomb, causing some fifty holes in the plane, which they then crashlanded just inside Republican territory. At the time neither he nor his navigator/gunner DOMBROVSKII were injured. Two days later during an attack on Torrijos, they were not so lucky. Both men were wounded, and DOMBROVSKII died of his wounds the next day. Awarded the Red Banner 2 Jan 1937. (*Vmeste, Pravda*, Abrosov)

BOGDANOV, Boris Sergeevich, Lt., born 1912

Was in the 56th IAB Kiev Mil. Dist. In Spain from 10 June to 15 September 1938. He was an I-16 Patrulla CO in the 5th Moscas. Flew thirty-two missions and fought in thirteen air combats claiming two aircraft, a Fiat CR 32 and a He 51. In August 1938 he became sick and could no longer participate in combat missions, so he was sent home ahead of schedule. Awarded the Red Banner 22 February 1939. At the start of WWII he was an Eskadril'ya CO in the 16th AD; on 27 July 1941 he failed to return from a mission. (Semenov"*Parol*," Kaminskii, *Pravda*)

BOGUSLAVCHIK, Leonid Dmitrievich, born 1914

Pilot in the 4th IAE and also communications chief of a detachment in the 56th IAB Byelorussian Mil. Dist. I-16 pilot in Spain from 10 June to 21 September 1938, member of the 2nd Escuadrilla Moscas under NEDELIN. On 24 August after an air battle, he found that his undercarriage had been shot up and was no longer working. So he had to make a belly landing at his airfield. Later on 31 August after a mission at Gandesa, he crashlanded his plane CM 200 at his base. The aircraft flipped over and was wrecked. Semenov in "*Parol*" pgs.301-302, lists as an I-16 pilot, killed in landing accident on 29 September 1938 at Partida de Fanjuanes (on the road between Villalba de los Arcos and Corbera), but in his *Tovarishch*. Semenov says KIA in air combat p.168, as does Abrosov who lists as KIA on 21 September 1938. Kaminskii reports that on either the 21st or 22nd he was shot down in an air battle with Fiat CR 32s near the Ebro, and that neither the crash site nor the pilot were ever found. Salas *Diario* indicates at the time he was flying I-16 CM 227. Awarded the Red Banner 22 February 1939. *Pravda* spells name BOGUSLOVCHIK. (Semenov "*Parol*," Semenov *Tov.*, Abrosov, Kaminskii, *Los Rusos, Pravda*)

BOLDYREV, Ivan Grigor'evich, Lt., born 1911

He was born in Dnepropetrovski in the Ukraine, and after working as a Metal worker, he joined the Navy. In 1934, he completed training at the Eisk School for Naval pilots. SB Navigator in Spain from 14 December 1937, he was killed in action on 7 February 1938. He was in the Aircraft flown by Ivan SMIRNOV, which along with another Soviet flown SB (SURZHIN) and two Spanish flown SBs were attacked and shot down by Messerschmitts from both 1. and 2.J/88. The pilot and gunner/radioman were able to bail out and get down alive, but BOLDYREV was machine gunned while hanging in his chute. This is one of ten SBs claimed by the Legion Condor on that day. Laureau lists only three losses, but all with Spanish crews. On the other hand, Semenov says only two Spanish flown and two Soviet flown SBs were downed. See SURZHIN for details of this mission, also see GORELOV, and LATYSHEV. Awarded the Red Star 14 November 1938. (Semenov"*Parol*," Berch, *Los Rusos*, R and R, *Pravda*)

BONDAR', Ivan Prokof'evich, Lt., born 1913

Navigator SB in Spain from 30 December 1937 until 13 July 1938. Awarded the Red Banner 14 November 1938. (Berch, Semenov"*Parol*," *Los Rusos, Pravda*)

BONDARENKO, Nikolai Ivanovich, born 22 November 1908 (Abrosov says 1909)

Before going to Spain he was CO of a Zvena in the 121st IAE 95th IAB Transcaucasian Mil. Dist. He was an I-15 Fighter pilot in Spain from 14 January to 2 July 1937, where he was a Patrulla CO most likely in ZOTSENKO's Esc. Awarded the Red Banner on 17 July 1937. In June 1941 he was second-in-command of 10th SAD. Later was second-in-command of the 320th IAD. Awarded the Red Banner, Red Star, Medal for Courage 14 November 1938 and the Medal for the Battle of Moscow on 1 May 1944. Died 19 February 1982. (Abrosov, Kaminskii)

BORISHPOL

Navigator on SB according to POLUSHKO (in Vmeste This is undoubtedly a mistake for BARYSHPOL, V.P see listing.)

BOROZDKIN, Vasilii Fedorovich, born 1909
Aviation Engineer in armaments with the 5th Escuadrilla (Moscas). Served from 26 March to 26 October 1938. Awarded the Red Star 22 February 1939. (*Los Rusos, Pravda*)

BRATENKOV, Ivan G., born 1907
Aviation Technician with the Bomb Group, October 1936 to 29 September 1937. Awarded the Red Banner 27 June 1937 and Red Star 2 January 1937. (*Los Rusos, Pravda*)

BROVKIN, Aleksei Vasil'evich, NCO, born 1913
Radio/Gunner of SB, in Spain from 28 May until killed on 24 August 1937 when a Spanish I-15 pilot mistakenly attacked his SB. The SB from OSTRYAKOV's Detachment, was flown by ZOBOV with SIMONYAN as Navigator, they were making a sweep over the sea watching for He 59s coming from Mallorca. They discovered three He 59s heading for the Port of Rosas and after sometime were able to divert them; then a lone I-15 approached and believing them to be enemy, attacked the SB and BROVKIN was killed. *Los Rusos* say buried at Reus. Awarded the Order of Lenin. (Abrosov, *Los Rusos*)

BROVKO, Ivan K., Lt., born 1908
Navigator SB, 2nd Esc. from October 1936 to 27 May 1937. Awarded the Red Banner 2 January 1937. Listed as having flown over 100 combat missions. After his return he was appointed CO of a BAE, then became CO of the 98th (10th Guards) BAP. Later he became CO of the 3rd Guards DBAD. (*Bajo la B., Vmeste, Pravda*, Bochkarev, P and Paryqin, N., *Los Rusos* says R.B. twice)

BRUDNITSKII, Mikhail Efremovich, NCO, born 1913
SB Radio/Gunner, from 26 March to 3 September 1938. Awarded the Red Banner 22 February 1939. (*Bajo la B.*, Semenov "*Parol*," *Los Rusos, Pravda*)

BUDIM, Fedor Zakharovich, Lt., born 1913
He was a pilot in the 57th IAE 142nd IAB Byelorussian Mil, Dist. An I-16 pilot in Spain from 28 March to 18 May 1938. Abrosov says He was not allowed to fly at the front, but Kaminskii says: Because of several failures and accidents with the new I-16s, which occurred in Spain in the spring of the year, he together with a group of other pilots had refused to fly operations in the badly made aircraft. He was sent back to the Soviet Union. (Abrosov, Kaminskii)

BUKHARIN, Iosif S.
Fitter from Aircraft Factory #21 assembling I-16s. In Spain October 1936 to 27 April 1937. Awarded the Red Star 2 January 1937. (*Los Rusos, Pravda*)

BULKIN, Sergei Georgievich, Lt., born 1908
Before going to Spain, he was a Zvena CO in the 118th IAE Moscow Mil. Dist. He was an I-15 pilot in TURZHANSKII's Esc. on the Northern front from October 1936 to 7 April 1937. On 4 January 1937 he shot down a Ju 52 of 3.K/88 near Bilbao. Claimed a total of two aircraft. Awarded the Order of the Red Banner on 2 January 1937. After Spain he was a Detachment CO in the 26th IAE Moscow Mil. Dist. During WWII, from August 1941 to October 1942, he was CO of the 130th AE flying Polikarpov U-2s on the Ukrainian front. Died in the war. (Lukes, Abrosov, Kaminskii, *Pravda*)

BULYGIN, Vladimir Dmitrievich, born 1912
Mechanic who assisted I. A. PRACHIK to make modifications on I-16s, from 26 March to 26 October 1938. Awarded the Red Banner 22 February 1939. (Semenov "*Parol*," *Vmeste*, Los Rusos, *Pravda*, Gagin claims spelled Bulypin)

BURAKOV, Sergei Nikiforovich, Capt., born 1908
He was a pilot in the 40th IAE 83rd IAB Byelorussian Mil. Dist. An I-16 Pilot, he arrived in Spain on 10 May 1937 and returned on 28 January 1938. Flew 160 missions and claimed two enemy aircraft, one personal and one in group. Awarded the Red Banner on 2 March 1938. In 1939 he was CO of a Regiment. Gagin claims he flew in PLESHCHENKO's 2nd Esc. (Berch, Pritsker, Abrosov, Kaminskii, *Pravda*)

BURDENINSKII, Pavel A., Lt., born 1908
SB Navigator in the 1st Esc. October 1936 to 7 April 1937. Awarded the Red Banner 2 January 1937. (*Pravda, Bajo la B.* spells it BURDENIN, *Los Rusos* spell it BURDENINEI)

BUROV, Petr Ivanovich, born 1913
Was Zvena CO in the 107th IAE 83rd IAB Belorussian Mil. Dist. An I-16 pilot, he arrived in Spain on 10 May and on the morning of 14 June 1937, while participating in an air combat against Fiat CR 32s near Valencia, his aircraft went down

for an unknown reason (possibly due to a wing coming off) and he crashed in Republican territory. He was buried at the crash site. Awarded the Red Banner 11 November 1937. Abrosov, Kaminskii, *Pravda*, Pritsker lists as Sergei P., *Los Rusos* list as Ivan.

BURYAK, Ivan Markiyanovich, NCO, born 24 January 1909
Joined the RKKA in 1933, He was in the 36th IAE of the 56th IAB Kiev Mil. Dist. I-16 pilot, he departed for Spain on 20 August 1937 and returned on 25 April 1938. Flew 120 missions and fought in thirty-six air combats, claiming one Bf 109 plus three aircraft in patrulla (Kaminskii says five in Patrulla). Flew Mosca CM-060. Awarded the Red Banner twice, on 2 March and 14 November 1938. In 1942 he was wounded and served the rest of the war at the Air War Acadamy. Served in Korea and retired in 1954, passing away in 1991. (Abrosov, Kaminskii, *Pravda*)

BUTRYM, Petr Pavlovich, Lt., born 1906
Before Spain he was CO of a Zvena in the 116th IAE Moscow Mil. Dist. Served in Spain from 13 May 1937 to 28 January 1938. He was a member of the 3rd Escuadrilla I-16 Moscas under MINEAV, VEREVKA and SMIRNOV. Codename "Pedro," EVSEV'EV in Vmeste says he was to be the ninth man in their Esc. under UKHOV going to Santander, but he had engine problems and had to abort the mission. Led a Patrulla in the Escuadrilla under B. SMIRNOV. He temporarily took over command of the 3rd when PTUKHIN moved SMIRNOV to the Asturias with an Escuadrilla of new Spanish pilots just returned from flight training in the Soviet Union. Listed as having three aircraft to his credit. Awarded the Order of Lenin on 2 March 1938, and the Red Banner 3 November 1937. During WWII, he was CO of the 425th IAP. Shot down and captured in September 1941, he was able to escape in the fall of 1942. Became a test pilot at aircraft factory #153. Died 18 August 1982. (Gusev 68, Smirnov, *Vmeste* 94, *Pravda*, Kaminskii, Abrosov)

BYCHKOV, A.G., born 1909
Aviation Mechanic in a Patrulla, October 1936 to 2 July 1937. Awarded the Red Star 2 January 1937. (*Pravda*, *Los Rusos* spell it BYCHIKOV)

BYKOVSKII, Sergei Dmitrievich, born 1912
Flew with the 4th IAE 56th IAB Kiev Mil. Dist. I-16 pilot, arrived in Spain 10 June and returned 26 October 1938. Flew in the 5th Escuadrilla at first commanded by GLUSHENKOV and then by KOROBKOV. Claimed two Fiats. Crashlanded CM-209 after running out of fuel on 5 August, the aircraft was destroyed.[1] Awarded the Red Banner 22 February 1939, died in 1941 during WWII. (Semenov"*Parol*," Semenov *Tov.*, *Vmeste*, *Pravda*, Abrosov, [1]Salas lists as lost on 4 August)

BZELIEV, Sergei, Lt., born 1909
Bomber pilot, in Spain from 7 March to 18 October 1937. Awarded the Red Banner. (*Los Rusos*)

"CASIMIRO"
Commander of an I-15 Detachment, shot down and killed 1 February 1937 over Malaga. Ries and Ring p.51 correctly claim this was KOWALEWSKIJ (KOVALEVSKII, A.), but Lacalle says no, but see photo on p.178 of Lacalle's book. See also KOVALEVSKII listing. (R and R, Lacalle, Salas)

CHERENKOV, Mikhail Zakharovich
Radio/gunner on SB, arrived in June 1938. Awarded the Red Banner 22 February 1939. (Berch, Semenov "*Parol*," *Pravda*)

CHEREPKO, Pavel S., Lt., born 1907
Before going to Spain he was in the 16th ShAE 114th ShAB named the "Ultimatum" based at Gomel, Byelorussian Mil. Dist. From what his biography and Kotelnikov say, it would seem that all or most of the SSS pilots and Navigators came from this unit. He was an SSS navigator and served from October 1936 to 2 July 1937. Awarded the Red Banner on 2 January 1937. Retired in 1980 and passed away in 1982. (*Los Rusos*, Emelyanov, *Pravda*, Kotelnikov)

CHERKASOV, Aleksei Fedorovich, NCO, born 1914
Radio/Gunner on SB, in Spain from 15 June 1937 until 7 February 1939. He was shot down near Brunete on 12 July 1937. Age twenty-four, native of Kursk, he was tried and condemned to death along with Harold E. Dahl, an American flying for the Republic. The sentence was commuted and later he was exchanged for a German flyer. Upon capture he gave his name as CHERKAROFF, Alexis Theodore (*Spain* August 15, 1938, Sanchis, RSA, Logoluso. Lukes, Abrosov, *Los Rusos*)

CHERNIKH, Sergei, Maj.
SB Commander of Escuadrilla in Grupo 24 under GUSSAEV according to Howson. Logoluso says flew both SBs and I-15s in Spain. (Howson 278, Salas, Logoluso, *Alas Plegadas* Dic 1996. This is incorrect, see listing for CHERNYKH below and also GUSSAEV.)

CHERNOV, Aleksandr A., born 1911
Aviation Technician in Spain from October 1936 to 16 May 1937. Awarded the Red Star 2 January 1937. (*Pravda, Los Rusos*)

CHERNOV, Gavril E.
Worker from Factory #22 assembling SB aircraft in Spain from October 1936 until 8 May 1937. Awarded the Red Star 2 January 1937. (*Pravda, Los Rusos*)

CHERNYAVSKII, Pavel Mitrofanovich, Capt., born 1902
Navigator SB, arrived 30 May and returned 11 November 1938. His SB was one of the group of six attacked by Bf 109s on 23 September 1938. Two of the group were badly damaged and had to land at Valls and Reus. Awarded the Red Banner 22 February 1939. (Semenov "*Parol*," *Los Rusos, Pravda*, Abrosov)

CHERNYKH, Sergei Aleksandrovich, Lt., born 23 January 1912
Joined the army in 1930, attended the Stalingrad Military Aviation School for pilots in 1930. Was a Zvena CO in the 107th IAE 83rd IAB Byelorussian Mil. Dist. Awarded the Red Star on 25 May 1936. As a Lt. he arrived in Spain in October 1936 and returned on 6 February 1937. Commander of a Patrulla of I-16s in KOLESNIKOV'S Escuadrilla (Kaminskii says he then was a Detachment CO). Used codename Garcia, he flew ninety combat missions and downed three enemy aircraft (Kaminskii says he claimed seven aircraft, five personal plus two in patrulla). In Icare p.130 ZAKHAROV says he shot down the first Bf 109 (but only two Bf 109s were flying at the time he left Spain, one being lost on 11 February 1937 in an accident). Awarded the H.S.U. on 31 December 1936. After his return from Spain, he commanded a Mixed Aviation Division. On 22 June 1941, the first day of the war, he was in command of the 9th SAD, of its 409 aircraft 347 were destroyed on the ground that day. *Geroi*, The book on Heroes of the S.U. says, "General Major of Aviation, was killed on 27 July 1941" (Kaminskii says he was arrested on 8 July 1941, tried on 28 July and shot 16 October 1941, but Abrosov claims he was killed on 27 June). Murphy says "He was so devastated by the loss of most of his aircraft on the ground, that he fled. He was later found in Bryansk and immediately shot." Awards were H.S.U., Order of Lenin, Order of Red Star. He was rehabilitated on 5 August 1958. (*B. la B, Vmeste, Solidarity*, Zakharov, Pritsker, Rumyantsev "*Antonio*," Boyd, *Aviatsiya, Geroi*, Abrosov, Kaminskii, *Pravda*, Murphy)

CHERVOTKIN, Nikolai Matveevich, Lt., born 1905
Before Spain he was an Zvena CO in th 40th IAE 83rd IAB Byelorussian Mil. Dist. In Spain he was an I-16 pilot in TARKHOV's Esc. from November 1936 to 7 April 1937. He commanded a Patrulla in DENISOV's Detachment. Flew 25 combat missions, awarded the Red Banner on 2 January 1937. On returning home to the Soviet Union, he was put on the Staff of the 17th IAE. In 1939 he was a Major in the 142nd IAB. (Rumyantsev, Abrosov, Kaminskii, *Pravda*)

CHERVYAKOV, Efim Stepanovich, Lt., born 1906

In Spain November 1936 – July 1937. Patrulla leader in the 3rd SSS Escuadrilla under GUSEV. Says his Rasantes were off loaded at Cartagena in November 1936, and that the port was attacked by 30 Junkers. The aircraft went to the airfield at Murcia, then later to Alcala de Henares. After TUPIKOV was shot down on 4 December 1936, he assumed command of the 3rd Escuadrilla. Awarded the Red Banner 2 January 1937. He was listed in 1986 as a retired Colonel. (*Vmeste, Pravda*)

CHESNOKOV, Ivan D. NCO, born 1908

Radio/gunner SB from 28 May 1937 until 11 January 1938. Awarded the Red Banner 2 March 1938 as a Sr.Lt. (*Los Rusos, Pravda*)

CHIGIRINCKII, M.D., born 1908

Aviation Technician, served from October 1936 to 17 April 1937. Awarded the Red Star 2 January 1937. (*Los Rusos, Pravda*)

CHIGRIK, Petr A., Lt., born 1915

Pilot SB, in Spain from 14 December 1937 to 21 March 1938. (Berch, Semenov "*Parol*," *Los Rusos*)

CHISTOV, Vladimir Aleksandrovich, born 1892

A Doctor with the Air Group. In Spain 29 April 1937 to 25 April 1938. Awarded the Red Star on 28 October 1937. (Semenov "*Parol*," *Pravda*)

CHISTYAKOV, Aleksei Aleksandrovich

SB-2 Navigator, he arrived in April 1938. Awarded the Red Banner 22 February 1939. (Berch, Semenov "*Parol*," *Pravda*)

CHIZHOV, Aleksandr E., born 1912

Fitter from Aircraft Factory #22 assembling SBs in Spain from October to 12 December 1936. Awarded the Red Star 2 January 1937. (*Pravda, Los Rusos*)

CHUGUNOV, Vasilii Dmitrievich, Lt., born 1908

SB Navigator arrived 26 March and returned 13 August 1938. Slightly wounded on 6 June by AAA fire, while bombing enemy troops near Barracas. Awarded the Red Banner on 22 February 1939. (Berch, Semenov "*Parol*," *Los Rusos, Pravda*, Abrosov)

CHURINOV, Aleksei, born 1902

Engineer in a workshop (Aviation?). In Spain 12 November 1938 to 27 February 1939. (*Los Rusos*)

DANILOV, Stepan Pavlovich, Sr.Lt., born 15 December 1909

Joined the Army in 1931, and in June began attending the 7th Military Flying School from which he graduated in 1933. He then became a leader of a Zvena (flight) in the 121st IAE 95th IAB Transcaucasian Mil. Dist. In late 1936 he volunteered for duty in Spain, and saw service there from 14 January until 26 July 1937. Flying I-16s in the Escuadrilla under KOLESNIKOV, where he commanded a Patrulla. Awarded the Red Banner on 27 June 1937. Upon returning to the Soviet Union, he became commander of the 44th IAP. In 1938, he was promoted to rank of Major and put in command of the 56th IAP. This unit was to see extensive fighting in the battles for Khalkhin-Gol in Mongolia, from 17 July to 16 September 1939. During this time DANILOV flew sixty combat missions and claimed eight victories (six fighters and two bombers). For his actions at the Khalkhin, he was awarded the H.S.U. and Order of Lenin on 17 November 1939. He was also awarded the Mongolian Order of the Red Banner on 10 August 1939. Next he participated in the Russo-Finnish Winter war of 1939/40, after which he was promoted to the rank of Polkovnik (Colonel). He was then assigned to the General Staff of the RKKA, which commanded the 42nd Aviabrigade and 3rd Aviadivision. In June of 1941, when the Germans attacked, he was in command of the 7th IAK-PVO. He later would command several other units including in the fall of 1942, the 287 IAD and finally commanding the 14th IAK on the Leningrad front. At this time he was promoted to General Major. Danilov was killed in an accident of unknown circumstances on 24 May 1945 in the Riga region. During WWII, he flew 112 combat missions and fought twenty-three air combats adding another three victories to his score for a total of eleven. There is no information as to any claims by him in Spain. For his service to the Motherland, he received the following awards: H.S.U.,

Order of Lenin, Order of the Red Banner (twice), Orders of Kutuzov 2nd cl. and Suvorov 2nd cl., Order of the Patriotic War 1st cl. and Mongolian medal for service in the Khalkhin. (Rumyantsev *Geroi*, Boyd, Seidl. Polak, Kaminskii, *Pravda*)

DAN'KO, Ilya Ivanovich, born 1913

Gunner and radioman on SB, arrived 29 May and served until 17 October (15 November) 1938. Awarded the Red Banner 22 February 1939. (Berch, *Los Rusos, Pravda*)

DEMENCHUK, Kuz'ma Terent'evich, Lt., born 1909

In Spain from September to 12 December 1936, sent home early due to illness. He was a Navigator on Br 19 and Potez 540 aircraft in the 1st Escuadrilla Internacional based at Albacete in October 1936. this unit was commanded by Capt. Antonio Martin Luna and consisted of three Patrullas, two of which operated Potez 540s (three in each Pat.) while the third had two or three Br. 19s. The members of this unit included men from several countries and the following Soviets: PROSKUROV, I.I./BIBIKOV, V.N./SOKOLOV, I.N./AGUREEV, V.A./VOLODIN, V.F./TKHOR, G.I./TUPIKOV, G.N./SHAROV, V.V./PETROV, G.Kh. plus the Bulgarian ZAKHARIEV, Z. (who used the name GORANOV, V. in the S.U.). The crew of the Potez 540 he flew in consisted of GORANOV pilot, three Spaniards (co-pilot, flight Mech., and a gunner), DESNITSKII, P. and IVANOV[1] gunners and DEMENCHUK navigator. PROSKUROV was their detachment CO., they flew their first mission on 28 October 1936 against the enemy airfield at Talavera, where they claim to have destroyed fifteen enemy aircraft on the ground. On 30 October, on a mission in the Navalcarnero region, their three Potez were attacked by Fiat CR 32s commanded by A. Mantelli. Both his Potez "N" and the one flown by PROSKUROV were shot up. GORANOV, after both engines were knocked out, struggled to get to Republican territory but could not. The bird came down wheels up plowing into the earth in No Man's Land. The pilot and one gunner were wounded, but they were all able to reach Republican trenches and then to the hospital. He had also served in the crew of a Potez flown by TKHOR. Next he transferred to Grupo 12 flying the SBs, which he says had arrived in October 1936. There were three escuadrillas of 9-10 aircraft each. The Group CO. was ZLATOTSVETOV, A.E. with KOTOV, P.A. as Chief of staff. He was put in the 2nd Escuadrilla under command of KHOL'ZUNOV, this unit was based at San Clemente. The 1st Esc. under SCHACHT, was based at Tomelloso. Awarded the Order of the Red Banner 2 January 1937. In December he returned to the USSR on the Soviet ship "Chicherin" along with GORANOV and DESNITSKII. During WWII, he served in the Directorate of the VVS, reaching the rank of Colonel. (Meroño, *MY*, Logoluso, Berch, *Vmeste, Pravda*, Demenchuk. [1]Demenchuk lists him as Anatoli Ivanov, but could find no listing for this name.)

DEMIDOV, Nestor Fillipovich, born 1909

Was the CO of a Zvena in the 40th IAE 83rd IAB Byelorussian Mil. Dist. Arrived in Spain on 17 May and returned home on 29 September 1937. When he first arrived he was put into the 3rd Escuadrilla de Moscas, but on 2 July he went to the Santander area with a newly formed Escuadrilla under UKHOV. There he became an I-16 Patrulla leader under EVSEV'EV when the latter assumed command on the northern "Santander" front from August to September 1937. Flying out of the Gijon pocket in September just before EVSEV'EV, he had originally been in a Patrulla along with EVSEV'EV and BUTRYM in SMIRNOV's 3rd Esc. Awarded the Order of Lenin on 22 October 1937. After Spain, he was named CO of the 9th IAE and fought in the Russo-Finnish Winter war. At the beginning of WWII he at first was second-in-command of the 28th IAP. This unit is said to have flown 157 combat missions and shot down six enemy aircraft on that first day. He was then named as the CO of the Regiment, which in January 1943 was flying MiG-3s, P-40 Kittyhawks and P-39 Aircobras. In June 1943 he took command of the 318th IAD PVO. Awarded Red Banner 4 March 1942. Died April 1989. (Logoluso, Laureau, Shingarev, *MY, Vmeste*, Pritsker, Abrosov, Kaminskii, *Pravda*)

DENISOV, Aleksei Aleksandrovich, Lt., born 1 October 1907

in the Village of Petrovka, later named Dubenskii in the Mordovian region ASSR. Russian by birth. Lived in Moscow, where he worked as a seasonal Construction worker before joining the military in 1929. In 1932 he attended Naval

Flight School, graduating in 1934. He then began to serve with the 3rd IAE 31st IAB VVS KBF Red Banner Baltic Fleet, where he was a Zvena CO. Volunteered for Spain in 1937, arriving there on 14 December 1937 and returning 24 April 1938. In Spain he was an I-16 pilot in DEVOTCHENKO's 2nd Escuadrilla. Wounded on 21 February 1938 while flying CM-034 in an air battle with Messers and Fiats near Teruel. He claimed a Bf 109 but was himself shot down and had to bail out. In this same battle his squadron mate Viktor TROSHKIN was shot down and killed. In Spanish service, he flew thirty-five combat missions and fought in ten air combats, claimed seven victories personal and in group and was awarded the Order of the Red Banner on 14 November 1938. During the Winter War with Finland, he commanded the 12th OIAE (Independent Fighter Squadron) of the 61st AB KBF (Aviation Brigade Red Banner Baltic Fleet). Named H.S.U. on 21 April 1940. During the first months of the Great Patriotic War he commanded the 13th Red Banner IAE VVS KBF of the 4th IAP. After being badly wounded, he was made regimental chief of staff. In the fall of 1941, he became CO of the 12th IAP TOF (Pacific Fleet). He left the military in 1946. Died on 14 April 1976. (Semenov "*Parol*," Pritsker, L'vov, Polak, Kaminskii, *Pravda*)

DENISOV, Sergei Prokof'evich, Sr.Lt., born 25 December 1909

He joined the army in 1929, attending Military Flying School from which he graduated in 1931. Before going to Spain, he was a Detachment CO in the 41st IAE 83rd IAB Byelorussian Mil. Dist. Volunteered for duty in Spain, arriving in November 1936 with the first large group of Soviets. He used the name RAMON in Spain. At first he commanded a Patrulla in KOLESNIKOV's Detachment in TARKHOV's enlarged I-16 Escuadrilla. Later he became the commander of a Detachment, which claimed forty-nine enemy aircraft shot down. During his time in Spain, he had flown 200 missions and claimed seven aircraft (three personal and four in group). Others say he had thirteen victories, but Bodrikhin and Kaminskii both give him only seven kills. Awarded the Red Banner 2 January 1937. He returned from Spain on 7 April 1937. After his return to the S.U., he was awarded the H.S.U. on 4 July 1937. Also on his return he submitted a memorandum to the VVS in 1937, RE: the relative merits of syncro. cannon in the nose vs. wide spaced machine guns on fighters, etc. No action taken then. Spoke with aircraft designer Yakolev about fighter design in July 1939. Became CO of the 142nd IAB and then in 1938, CO of the 2nd Air Army. As CO of the 56th IAB, he fought against the Japanese in the Khalkhin-Gol conflict, where he was awarded a second Red Banner on 29 August and the Mongolian Red Banner on 10 August 1939. He was awarded his 2nd H.S.U. on 21 March 1940, for service in the Winter War against Finland where he commanded the 7th VVS Air Army. In 1940, he was promoted to the rank of General Lieutenant. In WWII, he commanded the 283rd IAD 16th Air Army. He retired from the Army in 1947. Passed away on 16 June 1971. He was awarded the H.S.U. twice, Order of Lenin, Order of the Red Banner three times, Order of Aleksandr Nevskii 2nd cl., Order of the Red Star. (R and R, Yakolev, Howson, Ha 24, *Lexikon*, *Vmeste*, Pritsker, Rumyantsev "*Antonio*," Boyd, *Geroi Sovetskogo Soiuza*, Gagin, Polak, Bodrikhin, Kaminskii, *Pravda*, Abrosov)

DESNITSKII, Petr Pavlovich, born 13 June 1911

Joined the Army in 1933. In Spain from September through December 1936 in the 1st Escuadrilla Internacional. Initially a Gunner on a Br 19, then the Potez 540 "N" flown by GORANOV where he was the lower turret gunner. On 28 October they had attacked the Nationalist airfield at Talavera where they are said to have destroyed several enemy aircraft. He was badly wounded during a mission on 30 October when the aircraft was attacked by Fiat CR 32s. He kept firing his machinegun even after he was hit, downing an attacking plane. He was pulled from his position and replaced by DEMENCHUK, who was also pulled from the turret just before the plane crashlanded in no man's land. Dragged by the other crewmembers to

Republican lines, he was then sent to a hospital. After over a month in the hospital, he returned to the USSR in December 1936. Awarded the H.S.U. 31 December 1936. Fought in WWII as Senior Chief of Operational Services Division 76th IAD. As a Major, he entered the reserves in 1948. Passed away in 1993. (Meroño, *Bajo la B., G. y Rev 2,* Berch, *Vmeste, MY,* Gagin, *Geroi, Pravda,* Demenchuk)

DEVOTCHENKO, Ivan Georgievich, Sr.Lt., born 1902

Before Spain he had been a detachment CO in the 11th IAE 111th IAB Leningrad MD. He along with EVTIKHOV, KUSTOV, GOROKHOV, KOTYKHOV, POPOV, STEPANOV, and SIUSIUKALOV had flown from La Bourget (Paris) to Toulouse on 26 August 1937 in an Air France Farmen. From there they next flew to Barcelona arriving on the 28th. Used the codename "Pedro." At first, he was in GUSEV's Esc., but later in October was made CO of the new 5th I-16 Esc. de Moscas,[1] based at Caspe. Participated in the 15 October 1937 attack on Sanjurjo Airfield (Garrapinillos) where the I-16s flew top cover for the Chatos which attacked the field. During an air battle in late December, he downed a Fiat. From 22 December 1937 until February 1938 he filled in for GUSEV as commander of Grupo 21. He was in command of the fighter escort on 7 February 1938 when four SBs were lost because he went off hunting. After that he was transferred to command the 2nd Escuadrilla de Moscas. The members of his 2nd Escuadrilla in February 1938 were Boris TAKHTAROV, Vasilii BAGROV, Arsenii SHUBIKOV, Nikolai NIKITIN, Andrei BELOV, Arkadii SVIRIDOV, Viktor TROSHKIN, Vyacheslav PRESNUKHIN, and Aleksei DENISOV. He left Spain with some of the pilots of his Esc. and returned home on 25 April 1938. He had flown 100 missions and fought in thirty air combats, claiming a total of eight kills, but Abrosov says only one Fiat on record. Awarded the Red Banner twice, on 2 March and 14 November 1938. After returning, he was made CO of the 49th IAB and fought in the Winter War with Finland where he received a third Red Banner on 21 May 1940. From January to June 1941 was CO of the 120th IAP, and from July 1942 to September 1943 commanded the 126th IAP flying MiG-3s and P-40 Tomahawks. From August 1944 until end of the war he was CO of the 127th IAD. (Semenov "*Parol,*" Lacalle, Shingarev, Arias, Pritsker, Laureau, Logoluso, Gusev, Kaminskii, *Pravda*, Abrosov, R and R says CO of I-15s! [1]The memoirs of both Airas and Bravo state that DEVOTCHENKO commanded the 1st Escuadrilla Moscas with N. IVANOV as second-in-command at the beginning of August 1937, but see IVANOV. As a possible explaination for this, the 1st Esc. was being reformed with all Spanish pilots and the 6th was just being started with all Soviets. Devotchenko could well have been lent to the 1st for the short period before he took over the 5th Esc.)

DMITRIEVSKII, Vladimir V., born 1918

Radio/gunner SB from 21 January to 21 July 1938. Awarded the Red Banner 14 November 1938. (Berch, *Los Rusos, Pravda*)

DOBRONITSKII, Konstantin Petrovich, born 1910

Before going to Spain, he was a Zvena CO in the 11th IAE 111st IAB Leningrad Mil. Dist. "Kosti," an I-16 pilot, departed for Spain on 20 August 1937 and served until 25 April 1938. GUSEV says he came with him and that he was a Patrulla CO in DEVOCHENKO's 5th Esc. The Diario indicates he was in the 5th Esc. under SIL'VERSTOV, which shows he remained in that Esc. and did not transfer when Devotchenko took over the 2nd Esc. Wounded on 30 December 1937 when his plane CM-132 was hit by AAA fire. On trying to land he collided with a tree receiving a severe head trauma. He was sent to the same hospital as GUSEV. Others sources say that he was shot down in air combat with a Fiat CR 32 and was injured when he bailed out and that after two and half months was sent back to USSR. Salas in *Diario* p.104, says CM 132 collided with a tree, while Abrosov says hit a wall. Gagin mistakenly says he was in SIUSIUKA'LOV's Esc. Awarded the Red Banner on 2 March 38. After Spain he was an Eskadril'ya CO in the 26th IAP, and participated in the Winter war where he won a second Red Banner on 7 April 1940. During WWII, he was Chief of the operations section 7th IAK PVO Leningrad. (Gusev, Pritsker, Gagin, Kaminskii, *Pravda*, Abrosov, Salas)

DOLGIJ, Vasilii Pavlovich, born 1906

Before Spain he was a Detachment CO in the 34th IAE 56th IAB Kiev Mil. Dist. An I-16 pilot in Spain from 31 May 1937, he had flown some missions by 18 July 1937 when in the morning in an air combat in the Sierra de Guadaramma area he shot down a Ju 52. But he was in turn shot down by an escorting Bf 109 thought to have been flown by *Oberfeldwebel* Fritz Hilmann and was KIA. One Aircraft to credit, awarded the Order of Lenin on 2 March 1938. (Abrosov, Kaminskii, *Pravda*)

DOLGOPOLOV, Ivan Afanasievich, NCO, born 1 Jan, 1913
SB Gunner in the 1st Esc. under SCHACHT. In Spain from October 1936 to 7 April 1937. Awarded the Red Banner 2 January 1937. (*Bajo la B., Vmeste, Los Rusos, Pravda*)

DOMBROVSKII, Fedor Pavlovich, Lt., born 1907
Navigator/gunner on an SSS, he arrived in November and died of wounds received on 7 December 1936 during an attack on Torrijos airfield. The Pilot of the aircraft, BOGACHEV was also wounded. These two had narrowly escaped death or injury during an attack on Navalmora de la Mata airfield back on 4 December They had dropped a bomb and it exploded as they flew over it, causing some fifty shrapnel holes in their aircraft. They had to crashland the aircraft, but neither crewman was injured at that time. Posthumously awarded the Red Banner 2 January 1937. (Abrosov, *Los Rusos, Pravda*)

"DOUGLAS"
See listing for SMUSHKEVICH, YA.

DOYAR, S.A., Maj.
SB pilot in SENATOROV's 1st Esc. 12th Grupo. In Spain from 31 May 1937 to 28 January 1938. Awarded the Red Banner on 28 October 1937 and the Order of Lenin on 2 March 1938. (*Solidarnost*, Logoluso, Shingarev, *Pravda*)

DUBKOV, Konstantin Stepanovich, born 1908
Before going to Spain, he was a pilot in the 40th IAE 83rd IAB Byelorussian Mil. Dist. In Spain he was an NCO Pilot of an I-16 in TARKHOV's enlarged Escuadrilla. Served from November 1936 to 26 July 1937. Listed as downing two aircraft on 18 February 1937, plus had one more in group. Awarded the Red Banner twice, 2 January and 4 July 1937. (*Vmeste*, Abrosov, Kaminskii, *Pravda*)

DUSHKIN, Ivan Ivanovich, Sr.Lt., born 23 February 1905
Joined the Army in 1927. Attended Kursk Navigators School in 1934, after which he taught Navigation courses at the Yey'sk school on the Azov Sea, for Naval airmen. An SB Navigator, he arrived in Spain on 27 May 1937 and returned on 15 January 1938. Shingarev says he was SENATOROV's Navigator on the flight guiding the Spanish pilots to the North. Awarded the H.S.U. on 14 March 1938 and the Red Banner on 22 October 1937. Later in 1939 he fought in the Khalkhin-Gol, for which he was awarded a second Red Banner plus the Mongolian Order of the Red Banner. Fought in the Winter War against Finland. In 1942 he attended the Air War Academy and in 1943-5 headed the Strelkov Bombardiers School. After the war, he headed Combined Aviation Battle Preparations. Retired in 1956 as a General Major. Died 10 June 1976. Awards were Order of Lenin twice, Order of the Red Banner three times, and Order of the Red Star twice. (Berch, Shingarev, *Vmeste*, Pritsker 153, *Pravda*)

DUSHUTIN, Nikolai Ivanovich
Gagin p.61 says he was Advisor for Bombers (but I found no proof in *Pravda* etc.)

D'YAKONOV, Nikolai Aleksandrovich, born 1910
Zvena CO in 40th IAE 83rd IAB before Spain. An I-16 pilot he arrived 14 June 1937. On the morning of 7 July 1937 he was participating in a large air combat with Fiat CR 32s of the 23rd Grupo Asso di Bastoni over the Casa de Campo outside Madrid, and was shot down and died of his wounds. Awarded the Red Banner 28 October 1937. (Abrosov, Kaminskii, *Pravda*)

EDAMSKII, Vladimir I., born 1916
Worker from Aircraft Factory #1 assembling I-15 and SSS aircraft. In Spain from October 1936 to 18 October 1937. Awarded the Red Star 2 January 1937. (*Pravda, Los Rusos*)

ELAGIN, Vasili Ignat'evich

Navigator SB, arrived March 1938, was in the crew of aircraft flown by LIPASHOV. Awarded the Red Banner 22 February 1939. (Berch, *Vmeste*, Semenov, *Pravda*)

EMEL'YANENKO, Mikhail Ivanovich, Lt., born 25 August 1914

I-16 Fighter pilot in the 57th IAE 142nd IAB Byelorussian Mil. Dist. He arrived in Spain on 26 March and flew in RODIN's 2nd Esc., returned home on 13 August 1938. Awarded the Red Banner on 22 February 1939. Participated in the Winter War against Finland, and at the beginning of WWII (22 June 1941), was an Eskadril'ya CO in the 122nd IAP. In December 1942 he was shot down during an air combat and had to make a crashlanding in the woods. When landing he was knocked unconscious and sustained a serious head injury. He was in hospital for about three months, after which he could not fly for several months. In July 1943 he was able to fly again and fought until the end of the war. Awarded the Order of the Patriotic War, he continued in aviation after the war. Died 1 May 1957. Gagin spells it EMEL'YANOV. (Semenov "*Parol*," Gagin, Abrosov, Kaminskii, *Pravda*)

EREMENKO, Ivan Trofimovich "Ramon," born 7 July 1910

Ukrainian by birth. Joined the Soviet Army VVS in 1927. Attended Leningrad Military Theoretical Aviation School in 1928. In 1929 attended Military Flyers School at Sevastopol. In 1936 he was a Detachment CO in the 119th IAE 95th IAB Transcaucasian Mil. Dist. flying Type 4 I-16's and in April 1937 he was made commander of this unit. Volunteered for Spanish duty and arrived on 31 May 1937. In command of the 1st Escuadrilla de Chatos from June until September 1937. A.K.A. "Comrade Aragon" in Spain, his Escuadrilla was based at El Soto. His Patrulla leaders were SEROV, SOROKIN and RYBKIN. The second-in-command was Viktor KUZNETSOV. In September he became Commander of the Fighter Air group, replacing PTUKHIN. On the night of 14/15 September he downed Junkers Ju 52 number 22-61 flown by Jose Muntadas and V. Marchenko Larinov near Sariñena. The only crewmember to survive was Jose Ramon Blasco.[1] In command of the raid on Sanjurjo (Garrapinillos) airfield on 15 October 1937, during which he flew I-16 CM 141. Credited with fourteen kills, he was awarded the title of H.S.U. on 28 October 1937 and awarded the Red Banner on 2 March 1938. Returned from Spain on 6 February 1938. After his return, he continued to serve in the VVS, commanding the 95th Aviabrigade at Baku. In 1939 he completed courses at the Genshtaba Military Academy. In 1940 was a Major General of Aviation and just before WWII began, he was put on the Staff of the 9th Air Army. Next he commanded the 218th SAD Mixed Fighter Aviation Division. (Kaminskii claims after Spain he was CO of the 60th IAB Transcaucasan Mil. Dist. and from June 1938 to December 1940 was CO VVS Moscow Mil. Dist. In May 1941 he was second-in-command of the VVS 1st Red Banner Army and later CO of the 25th VVS Army. In July 1941 he was CO of the 9th Air Army on the southern front and from November 1941 to May 1942 CO of the VVS 18th Army) In late 1942, took over command of the 2nd SAK of the 8th Air Army. In 1949 he was a Lt. General in reserve. In 1952, he headed the VVS Urals Military District. Lived in Kiev. Died 1 December 1986. Awards were H.S.U., Order of Lenin twice, Order of the Red Banner three times, Order of Kutuzov 2nd Cl., Order of the Great Patriotic War 1st Cl. twice, Order of the Red Star plus others. Died 1 December 1986. BELOV, A.I. in Pritsker, says he left Spain in December 1937 as does Sukhachev. Shingarev, on other hand, lists him as leaving on 18 January 1938, and also states that KATROV, Vasilii (KOTROV) took over EREMENKO's job. But Semenov p.25, says that GUSEV, A.I. replaced EREMENKO. (RSA, Gusev, Laureau, Berch, Howson, Ha, *Bajo la B.*, Shingarev, *Vmeste*, Pritsker, Sukhachev, *Geroi*, *Pravda*, Polak lists six of his kills p.337, Kaminskii, airaces.narod.ru. [1]Abrosov says Marchenko survived.)

ERENKOV, Mikhail Dmitriovich, Lt., born 1911

SB Navigator, served from 27 May to 18 October 1937. Awarded the Red Banner 14 November 1938. (*Los Rusos, Pravda*)

ERGUNOV, Aleksandr V., Lt., born 1909

SB Navigator, 1st Esc. under SCHACHT, from November 1936 to 29 September 1937. At first he was in LINDE's crew, was later moved to OSTRYAKOV's Sea Detachment. On 26 July his aircraft flown by ZOBOV and with BROVKIN as gunner was off behind government lines doing some bombing practice where they were suddenly attacked by enemy Fiat CR 32s and He 51s. They were finally able to elude them and landed at Liria field, where they counted twenty bullet

holes in the plane. Awarded the Red Banner twice, on 2 January and 3 November 1937. (Abrosov, *Bajo la B.*, *Los Rusos, Pravda*)

ERLYKIN, Evgeni Efimovich, Sr.Lt., born 24 December 1909

Joined the Soviet Army VVS in 1928. In 1929 completed Military Pilots Theory School in Leningrad and in 1930 at the Borisogleb Flight School. Detachment CO 92nd IAB Moscow Mil. Dist. Fighter Pilot, he arrived in Spain in September/October 1936 with the first batch of volunteers and returned on 27 March 1937. According to PUZEIKIN in Pritsker, he was Commander of the 1st Internacional Escuadrilla de Caza, flying NI-52s and Dewoitine 372 aircraft. From November 1936 to January 1937 he was member of RYCHAGOV's I-15 Escuadrilla commanding a Detachment. Kaminskii says Patrulla CO. In Spain according to Kaminskii, he used the codename Pedro Rivera Soltero. Flew 214 combat missions, fought in eighty air combats and claimed five aircraft. Awarded the Red Banner twice 2 Jan, and 4 July 1937. During the Russo-Finnish war 1939-40, with the rank of Colonel, he commanded the 59th IAB (Fighter Aviation Brigade) 7th Army North-Western Front. This unit carried out many missions against enemy troops and airfields from the very first days of the war. They are said to have destroyed some thirty enemy aircraft on the ground and have shot down 101 in air combat, with few losses on their part. He was awarded the title of H.S.U. on 21 March 1940. During WWII, he commanded the 2nd Guards IAK (Fighter Aviation Corps) which was the old 7th IAK PVO from July 1943. (*Aviatsiya i Kosmonavtika* lists him in command of the 6th IAK of the 16th Air Army as does Boyd, but Kaminskii says fought in the Khalkin-Gol and in September 1941 was made CO of the 5th SAD and later to June 1943 was CO of the 7th IAK PVO Leningrad, and from July 1943 to May 1944 he was CO of the 6th IAK). Continued to serve in the VVS after the war and in 1956 was a Major General in reserve. After retirement he lived in Leningrad and died 18 April 1969. Awards were: Order of Lenin, Order of the Red Banner three times, Order of the Red Star, plus other medals. (Lacalle, Bajo la B., Salas, RSA, Zakharov, Pritsker, Geust, Boyd, *Geroi Sovetskogo Soyuza*, Kaminskii, *Pravda*)

ERMAKOV, N.K., born 1911

Aviation Technician, served from October 1936 to 9 July 1937. Awarded the Red Star 2 January 1937. (*Los Rusos, Pravda*)

EROKHIN, Leonid Matveevich, born 1910

Before Spain, he was an instructor in the 34th IAE 56th IAB Kiev Mil. Dist. Went to Spain as an I-16 pilot, beginning on 31 May. He was killed on a training flight from Murcia air field on 25 June 1937, when his plane failed to recover from a corkscrew, said to have been caused by an aileron malfunction. A Russian website also claims he died on a training flight, while Abrosov says KIA (Possibly instead of an aileron problem it was loss of the outer wing section, as this was in the time frame of that problem with the I-16). Awarded the Red Banner 2 March 1938. (Abrosov, Kaminskii, *Pravda*, airaces.narod.ru)

ES'KOV, Fedor L., born 1908

SSS Bomber pilot, in Spain from October 1936 to 2 July 1937. Awarded the Red Star 2 January and the Red Banner 4 July 1937. (*Los Rusos, Pravda*)

EVDOKIMOV, Ivan Vasil'evich

Navigator SB, arrived in June 1938 and returned home in November. Awarded the Red Banner 22 February 1939. (Semenov "*Parol*," Berch, *Pravda*)

EVSEV'EV, Ivan Ivanovich, born 18 October 1910

Joined the Army in 1929. He attended the Volsk Military Aviation School, graduating in 1930. He then went to Orenburg Military Aviation School, from which he graduated in 1934. Was Detachment CO in 34th IAE 56th IAB Kiev Mil. Dist. Began his Spanish service on 13 May 1937, and returned home on 29 September 1937. Abrosov indicates that he, DEMIDOV and BUTRYM upon arrival, all flew in the same Patrulla, this would seem to indicate they were in the 3rd Esc. as BUTRYM remained with the 3rd. (Kaminskii says he was detachment CO in the 1st Moscas.) He came to Spain with rank of Senior-Lt., "Ivanio" led a Patrulla in the Escuadrilla under UKHOV in the North from July 1937. When UKHOV left the "Santander" Front in August 1937, EVSEV'EV

took over command of the Escuadrilla, where he says he flew missions with Francisco Tarazona. Had four kills in combat plus twelve shared. He left the Northern front in mid-September 1937 together with Sergei KUZNETSOV and ADRIASHENKO. They were flown out by a French pilot who flew a small aircraft into the Gijon pocket. Awarded the H.S.U. on 28 October 1937 with rank of Colonel. In November 1937 after his return to the USSR he was put in command of the 71st IAE. In April 1938 he became CO of the 51st IAB Kiev Mil. Dist. Next in April 1939 he was made CO of the 51st ShAB. In August 1940, he became CO of the 38th IAD Transbaikal Mil. Dist. At the beginning of WWII in November 1941, he was transferred to the 102nd IAD-POV, and from June to September 1942 was CO of the 101st IAD which was fighting at Stalingrad. Later from September 1942 to August 1944 he was CO of the 8th IAK PVO at Baku. In March 1945 he became VVS Commander PVO Transcaucasian Front. After the war he returned to command the 8th IAK POV. Retired in 1964 as a General Lt., lived in Kiev, and died on 30 December 1991. Awards were H.S.U., Order of Lenin twice, Order of the Red Banner, Order of the Great Patriotic War 1st. Cl. three times, Order of the Red Star twice. (Berch, Shingarev p.135, *Vmeste* pgs.78, 86-108, Pritsker, *Pravda*, Kaminskii, Howson p.200 spells it VEVSEVIEV, and says he took over command of the Santander Esc. when UKHOV became CO Grupo 21 in July 1937. But see listing for UKHOV. Polak lists three of his kills.)

EVSTIGNEEV, S.E.

Worker from Aircraft Factory #1, assembling I-15 and SSS aircraft. In Spain from October 1936 until at least January-February 1937. Awarded the Red Star 2 January 1937. (*Pravda*)

EVTEEV, Aleksandr Aleksandrovich, born 1905

In 1936 he was the head Aviation engineer on SBs at Aircraft Factory #22. When the Soviet Union decided to send Spain some of the new SB Bombers, he was put in charge of a group of twenty-nine other workers and Engineers from Factory #22 to be sent to Spain. They would re-assemble the aircraft and prepare them for action. Ten of the crated SBs were loaded on to the Soviet ship *Stary Bolshvick* at the port of Feodosiya. The group from Factory 22 was joined on this ship by a group of airmen who would be flying these very aircraft in combat. The ship sailed on 7 October and arrived at Cartajena, Spain on 15 October 1936. When they began unloading, EVTEEV relates in his memoirs in MY, that it was in full view of everyone, friends and enemies. The aircraft were then moved to the airfield at Albacete. The team working under the overall command of Kombrig P.A. ALEKSEEV from October 1936 to at least January 1937, until they had sufficiently trained their Spanish counterparts, not only assembled and prepared the aircraft, but also repaired any which were damaged on bombing missions. These Factory workers all returned home to their jobs between December 1936 and February 1937. He was awarded the Red Banner on 2 January 1937. In the 1940s he was Director at Plant 18 building the Il-10 and in December 1955 he became Director of Factory 456 which was building Missiles. He died in 1980. (*MY*, Berch, *Pravda*)

EVTIKHOV, Semen Alekseevich

Pilot in the 12th IAE 111st IAB Leningrad Mil. Dist. Departed for Spain on 20 August 1937 and served until 25 April 1938. Flew an I-15 in the 1st Esc. under OSIPENKO. (Kaminskii says 2nd Esc.) Two aircraft to his record. Later fought in the Winter War, where he is believed to have been killed, but others say he served in WWII. (Logoluso, Lacalle, Shingarev, Kaminskii)

FEDIUNIN, Ivan N., born 1904

Navigator SB, in 1st. Esc. October 1936 serving until 8 March 1937, then sent home due to illness. Awarded the Red Banner on 2 January 37. (*Bajo la B., Los Rusos, Pravda*)

FEDORENKO, Timofei Nikolaevich, born 1914

Radio/gunner SB, arrived 26 March and served until 3 September 1938. According to *Los Rusos* his codename was Fadeev. Awarded the Red Banner 22 February 1939. (Berch, Semenov "*Parol*," *Los Rusos, Pravda*)

FEDOROV, Grigorii Mikhailovich, Sr.Lt., born 1911

SB pilot in the 1st Escuadrilla de Kats, killed on 12 November 1936 in a collision with another SB being flown by BAZHENOV. Also killed were the two navigators ROSHCHIN and SEROV plus two gunners whose names are unknown. Awarded the Red Banner on 2 January 1937. (Laureau, Howson, *Bajo la B.*, Abrosov, *Pravda*)

FEDOROV, Ivan Evgrafovich, born 23 February 1914

Joined army in 1932 and attended Military Flying School. A Zvena CO in the 35th IAE 56th IAB Kiev Mil. Dist. He volunteered for Spain in 1937 and left the S.U. for there on 31 May of that year. Used the codename "Juan." He flew an I-16 in the 2nd Escuadrilla under PLESHCHENKO. According to the *Airaces* site, on 17 June 1937, five bombers escorted by two Messerschmitts flew over the port of Cartagena. He jumped into a just fueled I-16, and only after takeoff did he realize he had no parachute. He claimed a Messerschmitt. Hidalgo de Cisneros is said to have awarded him the "Laurel of Madrid" – only five Soviets received this award. Returning from a recon flight on 21 August 1937, he was injured in a crashlanding at Sariñena airfield. He was hospitalized, but soon recovered. Flew 150 missions and claimed two aircraft shot down. He returned home from Spain on 28 January 1938. (Polak claims he had twenty-three victories, many of which were shared.) Awarded the Red Banner twice, on 28 October 1937 and on 2 March 1938. In 1939 he took Superior Officer Aviation courses, and then flew in China from November 1940 until February 1942, where he claimed two kills. Participated in the Patriotic War, as Commander of the 157th IAD in 1942, then CO of the 273rd IAD and later CO of the 269th IAD. Claimed a total of seventeen enemy aircraft. Kaminskii says during WWII he flew 114 missions and claimed twelve aircraft. He was awarded the H.S.U. on 5 March 1948. Retired in 1954 with rank of Polkovnik (Colonel). Other awards given were Order of Lenin, Order of the Red Banner (four times including 28 October 1937 and 2 March 1938), Order of Aleksandr Nevskii, Order Patriotic War 1st cl. (four times), Order Patriotic War 2nd cl., Order of the Red Star. Died 12 February 2011 in Moscow. (Berch, Pritsker, Bodrikhin, Polak, Kaminskii, *Pravda*, Abrosov, airaces.narod.ru)

FEDOROV, M.N.

Was a staff officer in the Fighter Group, killed flying an I-15 at Alcala de Henares airfield, July 1937. (*Vmeste* 280 Undoubtedly, this is really FEDOSEEV, N.I.)

FEDOSEEV, Mikhail Andreevich, born 20 September 1912

Joined the army in 1933. Attended Orenburg Military Flying School. Before going to Spain, was a Zvena CO in the 4th IAE 56th IAB Kiev Mil. Dist. Volunteered for Spanish duty and arrived there on 10 June 1938. He was posted to the 5th Escuadrilla commanded by GLUSHENKOV and later by GRITSEVETS. While making a landing at his field on 21 July, the starboard outer wing panel broke loose when a support bolt broke. The aircraft was damaged but FEDOSEEV was uninjured. At the beginning of August 1938 he temporarily took over command of the Escuadrilla when GRITSEVETS was called to Valencia. He was on the staff of the Grupo (2nd and 5th Escuadrillas). Scored his first victory on 4 August 1938 and by the time of his return home on 26 October 1938, he was credited with seven victories in 160 (88) sorties with forty air combats. Awarded the Order of Lenin for his service in Spain on 22 February 1939. After his return he was appointed commander of the 6th OAE (Independent Aviation Squadron). This unit later combined with some other units, became the 88th IAP and FEDOSEEV became its deputy commander. Next he assumed command of the 247th IAP of the 72nd IAD, and it was with this unit he went to war in June 1941. During the extremely hard day-to-day air combats, he added another thirteen victories to his score for a total of twenty (Kaminskii says he flew 169 missions, fought in twenty-seven air combats and claimed eighteen Aircraft). He was killed in aerial combat on 23 March 1942 over Semisotka in the Crimea. (Kaminskii says the 22nd). He was posthumously awarded the H.S.U. and a second Order of Lenin on 6 June 1942. His rank at the time of his death was Podpolkovnik (Lieutenant Colonel). (Semenov "*Parol*," Semenov/*Tov*. P.179, *Vmeste, Geroi*, Seidl, Polak, Bodrikhin, Kaminskii, *Pravda*, Abrosov)

FEDOSEEV, Nikolai Ivanovich, Col., born 1901

Was on Staff of the 40th LBAB Byelorussian Mil. Dist. Went to Spain in November 1936 and was posted to the Fighter Air Group Staff. He was named commander of the Fighter Group replacing PUMPUR on 21 April 1937, but died in an accident while flying an I-15 from Tembleque Aerodrome on 16 May 1937. Supposedly at a gathering for the change from PUMPUR to PTUKHIN, he arrived flying an I-15 and KOPETS an I-16. But, as he actually came between PUMPUR and PTUKHIN, he could not have attended the above mentioned meeting or perhaps this was in fact the meeting of 21 April where he was appointed to replace PUMPUR. Posthumously awarded the Red Banner on 27 June 1937. (Zil'Manovich/Berch, *Vmeste*, Pritsker, Abrosov, Kaminskii, *Los Rusos, Pravda*)

FEDOSOV, Dmitri I.

Worker from Aircraft Factory #22, assembling SB aircraft. In Spain October 1936 to 8 March 1937. Awarded the Red Star on 2 January 1937. (*Pravda, Los Rusos*)

FEDOTOV, Anatolii Vasil'evich, born 1907

SB pilot, arrived 14 December 1937 and served until 21 July 1938. According to *Los Rusos*, codename was "Fedchenko." Awarded the Red Banner on 14 November 1938 and the Red Star on 22 February 1939. (Semenov "*Parol*," Berch, *Los Rusos, Pravda*)

FEDULOV, Mikhail Yakovlevich, NCO, born 1912

Pilot in the 12th IAE 111th IAB Leningrad Mil. Dist. He departed for Spain on 31 May 1937 where he flew an I-16, as a member of PLESCHENKO's 2nd Escuadrilla. KIA, on the Madrid front 16 July 1937 in an air combat with Bf 109s during the Brunete operations. Both Abrosov and Kaminskii think it was Rolf Pingel that shot him down. Awarded the Red Banner 3 November 1937. (Berch, *Pravda*, Pritsker, Abrosov, Kaminskii)

FEERSTHEIN, Elena Naumova, born 1917

Served in Spain from 28 April 1938 to 27 February 1939 as translator for the Aviation Group. (*Los Rusos*)

FEL'DMAN, Mikhail E., born 1908

Mechanic/Technician I-15, served from 14 January to 27 August 1937. Awarded the Red Star on 4 July 1937. (*Bajo la B., Los Rusos, Pravda*)

FEODOR

Replacement pilot killed in action over Madrid front on 13 June 1937. Although Baumler lists this date, no Soviet pilot is listed as lost on the 13th. In fact neither Baumler nor Tinker, who were both in Lakeev's 1st Esc., flew that day. On the next day (14th) a new Soviet pilot Petr BUROV was killed in combat with CR 32s, but whether or not this was FEODOR is questionable. (Baumler)

FEODOROVICH, S.

Jefe I-15 Escuadrilla (?) (According to Salas, *Modelismo and Hist.*)

FEOKTISTOV, Stepan Petrovich, born 1913

SB Navigator in SENATOROV's 1st Esc. had arrived on 16 June 1937. He was KIA when his aircraft flown by TIKHOMIROV was shot down on 29 August 1937 in an air battle over Villamayor near Zaragoza. Abrosov attributes this to Monoplanes, but in fact it was CR 32s from the 19th Squadriglia "Asso di Bastoni" that attacked it. Giuseppe Ruzzin is listed as sharing in this kill. Awarded the Red Banner 22 October 1937. (Abrosov, *Los Rusos, Pravda*)

FERSKOV, I.

Pilot according to Laureau, but Logoluso says name was FORKSOV, Ivan and that he flew an I-15 that landed in France at Cenne-Monestier on 11 March 1938. But see listing for I. GORSHKOV. (Laureau, Logoluso, Abellan)

FILARETOVICH, K.E. (?)

In Spain September 1936 – July 1937 according to Lukes.

FILIPCHENKO, Fedor Vasil'evich, born 28 October 1915

Before going to Spain he was a pilot in the 36th IAE[1] 56th IAB (this later became the 28th IAP). An I-16 pilot using the codename "Federico," he arrived 10 June 1938. He became a Patrulla leader in early July when GRITSEVETS took command of an Escuadrilla. Later when GRITSEVETS had become Group commander, he was on the Staff. Fought in two air combats, claiming one Fiat CR 32. On 23 July 1938 at the beginning of the Ebro operation his and KHOTELEV's Moscas were badly shot up. He was wounded and could hardly see, but was led back to the airfield by a Spanish pilot who flew alongside of him. He returned to the USSR on 15 September 1938. Awarded the Red Banner 22 February 1939. Back in the USSR, he returned to service in the 28th IAP and participated in the Western Ukraine/Byelorussia Operation 15 September to 15 October 1939 (Occupation of Eastern Poland). From 1940 to June 1941 he was second in command of the 12th IAP. After which he fought on the Southern front from mid-June until July 1942 as an Eskadril'ya CO in the 13th IAP. After that, he was CO of the 73rd GIAP until April 1943, then moved as CO of an Eskadril'ya in the 22nd ZAP 3rd ZAB until June 1943. Next he was named CO of the 1st PAD which brought Lend Lease aircraft from Alaska to Yakutsk Siberia. Then he went onto the Staff of the 20th and 5th PAPs. He retired in 1958, and passed away 24 April 1992. [1]Kaminskii lists as the 36th while Abrosov lists as the 4th. (Semenov *Tov.*, *Vmeste,* Kaminskii, *Pravda*, Abrosov)

FINN, Il'ya Aleksandrovich, born 1911

Trained first at the Leningrad Military Theoretical School, and then the Serpukhov Military Pilots School. In 1935 he was a test pilot in the NII VVS Moscow Mil. Dist. He went to Spain on 5 September 1937. Was member of the 1st Esc. I-15 under SEROV, and according to Los Rusos had the codename "Ilio." Logged at least one night kill (S 81) on night of 25-26 September 1937 plus two others. Died in Spain, Salas in *Aeroplano* #6 p.86 states the Diario de la Escuadrillas list Fin (sic) as dying in an accident on 26 October 1937. He was killed when returning to Sabadell from a night mission, his wheels hit the trees causing the plane to crash. A photo of the Chato he died in is in Schroeder. He is said to have been awarded the Red Banner on 10 November 1937, but is not listed in Pravda for that day. Berch extract #5 says FINN buried at Sabadell along with VOLOSHCHENKO. Abellan, on the other hand, says (incorrectly) killed on 16 October 1937 while Shingarev (also incorrectly) says he was killed on 2 November 1937 and that he was awarded the H.S.U. posthumously, but there is no record of him in the H.S.U. lists. (Salas, Gusev 71, Berch, Ha 24, *G y Rev 3* photo facing p.160, Logoluso, Schroeder, Abellan, Shingarev, Lukes, Abrosov, *Los Rusos*, Kaminskii)

FIRSOV, Vladimir P., born 1914

Worker from Aircraft Factory #1, assembling I-15 and SSS aircraft. In Spain October 1936 to 27 March 1937. Awarded the Red Star 2 January 1937. (*Los Rusos, Pravda*)

FOMENKO, Igor T., born 1911

Mechanic in TARKHOV's I-16 group, in Spain from October 1936 to 27 August 1937. Awarded the Red Star 2 January 1937. (*Solidarity, Vmeste, Pravda*)

FOMENKO, Sergei Timofeevich, Lt., born 1913

Navigator SB, arrived in Spain 26 March and returned 18 August 1938. Awarded The Red Banner on 22 February 1939. (Berch, *Los Rusos, Pravda*)

FOMENKO, Vladimir

Pilot killed in Spain, says POLUSHKO in *Vmeste*.

FOMIN, Ivan Dmitrievich, Lt., born 1911

Fighter pilot in the 56th IAB Kiev Mil. Dist. Departed for Spain 20 August 1937 as an I-16 pilot and served in DEVOTCHENKO's 5th Esc. Died in an aircraft crash on 17 November 1937 while taking off from Caspe Aerodrome. Earlier on 9 August he and GORYAINOV had collided while taxing, damaging a wing on one of the fighters; neither pilot was injured. Awarded the Red Banner 2 March 1938. (Kaminskii, *Pravda*, Abrosov in his 2003 edition lists as Nikolai, but this is corrected in the 2008 edition, *Los Rusos* list date of death as 17 January 1937.)

FOMIN, Nikolai Yakovlevich, Lt., born 1916
I-16 Pilot in the 4th IAE 56th IAB Kiev Mil. Dist. Arrived in Spain 10 June 1938 and returned on 26 October 1938. He was in the 5th Moscas under KOROBKOV. Flew fifty-six combat missions and participated in twenty-five air combats One aircraft to credit, awarded the Red Banner on 22 February 1939. In September 1939 he was a Zvena CO in the 12th IAP. Participated in the operations for the western Ukraine, claiming one aircraft in Zvena. At the beginning of WWII he was a Eskadril'ya CO in the 17th IAP on the Southern front. He was KIA on 10 November 1941. (Semenov *"Parol,"* *Vmeste*, Kaminskii, *Pravda*, Abrosov)

FORTAKOV, V.I., born 1912
Worker from Aircraft Factory #1, assembling I-15 and SSS aircraft. Served from October 1936 to 7 April 1937. Awarded the Red Star 2 January 1937. (*Pravda, Los Rusos* list first name as Boris)

GAITOV, Gaskar D., born 1909
Bomber Aviation Technician (SSS), served from October 1936 to 7 April 1937. Awarded the Red Star 2 January 1937. (*Los Rusos, Pravda*)

GALAICHUK, Ilya Anufrievich, NCO, born 1912
Radio/Gunner SB, arrived 26 March and returned 3 September 1938. Awarded the Red Banner 22 February 1939. (Berch, *Los Rusos*, Semenov *"Parol," Pravda*)

GALIMOV, Mukharam Nigametovich, Maj., born 1907
SB Navigator in Spain 14 December 1937 to 21 July 1938. Participated in the attack on the Baleares on 6 March 1938. During the 28 January 1938 attack on Salamanca he was one of the few who were able to endure the flight at high altitude and successfully come back to land at San Clemente airfield where the two Soviet Escuadrillas were based. GUDOVICH in *My* (1986) says GALIMOV was the Navigator for STECHISHIN. Awarded the Red Banner twice, 14 November 1938 and 22 February 1939. (Berch, Semenov *"Parol," My, Los Rusos, Pravda*)

GALIN, Aleksei
SB pilot, shot down on 21 July 1937. According to Abrosov, P. Boddem of 2J/88 shot down this aircraft flown by GALIN and wounded his Gunner ARONOV. One engine had caught fire, but they were able to put it out, then both engines quit running and they were forced to make an emergency crashlanding just inside Republican territory. The J/88 victory list in R and R indicates Boddem downed an I-16 that day, but there is no I-16 listed as lost on the 21st. (Abrosov, R and R)

GAL'TSEV, Ivan S., born 1901
He was the head of the political Dept. of the 40th LBAB Aviabrigade Byelorussian Mil. Dist. A.F. Staff Regimental Commissar. In Spanish service from October 1936 and returned home on 17 June 1937. Awarded the Red Star on 2 January 1937. (*Solidarity*, Zil'manovich, *Pravda*, Abrosov)

GALUNOV, Dimitrii Pavlovich, Sr.Lt., born 1904
In Spain 17 October 1936 to 2 July 1937, assistant commander/Chief of Staff of the SSS 1st Escuadrilla. While in Spain he used the codename "Ramon." Awarded the Red Banner on 2 January 1937. At the start of WWII, he was CO of the 21st ShAD, which is said to have performed very well claiming twenty enemy aircraft for the loss of six of their own on that first day. Next he commanded the 174th IAD and on 18 May 1943 became CO of the 8th GvIAD (217 IAD). On 5 July 1943 he took over command of the 5th IAK (Fighter Aviation Corps) of the 2nd Air Army, with rank of Major-General. After war he remained in the VVS, until 1961, after which he was put in charge of the Kiev Airport. (*Vmeste*, Boyd, *Aviatsiya i Kosmonavtika, Pravda* where name is misspelt as GOLUNOV)

GAMSHIEVICH, Isidor
Translator for Hidalgo de Cisneros and TARKHOV. (Rumyantsev *"Antonio"*)

GAVRILIN, Ivan A., born 1912
Worker from Aircraft Factory #22 assembling SB aircraft. In Spain October to 13 December 1936. Awarded the Red Star 2 January 1937. (*Los Rusos, Pravda*)

GAVRISH, Sergei Tikhonovich, NCO, born 1914
Radio/gunner SB, Arrived in April and returned 3 September 1938. Codename "Finenko." Awarded the Red Banner 22 February 1939. (Berch, Semenov *"Parol," Pravda, Los Rusos* where it is spelled GAVISH)

GAVRYAT, Stepan A., Lt., born 1906

Bomber pilot SSS served from October 1936 to 8 May 1937. Awarded the Red Banner 2 January 1937. (*Los Rusos, Pravda*, Abrosov p.376 lists as GOVRYAT, Navigator on SSS)

GENOV, Naum A., born 1909

Engineer from Aircraft Factory #22 assembling SB aircraft. In Spain October to 12 December 1936. Awarded the Red Banner 2 January 1937. (*Pravda, Los Rusos* spell it GUENOV)

GERASIMOV, Aleksandr Ivanovich

Gagin says was in RYCHAGOV's esc. (Semenov "*Parol*," Gagin)

GERASIMOV, Nikolai Semenovich Senior, Lt., born 6 December 1911

Joined the Soviet Army VVS in 1934. Attended Borisogleb Flight School in 1937. Before going to Spain he was a Zvena CO in the 56th IAB Kiev Mil. Dist. He arrived in Spain on 10 June and returned home on 26 October 1938. He was wounded during an air battle on 29 July 1938, later in August became a Patrulla leader in the 2nd Moscas under SEMENKO. Next he was put on Group Staff, then became second in command of the Group under GRITSEVETS, which was comprised of the 2nd and 5th Moscas during the Battle of the Ebro. Flew eighty missions and fought in thirty-eight air combats claiming five enemy aircraft. At end of the war he had reached the rank of Major. Awarded title of H.S.U. on 22 February 1939. He fought in the Battles of Khalkhin-Gol in 1939 with the 70th IAP flying I-153s, where he shot down two Japanese Ki-27 fighters. Awarded the Red Banner on 29 August 1939 and the Mongolian Order of the Red Banner 1st Cl. on 18 August 1939. He participated in the campaign of liberation in Western Ukraine September 1939. Fought in the Russo-Finnish war 1939-40 as assistant CO of the VVS 7th Army. At the beginning of WWII, he was Chief flight instructor VVS, then on Staff of the 129th IAP. In September 1941 became CO of the 512th IAP until September 1942 when he was wounded. After recuperating, became replacement Commander of the 256th IAD from July 1943 until November 1944. During WWII, he flew 500 combat missions and claimed twenty-six aircraft (sixteen personal and ten in group) and was wounded ten times. Continued to serve in VVS until 1954 when he retired as a Colonel. Died 29 June 1960. Awards were Order of Lenin twice, Order of the Red Banner three times, Great Patriotic War 1st Cl., Order of the Red Star twice plus other medals. (Semenov *Tov*. Merono 204, *Solidarity, Vmeste, Geroi*, Kaminskii, *Pravda*)

GIBELLI, Primo, born 27 December 1893

Born in Italy, emigrated to the USSR in 1921. In 1933 he was a test pilot with the NII VVS. While attempting to fly under a Moscow bridge, he crashed and the aircraft was destroyed. After his release from the hospital, he was dismissed from the Army. He then began working at a job repairing engines after which he went to work at an automobile factory in Moscow. One of the first Soviet volunteers to arrive in Spain in September 1936. In Spain he used the Nom de guerre "Jose Cordero," and served in the 1st Escuadrilla Internacional. When he first arrived, he flew a Br 19 in a Patrulla commanded by KHOL"ZUNOV. Later in October was appointed crew commander of a Potez 540. On 4 November two Potez under command of Gibelli went on mission over the Madrid front and were attacked by Heinkel 51s, four of which were said to have been downed by the escorting I-15s. On a mission 10 November he was flying Potez 540 "A," the aircraft was shot down by AAA and he was killed. Howson found the following information in Madrid: On 10 November 1936, Potez A, one of two sent out, was shot down near Alcorcón (a small town about 7-8 miles southwest of Madrid on the road to Navalcarnero.) The crew consisted of (Pilot) Cordero. (2nd Pilot) Sgt. Paul. (Bombardier) Brig. Chardell, Sgts, Carnero, Soto and Corporal Virgilio Gonzalez (Gunners) and Montilla (Mech.). (A note by J. Carmody says that this aircraft was perhaps named "Marat.") This aircraft had not been claimed by the Nationalist Air Force, and there was no indication of how it was shot down, nor how many casualties. But DEMENCHUK in *MY* (1986) p.31 says that while carrying out the mission the aircraft was shot down by AAA, caught fire and fell in enemy territory. Abrosov also says downed by AAA on 10 November 1936. Posthumously awarded the H.S.U. 31 December 1936. *Solidarity* lists him as DJIBELLI, P.A. Some sources

have said he was the "Man in the Box," which the Nationalists sent back, but see listing for BOCHAROV. The Enciclopedia dell'antifascismo e della Resistenza lists him as Luigi GORELLI (?). See also Malraux Man's Hope, pgs.278-282, where he possibly gives a fictionalized version of this mission, calling the pilot Carnero. (Salas, Osipenko, Stuani, *Bajo la B.*, Berch, *Vmeste*, *MY, MY* (1986), Pritsker, Howson, Abrosov, Carmody)

GLADINTSEV, Vladimir P., Lt., born 1911

Navigator SB, arrived 30 December 1937 and returned 13 July 1938. Participated in the attack on the Baleares on 6 March 1938. Awarded the Red Banner on 14 November 1938. (Berch, Semenov "*Parol,*" *Los Rusos, Pravda*)

GLOMOZD, Vasilii D., born 1913

Bomber Aviation Technician, served from October 1936 to 8 March 1937. Awarded the Red Star on 2 January 1937. (*Los Rusos, Pravda*)

GLUKHOVTSEV, Ivan A., Lt., born 1907

Navigator on SB in Spain from 3 January to 30 June 1937. On 21 February 1937 he mistakenly bombed the Town of Alcala, 5km from the airfield. Awarded the Red Banner 17 July 1937. (Abrosov, *Vmeste* spells it GLUKHOVSKII, *Los Rusos, Pravda*)

GLUSHENKOV, Nikifor Emmanuilovich, Capt., born 1902

Before Spain he was a flight inspector in the 107th IAE 83rd IAB Byelorussian Mil. Dist. He arrived 26 March 1938 and returned to the USSR on 23 August 1938. He was CO of the 5th Escuadrilla (Kaminskii says 2nd) de Moscas (I-16) from the start of April and later became Commander of Grupo 21 until his return. Beginning on 25 May until 30 June, he was sick and after recuperating began forming the Fighter Group. During that time PROKOPENKO was technically in command of the 5th Esc. While in command of the group, he wrote reports back to Moscow complaining about the M-25A and V (B) engine problems. Listed as having ten victories, seven Fiats, one Bf 109 and two He 111, he had flown ninety missions and fought in fourteen air battles. Awarded the Order of Lenin on 22 February 1939. Served in WWII as a VVS commander and after the war from 1946 to 1952 was VVS Commander of the Siberian Mil. Dist. Died 5 January 1960. (Semenov "*Parol,*" Semenov *Tov.*, *Vmeste*, Abrosov, Kaminskii, Salas "*Diario,*" *Pravda*)

GLUSHKOV, Petr Gerasimovich, Sgt., born 1913

Was a pilot in the 36th IAE 56th IAB Kiev Mil. Dist. before going to Spain, I-16 Pilot, served from 10 June until 26 October 1938. A member of the 5th Esc. he had flown thirty-nine missions and participated in twenty air combats. On 3 August, he along with ZYUZIN 5th Esc. and ZHURAVLOV from the 2nd Esc. all destroyed their aircraft in landing accidents. After having the engine on his replacement aircraft repaired, on 18 August he made a return flight to Valls, where he forgot to lower the landing gear and came in on the belly. The aircraft had to be repaired. In an air combat on 23 August both his and ONISHCHENKO's Mosca were shot up, but able to return to the airfield without problems. Later on 27 September 1938 in an air battle his aircraft CM-210[1] collided with another Mosca flown by V. STARKOV. GLUSHKOV was able to bail out, but STARKOV was killed. Awarded the Red Banner 22 February 1939. Fought in the Russo-Finnish Winter War where he claimed two aircraft shot down. During WWII, he was the assistant CO of the 721st IAP., flew 400 missions and claimed fifteen enemy aircraft. On 10 April 1945 he went missing during a flight in the Mezeritts area. TUROV in *Vmeste* lists him as Pavel (Semenov "*Parol,*" *Vmeste*, Abrosov, *Los Rusos*, Kaminskii, *Pravda*. [1]Salas in "*Diario*" says this Aircraft was flown by E. Fernandez Plaza. There is also a problem with the listing of the three Aircraft destroyed on 3 August On p.27 of *Diario*, Salas lists CM 092, 176 and 165 as from the 5th and CM 139 as in the 4th. But on p.216 he lists CM 165 and 176 as 2nd Esc. CM 139 no Esc. mentioned and CM 092 no Esc. but flown by A. Dominguez Lopez. Bodrikhin lists as MIA April 1942.)

GODUNOV, Viktor Aleksandrovich, Lt., born 1911
Prior to Spain, he had been a senior pilot in the 17th IAE 142nd IAB Byelorussian Mil. Dist. I-16 Pilot, served from 20 August 1937 until 28 February 1938. Member of GUSEV's 6th Esc., he fought in fifteen air battles and claimed two enemy aircraft. On 12 October 1937 in a combat with Fiats, he was badly wounded in the left arm while flying CM-156; the aircraft was destroyed on landing. After his release from the hospital he returned to the USSR. Awarded the Red Banner on 2 March 1938. During WWII at the beginning of 1943 he was on staff of 247th IAD (Abrosov says the 210th IAD), this was renamed the 4th GvIAD. In October 1944 he was made CO of the 5th Reserve Aviation Group. Passed away 17 May 1988. (Gusev, Shingarev, *Pravda, Los Rusos,* Kaminskii, Abrosov)

GOLOVKO, Ivan L., Lt., born 1907
Bomber/navigator, in Spain October 1936 to 30 June 1937. Gagin says was in K. GUSEV's 15th Grupo (SSS). Awarded the Red Banner 2 January 1937. (Gagin, *Los Rusos, Pravda*)

GOLOVKO, Pavel P., born 1903
Mechanic (Aviation?) in Spain from October 1936 to 27 March 1937. Awarded the Red Star 2 January 1937. (*Los Rusos, Pravda*)

GOLOVNEV, Pavel Fedorovich, Lt., born 1912
Was a pilot in the 121st IAE 95th IAB transcaucasian Mil. Dist. I-15 Pilot, he was in Spain from 14 January until 5 August 1937. Wounded in a landing accident on 14 April 1937. Gagin says he was in SEROV's esc., but this is impossible as SEROV only arrived in Spain in June, and did not take over the 1st Escuadrilla until September 1937. Had to have been in either OSADCHII's or ZOTSENKO's Escuadrilla. Awarded the Red Banner 17 July 1937 plus the Medal for Bravery on 14 November 1938. In 1940 he was the assistant CO of the 67th IAP, flying 1-16s. (Berch, *Bajo la B.*, Gagin, Abrosov, Kaminskii, *Pravda*)

GOLUBEV, Konstantin Ivanovich, Lt., born 1911
Fighter pilot in the 107th IAE 83rd IAB Byelorussian Mil. Dist., flew the I-16. He arrived on 26 March 1938 and became ill right after he arrived. He was sent to the hospital and after release was sent home, returning to the USSR on 10 June 1938. He did not fly any missions while in Spain. After returning he again served in the 107th IAE. (Abrosov, Kaminskii, *Los Rusos* claims was awarded the Red Banner, but no listing found in *Pravda.*)

GOLUBEV, Valentin D., born 1904
Armaments worker from Aircraft Factory #1, assembling I-15 and SSS aircraft. In Spain October 1936 to 30 January 1937. Awarded the Red Star 2 January 1937. (*Los Rusos, Pravda*)

GONCHAROV, Ivan
White Russ. Lacalle Esc. Var.sp GONTCHAROV (Logoluso)

GONCHAROV, Pavel Artemovich, Lt., born 11 August 1913
He was CO of a Zvena in the 36th IAE 56th IAB Kiev Mil. Dist. An I-15 pilot, he left for Spain in October 1936 actually arriving at Bilbao on the night of 1 November and was a member of TRUZHANSKII's Esc. on the Northern or Basque Front. Later in 1937 he flew I-16s. Returned home 27 May 1937. He had fought in eighty air combats and shot down three enemy aircraft, and was awarded the Red Banner on 2 January 1937. Between October 1937 and March 1938 he went from a detachment CO to Commander of the 5th IAE 8th IAB. From November 1939 to December 1940 he was the CO of the 13th IAP VVS Baltic Fleet where he fought in the Winter War from 30 November 1939 to 12 March 1940. He was awarded the Red Banner for his actions on 21 April 1940. From December 1940 to February 1942 was head of the Aviation Dept. Naval War Academy. In March 1942 he became CO of the 14th IAP VVS Pacific Fleet, and later in October 1946 became CO of the 12th IAP Pacific Fleet. He continued to serve in the Naval Air Force until the mid 1950s. Passed away 24 October 1982. (Lukes, *Pravda*, Abrosov, *Los Rusos*, Kaminskii, *Pravda*)

GORANOV, Vulkan Semenovich, born 4 February 1904
Real name ZAKHARIEV, Zakhari Simeonov, a Bulgarian in the Soviet Army. Before going to Spain he was an instructor at the Tambov Aviation School.

He volunteered for foreign duty and came to Spain in September 1936. Where he flew in the 1st Escuadrilla Internacional, which consisted of Potez 540s and Br 19s, later in November 1936 he switched to flying SBs in the 12th Grupo. Awarded the H.S.U. on 31 December 1936 with the rank of Colonel. Passed away 29 April 1987. See main listing under ZAKHARIEV. (Berch via RSA, *Bajo la B.*, Zil'manovich, *Vmeste* Salas, Logoluso, *Solidarity, Pravda*)

GORBATENKO, Aleksii G., Lt., born 1909
Navigator/gunner on SSS Attack Aircraft, served from October 1936 until 3 August 1937. Injured on 22 January 1937 while landing after a mission. Awarded the Red Banner 2 January 1937. (Semenov, Abrosov, *Pravda*)

GORBATOV, Vasilii Ivanovich, born 1908
Armaments Technician on ShKAS machine guns mounted on the I-16 and SB. In Spain from October 1936 to 17 September 1937. Awarded the Red Star 2 January 1937. Also awarded Order of the Red Banner on 27 June 1937. (*Vmeste, Los Rusos* list as I-16 tech., *Pravda*)

GORBUNOV, Nikolai Nikolaevich
Gunner SB, arrived in April 1938. Awarded the Red Banner on 22 February 1939. (Berch, *Pravda*)

GORELOV, Anatolii Andreevich, NCO, born 1911
Radio/Gunner SB, arrived 14 December 1937 and was killed in action on 7 February 1938. He was a member of SURZHIN's crew. When the aircraft he was in burst into flames he jumped, but apparently opened his parachute too soon, where it was struck by flaming debris. His chute burned up and he fell to his death. See SURZHIN listing. He was from Leningrad. He was buried together with LATYSHEV and BOLDYREV in Mora de Rubielos. Awarded the Red Star on 14 November 1938. (Semenov "*Parol*," Berch, Los Rusos, *Pravda*)

GOREV, Vladimir Efimovich, born 1900
Although not Air Force, he was one of the top Military attaches; he arrived in Spain along with first Soviet Ambassador MARCEL ROSENBERG in August 1936. Later in November 1936 he was a Brigade Commander on the Madrid front. Went to the North at the end of 1936, where he was an advisor in the defense of Bilbao and later Santander. As the Northern front collapsed, GOREV became trapped at Gijon along with twenty-five other Soviet officers and his interpreter Emma Wolff. Ehrenberg, pgs.376-377, goes on to say that most of the Soviets were rescued by ABEL GUIDEZ in three flights. On the fourth flight 7 September 1937[1] GUIDEZ was shot down. When the Gijon pocket fell (21 October) GOREV and the few remaining Soviets "took to the Mountains with the Guerrillas" and were later rescued by Soviet aircraft. Approximately six months later he would fall in Stalin's purge of the military. He was arrested on 25 January 1938 and tried and executed on 20 June 1938. Howson, p.40, says that GUIDEZ was flying on 7 September 1937 to Gijon to rescue some Russian airmen when his Envoy III F-AQCS was downed by Bf 109s, GUIDEZ being killed. Ries and Ring mentions only that HARDER claimed a French twin engine aircraft on the 7th of September; Garriga has same information from above, but says the Spanish destroyer "Ciscar" had been sent to pick up the Russians (against orders) and was sunk by Legion Condor Aircraft on 20 October 1937. Awarded the Red Star in 1936 and the Order of Lenin and Red Banner in 1937. (Berch, *Icare 130*, Ehernberg, Howson, R and R, Garriga pgs.154-155, Suvenirov[1] Castells, A. *Las Brigadas Internacionales de la Guerra de España*, Ariel, Barcelona 1974 p.482 says Guidez died in October 1937.)

GORLACHENKO, Mikhail Iosifovich, Capt., born 1905
Pilot of SSS Rasante in 1936 says KARPENKO in *Vmeste* p.166, but Lugoluso thinks he was an SB Pilot. *Los Rusos* say he arrived May 1936 (?) and returned 2 July 1937. Awarded the Red Banner 17 July 1937. At the start of 1942 he was CO of the 226th ShAD and then in 1942-45 Major General commanding the III ShAK operating the Il-2 Shturmovik. Passed away in 1976. (*Icare 130*, Semenov "*Parol*," *Los Rusos*, Lugoluso, *Pravda*)

GORODNYAKOV, Makar G., Lt., born 1907
Bomber Navigator (SSS?), served from October 1936 to 8 May 1937. Awarded the Red Banner 2 January 1937. (*Los Rusos, Pravda*)

GOROKHOV, Aleksei Mikhailovich, Lt., born 1912
Originally in the 12th IAE 111th IAB Leningrad Mil. Dist. before Spain. An I-15 pilot he served from 20 August 1937 to 2 March 1938 as CO of a Patrulla in the 1st Escuadrilla de Chatos. He had arrived in Spain along with DEVOTCHENKO, KOTYKHOV, POPOV and others. Logoluso lists as nightfighter pilot. In one of the air battles, his Aircraft was shot up and had to make a crashlanding. After his return to the USSR, he was CO of an IAE in the 26th IAP and fought in the Winter War with Finland and it is thought that he was KIA in Finland. Awarded the Red Banner 15 January 1940. Salas lists as GOROJOV. (Laureau, Salas, *Bajo la B.*, Shingarev, Kaminskii)

GORSHKOV, Ivan Aleksandrovich, Lt., born 1910
Fighter pilot and Zvena CO in the 6th IAE 116th IAB Byelorussian Mil. Dist. In Spain flew an I-15, serving in the 1st Esc. from 30 December 1937 to 25 April 1938. On 20 January 1938 during an air battle, while flying Chato 9963, he collided with another I-15 flown by a Spanish pilot and had to bailout. On 10 March he along with OSIPOV while flying to Caspe, became disoriented and landed their I-15s at Cennes-Monestié France.[1] It took a week before they were allowed to return to Spain. He is thought to have served during WWII on the staff of the 434th IAP. (Abrosov, Kaminskii, Saiz, [1]Masse p.101 lists them as A. Ozipoff and Ivan Forksov.)

GORYAINOV, Nikolai Aleksandrovich, Lt., born 1909
Was a Zvena CO in the 2nd IAE 56th IAB Kiev Mil. Dist. Served in Spain as an I-16 Pilot, from 10 June until 12 October 1938. He was a member of 5th Esc. under KOROBKOV. Flew thirty-one combat missions and fought in twenty-four air battles. Awarded the Red Banner 22 February 1939. During WWII, he was the CO of the 163rd IAP flying Yaks. On 27 March 1944 he along with the assistant CO V.S. Bogatyrev had taken off on a "Free Hunt" in the Lake Synovo area near Kovel Volynsk. Both men failed to return from this mission. (Semenov "*Parol*," *Vmeste*, Abrosov, *Los Rusos* list as GARIAINOV, Kaminskii, *Pravda*)

GRACHEV, Grigorii Nikolaevich, Lt., born 1907
Pilot SB, arrived in Spain 30 May and returned home on 15 November 1938. Awarded the Red Banner on 22 February 1939. (Berch, Semenov "*Parol*," *Los Rusos, Pravda*)

GRACHEV, Mikhail N., born 1912
Aviation Technician, served from October 1936 to 27 August 1937. Awarded the Red Star 2 January 1937. (*Los Rusos, Pravda*)

GRIBANOV, Petr Georgievich, Lt., born 1911
Fighter pilot and Zvena CO in the 6th IAE 116th IAB Byelorussian Mil. Dist. Served in Spain from 30 December 1937 to 2 March 1938 flying an I-16. He was sent home early due to illness. During WWII, from 11 July 1941 he was the assistant CO of an IAE in the 32nd IAP flying I-16s. On 13 January 1942 he was KIA when his plane was shot down during an air combat with Me 109s over the Barbinino-Moscow area. Kaminskii thinks that the pilot who shot him down was *Feldwebel* Karl Ruitter of JG 52. (Abrosov, Kaminskii)

GRIBOV, Andrei I., Capt., born 1915
I-16 pilot, KIA on 24 October 1937 when he is said to have rammed a Bf 109[1]. Awarded the Red Star on 2 March 1938. (Kaminskii pgs.358-359, *Pravda*. [1]There is no info on him in Abrosov)

GRIBOV, Nikandr S.
Before Spain, he was in the 147th SBAB Leningrad Mil. Dist. An SB Pilot, he arrived in Spain December 1937 and returned approx. July 1938. On 28 January 1938, he aborted a mission to Salamanca without sufficient reason (Abrosov p.201). Did not receive any awards for Spanish duty. (Berch, Semenov "*Parol*," Abrosov)

GRIGOR'EV, Anton Grigor'evich, Lt., born 1910
I-16 Fighter pilot in the 107th IAE 83rd IAB Byelorussian Mil. Dist. In Spain from 26 March to 10 June 1938, where he flew thirty missions and fought in five air combats (some information says he did not fly any combat missions) and returned home early due to health problems. It is thought that he participated in the fighting at the Khalkhin-Gol, and that in June 1943 was on the Staff of the 299th ShAD. (Abrosov, *Los Rusos*, Kaminskii)

GRIN'KO, Platon P., born 1906
Worker from Aircraft Factory #22, assembling SB aircraft. In Spain from October to 13 December 1936. Awarded the Red Star 2 January 1937. (*Los Rusos, Pravda*)

GRITSEVETS, Sergei Ivanovich, Sr.Lt., born 19 July 1909
Joined the army in 1931. Attended Orenburg Military Flying School. Prior to going to Spain he was VRIO Zvena CO at the 8th Odessa Pilots School in Kiev and is also said to have trained Spanish pilots at Kirovabad on the U-2, I-5 and I-16 types along with Nikolai ROMANOV. He departed for Spain on the 10th of June

1938 on the Andrei Zhdanov. "Comrade Sergio" was put into the 2nd Escuadrilla de Moscas stationed at Utiel airfield under the command of RODIN on 21 June. Later at the beginning of July, with RODIN in the hospital after being wounded, he took over command of the 2nd and began putting together his own Escuadrilla from the new pilots that had arrived with him. His second-in-command was NEDELIN, with FILIPPCHENKO, KOROBKOV, and SEMENKO as his Patrulla leaders. Later in August when GLUSHENKOV returned home, he was given command of the entire Group. This Group was made up of two Mosca Escuadrillas, the 2nd under NEDELIN and the 5th at first under GRITSEVETS and then KOROBKOV, with GRITSEVETS as overall leader. When this Group was initially put together it had thirty-four pilots on its roster, and during the course of operations had lost nine of its pilots. On 20 October the aircraft from the group were taken over by Spanish pilots with the 2nd going to Pereira. (Tarazona claims Pereira had the 2nd on 21 September.) Every member of the Group was awarded the Order of the Red Banner. He had six kills to his credit, five fighters and one bomber plus twenty-four more in Group. ANDREEV in *Vmeste* claims GRITSEVETS shot down two Fiats on 18 August 1938, but I think he means the 14th. In one air battle on 13 August 1938 he, together with the Spanish pilot Luis Margalef, succeeded in forcing a He 111 to land in Republican territory where the aircraft was captured and the crew taken prisoner. During his time in Spain, the airfields used by his units were Utiel, Villar, Liria and Figueras. By the end of his tour in Spain he had become a Major and he returned home on 26 October 1938. Awarded the H.S.U. and Order of Lenin on 22 February 1939. After Spain he served in the Battle for Khalkhin-Gol, where he was at first deputy commander of the 70th IAP until mid July 1939, then commanded a unit of I-153s (100th Mixed Aviation). On 26 June 1939, during an air combat, the commander of the 70th IAP Major Zabaluev was shot down. His aircraft crash-landed behind Japanese lines, GRITSEVETS landed his I-16 and sharing the cramped cockpit with Zabaluev took off again under fire from approaching Japanese forces. (Polak in his book mistakenly lists date as 23 August 1939.) For his actions in the Khalkhin-Gol he received a 2nd H.S.U. on 29 August 1939. At the beginning of September 1939, the Soviets began concentrating their most experienced pilots on their Western frontier border with Poland, in readiness for what they would call "The Campaign for the Western Ukraine and Byelorussia." GRITSEVETS was appointed as an advisor to the Fighter Aviabrigade based in Orsha. On 16 September 1939 at approximately 7:00pm one day before the invasion, the Fighter Group was given a mission to do a recon. Three aircraft took off on this mission from their base at Balbasovo at 7:30pm. After completing the mission, two of these fighters, those flown by "Spaniards" GRITSEVETS and KHARA, collided with each other while attempting to land at the airfield. KHARA survived but GRITSEVETS was killed in the crash. An investigation seems to have indicated that Captain KHARA was at fault[1]. Information listed in Rumyantsev *Geroi* credits him with thirty kills in Spain as does the Finnish book *Red Stars* also twelve more at Khalkhin Gol. (Semenov "*Parol*," Semenov *Tov*., Berch, *Pravda, Vmeste*, Polak, Seidl Kaminskii, Slyusarev in *Soviet Volunteers in China 1925-1945*, Progress Publishers, Moscow 1980 p.258 says GRITSEVETS was involved in fighting around Hankow China on 29 April 1938 as does "V Nebe Kitiya," but it is not mentioned in any of his biographies. Boyd says the Aviation School in Khar'kov is named after him. Note: In the supposed list of his victories in Polak p.138, the author is mistaken in his note about the He 111. Margalef was in fact a Republican pilot with the 3rd Moscas. He had trained in the USSR, and was KIA over the Ebro on 22 September 1938. [1]For more details on his death, see "The Fate of Two Majors" at airaces.narod.ru. This site also has a drawing of CM-215 that they say was his aircraft, but the CM is black and not the usual white of command.)

GRITSUK, Vladimir N., born 1901

Rasante (SSS) Group Engineer says GALUNOV in *Vmeste*, In Spain from October 1936 to 2 July 1937. Awarded the Red Star 2 January 1937. (*Vmeste, Los Rusos, Pravda*)

GROMOV, Ilya N., born 1906

Armaments specialist from Aircraft Factory #22 assembling SB aircraft. In Spain from October to 12 December 1936. Awarded the Red Banner 2 January 1937. (*Los Rusos, Pravda*)

GROMOV, Mikhail

Listed by AKULENKO as an I-16 Pilot in the Escuadrilla under KOLESNIKOV, His Bio. on the internet says nothing about a service in Spain. Very doubtful (*Vmeste,* OnAirpower.org.)

GUBENKO, Anton Alekseevich, born 12 February 1908

Some sources say he was a Volunteer in Spain 1937, but there is no listing of him in Abrosov, Kaminskii or on airaces.narod.ru, the site for Soviet pilots in Spain. In March 1938 he was sent to China where he downed five Japanese aircraft. He returned home in August 1938. Awarded H.S.U. 22 February 1939. (*Lexikon*, Smirnov, Polak. Information on his service in China and subsequent death on 31 March 1939 can be found

in "Protecting China's Airspace" by S.V. SLYUSAREV in the book *Soviet Volunteers in China 1925-1945* Progress Publishers, Moscow 1980.)

GUDOVICH, Solomon Aronovich, Lt., born 1914

Navigator SB, in Spain from 26 March to 13 August 1938. In his memoir in *My* (1986), he says he arrived at Gerona Airfield on 15 March 1938, this field was shared by the two Soviet SB Escuadrillas, the other having arrived three months earlier from Leningrad. He also states that the Commander of his Escuadrilla was Lt. KRASHOGLAZOV, Nikolai but that in battle the Escuadrillas were led by "Comrade Andresu" Lt. STECHISHIN, Andrei. The crew of his aircraft was VALUEV, I., pilot, and POPOVKIN, gunner. In April, his Escuadrilla was transferred to the airfield at Lerida from which they flew missions against Mallorca. He also participated in attacks against other airfields like La Cenia. His Escuadrilla received orders to return to the Soviet Union at the end of August 1938, leaving only one (the last) Soviet SB Escuadrilla commanded by Lt. Mikhail KARPENKO remaining in Spain. Awarded the Red Banner 22 February 1939. During WWII, he was Chief of Staff of a Bomber Group, and later from 1947-1962 he taught at the Air Force Academy. In 1986 he was a retired Colonel. These memoirs of GUDOVICH seem to be at some odds with those of LIPASHOV in *Vmeste*, who even though they do not mention each other seem to have been in the same Escuadrilla. LIPASHOV wrote that STECHISHIN and his Escuadrilla was at Gerona when he arrived, but were getting ready to rotate home and was replaced by SEREBRYAKOV. He also says that KRASNOGLAZOV became CO of his Escuadrilla after its second operational flight. (Berch, Semenov "*Parol*," *My* (1986), *Vmeste, Los Rusos, Pravda*)

GUEORGUI

Jefe de Partulla SB 1936-7 (*Bajo la B.* p.377)

GULYAEV, Vyacheslev P., Sr.Lt., born 1906

Bomber navigator, served from October 1936 to 30 June 1937. Awarded the Red Banner 2 January 1937. (*Los Rusos, Pravda*)

GUMENNYI, Nikolai Gerasimovich, Lt., born 1911

Navigator on SB served from 3 January to 13 August1937. In January 1937, he had left his Base at Bykhov in Byelorussia and traveled to Moscow where his group of volunteers were assembled, they then took the Moscow-Paris Express, crossing Poland and Germany. From Paris they went on to southern France and into Spain at Port Bou. He was navigator of the SB flown by SENATOROV, which led the first group of I-16s under UKHOV to Santander. The radio/gunner on that mission was an Italian named Antonio. Awarded the Red Banner 17 July 1937. Died in 1980. (*Vmeste, Los Rusos, Pravda*)

GURIN, M.

Navigator SB, arrived in April 1938. (Berch, Semenov "*Parol*," but are they confused with the fighter pilot below?)

GURIN, Mikhail Mikhailovich, Lt., born 1913

Fighter pilot, was in the 107th IAE 83rd IAB Byelorussian Mil. Dist. He served in Spain from 26 March to 13 August 1938, as a Patrulla CO in an I-16 Escuadrilla. Fought in ten air battles and claimed four Fiat CR 32s (two personal and two in Group). Awarded the Red Banner on 22 February 1939. He was on the staff of the 80th SAP during the Winter War against Finland, for which he was awarded a 2nd Red Banner on 21 May 1940. In late-1940, he was in the 143rd IAP and later made second-in-command of an IAE when the war began in June 1941. He failed to return from a mission near Murmansk on 3 July 1941. (Abrosov, Kaminskii, *Pravda*)

GUSEV, Aleksandr Ivanovich, Sr.Lt., born 24 August 1910

Joined the Army in 1928 and later attended the Borisoglebsk Military Flying School. Detachment CO in the 17th IAE 142nd IAB Byelorussian Mil. Dist. Volunteered for Spanish service, departing on 20 August 1937, and returned on 25 April 1938. Using the codename "Alejandro" he commanded the 6th escuadrilla de Moscas on the Aragon front. The COs of three of his Patrullas were PANFILOV, "Victor" GODUNOV, and "Juanito" SMOLYAKOV. He commanded the I-16 Escuadrillas which took part in the attack on Garrapinillos Aerodrome on 15 October 1937, under the overall command of EREMEMKO. On 30 December 1937 he was wounded in an air combat against Bf 109s and Fiats (flying either CM 143 or 154) over Teruel. It was in that same 30 December battle that SUMAROV had been KIA and IL'IN wounded. He had just replaced EREMENKO as the CO of Fighter Air Group, when the latter returned home in January 1938 during the Teruel operations. He was temporarily replaced in that position by DEVOTCHENKO, until his return from the hospital in February 1938. He then resumed command of the Fighter Group, and was flying CM-157. He is said to have flown 100 combat mission and fought in thirty-two air battles, he claimed four aircraft (three personal and one in Group). He was awarded the H.S.U. and Order of Lenin on 14 November 1938 plus the Red Banner on 2 March 1938 for his sevice in Spain. As CO of the 1st VVS Army, he was initially directing the air operations at the beginning of the Khalkhin-Gol fighting, in May 1939, but with the battle escalating SMUSHKEVICH took over command. For this service in the fighting he was awarded the Mongolian Order of the Red Banner 1st class on 18 August 1939. GUSEV also was part of a Soviet delegation sent to Germany in October 1939 for the purpose of buying military aircraft. Yakovlev, also a member of this group, quoted GUSEV as saying "the aircraft shown them were all old junk!" He had also recommended that the three plane Zveno be changed to four planes (like the Germans), but this went unheeded. In 1940, he was the Deputy Commander VVS with the 8th Army during operations in Finland and was awarded the Red Banner 20 May 1940. During the Great Patriotic War, he commanded the 17th SAD until September 1941, the 106th IAD-PVO from December 1941 until November 1942 and then from November 1942 to July 1944 the 104th PVO. After which he led the 328th IAD-PVO for two months, with the rank of General Major. He retired in 1960, and died on 26 July 1978. Awards were H.S.U. on 14 November 1938, Order of Lenin twice, Order of the Red Banner five times, OPW 1st Cl., Order of the Red Star. (Gusev, Salas, Howson, Vasilevskii, RSA, Berch, Shingarev, Semenov "*Parol*," Yakovlev, Boyd, Sukhachev p.197, *Geroi Sovetskogo Soiuza*, Polak, Seidl, Kaminskii, *Pravda*, Abrosov)

GUSEV, Konstantin Mikhailovich, Major, born July 1906

In the PKKA since 1926. In 1926 he graduated from Leningrad military-theoretical school of pilots, and in 1928, the 2nd Borisglebsk military school for pilots. From July 1930 he was the commander of a Detachment of the 52nd IAE, and from November 1931 he first became CO of a Zvena then a Detachment and later Commander of the 9th ShAE (assault squadron) 114th ShAB at Gomel Byelorussia. He was Commander of the Rasantes (SSS) Grupo 15, in Spain from October 1936 until 17 June 1937. When the decision was first made to supply the Republic, a complete Eskadril'ya of 31 SSS with its corresponding crews of pilots and navigators, and ground personnel, totaling 109 men, plus spare parts, engines, ammunition and fuel was put together, with most of the men coming from the 114th ShAB Byelorussian Mil. Dist. Upon arrival in Spain, the Group Command and First Escuadrilla were based at Quintanar, while the second was at Santa Cruz de la Zarza and the third at Villamayor.[1] COs were LEVSKII (first), STRELKOV (second) and TUPIKOV/CHERVYAKOV (third).[2] Awarded the Red Banner twice, on 2 January and 21 June 1937. *Solidarity* says he was Commander of RZs, but *Solidarnost'* correctly lists as SSS. His codename was "Vochev," but GALUNOV in *Vmeste* p.153, says he used the name "Fernando" in Spain. In 1937-39 he was the commander of Air Forces BVO, Byelorussian Military Dist. In 1940-41 as a lieutenant general of aviation, he was commander of the Air Forces on the Far Eastern front. On 11 or 17 July 1941 (at least one internet site plus Murphy list as 17

June 1941) he was arrested. He never admitted to any guilt, but was sentenced at the People's Commissariat for Internal Affairs on 13 February and on 23 February 1942 he was shot. He had been awarded the Order Lenin and two awards of the Red Banner. (Zakharov, Lugoluso, Pritsker, *Los Rusos, Pravda*, KARPENKO in *Vmeste* p.161. [1]GALUNOV, Vmeste p.151. [2]Kotel'nikov in *Aviatsiya Vremya* #6 2001 indicates that Strelkov was CO of the 1st and LEVSKII CO of the 2nd, but KARPENKO, writing in *Vmeste,* states he was based at Santa Cruz and the CO was STRELKOV.)

GUSSAEV, A.I.

Said to have been Commander of the 24th Grupo de Kats (SB), reportedly under the codename "Gold," but see listing for ZLATOTSVETOV. Var.sp. GUSSEV. (Laureau, Martinez *AEQ 32*, Howson 278. It is possible that they are confusing him with the "Grupo Gusev" fighter unit Commanded by GUSEV, A.I.)

GUTSOL, Nikolai N., born 1909

Technician on I-15s from October 1936 until 7 April 1937 says KAL'CHENKO in *Vmeste*. Awarded the Red Star 2 January 1937. (*Vmeste, Los Rusos* spells it GUTSOV, *Pravda*)

IEVLEV, Anatoli P.

Worker from Aircraft Factory #21, assembling I-16 aircraft. Served from October 1936 to 3 June 1937. Awarded the Red Star 2 January 1937. (*Pravda, Los Rusos* spell it IVLIEV)

IGNATENKO, Andrei T., Lt., born 1908

Navigator SB in SENATOROV's Esc. In Spain from 15 June 1937 until 2 March 1938. Awarded Red Banner twice, 28 October 1937 and 2 March 1938. (*Solidarity, Pravda, Los Rusos* say pilot)

IHOSIAINOFF, G.

Prisoner of war (real name KHOZYAINOV, G. N.), see also JHOSIANOV, G. in Salas, and also JHOSIAINOFF, GREGORY NICHOLAS (name Anglicized) in *Spain* magazine August 15, 1938 p.17 which also mentions he was a twenty-three-year-old fighter pilot. (Hericourt, Salas, Berch, Logoluso)

ILIEV

Wounded six times by explosive bullets 2 June 1937 according to Baumler, see IL'IN, S.

IL'IN, Aleksandr N., born 1910

Aviation Technician (SSS?), in Spain October 1936 to 9 July 1937. Awarded the Red Star 2 January 1937. (*Pravda, Los Rusos* give end date as 1938)

IL'IN, Aleksandr Vasil'evich, born 12 February 1910

Before departing for Spain, he was a Zvena CO in the 142nd IAB Byelorussian Mil. Dist. Served in Spain from 20 August 1937 to 8 April 1938. He was an I-16 pilot in DEVOTCHENKO's Esc., later he became a Patrulla CO. He was wounded in a battle with Messerschmitts and Fiats on 30 December 1937, but was able to bring his aircraft (he was flying either CM-143 or 154) back to the airfield. After his release from hospital, he returned home. He had flown fifty combat missions and claimed one aircraft in patrulla. Awarded the Red Banner on 2 March 1938. From 25 December 1939 to 13 March 1940 he was the CO of the 4th OIAE and fought in the Winter War with Finland. Awarded the Red Banner 22 February 1941. During WWII he was second-in-command of the 13th IAP from January 1942 on the Leningrad front, this unit was later renamed the 4th GvIAP. On 30 September 1942, during an air combat, his aircraft was shot down and he was badly wounded. From March 1943 he was on the staff of the 3rd IAD (before the war this had been the 61st IAB), which in June 1943 was renamed as the 1st GvIAD. He flew 157 combat missions and fought in seventeen air battles, claimed five aircraft personal and in group. For service in WWII, he was awarded the Red Banner on 20 May 1944. After the war he was awarded another Red Banner on 21 August 1952 and a Red Star on 6 November 1947. Died in a plane crash on 25 October 1954. (Kaminskii, Berch, Gusev, Pritsker, *Pravda*)

IL'IN, Nikolai Ivanovich, NCO, born 1912

Radio/Gunner SB, arrived 28 June and returned 15 November 1938. His aircraft was one of six SBs that took off on a mission 10 October 1938. One of the group immediately turned back with engine problems and shortly after this, the five remaining SBs were attacked by six Bf 109s. During the ensuing battle, one of the SBs in the lead group was shot down and the other two damaged. The 109s then turned on the two aircraft in the second group, but the 109 flown by Gamringer[1] was shot up by the gunners in three of the SBs IL'IN, TERTYCHNYI and KOZHEMYAKO and had to abandon the combat. Awarded the Red Banner 22 February 1939. (Semenov "*Parol,*" *Los Rusos, Pravda*, Abrosov, [1]Ries and Ring say his aircraft had to force land.)

IL'IN, Semen Grigor'evich, born 1906

Was a pilot in the 120th IAE Transcaucasian Mil. Dist. In Spain he served as an I-15 pilot, from 14 January to 26 July 1937. On 2 June 1937 during an air combat he was badly wounded, but was able to return his aircraft to base. After release from the hospital he returned home. He had flown ninety-six combat missions and fought in many air battles. Awarded the Red Banner twice, 27 June 1937 and 2 March 1938. In the spring of 1941, he was on the Staff of the 21st ShAD, and from 23 June 1941 he was the Flight Inspector for the 5th VVS Army. He was captured near LUTSK on 30 June 1941, and sent to Camp #62 on 18 August 1941 where he was interrogated by the Germans. He is assumed to have died in captivity and was listed so on 27 August 1943. (Abrosov, *Los Rusos*, Kaminskii, *Pravda*)

IOFFE, Zelik Aronovich, born 1903

SB Engineer, outstanding at field design and fixing problems. Among the first volunteers to arrive in September 1936, he was initially in the 1st Escuadrilla Internacional, where he helped to make bombers of some of the civilian types. Next he transferred to the newly arrived SB Grupo 12. *Los Rusos* give his dates of service as from October 1936 to 3 June 1937. Awarded the Red Star on 2 January and the Red Banner 4 July 1937. During WWII, he was Chief Engineer of an Air Army. After the war he continued to serve with the VVS; in 1960 he was Head of the Institute for Space Technology in Moscow. In 1963 he was promted to General Lieutenant of the Engineer Corps. Passed away in 1980. (*Solidaity*, Berch, *Bajo la B.*, *Vmeste*, Pritsker, *Los Rusos, Pravda*)

IONOV, Aleksandr Makeniovich, Lt., born 1908

Navigator SB arrived 14 February and returned home 21 July 1938. Awarded the Red Banner on 14 November 1938. (*Los Rusos*, Berch, Semenov "*Parol*" seems to indicate he came earlier around December 1937)

IRODOV, Ivan L., born 1907

Aviation Technician SSS, served from October 1936 to 30 June 1937. Awarded the Red Star 2 January 1937. (*Los Rusos*)

IVANOFF

Escuadra España, White Russian. *My* lists him as serving with the Maquis after Spain, and that he was killed in France. Berch spells name IVANOV. (Laureau, Berch, *MY*)

IVANOV, Andrei Timofeevich, Lt., born 1909

Navigator SB, in Spain from 14 December 1937 to 21 July 1938. Awarded the Red Banner 14 November 1938. (Berch, Semenov "Parol," *Los Rusos, Pravda*)

IVANOV, Boris Konstantinovich, born 1912

Flyer in the 107th IAE 83rd IAB Byelorussian Mil. Dist. In Spain he flew an I-16 in the 5th Esc. from 26 March to 5 August 1938. His aircraft CM-095 was shot down on 23 May 1938 during air combat and collided with a Fiat CR 32; he was wounded and bailed out. Returned home after release from hospital. Awarded the Red Banner 22 February 1939. In May 1939 he was on the Staff of the 22nd IAP and fought in the Khalkhin-Gol, where on 22 June 1939 during an air battle with Japanese Ki-27s he was shot down and KIA. (Semenov "*Parol*," Abrosov, *Los Rusos*, Kaminskii, *Pravda*)

IVANOV, Ivan G., born 1906

Bomber Aviation Technician (SSS?), in Spain from October 1936 to 30 June 1937. Awarded the Red Star on 2 January 1937. (*Los Rusos, Pravda*)

IVANOV, Mikhail Ivanovich, Sr.Lt., born 18 July 1910

He joined the army in 1929 and finished training at the Stalingrad Military Aviation School for Pilots in 1932. After 1932, he was a member of various bomber Eskadril'ya in the Byelorussian, Caucasus, and Far East Military Districts. Volunteered for Spain and served there from October 1936 until 23 January 1937 as commander of an SB Patrulla in the 1st Esc. Awarded the Red Banner 2 January 1937. From 1939 to 1941, he test flew aircraft at the #301 factory (Khimkis) including the UT-2 and Yak-1 fighter. From 1941 to 1945, he tested aircraft at factory #31, which included the LaGG-3, La-5FN, and Yak-3. During this time he also served on air defense of the factory, flying some sorties. In February 1945 he became senior test pilot at the Yakovlev OKB, and on 24 April 1946 test flew the Yak-15. Later he tested

the Yak-19 and -23 jet fighters. Awarded the H.S.U. on 5 March 1948. Other awards were Order of Lenin, Red Banner twice, Order GPW 1st cl., and Red Star. Died in a crash 14 July 1948 while flying a Yak-23 in preparation for an aviation parade. He had lived in and is buried in Moscow. (airforce.ru/staff/who_is_who/index.htm, *Bajo la B., Los Rusos, Pravda*)

IVANOV, Nikolai Semenovich "Panas," Capt., born 1914

Before Spain he was a pilot in the 34th IAE 56th IAB Kiev Mil. Dist. Began his Spanish mission on 31 May 1937 and returned home 28 January 1938. Traveled to Spain in a group together with A. MINAEV, B. SMIRNOV, P. BUTRYM, A. SEROV and N. VOLOSHCHENKO. According to SMIRNOV's memoirs they traveled on the Spanish ship *Aldecoa*, which is listed as arriving in Spain on 21 June 1937.[1] All of the group except SEROV were put into the new 3rd Escuadrilla de Moscas with MINAEV as commander. He remained with the 3rd for his entire time in Spain, and according to SMIRNOV's memoirs, sometime in early December 1937 his aircraft was shot up in a battle and he had to bail out. But to add confusion to this, according to the memoirs of both Airas and Bravo, IVANOV was second-in-command of the 1st Moscas under DEVOTCHENKO. From August-October 1937, where they say he flew I-16 CM 124. Arias further states that he flew as his wingman in the 1st and that when the Escuadrillas were Spanishized after the attack on Garrapinillos, that both DEVOTCHENKO and IVANOV went to the 2nd Esc.[2] But according to the *Diario de Operaciones* (Salas) DEVOTCHENKO is listed with the 2nd from the 16th of January 1938. It also indicates that IVANOV led the 5th Moscas on the Aragon front from 11 October until 11 November 1937, while GUSEV says he was lent to his Escuadrilla (6th) to teach shooting techniques to his pilots, and that he was a member of the SMIRNOV/BUTRYM Escuadrilla. But this must have been at the time the 6th was being formed at the beginning of September 1937. GUSEV also states that he returned to his old Esc., as does SMIRNOV. During his time in Spain, he flew 150 combat missions and fought in fifty air combats and had five aircraft to his credit (three personal and two in patrulla). He also trained Spanish pilots in the Soviet Union. He was killed while testing an aircraft in the S.U. Awarded the Order of Lenin 2 March 1938, and Red Banner 3 November 1937. (Tarazona, Salas, Gusev 61, Berch, Howson 199, Laureau, Smirnov, Arias, Abrosov, *Los Rusos* give end date as 23 September, Kaminskii, Pravda [1]SMIRNOV states they arrived on 26 May. [2]I do not believe this to be accurate as they give the start date of 8 August 1937, but Abosov mentions that DEVOTCHENKO did not arrive in Spain until 28 August.)

IVANOV, Petr Mikheevich, born 19 October 1913

Joined the Army in 1933, and in 1934 attended the Okonchil Military Pilots Aviation School. After graduating he flew with the 56th IAB Kiev Mil. Dist. Volunteer in Spain from 20 August 1937 to 25 February 1938. Flew I-15 #CC-020 in the 1st Escuadrilla (Kaminskii says he flew the I-16, but he seems to be mistaken). Flew fifty combat missions and fought in many air battles. On 9 December 1937, at Sabadell Airfield, while flight testing his engine, almost immediately after take-off the plane caught fire and he was forced to bail out. He was badly burned and spent the next two months in the hospital, returning home after his release. Awarded the Red Banner 2 March 1938. Later fought in the Winter War against Finland 1939-40. At the beginning of WWII, he was a member of the 17th IAP and then in 1942 was on the Staff of the 23rd IAP. Later became the commander of the 866th IAP in the 288th IAD (which was led by another Spanish veteran, Boris SMIRNOV) of the 1st SAK (mixed Av. Corps), 17th Air Army. A Lt. Colonel, he flew 299 sorties and fought in eighty aerial combats downing twelve (some say seventeen) aircraft. He was KIA on 28 November 1943 during an air combat with Me 109s. His aircraft was hit around 300 meters from the ground; he jumped, but his parachute was said to have become entangled with the tail and never fully opened and he fell to his death. Awarded the title of H.S.U. (posthumously) on 26 October 1944. Other awards were Order of Lenin, and Order of the Red Banner three times 2 March 1938 for service in Spain, and twice in WWII. (Kaminskii, *Geroi*, Abrosov, *Los Rusos, Pravda*)

IVANOV, Pavel I., born 1910
Mechanic in TARKHOV's I-16 group sent in October 1936 and returned 27 August 1937. Awarded the Red Star 2 January 1937. (*Vmeste, Pravda*)

IVANOV, Pikar Ivanovich
Pseudonym of Bulgarian Nikolai VATOV. See main entry.

IVANOV, Stepan Ivanovich, born 1910
Radio/Gunner SB, in Spain 14 June 1937 to 28 January 1938. Was in the 3rd Escuadrilla. Awarded the Red Banner 2 March 1938. (*Solidarity, Los Rusos, Pravda*)

IVANOV, Vladimir P., NCO, born 1913
Radio/Gunner on SB, in Spain from 15 June 1937 to 11 January 1938. Awarded the Red Banner 2 March 1938. Said to have shot down a monoplane (Bf 109) on 21 July 1937. (*Los Rusos* Abrosov, *Pravda*)

JANSON, Kirill Ivanovich, Gen., born 1894 in Latvia
While not Air Force Personnel, he was the Chief advisor on the Northern Basque front, in Spain from 1 October 1936 until 20 May 1937, and as such had control over air operations. After he returned to the USSR he was placed in command of the 64th Rifle Division and awarded the Order of Lenin. He was arrested on 2 December 1937 and tried and executed on 22 August 1938. (Fernandez p.5, Aizpuru p.255, Suvenirov p.414, Russian site on members of the Communist Party list as Yanson, *Los Rusos* also list as Yanson, Pritsker, Talon 279, Alcofar)

JHOSIANOV, Gregorio Nikoli
(Var. Sp. THOSIAINOFF, and IHOSIAINOFF see above) Pilot of I-16 shot down near Brunete on 6 July 1937, tried and condemned to death along with CHERCASOV and H.E. Dahl. Later released. (RSA, Sanchis, Salas, Logoluso and Berch, but see KHOZYAINOV.)

"JOSE"
See KOPETS, Ivan.

"JULIO"
See PUMPUR, P., Col.

KABANOV, Isaj Trofimovich, born 1904
Armaments specialist in TARKHOV's Esc. In Spain from November 1936, he was badly wounded and died of wounds on 25 November 1936. Awarded the Red Star 2 January 1937. (*Vmeste, Pravda, Los Rusos*)

KACHAN, Georgii Dmitrievich, Lt., born 1914
Joined the Red Army in 1933, was a pilot in th 107th IAE 83rd IAB Belorussian Mil. Dist. In Spain he was an I-16 fighter pilot in the 5th Moscas under command of GLUSHENKOV/GRITSEVETS from 26 March to 13 August 1938. He was wounded in an air battle with Bf 109s on 18 May 1938. Flew forty combat missions and fought in seven air battles, claiming two enemy aircraft (CR 32 and Bf 109). At the beginning of WWII he was the CO of an Eskadril'ya in the 178th IAP PVO. Died in 1941. (Semenov "*Parol*," Abrosov, *Los Rusos*, Kaminskii)

KACHANOV, Kuz'ma Marksimovich, Col., born 1901
Air Force advisor at the Estado Mayor. In Spain from 11 October 1937 and returned on 27 February 1939. Went to China in September 1939 as an Advisor to the People's Liberation Army. At the beginning of WWII, he commanded a Rifle Corps and then the 34th Army on the Northwestern Front. In August 1941, his unit got into a very difficult situation while trying to counter-attack, and had to retreat. Accused of cowardice and willfully withdrawing his troops, on 12 September 1941 he was executed. The charges were dropped in 1958. Awarded the Order of Lenin 2 March 1938. (Berch, Semenov "*Parol*," *Los Rusos*, Voronkova)

KAKUTICH, Ivan Iosifovich, born 1914
Zvena CO in the 4th IAE 56th IAB Kiev Mil. Dist. Arrived in Spain 10 June, returned 15 September 1938. I-16 Pilot in the 2nd Moscas under SEMENKO, where he was a Patrulla leader. He was one of a group of thirty-four fighter pilots who had arrived in Spain in June 1938. Flew eight combat missions and fought in two air combats. According to Abrosov, he

was wounded in combat over the Ebro on 14 August his engine was shot up by machine gun fire from the He 111s and he had to make a forced landing 10km from his base. While attemping to land, he was attacked by Fiats, but these were driven off by FEDOSEEV. (Kaminskii says it happened on the 20th when his plane was hit by AAA). Returned home after release from the hospital. Awarded the Red Banner 22 February 1939. During the Russo-Finnish war, he was an Eskadril'ya CO in the 23rd IAP. On 10 March 1940 he was killed in an air crash (some say KIA in battle with a Finnish fighter). Awarded the Red Banner. (Kaminskii, Semenov *Tov.*, *Vmeste*, Abrosov, *Pravda*)

KALACHIKOV, Andrei Andreevich, Capt., born 1907
Pilot SB, served from 30 May to 15 November 1938. Detachment commander in KARPENKO's Escuadrilla, this was the last Soviet air unit to leave Spain. On 31 August, on a mission near Batea, his Detachment was attacked by Fiat CR 32s. One SB flown by NAKONECHNIKOV lost power on one engine and began falling behind with the Fiats attacking it. KALACHIKOV, in order to help the crippled SB, slowed the formation down allowing it to keep up and fought off the Fiats. Awarded the Red Banner 22 February 1939. (Berch, Semenov "*Parol*," *Los Rusos*, Abrosov, *Pravda*)

KAL'CHENKO, Leonid Lavrent'evich, born 1906
I-15 engineer with RYCHAGOV's Esc. Codename "Lucas." Arrived in Spain on the ship Karl Lepin in October 1936 and served until 27 March 1937. Awarded the Red Banner 17 July 1937 and the Red Star on 2 January 1937. (Berch, Logoluso, *Icare 130*, *Vmeste*, Zakharov, *Los Rusos*, *Pravda*)

KALININ, Ivan Sergeevich, born 1908
Aeronautical Engineer at Reus SAF 3 from 10 October 1937 until 15 September 1938, working on construction of the Polikarpov I-15s being built in Spain. Awarded the Red Star 22 February 1939. (*Los Rusos*, *Pravda*)

KAPUSTIN, Iosif Egorovich, born 1908
Before going to Spain he was in the 109th IAE 36th IAB Kiev Mil. Dist. In Spain from 20 August 1937 until 25 April 1938. Both Kaminskii and Abrosov say he flew I-16s, but Sayos p.61 indicates he was second-in-command of the 1st Chatos Escuadrilla under SIUSIUKA'LOV, to which Sayos was attached. Flew seventy combat missions and fought in thirty-two air combats and claimed two enemy aircraft (Bf 109 and CR 32). According to Abrosov, his aircraft was shot down on 4 January 1938 and he bailed out, but I found nothing to substantiate this in Salas "*Diario*." In 1940 he was an IAE CO in the 69th IAP at Odessa. In July 1941 he was wounded in air combat, after release from the hospital he became commander of the 788th IAP-PVO, on the Stalingrad front. On 23 August 1942 he and three other Soviets fighter pilots fought an air battle with some twenty Ju 87s escorted by six Me 109s. In a frontal attack he shot down an Me 109, but was himself badly wounded. He made a wheels-up landing and died. According to Milany (Sayos) KAPUSTIN and SIUSIUKA'LOV left and then OSIPENKO took over the command of the 1st Escuadrilla. R and R list him as CAPUCHIN and Laureau as KAPUCHIN. Abellan incorrectly lists him as CO of 1st Chatos in April 1938. (*My* (1986), Milany 63, R and R, *Los Rusos*, Laureau, Abellan. Abellan in his book on Soviet fighters also says Kapustin left Spain with SIUSIUKA'LOV and OSIPENKO took over command. But according to Sirvent, SIUSIUKA'LOV did not leave Spain at that time, he went to head the combined 2nd and 5th escuadrillas de Mosca, but see his main listing.) Awarded Order of Lenin 14 November 1938 and Red Banner 2 March 1938.

KARMANOV, Afanasii Georgievich, born 18 January 1907
While Polak list him as having flown in Spain, his Biog. in *Geroi Sovetskogo Soiuza* vol.1 p.629 makes no mention of this. It lists only the Winter War in Finland.

KARMAZIN, Aleksei Vlasovich, Lt., born 1910
Navigator SB, served from 14 December 1937 to 13 July 1938. Participated in the attack on the Nationalist Cruiser Baleares on 6 March 1938. Awarded the Red Banner 14 November 1938. (Berch, *Los Rusos, Pravda*)

KARP, K.
Pilot I-15 in photo in *Icare #130* p.42, but both Shingarev and Lacalle contain same photo and claim he is KOVAL'CHUK, while at same time ZAKHAROV in Ya Istrebitel' rightfully says he is KOVTUN. See same photo in illustration section of this book. (*Icare 130*, Shingarev, Lacalle, Zakharov)

KARPENKO, Mikhail Spiridonovich "Miguel," Lt., born 1913
Pilot SB, in Spain from 30 May to 15 November 1938. After KRASNOGLAZOV left for home at the end of August 1938, KARPENKO took over as commander of the last Soviet SB Escuadrilla in Spain. Awarded the Order of Lenin 22 February 1939. (Berch, Semenov "*Parol*," *My* (1986), *Los Rusos, Pravda*)

KARPENKO, Stepan Mikhailovich, Lt., born 1904

Before going to Spain he was a member of the 114th ShAB Byelorussian Mil. Dist. stationed at Gomel. In Spain from October 1936 until 30 June 1937, he was a Navigator in the 2nd Escuadrilla de Rasante (SSS) 15th Grupo, stationed at Santa Cruz de la Zarza. The CO of his escuadrilla was STRELKOV. On 2 December 1936, while attacking the Railway Station at Illescas, his aircraft was damaged by shrapnel from the exploding bombs of the aircraft they were following. The pilot POLIVALOV made an emergency landing inside Republican territory, but in their confusion they thought it was enemy ground and burned their plane. Awarded the Red Banner 2 January 1937. Passed away in 1978. (*Vmeste, Los Rusos, Pravda*)

KARPOV

OSADCHII claims he was in first group of volunteers to come to Spain in the fall of 1936. Says he was in a Patrulla with the Spaniard Jimenez, and that during an air battle in February 1937 he was shot down. OSADCHII goes on to say that in this battle his Chatos downed three Fiats and one Heinkel, with KARPOV getting the Heinkel. Possibly OSADCHII was thinking of Ivan KARPOV who was shot down in July. I checked with Baumler's flight log; he only lists for 11 February 1937, "Stolck fatally wounded," and on 12 February, "Stolck dead. R.I.P." Baumler was in OSADCHII's (KAZAKOV) Escuadrilla, but this was not a squadron member that Baumler wrote of (i.e. KARPOV), but rather Jan-Fredericus Stolk, the pilot of one of the two Potez 540s of the Escuadrilla Malraux lost on February 11th. (*Vmeste*, Baumler)

KARPOV, Ivan Matveevich, NCO, born 1908

Was a pilot in the 35th IAE 56th IAB Kiev Mil. Dist. Arrived in Spain on 18 April 1937, he was an I-15 Pilot KIA near Brunete on 7 July 1937.[1] While on a mission (some say near the Casa de Campo), four Russians (others were SEROV, YAKUSHIN, and SHALIGANOV) became involved in a battle with twenty-two enemy aircraft. KARPOV is said to have downed a CR 32 in the first minutes and then was himself shot down. SHALIGANOV was wounded in this same engagement. KARPOV was a member of EREMENKO's 1st Escuadrilla, and flew in RYBKIN's Patrulla. Awarded the Red Banner twice, 27 June and 11 November 1937. According to Abrosov p.89, KARPOV and two other Soviets had been arrested in Switzerland on 23 January 1937 while trying to get to Spain. After his release, he made a second try and finally got through. (Salas, *Bajo la B.*, Shingarev, Abellan, Lukes, Abrosov, Kaminskii, *Pravda*, [1]Abellan says date was 12 July as does Lukes, while *Los Rusos* list as 8 March 1938 as does the 1991 Soviet list.)

KASHTANOV, Ivan Stepanovich, Lt., born 1909

SB pilot, in Spain from 28 June to 15 November 1938. Awarded the Red Banner on 22 February 1939. (*Pravda*, Semenov "*Parol*," *Los Rusos* spell it KASHTAKOV, Berch spells it KOSHTAKOV)

KAS'KOV, Semen R., Lt., born 1906

Navigator in the SSS grupo from October 1936 to 3 June 1937. Awarded the Red Banner twice, 2 January and 4 July 1937. (*Pravda, Los Rusos* spell name KAZLOV.)

KAZAKOV

Var. sp. KOSAKOV, KOSOKOV. Nom de guerre of Leader of Baumler's I-15 squadron in January to April 1937. See listing for OSADCHII. (Baumler, Tinker, Berch, Howson 194, Abellan)

KERENKO

Tarazona's QUERENKO? If so, he was one of the Soviet pilots who went North with UKHOV and saw service in the I-16 escuadrilla under EVSEV'EV and SMIRNOV, who Tarazona called "PLYGUNOV." (Laureau 98, Tarazona)

KETOV, Aleksandr Ivanovich, Lt., born 20 October 1907

CO of a Zvena in the 5th IAE 36th IAB Kiev Mil. Dist. Arrived in Spain on 1 November 1936 and returned home on 27 May 1937. I-15 Patrulla CO in TURZHANSKII's Esc. fighting on the Northern front. Shot down three enemy aircraft (two personal and one in group). Awarded the Red Banner 2 January 1937. Fought in the Winter War against Finland, where he was awarded a second Red Banner on 7 April 1940. In WWII from October 1942 he was CO of the 293rd IAP and fought at Stalingrad, Kursk and the Kuban. Flew 200 missions and participated in fifty air combats shooting down several enemy aircraft. Died 13 April 1964. (Lukes, Abrosov, *Pravda*, Kaminskii)

KHABASHEV, Aleksandr P., born 1911
Aviation technician for fighter group. Served from October 1936 until 30 June 1937. Awarded the Red Star 2 January 1937 and Red Banner on 17 July 1937. (*Los Rusos, Pravda*)

KHARA, Petr Ivanovich, Lt., born 15 May 1908
Zvena CO in the 107th IAE 83rd IAB Byelorussian Mil. Dist. Member of TARKHOV's/ KOLESNIKOV's I-16 Escuadrilla, served from November 1936 to 26 July 1937. Said to have downed a Ju 52 over Madrid on 4 December 1936. On 12 February 1937, in an air combat with three Ju 52s and sixteen He 51s, he claimed a He 51 (one of five He 51s claimed by the I-16 group). All told they claimed seven aircraft in this battle, one each for KHARA, PUTIVKO, SHEVTSOV, AKULENKO, TARASOV, MOROZOV and one shared by LESNIKOV/VINOGRADOV. On 16 February KHARA claimed a CR 32, MOROZOV claimed a second CR 32 and DENISOV a Ju 52. In another battle on 18 February 1937 even though the Republicans lost four fighters (one I-16 and three I-15s) KHARA together with MINAEV were able to down a Fiat. Awarded the Red Banner twice, 2 January and 4 July 1937. After Spain he returned to command a Detachment in the 107th IAE until May 1938 and then until October was second-in-command of the Regiment. In September 1939 he was given the rank of Major and appointed as CO of the 21st IAP. On 16 September 1939, while returning from a recon mission at the beginning of the Soviet invasion of Poland, his aircraft collided on landing with S. GRITSEVETS Aircraft with the latter being killed. From October 1940 to February 1941 he was CO of an Eskadril'ya in the 167th IAP, then became second-in-command. Later he was CO of the 352nd IAP until the end of the war. He retired on 5 July 1946 as a Lt.Col. And passed away 17 November 1967. (*Vmeste* p52, Abrosov, *Los Rusos*, Kaminskii, airaces.narod.ru, *Pravda*)

KHARAMSKII
SBs according to Shingarev, *Vmeste*.

KHARITONOV, Filipp Vasil'evich, born 1910
Navigator SB, arrived on 26 March and served until 3 September 1938. Awarded Red Banner on 22 February 1939. (Semenov "*parol*," Berch, *Los Rusos, Pravda*)

KHAR'KOVSKII, Anastasi M.
Abrosov says SB Esc. Commander. Could well be same person as below, with first name and initial reversed (Gusev, G. y Rev. 2, Logoluso, Abrosov)

KHAR'KOVSKII, Maxim A., born 1907
SB pilot, in Spain from 3 January until 13 August 1937. Awarded the Red Banner 21 June 1937. (*Los Rusos, Pravda*)

KHAUSTOV, Aleksei V., born 1912
Electricial engineer for air group. Served from October 1936 to 27 August 1937. Awarded Red Star 2 January 1937. (*Los Rusos, Pravda*)

KHAUSTOVICH, Vladimir S., born 1905
Worker from Aircraft Factory #22 assembling SB aircraft. In Spain from October to 12 December 1936. Awarded the Red Star 2 January 1937. (*Pravda, MY*, Berch, *Los Rusos* mistakenly lists by first name)

KHEVESHI, Akosh Akoshevich, Lt.
Hungarian with the VVS, Observer on SB, arrived in Spain in September (October) 1936 and returned to the USSR on 27 August 1937. Flew with the 1st Escuadrilla Internacional, then transfered to Grupo 12 SBs. BIBIKOV in *Vmeste* p.17 says he was KHOL'ZUNOV's navigator. Awarded the Red Banner twice, 2 January and 17 July 1937. Var. Sp. CHEVESKI (Logoluso, Berch, *Vmeste, Solidarity, Bajo la B., Pravda, Los Rusos* list as JEVESCI and give end date as 27 May.)

KHIMOCHKO, Fedor Zinov'evich, born 1902, died 1978.
Air Force Commissar, in Spain from October 1936 to February 1939. (*Vmeste*, but not listed in Abrosov.)

KHLUSOVICH, Ivan Mikhailovich, Lt., born 1911
Zvena CO in the 107th IAE 83rd IAB Byelorussian Mil. Dist. I-16 pilot/Patrulla CO, he arrived in Spain 31 May 1937 and left 28 January 1938. Flew 140 missions

and fought in twenty-five air combats. Awarded the Order of Lenin 2 March 1938 and Red Banner on 22 October 1937. After his return home, from 15 July to 16 September 1939 he fought in the battle of Khalkhin-Gol as assistant CO of the 56th IAP. From August to October 1941 he was assistant CO of the 180th IAP and then became the CO until December 1943. In 1943 this unit was re-designated as the 30th GIAP. From December 1943 to May 1944 he commanded the 10th GIAP on the 1st Ukrainian front and in September 1944 took over the 3rd IAD. He had twelve aircraft to his credit and was awarded numerous medals during and after the war. He retired 15 May 1958 and passed away 12 July 2001. (*Los Rusos,* Kaminskii, Abrosov, *Pravda*, airaces.narod.ru.)

KHMELOV, Arsenii, born 1910
Fitter with the Aircraft repair unit. In Spain from 21 July to 10 November 1937. (*Los Rusos*)

KHOKHLOV, Andrei I., born 1912
Bomb group technician, served from October 1936 until 27 May 1937. Awarded the Red Banner on 4 July and the Red Star 2 January 1937. (*Los Rusos, Pravda*)

KHOLOD, Grigori Trifonovich, Lt., born 1912
Pilot SB. Arrived October 1936, and was a member of the 2nd Escuadrilla. DEMENCHUK as was his gunner. Returned home 23 January 1937. Awarded the Red Banner 2 January 1937. (*Vmeste, Pravda, Los Rusos* say first name was Georgii)

KHOL'ZUNOV, Viktor Stepanovich, Maj., born 31 January 1905
Fought in the Russian Civil War. Attended the Leningrad Aviation School in 1929. In 1931 attended the 2nd Military Flying School Borisoglebsk, where he commanded first a Zvena and then a Detachment. Next he was appointed CO of an Eskadril'ya at the 7th Stalingrad Military Pilots School. He volunteered for duty in Spain, and was in the first group of volunteers that arrived in late September 1936. Here he was put in the 1st Escuadrilla Internacional and first flew a Breguet Br 19 and then the Potez 540. Next he transferred to the newly arrived SB Grupo 12 as a pilot. Became commander of the 2nd Escuadrilla de Kats based at San Clamente. After his return to the Soviet Union on 29 March 1937, he was made commander of an Aviabrigade. He was also at this time interviewed by Alksnis, Head of the VVS, regarding operations in Spain. He was very critical of the commanding officers ZLATOTSVETOV and K.M. GUSEV, saying they did not fly and did not manage or supervise well. He was also critical of the SB bomber, especially the pilots seat, saying it had no armor plate and was constructed in such a manner as to make the pilots legs go numb after several hours of flight.[1] In November 1937 he was CO of the 1st Army Special Forces (one of three Army Air Reserves). Died on 28 July 1939 when an aircraft he was testing exploded in midair. Awarded title of H.S.U. on 27 June 1937 (the award lists him as Kombrig, Komandir 49th Aviabrigady). Other awards were Order of Lenin and Red Banner. (Berch, *Solidarity, AEQ 32*, Howson 277, *Bajo la B.*, Salas, *G. y Rev. 2*, *Vmeste*, Pritsker, Boyd, *USSR*, *Geroi*, *Los Rusos*, Abrosov, *Pravda*, [1]Kholzunov VS (Oleg Shushakov)/ History and Politics/Proza.ru)

KHOMYAKOV, Valentin Ivanovich, Lt., born 30 August 1910
Was a Zvena CO in the 120th IAE Transcaucasian Mil. Dist. In Spain he was an I-15 Patrulla leader, served from 14 January to 26 July 1937 participating in the battle of Guadalajara. Awarded the Red Banner 27 June 1937. After his return to the USSR, he spent many years in the NII VVS (Air Force Research Institute). Bodrikhin indicates he scored six victories in Spain, plus nine more in WWII (Kaminskii says twelve in WWII). CO of the 401st IAP from 23 June 1941. At end of war he was a Lt.Col. (R.S.A., Logoluso, *Bajo la B.*, Shingarev, Lukes, Bodrikhin, Kaminskii, *Pravda*)

KHOR'KOVSKII
SB Escuadrilla commander says Kotelnikov, but see KHAR'KOVSKII above.

KHOTELEV, Iosif Sidorovich, Lt., born 1910

Was flight instructor at the 8th Odessa Pilots School Kiev Mil. Dist. I-16 Pilot/Patrulla CO arrived in Spain 10 June 1938 and returned home 26 October 1938. First flew in the Escuadrilla under RODIN, then with the GRITSEVETS Group. Flew in Patrulla with FILIPPCHENKO and Nikolai ROMANOV. All three were hospitalized after being wounded in an air battle on 23 July, in which he is said to have shot down two Bf 109s. During this battle, he was badly wounded but with the aid of a Spanish pilot who flew alongside him, was able to bring his plane back to the airfield. After being released from the hospital he returned to the USSR. He had flown twenty-five combat missions and participated in six air battles. Awarded the Red Banner on 22 February 1939. In 1939 he was CO of an Eskadril'ya and fought in the Winter war against Finland. He was awarded the Red Banner on 7 April 1940 and was elevated to the rank of major. In 1940 was made CO of the 92nd IAP. From October 1944 to January 1945 he was CO of the 304th IAD (which became the 23rd GIAD). Awarded the Red Banner twice more, 3 November 1944 and 9 May 1945. Passed away 21 January 1979. (Semenov *Tov.*, *Vmeste*, *Los Rusos*, Kaminskii, *Pravda*)

KHOVANSKII, Ivan Andreevich, Lt., born 1908[1]

Attended Military Flying School, then was a pilot in the 107th IAE 83rd IAB Byelorussian Mil. Dist. Volunteered for Spanish duty, arriving there on the Soviet ship *Kursk* in October 1936. Was an I-16 Patrulla leader in TARKHOV/KOLESNIKOV Escuadrilla. KIA on 6 January 1937 near Majadahonda when his aircraft collided with an enemy fighter. His aircraft was said to have crashed on the slopes of the Sierra de Guadarramas. Two aircraft to his credit. Awarded the H.S.U. on 4 July 1937. Other awards were Order of Lenin, Order of the Red Banner on 2 January 1937, and Badge of Honor. (*Solidarity*, *Vmeste*, Rumyantsev "*Antonio*," *Geroi*, *Pravda*, [1]Abrosov lists date of birth as 1907 as does *Los Rusos*, but Kaminskii and *Geroi* say 1908.)

KHOVANSKII, M.G.

POLUSHKO in *Vmeste* pgs.214-215 says he was the commander of an SB Escuadrilla at San Javier in May 1937. GUMENNYI in same work p.79 says he took over command from PROSKUROV. Abrosov p.104 also lists as CO of the 1st Escuadrilla taking over from PROSKUROV, also says it was he who flew the SB with Levinskii as navigator/bombardier which scored the hit on the German Battleship *Deutschland* at Ibiza on 29 May 1937. Whereas Saiz in Tomo II pgs.450, 469-471 list him as a Patrulla leader in the 2nd Escuadrilla under Pereira, but gives his initials as M.A. This could be another confusion with KHAR'KOVSKII. (*Vmeste*, Abrosov, Saiz)

KHOZYAINOV, Grigorii Nikolaevich, born 1909

Was a pilot in the 12th IAE 111th IAB Leningrad Mil. Dist. An I-16 pilot, he arrived in Spain on 31 May 1937. He was a member of PLESCHENKO's 2nd Esc. Shot down on 6 July 1937 in air combat with CR 32s near Villanueva de la Cañada, his aircraft crashlanded in enemy territory and he was captured. Released and returned home on 7 February 1939. Emilliani in an article in *Storia Militare*, August 2012, pgs. 48-54, indicates this aircraft had the number 35 on the tail and was shot down by Ten. Bruno Trevisan of the 19th Squadriglia Aviazione Legionaria. See also IHOSIAINOFF and JHOSIANOV. Abrosov claims he was shot down on 8 July. (Abrosov, Kaminskii, Lukes, Emilliani, Laureau, Logoluso, Pritsker)

KHRAMOV, Nikolai Ivanovich

Polak lists him as having flown in Spain, but there is no mention of this in his biography in *Geroi Sovetskogo Soiuza* vol.2, p.693 or other sources.

KHRAMTSEV, Aleksandr S., born 1907

Aviation engineer, served from October 1936 to 23 January 1937. Returned home early due to sickness. Awarded the Red Star 2 January 1937. (*Los Rusos*, *Pravda*)

KHREBTOV, I.K., born 1913
Aviation Engineer, in Spain from October 1936 to 27 August 1937. Awarded the Red Star 2 January 1937. (*Los Rusos, Pravda*)

KHRYUKIN, Timofei Timofeievich Lt., born 21 June 1910
Joined the Army in 1932. Graduated from Flying School in 1933. He was then posted to the 5th LBAE (Light Bomber Eskadril'ya), after which he was a senior pilot in the 10th SBAB (High Speed Bomber Aivabrigade). An SB pilot, he was one of the first Soviet volunteers to go to Spain, arriving in October 1936. In Spain he commanded the 2nd Escuadrilla SBs in the 12th Grupo. Awarded the Red Banner 2 January 1937. He returned to the Soviet Union on 8 March 1937. In 1938 he went to China, first as an Eskadril'ya commander, then he became group Commander. Flew 100 combat sorties including an attack on Formosa. Given title of H.S.U. on 22 February 1939. After China he became CO of the 10th SBAB. During the Winter War against Finland, he was VVS commander of the 14th Army. In May 1941 he became CO of VVS forces with the 12th Army Kiev Mil. Dist. In August 1941 he was put in charge of VVS Forces on the Karelian Front, then in June 1942 became Commander of the 8th Air Army on the South Western Front. Later in July 1944 he was appointed as CO of the 1st Air Army and remained there until the end of the war. Received a second H.S.U. on 19 April 1945. Remained in the VVS after the war. In 1950, he graduated from the Genshtaba Military Academy. Other awards were Order of Lenin, Order of the Red Banner three times, Orders of Suvorov 1st and 2nd classes, Order of Kutuzov 1st cl. twice, Order of the Great Patriotic War 2nd cl, and Order of the Red Star. Died 19 July 1953. (*Lexikon* via Haycraft, *Bajo la B.*, Boyd, *Geroi*, OnAirpower.org., *Pravda*)

KIRICHENKO, Ivan S., born 1906
Pilot of either SB or SSS, served from October 1936 to 27 May 1937. Awarded the Red Banner 2 January 1937. (*Pravda, Los Rusos* spell name KIRILENKO)

KIRILLOV, Aleksandr Ivanovich, Lt., born 1908
Was Zvena CO in 12th IAE 111th IAB Leningrad Mil. Dist. Volunteered for Spanish duty, leaving for Spain on 31 May 1937 and returned home on 28 January 1938. Flew an I-16 as a member of PLESCHENKO's 2nd Esc. Claimed five victories; in one battle he claimed three bombers, but was wounded and had to bail out. Flew 100 combat missions. Twice awarded the Order of the Red Banner, 3 November 1937 and 2 March 1938. From 30 November 1939 he was CO of the 26th IAP 54th IAB and participated in the Winter War. Fought in the Great Patriotic War, and in 1945 commanded the 761st IAP. (Berch, Pritsker, Polak, *Los Rusos*, Kaminskii, *Pravda*)

KIRILOV, Kiril Aleksandrov
Bulgarian in the VVS. Bomber Pilot, arrived in late September 1936. Served first in the 1st Escuadrilla Internacional and then later in November 1936 went to the new SB Grupo 12. Awarded the Order of the Red Banner 2 January 1937. See BENKOVSKI. (*Solidarity*, Berch)

KIRIUKHIN, Aleksandr A., born 1913
Mechanic (Aviation?) in Spain 18 July 1937 to 25 April 1938. Awarded the Red Star on 2 March 1938. (*Los Rusos, Pravda*)

KISCHEV, Dmitri
Could be KISELEV below – has same exact information. (*Los Rusos*)

KISELEV, Dmitrii Alekseevich, Lt., born 1909
Was Zvena CO in the 107th IAE 83rd IAB Byelorussian Mil. Dist. I-16 Fighter pilot/Patrulla CO in the 5th Esc. under GLUSHENKOV from 26 March to 13 August 1938. Flew seventy-seven missions and fought in fifteen air combats, two Fiats to credit. Experienced a problem on 30 June when the leading edge of his port wing began to come apart, but he was able to bring it in for a landing. Awarded the Red Banner 22 February 1939. During WWII was on the Staff of the 1st GIAP. (Abrosov, *Pravda*, Semenov spells it Kirselev, Kaminskii spells it KISILEV)

KLIMOV, A.I., Lt.
Listed by KAL'CHENKO in *Vmeste* as an armaments man in RYCHAGOV Esc. Awarded the Red Banner 2 January 1937. But there may be some confusion with the person listed below, as *Los Rusos* lists a KLIMOV, A.I. with the armor group. (*Vmeste, Pravda, Los Rusos*)

KLIMOV, Leontii Aleksandrovich, Sr.Lt., born 1908
Zvena CO in the 107th IAE 83rd IAB Byelorussian Mil. Dist. Pilot I-16, arrived 26 March 1938 and was KIA on 18 May 1938.[1] During an attack on La Cenia by SBs with I-16 escort, while trying to protect the bombers, his aircraft was attacked by two Messerschmitts. Hit, the aircraft went into a dive,

crashing to the ground. KLIMOV was unable to get out. He was a member of PLYASOV's Patrulla in the 5th Esc. Abrosov indicates he was shot down by Handrick, but three others from 2.J/88 claimed "Ratas" that day. (*My* (1986), Abrosov, Salas *Diario*, [1]Semenov says KIA 20 May as does Kiminskii and *Los Rusos*)

KLIMOV, Vladimir V., born 1909

Aeronautical technician, from 30 October 1936 to 27 April 1937. Awarded the Red Star 2 January 1937. (*Los Rusos, Pravda*)

KLIMOVSKI, Anatoli S.

Fitter from Aircraft Factory #21 assembling I-16s. In Spain from October 1936 to 8 May 1937. Awarded the Red Star 2 January 1937. (*Los Rusos, Pravda*)

KOBYLYANSKII, Kazimir V., born 1904

Intepreter with the Air Group, nom de Guerre BERTOLI. In Spain from October 1936 to 2 March 1938. Awarded the Red Star. Var. Sp. KOBILYANSKI (Berch, Zil'manovich, *Bajo la B.*, Logoluso, *Los Rusos* spell it KOBELYANSKI)

KOGRUSHEV, Grigorii Aleksandrovich, Lt., born 20 November 1909

I-16 Fighter pilot, before going to Spain was a Zvena CO in the 57th IAE 142nd IAB BVO. Patrulla CO in the 2nd Esc. under RODIN, served from 26 March until 5 August 1938. Flew seventy combat missions and participated in twelve air battles. Awarded the Red Banner 22 February 1939. He was CO of an Eskadril'ya in the 11th IAP from 1939 and in June 1941 became the commander of the 11th IAP. From November 1941 until January 1943 he was CO of the 172nd IAP and from November 1943 until the end of the war was CO of the 168th IAP. Awarded many medals during the the war. Semenov spells it Kogrushchev. (Semenov "*Parol*," Abrosov, *Los Rusos*, Kaminskii, *Pravda*)

KOKAEV, Andrei, born 1906

Aviation Technician, served from 14 January until 23 December 1937. Awarded the Red Star 4 July 1937. (*Los Rusos, Pravda*)

KOKIN, Nikolai V., born 1906

Armaments specialist from Aircraft Factory #22 assembling SB Bombers. In Spain October to 12 December 1936. Awarded the Red Star 2 January 1937. (*Los Rusos, Pravda*)

KOKKINAK, K.

Flight Instructor for Spanish pilots in USSR. (*Vmeste*)

KOKOREV, Dmitri I., born 1913

Aeronautical engineer with the Bomber Group. In Spain from October 1936 to 9 July 1937. Awarded the Red Star 2 January 1937. (*Los Rusos, Pravda*)

KOLBASOVSKII, Ivan G., born 1907

Pilot, patrulla leader in SSS Escuadrilla from October 1936 to 2 July 1937. Awarded the Red Banner twice, once on 2 January and 22 October 1937. (*Vmeste, Los Rusos, Pravda* spells name KOVBASOVSKII)

KOLEGAEV, Fedor M., born 1908

Armaments specialist from Aircraft Factory #22 assembling SB Bombers. In Spain October to 12 December 1936. Awarded the Red Star 2 January 1937. *Pravda, Los Rusos*)

KOLESNIKOV, Aleksandr Karpovich, Lt., born 1910

Navigator SB from 30 December 1937 to 21 July 1938. Codename was "Krovkin" according to *Los Rusos*. Awarded the Red Banner 14 November 1938. (Berch, *Los Rusos, Pravda*)

KOLESNIKOV, Konstantin Il'ich, born 21 May 1908

Joined the Army in 1927. Graduated from War Theory School in 1928 and in 1930 entered the VVS. He attended the Borisoglebsk Military Flying School, after which he was a Detachment CO in the 107th IAE 83rd IAB Byelorussian Mil. Dist. Volunteered for service in Spain, arriving as a Sr.Lt. in October 1936. Commander ("Kostya") of an I-16 Detachment based at Guadalajara, in TARKHOV's enlarged (thirty-one

aircraft) 1st Escuadrilla in October/November 1936. Ordered by SMUSHKEVICH on 14 November to take over command of the TARKHOV Escuadrilla after its leader was badly wounded and dying. He flew to Alcala de Henares the next day after turning over the command of his Detachment to Andrei MOROZOV. At the time, the members were SHEVTSOV, BALANOV, MOROZOV, POLYAKOV, PAVLOV, KUZNETSOV, ZHEDANOV, MATVEEVICH, LAKEEV, MINAEV, NEGOREEV, CHERNYKH, and DENISOV, KRAVCHENKO, ZAMASHANSKII. BELOV in *Vmeste* says he was the CO of the Escuadrilla, which BELOV served in. Killed in an accident on 12 May 1937 when the left wing of his Aircraft came off in flight and it crashed into a hill. Buried with full military honors at Albacete. Awarded the H.S.U. 4 July 1937, Order of Lenin, and Order of the Red Banner 2 January 1937. Seven aircraft to his credit. (*Solidarity*, Gusev 89 and 91, Berch, Howson 198, *Vmeste*, Rumyantsev "*Antonio*," *Pravda*, Kaminskii, Abrosov, *Pravda*)

KOLESNIKOV, Vasilii I., born 1915
Worker from Aircraft Factory #1 assembling I-15 and SSS aircraft. In Spain from October 1936 to 17 April 1937. Awarded the Red Star on 2 January 1937. (*Pravda, Los Rusos*)

KOLLONTAI, A.M.
Latvian SB pilot, who went to Spain with POLUSHKO in March 1937. (*Vmeste*)

KOLOMIETS, Kirill Pavlovich, Lt., born 1915
Navigator SB, served from 30 May to 15 November 1938. During a mission in the Batea region on 31 August 1938, the SB he was in was attacked by Fiat CR 32s. One engine was shot up and the plane began to fall behind the group. The Detachment commander KALACHIKOV seeing this had the other four aircraft slow down to protect the stricken bomber. Crashlanded at Valls fighter field on 21 September 1938. Awarded the Red Banner 22 February 1939. (Semenov *Tov*, Berch, *Los Rusos, Pravda*, Abrosov)

KOLOSKOV, Nikolai Nikolaevich, Sr.Lt., born 1911
Was a Detachment CO in the 57th IAE 142nd IAB Byelorussian Mil. Dist. before going to Spain. An I-16 pilot in 2nd Esc. under RODIN, he arrived 26 March 1938 and was KIA in a battle with Fiat CR 32s near the airfield at Villar on 13 May 1938. According to *Los Rusos* his codename was "Kosheval." He was posthumously awarded the Red Banner on 22 February 1939. (Semenov "*Parol*," *Vmeste*, *My* (1986), Abrosov, *Los Rusos, Pravda*, Kaminskii says date of death was the 12th as does the 1991 Soviet list of dead.)

KOLOSOV, Fedor Pavlovich, Lt., born 1906
Zvena CO in the 11th IAE 111th IAB Leningrad Mil. Dist. An I-16 pilot, he arrived in Spain on 31 May 1937. He was KIA on 13 July 1937 in combat with Bf 109s, his aircraft crashing in enemy territory on the Madrid front. He had been a member of the 2nd Esc. under PLESHCHENKO. According to *Los Rusos*, his codename was "Kostin." He was awarded the Red Banner 2 March 1938 posthumously. (Berch, Pritsker, Abrosov, *Pravda*. On p.336 Abrosov lists 11 July, but on p.97 it says 13 July. Also airaces.narod.ru says the 11th, yet gives date as 13th, *Los Rusos* give date as 13th.)

KOLOSOV, Konstantin A., born 1909
Radio /Gunner on SB flown by TKHOR in April 1937. In Spain from 3 January to 25 May 1937. Awarded the Red Banner on 21 June 1937. (Abrosov 94, *Los Rusos, Pravda*)

KOMAROV, Dmitrii Ivanovich, Lt., born 1909
An I-16 pilot, before Spain he was in the 40th IAE 83rd IAB Byelorussian Mil. Dist. Served in Spain from 17 May 1937 until 28 January 1938. Flew 130 missions and fought in several air battles. Awarded the Red Banner twice, 28 October 1937 and 2 March 1938. Participated in fighting at Khalkhin-Gol, for which he was awarded the Order of Lenin on 29 August 1939. In 1940 he was assistant CO of the 129th IAP and in June of that year became CO of the 181st IAP on the Southern Ukrainian front. KIA 17 September 1941. (Pritsker, Abrosov, *Los Rusos*, Kaminskii, *Pravda*)

KOMIN, Aleksandr I., Sr.Lt., born 1912
Aviation Technician with the Air Group. In Spain October 1936 to 30 June 1937. Awarded the Red Star 2 January 1937. (*Los Rusos, Pravda*)

KOMOV, Vasilii, born 1908
Aviation technician with the fighter group. Served from 14 January to 23 December 1937. Awarded the Red Star on 21 June 1937. (*Los Rusos, Pravda*)

KONDRASHEV, Petr P., NCO, born 1913
Radio/gunner SB, 1St Esc. from October 1936 to 7 May 1937. Claimed to have shot down an enemy fighter on the Southern Front on 2 January 1937. Awarded the Red Banner twice, 2 January and 4 July 1937. (*Bajo la B., Los Rusos, Pravda*)

KONDRAT, Emel'yan Filaretovich, Lt., born 8 August 1911

Joined the Army in 1932. Attended the Kacha Military Air College. From October 1933 to October 1936 was a pilot in the 34th IAE 56th IAB Kiev Mil. Dist. I-15 pilot in Spain from 20 October 1936 until 7 April 1937. Used the codename Konrad. Initially in the Escuadrilla under RYCHAGOV, he was in a Detachment along with "CASIMIRO" KOVALEVSKII sent to Malaga in late January 1937. The other members of this group were MATYUIN, MIROSHNICHENKO, Alonso Jimenez, Emilio Galera and Jose Cuartero. After the death of KOVALEVSKII the remainder of the Detachment was absorbed into OSDACHII's new Escuadrilla. Flew 180 missions and claimed at least two He 51s and one S.81 personal plus one He 51, one S.81 and one He 59 in pair. This last aircraft in fact was badly shot up, but managed to land next to the Nationalist Crusier Canarias. Awarded the Red Banner twice, 2 January and 4 July 1937. He returned home in April 1937 and from September 1937 to June 1938 he was a Detachment CO in the 26th IAE and fought at Lake Khasan against the Japanese. In 1939, he fought in the battles for the Khalkhin-Gol. Then in the Russo-Finnish Winter War from 15 February to April 1940 as CO of the 152nd IAP, where he flew fifty-one missions. Awarded his third Red Banner on 21 May 1940. In April 1940 he became CO of the 131st IAP and in February 1942 he took over the 274th IAP. Became commander of the 2nd GuIAP of the 215th IAD of 14th Air Army in June 1942 and remained there until July 1943 after which he became CO of the 249th IAD. Awarded title of H.S.U. plus the Order of Lenin on 1 May 1943. By the end of the war, he was a Lieutenant Colonel and had had flown 308 missions and claimed sixteen victories. From April 1954 until October 1957 he served as an Air Force Advisor in China. Retired as a Major General in 1969 and passed away on 16 August 2002 in Kiev. Awards given were H.S.U., Order of Lenin, Order of the Red Banner five times (twice for Spain), Order of the GPW 1st Cl., and Order of the Red Star. (*Icare 130, Vmeste,* Zakharov, *Geroi Sovetskogo Soiuza*, Kondrat, Kaminskii, Abrosov)

KONDRATENKO, Mikhail N., born 1907

Mechanic/technician for a Patrulla de Asalto SSS, from October 1936 to 26 July 1937. Awarded the Red Banner on 4 July and Red Star on 2 January 1937. (*Los Rusos, Pravda*)

KONDRAT'EV, Vladimir Mikhailovich, Lt., born 1909

Pilot in the 109th IAE 36th IAB Kiev Mil. Dist. He was an I-15 pilot in RYCHAGOV's Escuadrilla, in Spain, arrived on 20 October 1936. Both he and ZVEREV on 3 November 1936 lost their orientation while flying to Alcala de Henares and wound up landing instead at a Rebel airfield, where they were captured. KONDRAT'EV says he was taken to Germany on 12 March 1937 where they tried to recruit him. In May 1937 he was exchanged for a German pilot and returned home on 13 June 1937. After which he served in the 109th IAE. Awarded the Red Banner 2 January 1937. (*Vmeste*, Lukes, Abrosov, *Pravda*, Kaminskii)

KONDRAT'EVA, Adelina

Translator. See ABRAMSON. (Shingarev)

KONDRATIUK, Vasilii P., born 1910

Aviation technician from October 1936 to 27 August 1937. Awarded the Red Star 2 January 1937. (*Los Rusos, Pravda*)

KONDRATOVICH, Vladimir I., born 1907

Armaments technician with the Air Group. Served from October 1936 to 30 June 1937. Awarded the Red Star 2 January 1937. (*Los Rusos, Pravda*)

KONEV, Fedor

GUSEV claims he flew in the 2nd Escuadrilla de Moscas. Further claimed he had six victories plus four shared, and that he was KIA 11 March 1938 during a combat with messerschmitts. (Gusev pgs.280-281, but see listing for KOVENEV; also no I-16s are listed as downed on 11 March 1938.)

KON'KEV, Gennadii Y.A., born 1912

Mechanic in first group sent, he served from October 1936 and returned home on 28 August 1937. Awarded the Red Star 2 January 1937. (*Los Rusos, Pravda, Solidarnost* spells name KON'KOV)

KONOTOPOV, Andrei Efimovich, Lt., born 1908

SB navigator in Spain from 3 January to 27 August 1937. Flew with TKHOR. Awarded the Red Banner 2 March 1938. (Berch, Pritsker, *Los Rusos, Pravda*)

KONOVALOV, Aleksei Nikolaevich, born 21 July 1912
Before going to Spain he served as a pilot in the 35th IAE 56th IAB Kiev Mil. Dist. I-16 pilot in the 2nd Moscas, under RODIN/SEMENKO, from 10 June until 4 October 1938. Came to Spain along with thirty-three other pilots. Fought in ten air battles and was wounded on 12 August 1938. While escorting SBs his aircraft was shot up by a Bf 109 flown by Otto Bertram. Fortunately he was able to get back to his airfield. After leaving the hospital he returned to the USSR. Awarded the Red Banner on 22 February 1939. In 1940 he was a captain serving in the 28th IAP in the Kiev Mil. Dist. During WWII he commanded first an IAP then an IAD. Died in September 1992.[1] (Kaminskii, *Pravda*, Semenov *Tov*. Claims he was wounded on the 21st, *Vmeste*, *Los Rusos* says name is Aleksandr, [1]Abrosov claims died in 1993)

"KONRAD"
Flew in "KAZAKOV's" I-15 Escuadrilla with Baumler. This was a KONDRAT who was a member of that Esc. (Baumler)

KONSTANTINOV
Lt.Col. "Alejandro," Co. of R-5s says note on p.49 of *Icare 130*. This is undoubtedly a reference to GUSEV, K.)

KONSTANTINOVSKAIA, Elena E.
Translator. (Shingarev)

KOPETS, Ivan Ivanovich "Jose," Sr.Lt., born 19 September 1908
Joined the Soviet Army VVS in 1927. In 1928 finished Leningrad Military Theoretical School for Flyers. In 1929 attended Kachin Military Aviation Flyers School, and in 1935 took courses in higher command at Genshtaba Military Academy. He was a Detachment CO in Zhukovskii's VVA 70th OIAO. Went to Spain as a Sr.Lt. in September 1936 where at first he flew a Ni 52c in the 1st Escuadrilla Internacional. In November 1936, he was made a Patrulla leader in RYCHAGOV's newly arrived I-15 Escuadrilla. Next he became Commander of an Escuadrilla with Andres Lacalle as a patrulla leader. Later made Commander of Grupo 26 (I-15) with Lacalle commanding one of the Escuadrillas. Next he became commander of Escuadra 11, which encompassed both Grupos 26 (I-15) and 21 (I-16). Flew more than 200 combat sorties, shot down six aircraft (two personal and four in group). Returned home on 17 June 1937. Given title of H.S.U. on 21 June 1937 plus the Red Banner 2 January 1937. Participated in the Russo-Finnish War 1939-40 commanding the VVS 8th Air Army. On the eve of WWII, as a Major General, he commanded the VVS Special Western District. On the first day of the Great Patriotic War, June 22, 1941, the Air Force western District suffered catastrophic losses: of 1,560 aircraft available, 738 had been destroyed, which was almost half of the combat aircraft. Shaken by this tragedy, Major General I. Kopets that same evening (other data says the following day), without waiting for his arrest and trial, committed suicide at his headquarters in Minsk. Murphy says, committed suicide in Minsk, at 5:00pm on 22 June 1941 after seeing all his aircraft destroyed on the ground. Awards given were the Order of Lenin twice, and Order of the Red Banner. (Lacalle, RSA, *Vmeste*, Zakharov, Pritsker, Gusev, Boyd, *Geroi Sovetskogo Soiuza*, Murphy, Kaminskii, *Pravda*, airaces.narod.ru.)

KORNEV, Mikhail, born 1905

Armaments engineer (aviation?), served from 11 January to 14 April 1938. (*Los Rusos*)

KOROBKOV, Fedor Grigor'evitch, Col., born 7 June 1898

In 1933 he was the CO of the 23rd BAE based at Khotunke. In Spain he was an advisor from October 1936 to 29 September 1937, where he used the codename "General Pavlovich." *Los Rusos* list him as CO of an Escuadrilla. Awarded the Order of Lenin and Red Banner 2 January 1937. From June 1941, he was commander of the Baltic Fleet VVS, then Deputy CO Naval VVS. On 24 April 1942, Major Gen. KOROBKOV was inspecting a workshop at the Sevastopol Naval Base along with another "Spaniard" OSTRYAKOV plus some accompanying officers. All were killed when the building was hit by a bomb dropped by an attacking German aircraft. (*Los Rusos*, *Pravda*, warheroes.ru)

KOROBKOV, Pavel Terent'evich, Capt., born 5 October 1909

Joined the Army in 1931, attended the Lugansk Military Flying school and graduated in 1933. From 1936 until May 1938 he was flight inspector at the 8th Odessa Pilots School Kiev Mil. Dist. Sent to Spain as a Senior Lt. "Comrade Pablo." Served from 10 June until 26 October 1938, first in RODIN's 2nd Escuadrilla, then with GRITSEVETS as second-in-command of the Group until early August 1938. Semenov says, he took over the 2nd Moscas when NEDELIN became incapacitated on 21 August, but Abrosov indicates that he took over command of the 5th Esc. In a landing on 26 August an undercarriage bolt broke causing the port wing to hit the ground breaking the outer wing panel, but he escaped without injury. Flew 121 sorties (Kaminskii says flew ninety combat missions and fought in thirty-two air combats) claiming six victories. By the end of service in Spain he had become a captain. Awarded the H.S.U. and Order of Lenin on 22 February 1939. Fought against the Japanese in the Khalkhin-Gol in the summer of 1939 as a Eskadril'ya CO in the 70th IAP. Flew 109 missions and fought in thirteen air battles claiming one Ki-27. Was awarded the Mongolian Order of the Red Banner on 18 August 1939, also a Red Banner on 29 August 1939. Fought in the winter war against Finland 1939-40 with the 25th IAP, awarded the Red Banner 7 May 1940. In June 1941 he was commander of the 12th IAP with rank of Major and claimed two victories on the first day of the war. Promoted to Lieutenant Colonel and given command of the 265th IAD in 1942. Retired in 1960 and died on 12 April 1978[1]. Awards were H.S.U., Order of Lenin (three times), Order of the Red Banner (three times), Order of the GPW both 1st and 2nd classes, and Order of the Red Star. (*Solidarity*, Berch, Semenov *Tov.*, *Vmeste, Geroi*, Abrosov, Kaminskii, *Pravda*, [1]Polak lists as 1974.)

KORZINNIKOV, Grigorii Mikhailovich, Lt., born 1910

Pilot SB, in Spain 26 March to 3 September 1938. Codename according to *Los Rusos* was "Korzan." He was a Patrulla leader in KRASNOGLAZOV's escuadrilla. At the end of an attack on enemy troops on 24 May, his aircraft received a hit from AAA, and he and his navigator TYAGUNOV were both wounded. The aircraft began to fall back from the formation, and then suddenly began to go down as KORZINNIKOV could no longer control it. The crew including the radio/gunner UDOVCHENKO were all able to bail out, saving themselves. Later at the end of June his aircraft was again hit and started to lag behind, but he was able to return to base after being rescued from attacking enemy fighters by the I-16 escorts. Semenov says he died in Spain, but GUDOVICH in *My 2* has a note saying this is incorrect, and that he had served in WWII and was at the time (1986) retired, living in the Ukraine. Awarded the Red Banner on 22 February 1939. (Semenov "*Parol*," Berch, *Pravda, My* (1986), *Los Rusos* spell it KOTZHINNIKOV.)

KOSENKOV, Ivan Ivanovich, born 1911
Zvena CO in the 119th IAE 95th IAB Transcaucasian Mil. Dist. In Spain he was an I-16 pilot in PLESHCHENKO's 2nd Esc, arrived 31 May 1937 and returned home 28 January 1938. Flew 150 combat missions and claimed two aircraft (one personal and one in Pair). Awarded the Red Banner twice, 28 October 1937and 2 March 1938. After his return he served in the 16th IAP Moscow Mil. Dist. In 1941 he was an Eskadril'ya CO in the 45th IAP. From July 1941 he was the head of the 20th Military Pilots School in the Caucasus. (Berch, Pritsker, Kaminskii, *Pravda*)

KOSHEL', Fedor Fedorovich, NCO, born 1910
SB radio/gunner, served from 26 March to 3 September 1938. Awarded Red Banner on 22 February 1939. (*Los Rusos* spell it KASHEL, Berch, Semenov "*Parol*," *Pravda*)

KOSHKIN, Pavel V., born 1912
Aviation technician, in Spain from 14 January to 28 August 1937. Awarded the Red Star on 4 July 1937. (*Los Rusos, Pravda*)

KOSHUBA, Yakov, born 1909
Aviation technician, served in Spain from 14 January 1937 to 11 January 1938. Awarded the Red Star. (*Los Rusos*)

KOSTANDI, Nikolai Ivanovich, Lt., born 1912
Pilot in the 107th IAE 83rd IAB Belorussian Mil. Dist. I-15 pilot in Spanish service from 30 December 1937 to 1 May 1938. Patrulla CO in the 1st Escuadrilla de Chatos. Flew 100 combat missions and fought in twenty-four air battles, three aircraft to credit (two He 51s and one CR 32). Awarded the Red Star 14 November 1938. In 1939 he is listed as serving in the Trans-Baikal Mil. Dist. and is thought to have died in a plane crash. (Abrosov, Kaminskii, *Los Rusos*, *Pravda* spells it KONSTANDI)

KOSTIKOV, Aleksandr I., Sr.Lt., born 1918
Navigator/Bombardier SB. In Spain from October 1936 to 27 May 1937. Awarded the Red Banner twice, on 2 January and 11 November 1937. (Semenov "*Parol*," *Pravda*, *Vmeste*, *Los Rusos* who spell it KOSHTIKOV)

KOTOV, A.I.
Listed as on Northern front by Golobeshkin in *Krylya Rodiny* 11/1989, but I think this is KETOV.

KOTOV, Dmitri I.
Aircraft Factory #22 Engineer on SBs. In Spain October 1936 to 8 March 1937. Awarded the Red Star on 2 January 1937. (*MY*, Berch, *Los Rusos, Pravda*)

KOTOV, Pavel Aleksandrovich, Col., born 1894
Chief of Staff at Estado Mayor del Grupo de Aviacion according to YAKUSHIN in *Bajo la B.* p.361. Same is listed by GUMENNYI in *Vmeste*, and also by Shingarev. But second-in-command of the SB Grupo under ZLATOTSVETOV, October 1936 states PROKOFIEV in *Bajo la B.* p.378. If the latter is correct, then probably nom de guerre was BOSKOSICH. *Los Rusos* list as "Pavlov." Shingarev says that it was he, together with AGAL'TSOV and PTUKHIN, who decided to form a night fighter unit as a Detachment of EREMENKO's Esc., with KUZNETSOV as leader and SEROV, YAKUSHIN, RYBKIN and SOROKIN as members, but see listing in LOPATIN. KOTOV was in Spain from October 1936 to 19 August 1937, awarded the Red Banner on 27 June 1937. On 7 May 1940 he was made a Major General, and in 1941 was the VVS commander of the Orlovskii Mil. Dist. On 15 May of that year he was relieved of his command and placed under arrest. After his hearing he was cleared of charges and appointed as a Professor at the Military Academy and survived the purge. Site Generals.dk list 1966 as year he died (they also say, born 1899). (Berch, Lazaro Avila, Logoluso, *Vmeste*, Shingarev, *Los Rusos*, *Pravda*, Abrosov lists as Commander of RZ Grupo)

KOTROV, Vasilii Petrovich, Maj., born 1902
Commander of the 119th IAE Transcaucasian Mil. Dist. In Spain Major "Nikolas" was the advisor to Major Isidoro Gimenez Garcia, Commander of the Escuadra de Caza, replacing GUSEV in that post in April 1938. Arrived 17 January and returned 26 October 1938, towards the end of his tour he is said to have been sick and did not fly much. Overall he flew sixty combat missions and fought in thirteen air battles and had two aircraft to his credit (one Bf 109 and one CR 32). Awarded the Red Banner 22 February 1939. Ibañiz in *Icare* p.130 claims he was only an Aero Engineer and spelled it KOTOV. Shingarev

on the other hand claims he replaced EREMENKO rather than GUSEV, and spells it as KATROV. After he returned to the USSR he was promoted to a Brigade CO and in 1941 became the Deputy CO of the VVS in the Odessa Mil. Dist. defending Odessa during the siege in August-September 1941. After WWII he stayed in the Air Force. For his service he was awarded the Order of Lenin (twice), the Red Banner (three times, 22 February 1939 for Spain) plus other metals. (Semenov "*Parol*," Berch, Shingarev, Ibaniz in *Icare 130*, Arias, *Los Rusos* give end date as 28th, Abrosov, Kaminskii, *Pravda* spell it KATROV)

KOTYKHOV, Mikhail Vasil'evich, Lt., born 1913[1]

Was a pilot in the 111th IAB Leningrad Mil. Dist. Served in Spain as an I-15 pilot in the 1st Esc. under SEROV. He had arrived on 20 August 1937 and was KIA 10 Dec., 1937. He had claimed a Bf 109 on 24 August, the pilot was said to have been taken prisoner. On 12 October he downed a Ju 52. On 10 December 1937, during an air battle near Bujaraloz, seven I-15s engaged eighteen CR 32s. He shot down one of the Fiats but then his aircraft Chato #CC-022, was hit and caught fire. He bailed out, but was attacked and machine gunned by Fiats. PLESCHENKO in Pritsker says it was during an attack on Sanjuro airfield. His Esc. was at this time based at Bujaraloz and commanded by ANTONOV. *Note,* Some list as KIA on 12 October 1937, undoubtedly reversing the the day/month. Abellan on the other hand says he died in a collision with a CR 32 flown by Vittorio Barberio, and the *Diario de Caza* also indicates he died in a collision. Awarded the Red Banner 2 March 1938. (Berch, Lacalle, Shingarev, *Bajo la B.*, Pritsker, Abellan, Abrosov, *Diario, Los Rusos, Pravda*, [1]Kaminskii and airaces.narod.ru says 1915!)

KOVAL'CHUK, K.

I-15 pilot 1936. Logoluso says used nom de guerre KARP. (Shingarev, Lukes says Rychagov's esc. But see KOVTUN below.)

KOVALEVSKII, Anton Vikent'evich "Kasimir," Sr.Lt., born 1909 (some say 1908)

Attended the Orenburg School for Military Pilots. Was a Detachment CO in the 1st LBAE MVO Moscow Mil. Dist. He went to Spain with first group of Soviet fighter pilots, arrived in Spain 29 September 1936, and served first in the 1st Escuadrilla Internacional, flying the Nieuport Ni 52c and Lorie 46. Later in November, he became part of RYCHAGOV's Escuadrilla and leader of an I-15 patrulla. At the beginning of 1937 he was sent along with eight other pilots[1] to the Malaga region. He was shot down and killed at Malaga, on February 1, 1937 during a battle with an S-81. He got on the tail of the bomber and started firing. Smoke and flames started to come from the bomber. As he started to pass over the top of the bomber, one of its gunners was able to fire on Casimiro's underbelly. The chato began smoking and crashed to the ground. KOVALEVSKII was buried in the local cemetery of Malaga. Awarded the Red Banner 2 January 1937. He had three aircraft to his credit. Used nom de guerre "Casimiro," but Lacalle (wrongly) says no. (Salas, Lacalle, RSA, *Solidarity*, RandR, Howson 194, *Bajo la B.*, *Vmeste*, Zakharov, Pritsker, Lukes, Abrosov, *Pravda*, [1]Kondrat only lists seven names, but I think he forgot ERLYKIN and ARTEM'EV.)

KOVBASA, Aleksei A., Lt., born 1909

SSS pilot, served from October 1936 to 2 July 1937. Awarded the Red Banner 2 January 1937. (*Los Rusos* list as KORBASA, *Pravda*)

KOVENEV, Fedor Dmitrievich, Lt., born 1904

Joined Army at the age of twenty-six, and shortly afterwards attended the Lugansk Pilots Air School. Was a Zvena CO in the 5th IAE 36th IAB Kiev Mil. Dist. Requested duty in Spain, and departed for there on 20 August 1937. Flew the I-16 as a patrulla leader in DEVOTCHENKO's 2nd Escuadrilla. His rank in Spain was Lieutenant. KIA when his aircraft CM-141 was shot down during an air battle with Messerschmitts on 10 March 1938. He is listed as having shot down a Bf

109 but was then himself shot down by either *Uffz.* K. Rochel or *Oblt.* Schlichting. Listed as having six aircraft to his credit. He was awarded the Order of the Red Star posthumously on 14 November 1938. Note this person is undoubtedly the same as KONEV, F., listed above as KIA on the 11th, a date on which no I-16 is claimed. But two I-16s were claimed on the 10th by members of 2/J88. Semenov also says KIA on 11 March. (Semenov "*Parol*," Berch, Polak, Abrosov, Kaminskii, *Pravda*, Salas *Diario* also lists 10 March.)

KOVTUN, Karp Ivanovich, Lt., born 15 May 1908
Joined the Army in 1930. Attended the Voroshilovgrad Aviation Flying School in 1934, after which he then commanded a Zvena in the 109th IAE 36th IAB Kiev Mil. Dist. Volunteered for duty in Spain, and arrived there on 20 October 1936 as a Sr.Lt. There he became a Detachment leader in RYCHAGOV's I-15 Esc. Shot down several enemy aircraft. He was KIA on 13 November 1936, when he was shot down in air combat over the Madrid area. His plane crashed twelve kilometers from the base at Alcala de Henares says DEMENCHUK in *Vmeste*. One report says he tried to bail out but somehow his chute was not buckled correctly and he slipped out of the harness and fell to his death. Awarded the H.S.U. and Order of Lenin, his was one of seventeen H.S.U.s awarded on 31 December 1936, eleven going to flyers and six to armored personnel. (*Solidarity*, Berch, Zakharov, *Vmeste*, Pritsker, Rumyantsev, *Geroi*, Lukes, Abrosov, *Pravda*, Kaminskii, *Los Rusos* give date of birth as 1909 and dates of service as 26 March to 5 August 1938 (?))

KOZEK
Escuadra España. (*Bajo la B.*)

KOZHEMYAKO, Andrei Fedorovich, NCO, born 1912
SB radio/gunner in Spain from 28 June to 25 November 1938. He was wounded on 10 October 1938, when the Aircraft he was in was shot up by Bf 109s. The pilot SHARONOV was able to bring it back to the airfield, but crashed while landing. In this action he along with IL'IN and TERTYCHNYI gunners in two other SBs shot up the 109 flown by Gamringer of 3.J/88, which crashlanded. Awarded the Red Banner on 22 February 1939. (Semenov "*Parol*," Berch, *Pravda, Los Rusos* spell it KOZHEMIAKOV.)

KOZLOV, Mikhail M., Lt., born 1907
Navigator (SSS) in Spain October 1936 to 26 July 1937. Awarded the Red Banner 2 January 1937. (*Los Rusos, Pravda*)

KOZLOV, Vasilii Ivanovich, NCO, born 1914
Gunner/Radio SB, from 30 May to 15 November 1938. On a mission in the Batea region, his aircraft had an engine shot up and he claimed a Fiat. His aircraft made a crashlanding at Valls fighter field on 21 September 1938, no one hurt. Awarded the Red Banner on 22 February 1939. (Berch, Semenov *Tov., Los Rusos, Pravda*)

KOZYREV, Mikhail Ivanovich, Lt., born 1907
Pilot SB-2, arrived 26 March and returned 3 September 1938. Codename according to *Los Rusos* was "Koklin." Awarded the Red Banner on 22 February 1939. (Semenov "*Parol*," Berch, *Los Rusos, Pravda*)

KOZYREV, Nikolai Ivanovich, Lt., born 1913
Was a member of the 40th IAE 83rd IAB Belorussian Mil. Dist. I-16 pilot in Spain from 10 May until 29 September 1937. Kaminskii lists him as in the 1st Moscas, but on 2 July 1937 he went to Santander with UKHOV's new (4th) Esc. Awarded the Red Banner on 11 November 1937. Promoted to captain, in June 1938 he was a CO of one of the IAPs in the Kiev Mil. Dist. In WWII, he was CO of the 929th IAP on the Stalingrad front, where he was KIA on 17 August 1942. (Kaminskii, Abrosov, Shingarev, Berch, *Vmeste*, Pritsker, *Pravda, Los Rusos* give start date as 15 May and spell it KOZIREV)

KRAPIVYANSKII, Nikolai Emelyanovich, Lt., born 1915
Navigator in the 10th SBAE (Fast Bomber Escuadrilla) Byelorussian Mil. Dist. In Spain from 5 September 1937 to 10 June 1938 with the SB Group, Gagin says was in LISOV's Escuadrilla and was KIA 10 June 1938. Codename according to *Los Rusos* was "Krogan." Awarded the Order of the Red Banner 14 November 1938. (Berch, Gagin, *Pravda, Los Rusos* give start date as 14 February 1937 and that he died in a storm, while Semenov "*Parol*" shows him as coming at the end of 1937.)

KRASILNIKOV, Petr S.
An SB or SSS pilot in Spain from 17 November 1936 to 26 July 1937. Awarded the Red Banner 27 June 1937 and Red Star 2 January 1937. (*Los Rusos, Pravda*)

KRASNOGLAZOV, Nikolai Mikhailovich, Lt., born 1907

Pilot SB, arrived 26 March and returned home 3 September 1938. He was the commander of an Escuadrilla according to LIPASHOV in *Vmeste* and GUDOVICH in *My 2*. During the May 20th attack on La Cenia, he had to return to his field just after take-off due to both engines failing. Switching to a reserve aircraft he was soon able to rejoin the formation. Later the tanks of his aircraft were found to have water in them causing the engines to malfunction. Sabotage? Awarded the Order of Lenin 22 February 1939. (Semenov "*Parol*," Berch, *My 2, Vmeste, Los Rusos, Pravda*)

KRAVCHENKO, Aleksandr P., born 1909

Aviation technician, served in Spain from 14 January to 18 October 1937. Awarded the Red Star on 21 June 1937. (*Los Rusos*)

KRAVCHENKO, Ivan Ivanovich, Lt., born 1914

Served in the 40th IAE 83rd IAB Belorussian Mil. Dist. I-16 pilot in Spain from November 1936 – 26 July 1937. Was a member of TARKHOV's Escuadrilla. Together with POLYAKOV they downed a Junkers on 22 November 1936, which had been attacking positions held by the 11th International Brigade. Claimed a He 51 in the Madrid area on 6 December and shared another Junkers on 25 March 1937. Awarded the Red Banner twice, 2 January and 4 July 1937. On his return from Spain he went back to the 40th IAE and then in September 1937 became a Detachment CO in the 2nd IAE Kiev Mil. Dist. At the beginning of 1938 he was made a test pilot at Factory #21 in Gorky. In July 1941 he became CO of the 433rd AP ADD and fought in defense of Moscow. From January to July 1942 was CO of the 747th AP ADD and from July 1942 to January 1944 was CO of the 749th AP ADD (became the 9th Guards in March 1943). And from January to October 1944 he was Inspector with the 56th IAD and after that he was deputy CO of the 173rd IAP. Retired with rank of Colonel in 1957 and passed away 24 July 1986. (Kaminskii, Rumyantsev "*Antonio*," *Vmeste, Los Rusos, Pravda*)

KRAVCHENKO, Vyacheslav Mikhailovich, Lt., born 18 March 1912

From March 1936 was a test pilot with the NII VVS. I-16 fighter pilot, in Spain from 13 May 1937 until 11 January 1938. He flew eighty combat missions and fought in three air battles and it is thought that he shot down one enemy aircraft. After returning from Spain he worked again as a test pilot. Fought in beginning of WWII as a member of the 401st IAP on the Western front. In September 1941 went back to being a test pilot and was killed on 22 July 1943 while testing bombs for the Il-2, one of the bombs exploded prematurely. (Abrosov, *Los Rusos*, Kaminskii)

KRIGIN, Mikhail Viktorovich, Capt.

White Russian listed as having been a Colonel in the Russian Imperial Navy, who had left Russia after the civil war and emigrated to Spain. According to J.L. de Mesa in *Aeroplano* #18 pgs.4-10, He joined the Legion on 19 June 1922, enlisting in Malaga for the duration of the war in Morocco. Flying a seaplane out of Melilla, he flew many bombing missions against the enemy. In June 1927, the Seaplane he was flying experienced a problem and was stuck sitting in the water just off the coast of Alhucemas, but he was eventually rescued (ABC 19 June 1927). Before the Civil War, he worked with the Spanish National Airline L.A.P.E. On 18 July 1936 he and another pilot were sent to Son San Juan in Palma Mallorca to transfer an L.A.P.E. Fokker FVII back to Alcazares, which they were able to do just before the rebels took over there. During the war, he worked with the Russian fighter Escuadrillas since he could speak the language. From August 1937 until at least the end of the year, he was Chief of staff for the 6th Moscas, This was the I-16 escuadrilla commanded by A. GUSEV. Various spellings, Spanish use KRIGUIN or KIRIGUIN. He is also said to have been called Melokanov. De Mesa also mentions the possibility that he was a spy for Franco, but no proof is supplied. (Gusev, *Vmeste* 278, Semenov "*Parol*," Lacalle p.87)

KRIVONOGOV, Mikhail, NCO, born 1913

SB radio/gunner, served from 3 January until 7 September 1937. Awarded the Red Banner. (*Los Rusos*)

KRIVOSHEEV, A.I.

Listed as a radio/gunner on SB. (*Vmeste*)

KROMBERG, Zucharoff
Flew in "KAZAKOV's" I-15 Escuadrilla with Baumler. Asst. CO. See ZAKHAROV, G.N. See also Baumler list of squadron members in Illustration section. (Baumler)

KRUPENIN, Samuel M., born 1900
SB engineer/technician, served from 22 June 1937 to 25 April 1938. Awarded the Red Banner 3 November 1937 and Red Star 2 March 1938. (*Los Rusos, Pravda*)

KRUPENIN, Timofei E., born 1905
Mechanic in TARKHOV's I-16 group. In Spain from October 1936 to 27 August 1937. Awarded the Red Banner on 27 June and the Red Star 2 January 1937. (*Solidarity, Vmeste, Los Rusos, Pravda*)

KRUPMAN, Eduard Petrovich, Sr.Lt., born 1909
CO of a Zvena in the 103rd IAE[1] Pacific Fleet. An I-16 pilot and Patrulla CO in Spain from 1 March until 29 September 1937. On 14 March, while returning from a mission in the Guadalajara area, he was unable to land at his airfield due to bad weather. He tried landing in an open field but crashed, destroying his aircraft. He was shot down during an air combat on 14 June. He bailed out when the plane lost control and came down in enemy territory, but after three hours he was able to get to friendly territory. Awarded the Red Banner 17 July 1937. [1]Kaminskii lists as the 103rd, but Abrosov lists as 108th. (Pritsker, Abrosov, *Los Rusos* list as KRUMPAN, Kaminskii, *Pravda*)

KUDRYAVTSEV, Dmitri O., born 1908
Fitter from Aircraft Factory #22 assembling SB bombers. In Spain from October to 12 December 1936. Awarded the Red Star 2 January 1937. (*Los Rusos, Pravda*)

KUKHAREV, Vasilii Aleksandrovich, Lt., born 1912
Pilot in the 57th IAE 142nd IAB Belorussian Mil. Dist. I-16 pilot he served in Spain from 26 March to 18 May 1938. Had refused to fly at the front and was sent home early. In June 1941 he was CO of the 21st IAP, but when the war began he was moved to the 99th SBAP. Died 9 July 1941. (Abrosov, *Los Rusos*, Kaminskii)

KULAGUIN, Mikhail I., born 1911
Engineer on fighter aircraft, in Spain from October 1936 to March 1937. Awarded the Red Star 2 January 1937. (*Los Rusos, Pravda*)

KULIKOV, Ivan T., born 1909
Aeronautical engineer, in Spain October 1936 to 30 June 1937. Awarded the Red Star 2 January 1937. (*Los Rusos, Pravda*)

KULIKOV, Zinovii Matveevich, NCO, born 1913
Gunner/radio SB, from 30 May to 15 November 1938. Awarded the Red Banner 22 February 1939. (Semenov "*Parol*," Berch, *Los Rusos, Pravda*)

KUMAR'IAN, Ivan
Translator. (Smirnov)

KUPREICHIK, Aleksei Ya., born 1911
Aviation technician, served from October 1936 to 30 June 1937. Awarded the Red Star 2 January 1937. (*Los Rusos, Pravda*)

KURBATKIN, Pavel Semenovich, Col.
In Spain from 1 August 1937 to 21 July 1938. Awarded the Red Banner 2 March 1938. But *Los Rusos* list as an advisor to the 21st Cuerpo. (For Aviation?) (Berch, *Los Rusos, Pravda*)

KURYGIN, Andrei E., born 1912
Armaments technician (aviation?) in Spain October 1936 to 3 June 1937. Awarded the Red Star 2 January 1937. (*Los Rusos, Pravda*)

KUSTOV, Viktor Pavlovich, Lt., born 26 April 1909 in Moscow.
Attended the Stalingrad Military Flyers School. Was pilot in the 12th IAE 111th IAB Leningrad Mil. Dist. An I-15 reinforcement pilot in the 1st Esc. during the battle of Brunete in 1937, he departed for Spain as a Lt. on 20 August 1937[1] and arrived on the 28th flying from France. He had traveled along with DEVOTCHENKO and others. On 4 December he was put in commanded of a Patrulla. He was wounded in an air battle with Bf 109s on 24 December 1937 while flying Chato #CC-021, and returned home on 25 February 1938. He had shot down three enemy fighters. He was awarded the Red Banner on 2 March 1938. In 1938-39, he commanded a Zvena in the 38th IAP and then in the 44th IAP. In 1939, at the Khalkhin Gol he commanded a Zvena in the 22nd IAP and then became CO of an Eskadril'ya in the 56th IAP. He was killed in combat on 3 August 1939 in a Taran against a Ki 21 Bomber. Credited with three kills there, he was posthumously awarded the H.S.U. on 29 August 1939. Other awards were Order of Lenin and Order of the Red Banner. (*Bajo la B.*, Shingarev, Salas, Rumyantsev *Geroi*, Lukes, Abrosov, Kaminskii [1]Note Shingarev wrongly claims he and others arrived on 28 July.)

KUTSENKO, Andrei Stepanovich
Navigator SB, arrived in June 1938. Awarded the Red Banner 22 February 1939. (Semenov "*Parol*," *Pravda*)

KUZ'KIN, Ivan E., Lt., born 1908
Pilot of SSS, in Spain from October 1936 to 30 June 1937. On 19 December 1936, during an attack in the Boadilla area against ground troops, his Aircraft was hit by AAA fire and had to make a forced landing. Awarded the Red Banner 2 January 1937. According to POLUSHKO in *Vmeste*, he was an SB pilot, but is he mistaking him with KUZMIN below? Los Rusos say was a Navigator. (*Vmeste, Pravda*, Abrosov, *Los Rusos* spell name KUZ)

KUZMENKO, Konstantin "Kost'ya"
(Gusev 88, Berch, Logoluso)

KUZMIN, Sergei Alekseevich, Sr.Lt., born 1906
SB pilot in Spain from 9 September 1937 to 11 February 1938. Awarded the Red Banner on 14 November 1938. (*Los Rusos, Pravda*)

KUZNETSOV
Mentioned by CHERVYAKOV in *Vmeste*, who says he led a Detachment in the same SSS Escuadrilla he was in. (*Vmeste*)

KUZNETSOV, Petr Fedorovich, Lt., born 1911
Pilot in the 107th IAE 83rd IAB Byelorussian Mil. Dist. In Spain, he was an I-16 pilot in TARKHOV/KOLESNIKOV's Esc. He arrived in November 1936 on the Kursk with the first group. Rumiantsev claims he was the second-in-command of TARKHOV'S Esc. and that he downed a Heinkel He 51 on 7 November and on the 22nd claimed a Ju 52. He shot down a total of four enemy aircraft during his time in Spain. Returned home 26 July 1937. Awarded the Red Banner twice 2 January and 4 July 1937. EVSEV'EV in *Vmeste*, says he was in the North, but feel he made a typo and meant Sergei (below). (Gusev 89, *Vmeste*, Pritsker, Rumyantsev "*Antonio*," Kaminskii, *Pravda*)

KUZNETSOV, Sergei Alekseevich, Lt., born 1912
Zvena CO in the 40th IAE 83rd IAB Belorussian Mil. Dist. Patrulla leader in EVSEV'EV's I-16 Escuadrilla on the "Santander" Front in the Summer 1937 where he is said to have flown I-16 number 33. He had been one of the eight pilots UKHOV took to the North on 2 July 1937. Served from 10 May to 29 September 1937. Both Shingarev and ADRIASHENKO in *MY* (wrongly) claim it was he and not SMIRNOV who had led the Spanish pilots to the North. Shot down one enemy aircraft (in partulla). Awarded the Order of Lenin on 3 November 1937. (RSA, Berch, *MY, Vmeste*, Shingarev, Pritsker, Abrosov, Kaminskii, *Pravda*)

KUZNETSOV, Viktor Vladimirovich, Lt. Born 1909
Zvena CO in the 34th IAE Kiev Mil. Dist. Served in Spain from 7 February to 7 September 1937. I-15 pilot, second-in-command of the 1st Chato Esc. before EREMENKO arrived. Retained by PTUKHIN, and became EREMENKO's wingman. He was later made commander of the night fighter unit when it was first formed. Shingarev says he flew his last mission on 18 July and returned home, but records indicate he did not leave until September. Shot down five enemy aircraft (including personal, pairs and in group). Awards were Order of Lenin on 14 November 1937 and Red Banner 27 June 1937. In 1939 he was commander of an IAP and fought in the Khalkhin Gol. After the start of WWII, it is thought he commanded the 263rd IAP. He was KIA on 23 February 1943 in air combat against Me 109s of JG 54 in the Sinyavino region. (Kaminskii, Lario, Berch, RSA, *Bajo la B.*, Shingarev, Lukes, *Los Rusos* give start date as 7 January, Abrosov, *Pravda*)

LAKEEV, Ivan Alekseevich, Lt., born 23 February 1908
Entered the Soviet Army in 1931. In 1932, he completed courses at the Military Theoretical School for Pilots in Leningrad and in 1933, the Military Practical School for Pilots in Engels. Before leaving for Spain, he was a fighter pilot in the 107th IAE 83rd IAB Byelorussian Mil. Dist. He volunteered for service in Spain, shipping out in October 1936 along with the rest of the men pulled from different IAEs, which would make up Sergei TARKHOV's I-16 Eskadril'ya in Spain. The unit traveled along with their aircraft and equipment on two Soviet ships, the *Kursk* and the *Blagoev* arriving on the 3rd and 4th of November 1936 at Cartagena. After arrival he was put into the Detachment commanded by Konstantin KOLESNIKOV which was based at Guadalajara. (KOLESNIKOV would take over command of the Escuadrilla on 13 November 1936 after TARKHOV was shot down.) After the death of KOLESNIKOV in an accident on 12 May 1937, it is said by several Soviet/Russian sources, that LAKEEV took over command of the Escuadrilla. Both I.E. Pritsker 227

and *Vmeste* say that he took over KOLESNIKOV's Esc. upon the death of the latter. Whereas Frank Tinker who flew in the same Escuadrilla and had nicknamed him "Goofy," says that he was second-in-command under Valentin UKHOV and that only later near the end of June 1937 became CO of the Escuadrilla (1st Moscas). OSADCHII says his Escuadrilla and LAKEEV's were together at Castejon airfield near Barbastro in Cataluña for the battle of Huesca in mid-June 1937. He was among the pilots replaced by new flyers from the Soviet Union in mid-July, returning home on 13 August 1937. He had flown 312 missions and fought in thirty-two air combats and had four kills[1] (personal and in group). He was awarded the Title of H.S.U. on 3 November 1937, and was twice awarded the Order of the Red Banner, on 2 January and 4 July 1937. After Spain, he commanded an Eskadril'ya of the 16th IAP with the rank of Major. Fought in the battles of the Khalkhin Gol, 1939, where he downed two Japanese Ki-27 aircraft. He was awarded his third Order of the Red Banner on 29 August 1939, plus the Mongolian Red Banner on 18 August 1939. In September 1939, he took part in the "Liberation" of the Western Ukraine and Byelorussia. Later he participated in the "Winter War" with Finland. On 4 June 1940, he was given the rank of Major General VVS. During the Great Patriotic War (WWII), he commanded the 235th IAD (Fighter Aviation Division), which became the 15th Guards IAD of the 8th Air Army. For his services in WWII, he was awarded the Order of Lenin, plus his 4th Red Banner, the Order of Suvarov 2nd Class, Order of Kutuzov 2nd class, Order of Bogdan Khmel'nits 2nd class, the Red Star and other medals. In 1952, he graduated from the Supreme Military Academy. After an illness in 1955, he was placed on reserve and died on 15 August 1990. (Berch, R and R, Gusev 89, RSA, Tinker, Baumler, Salas, Solidarity 315, *Bajo la B.*, *Vmeste*, Zakharov, Pritsker, Rumyantsev "*Anonio*," *Geroi Sovetskogo Soiuza*, Polak [1]note, Polak and others now have changed his score to thirty-two (twenty of these as shares) in 312 sorties, Abrosov, Kaminskii, *Pravda*)

LANTUKH, Aleksei Petrovich, Capt., born 1910
A Detachment CO in the 57th IAE 142nd IAB Byelorussian Mil. Dist. I-16 fighter pilot in Spain from 26 March until 28 June 1938. He was in the 2nd Moscas under RODIN. His aircraft was shot down in combat with Bf 109s on 18 May 1938; he bailed out, wounded. After his release from the hospital he returned to the USSR. He was awarded the medal for "Courage" on 22 February 1939. In 1940 he was a Zvena CO in the 31st IAP. During WWII he was appointed as an Eskadril'ya CO in the 515th IAP. He failed to return from a mission in the Doroguska region of Poland on 27 July 1944. (Semenov "*Parol*," Abrosov, *Los Rusos* spell it LANTUIA, Abrosov, Kaminskii, *Pravda*)

LAPIN, Aleksei Alekseevich, born 1898
Aeronautical engineer, in Spain from 11 November 1937 until 24 May 1938. Awarded the Red Star on 22 February 1939. (Los Rusos, *Pravda*)

LARIONOV, Evgeni Aleksandrovich, Lt., born 1910
Zvena CO in the 35th IAE 56th IAB Kiev Mil. Dist. An I-16 fighter pilot in Spain from 20 August 1937 until 15 April 1938; eventually became a patrulla CO in the 5th Moscas. Flew 125 missions and had two aircraft to his credit (Bf 109 and CR 32). Awarded the Red Banner twice, 2 March and 14 November 1938. (Abrosov, *Los Rusos*, Kaminskii, *Pravda*)

LARIONOV
Listed by KAL'CHENKO in Vmeste as a Technician in RYCHAGOV Esc. (*Vmeste*)

LARIONOV, Konstantin Ivanovich, Sr.Lt., born 1914
Pilot SB, served from 30 May to 15 November 1938. Awarded the Red Banner on 22 February 1939. (Berch, Gusev 101, *Los Rusos, Pravda*)

LATYSHEV, Petr Ivanovich, born 1910
Navigator SB, arrived in Spain on 30 December 1937; he was KIA 7 February 1938. After bailing out of the burning SB, flown by SURZHIN, he was machine gunned on his way down by Bf 109s. See SURZHIN listing for details of this. Before enlisting in the Air Force, he had worked as a joiner in a Tram depot. He graduated from Vol'skoe Aviation School as a radio gunner and had flown in the Far East. Later he attended the 3rd Orenburg Military School and became a bomber/navigator. Awarded the Red Star 14 November 1938. (Berch, Semenov "*Parol*," *Los Rusos, Pravda*)

LAVRENTEV, Petr, born 1906
Advisor in a factory (Aviation?), served from 28 March to 16 December 1938. (*Los Rusos*)

LAVROV, Aleksei, born, Lt., born 1907
SB navigator, in Spain from May to 2 July 1937. Awarded the Red Banner 27 June 1937. (Kotelnikov, *Los Rusos, Pravda*)

LAVROV, G.
Pilot of an SSS Rasante, in the 2nd Esc. Grupo 15. (*Vmeste*)

LAVSKII, Viktor Mikhailvich, Lt., born 19 October 1914
Before going to Spain he was a member of the 10th BAB at Smolensk. In Spain he was an SB navigator in the 1st Esc. under command of SENATOROV, from 14 June 1937 to 28 January 1938. Awarded the Red Banner twice, 28 October 1937 and 2 March 1938. Fought in the Russo-Finnish Winter War, where he flew twenty-one missions. Participated in WWII, where he was a senior navigator in the 8th BAK. In 1994, he was a retired Lt.Gen. and head of the Soviet War Veterans, Spanish Section. See letter in *The Volunteer* Fall 1994. Passed away 19 June 2012. (*Solidarnost*, Logoluso, Künzi, *Los Rusos* list as LIABSKI, http://topwar.ru/15714)

LAZARIEV, Abram, born 1908
Armaments Technician on SBs. Served from October 1936 to 27 March 1937. Awarded the Red Star 2 January 1937. (*Los Rusos, Pravda*)

LAZARIEV, Iosif G., born 1901
Engineer (Aviation?) in Spain from 14 January to 18 October 1937. Awarded both the Red Banner? and Red Star 17 July 1937. (*Los Rusos, Pravda*)

LAZUTKIN, Semen P., born 1903
Fitter from Aircraft Factory #1 assembling/repairing I-15 and SSS aircraft. In Spain from October 1936 to 27 May 1937. Awarded the Red Star 2 January 1937. (*Pravda, Los Rusos*)

LEBEDEV, Viktor Grigor'evich, Lt., born 1911
Navigator on an SB, in Spain from 31 May until he was KIA when shot down over Segovia on 12 July 1937. (Abrosov, *Los Rusos* lists as 14 July as does the 1991 Soviet list of dead.)

LEITNER-NIKOLAEVA, Irina K.
Translator. (Semenov "*Parol*," Berch)

LESHCHINSKII
Armaments Engineer on SBs (possible codename). (Kotelnikov)

LESNIKOV, Dmitrii Artamonovich, Lt., born 1907
Pilot in the 107th IAE 83rd IAB Belorussian Mil. Dist. An I-16 fighter pilot, he arrived in Spain in November 1936 and died on 19 June 1937. He was an Instructor on I-16s at Alcala de Henares. On 19 June he took off from Castejón Aerodrome to test the engine in a new I-16. Suddenly the left outer wing panel came off his aircraft and it spun into the ground. He had been in Spain eight months as a member of the TARKHOV/KOLESNIKOV/UKHOV/LAKEEV Esc. (1st Moscas). Awarded the Red Banner on 2 January 1937. Had three aircraft to his credit (in pairs and Group). Baumler, who was a squadron mate, called him LASNIKOV. (Tinker, Baumler, Kaminskii, *Pravda, Vmeste*, Rumyantsev, "*Antonio*," *Los Rusos* say 16 June as date killed, Martinez in *AEQ 32* says name spelled LICHNIKOV and that he was an SB Pilot. Abellan says he was in 3rd Moscas.)

LEVENBERG, ILya A., Lt., born 1902
SB Pilot in the 2nd Esc., Grupo 12 from October 1936 to 8 May 1937. Awarded the Red Banner twice, 2 January and 17 July 1937. (Salas, *Bajo la, Vmeste, Los Rusos, Pravda*)

LEVIN, Mikhail I.
Worker from Aircraft Factory #22 assembling SB aircraft. In Spain October 1936 to 8 March 1937. Awarded the Red Star 2 January 1937. (*MY*, Berch, *Los Rusos, Pravda*)

LEVINSKII, Georgii K., Col., born 1910
Although Los Rusos list his dates of service as 3 January to 19 August 1937, it seems he really arrived in May of that year as a Sr.Lt., as PROKOFIEV states in *Bajo la B.* that LEVINSKII arrived to replace him as head navigator of the Grupo de Kats, detailed to bomb shipping in the Balearic waters. BOGDENKO writing in *Leningradtsy* p.177 (Pritsker Ed.) says G.K Livinskii (sic) was in the 1st Bomber Escuadrilla SB under PROSKUROV. Abrosov p.104 states he was the navigator/bombardier who scored the hits on the German Battle Cruiser *Deutschland* on 29 May 1937, and that the pilot listed in the documents was KHOVANSKII, M.G., but other sources say LEVINSKII was the navigator in the SB flown by OSTRYAKOV along with LOBOZOV as gunner and is credited with

making the hit on the *Deutschland*. Awarded the Red Banner 3 November 1937 as a colonel. Is it possible he was he elevated to this rank due to that attack? Name is spelt LIVINSKI in *Bajo la B.* and also *Los Rusos (Vmeste, Bajo la B.*, Salas, RSA, *Pravda*, Abrosov)

LEVSKII

I-16 instructor for Spanish pilots in the Soviet Union. (Laureau, Berch)

LEVSKII, Viacheslav V., Sr.Lt., born 1910

In Spain from October 1936 to 2 July 1937. Commander of the 1st Escuadrilla[1] of SSS Rasantes Grupo 15 under the overall Command of GUSEV, K.M. This Esc. and the Command were based at Quintanar in late 1936 and early 1937. Awarded Red Banner 2 January and 4 July 1937. (*Vmeste, Pravda, Los Rusos,* [1]see STRELKOV listing)

LINDE, Aleksandr Y.A., Capt., born 1904

Pilot SB Patrulla Commander in 1st Esc. from October 1936 to 23 January 1937. Returned home early due to illness. Awarded the Red Banner 2 January 1937. (*Bajo la B., Pravda,* Kotelnikov, *Los Rusos* where it is spelt without the E.)

LIPASHOV, Aleksei Aleksandrovich, Lt., born 1913.

SB pilot in Spain from 26 March to 13 August 1938. Flew aircraft with ELAGIN and MATVIENKO as crewmembers. Awarded the Red Banner on 22 February 1939. (Berch, *Vmeste* says was retired colonel in 1986, *Los Rusos* says first name Aleksandr and last spelt Lipashev. *Pravda* also list last name that way, but see his memoir in *Vmeste.*)

LIPIN, Pavel I., born 1909

Flight instructor for Escuadrilla from November 1936 to 10 November 1937. Awarded Red Banner on 21 June 1937 and a Red Star. (*Los Rusos, Pravda* (there is also a Red Banner listing 28 October 1938 as a Col.))

LISIN, Vasilii Timofeevich, Col., born 24 February 1908

Served in the 13th IAE as a Zvena CO and later was head Navigator for the 83rd IAB Byelorussian Mil. Dist. Became a Captain on 22 April 1937. In Spain from 14 December 1937 to 10 June 1938. Kaminskii says initially he was flying the I-15 on the Aragon front, but then transferred to the 5th Esc. under SMOLYAKOV while based at Caspe airfield. He was named commander of the 2nd Escuadrilla in late March 1938 and then in April became Fighter Group CO. Flew eighty sorties, fought in thirty-five air battles and claimed two aircraft plus six more in group. Awarded the Order of Lenin on 22 February 1939 and the Red Banner on 14 November 1938. After his return to the USSR, he was appointed as CO of the 5th IAP Siberian Mil. Dist. from September 1938 to April 1941. When the war began, he was from July 1941 the deputy CO of the 32nd IAD and later CO of the 69th ShAD. In March 1942 he became deputy CO of the VVS 2nd Assault Army and in August 1942 when the 14th VVS Air Army came into being, a part of it was the 278th IAD to which LISIN was appointed as CO. This Air Army operated on the Volkhov front, and he commanded the 278th until June 1944. From July to November 1944 he was on reserve status, where he was training to fly the Il-2 Sturmovik and from November 1944 to the end of the war he was CO of the 19th Guards BAD (Bomber Aviation Division). In August to September 1945 he was on the Far Eastern front fighting against the Japanese in Manchuria. He was placed on reserves 10 January 1956, and passed away on 9 February 1973. (Kaminskii, Semenov "*Parol*," Gusev 194, 302, Abrosov, Los Rusos, *Pravda*)

LISOV, Mitrofan Andreevich, Maj., born 1909

In 1935 he was the CO of an R-5 Esc. ShAE in the Leningrad Mil. Dist. In Spain from 30 December 1937 to 13 July 1938. Commander of one of the two Soviet SB Escuadrillas in 1938. His unit took part in the battles at Teruel and Alfambra in January and February 1938, where his and STECHISHIN's Escs. were escorted by the I-16 Escs. of SMOLYAKOV and DEVOTCHENKO. During the disastrous attack on Calamocha 7 February 1938 (on the road from Teruel to Zaragoza), four SBs were lost and his aircraft was damaged by the attacking Bf 109s. Fortunately he was able to safely reach the airfield at La Cenia, as did the aircraft flown by MOROZOV. His Esc. also participated in the attack on the Cruiser Baleares on March 6, 1938. Awarded the Order of Lenin on 22 February 1939 and the Red Banner 14 November 1938. Fought in WWII, in 1944-46, he was a General-Major Commander of the Tambov flying school. Passed away in 1986. (Berch, Semenov "*Parol,*" *Los Rusos, Pravda*, Gagin gives his dates of service in Spain as May 1938 to January 1939.)

LIVANSKII, Nikofor Ul'yanovich, Lt., born 1915

Zvena CO in the 57th IAE 142nd IAB Byelorussian Mil. Dist. He was an I-16 pilot in Spain from 26 March until 13 August 1938. Three aircraft to his credit (one personal on 23 May and two in pair). When he first arrived he was put with the 1st I-15 Escuadrilla until 3 June where he had fought in six air battles. He was then transferred to an I-16 Escuadrilla and flew sixty-three hours and fought in ten air combats. Awarded the Red Banner 22 February 1939. After returning home was in the 142nd IAB, and during WWII is said to have been CO of the 3rd IAE 170 IAP. He was KIA 8 September 1941 in aerial combat. (Semenov "*Parol,*" Abrosov, *Pravda*, airaces.narod.ru)

LIVINSKII, Georgii K. Sr., Lt., born 1910

SB navigator in Spain from 3 January to 13 August 1937. Awarded the Red Banner 17 July 1937. (*Los Rusos, Pravda.* (See LEVINSKII above, possibly these are two different people, as one is a Sr.Lt. and the other a colonel, but their dates of service and position are the same.)

LOBODA, Stepan, Capt., born 1913

Radio/Gunner SB from 3 January to 29 September 1937. Awarded the Red Banner twice. (*Los Rusos* – Undoubtedly this is LOBOZOV below, as no ORBs are found under this name and service and birth dates are the same.)

LOBOZOV, Vasilii Andreevich, NCO, born 1 February 1913

Joined the Army in 1935, graduated from the Voronezh School of Aviation Specialists as an air gunner/radio operator. Went to Spain and served as radio/gunner on an SB, in the 1st Escuadrilla under command of Ernst SCHACHT, from 3 January to 29 September 1937. He was said to have been in the crew that bombed the *Deutschland.* Completed 153 sorties in Spain. Awarded the Red Banner twice, 21 June and 22 October 1937. On his return home, he attended the Stalingrad Military Air School and graduated as a pilot. He then began service in 1939 with the 40th BAP in the Black Sea Fleet Air Force. He saw action from the beginning of the war in June 1941. Later became commander of the 30th RAP (Reconnaissance Air Regiment). This unit was involved in the defense of Odessa and Sevastopol. By March 1943 he had become a Major. He was KIA on 30 November 1944. He had claimed eight kills and awards were H.S.U. and Order of Lenin (16 May 1944), and Order of the Red Banner (three times) (*Vmeste, Bajo la B.*, Polak, *Geroi Sovetskogo Soiuza, Pravda, Bajo la B.* spells it LOBIZOV)

LOGUINOV, Nikolai I., born 1902

Armaments expert from Aircraft Factory #1 assembling/repairing I-15 and SSS aircraft. In Spain from October 1936 to 27 March 1937, Awarded the Red Star 2 January 1937. (*Los Rusos, Pravda*)

LOGUINOV, Vasilii V., born 1911

Patrulla mechanic, served from October 1936 to 26 July 1937. Awarded the Red Star 2 January 1937. (*Los Rusos, Pravda*)

LOPATIN, Vsevolod Nikolaevich, Col., born May 1898

In 1916 he joined the Army and after training was a Company CO in the area around Riga December 1916 to August 1917. Next became CO of a Machine Gun Regiment August to November 1917. In February 1918 he joined the Red Army and fought on the Eastern and Southern fronts. After taking courses on aviation in 1923, he was appointed Chief of Staff of the 1st ORE (Independent Reconnaissance Squadron). In 1924 he attained his pilot/observer title. Over the next three years he commanded the 14th ORE, the 2nd ORE and the 1st ORE. In November 1926 he was CO of the 2nd AB. In October 1927 he went to the 15th AB. In 1930 he was appointed as Commander of the Orenburg 3rd Military Pilots School and from October 1933 he was Assistant commander of the Leningrad Mil. Dist. Air Force Staff. In Spain from 26 May to 9 September 1937. He used the codename "General Montenegro"[1] and had replaced SMUSHKEVICH (Gen. Douglas) at end of May 1937, but he was pulled out of Spain early, due to pressure from I. Prieto and also some of the Soviet advisors whom he did not get along with. PUZEIKIN in Pritsker p155, claims that he and PTUKHIN were the prime organizers of the Chato Night Fighter unit, and says members were YAKUSHIN, SEROV, RYBKIN, ANTONOV, and SOBOLEV. On 14 January 1938 Vice Commander LOPATIN was arrested. From the report, he was arrested on the testimony of Corp Commander Vasili Khripin, which along with the word of Corp Commander Mezheninov named him among participants in an anti-Soviet conspiracy, and who together with them had conducted subversive work in the field of aviation. He was interrogated some twenty-eight times. On 29 July 1938, Aviation Division Commander V. N. LOPATIN was sentenced by the VMN and on the same day shot. He was posthumously rehabilitated on 12 December 1956. His date of execution is the same as that of Commander of the VVS Alksnis who had been arrested on 23 November 1937. Source *USSR* p.67, says LOPATIN received the Order of Lenin on 25 May 1936. Viñas in *Escudo* pgs.253-254 says he did not show much skill in air operations and this caused several deaths. (*Solidarity*, RSA, Berch, *Vmeste*, Pritsker, Boyd, Suvenirov-*Tragadija RKKA 1937-1938* gives 1899 as birth date, Abrosov. [1]OSADCHII in *Vmeste* p.179, confirms that he was indeed "Montenegro," GUMENNYI in *Vmeste* p.78 says the same thing. *Los Rusos* say his codename was "Donstov.")

LOSKUTOV, Aleksei Vasil'evich, Lt., born 1908

Before going to Spain he was a pilot in the 12th IAE 111th IAB Leningrad Mil. Dist. In Spain from 20 August 1937, he was KIA on 5 January 1938. During an air battle with Bf 109s and Fiats at around 3:00 in the afternoon while protecting RZs in the Barrios de San Blas area, his aircraft was shot down. While both Abrosov and Kaminskii say he flew an I-15, only one Aircraft is listed in the *Diario de Caza* as being lost in combat that day. This was CM 118 of the 5th Esc., so most likely LOSKUTOV had been switched to the Moscas. Awarded the Order of the Red Banner twice, on 27 August 1937 and 2 March 1938. (Pritsker, Lukes, Abrosov, Kaminskii, *Pravda*, Salas "*Diario*," *Los Rusos* claims died on 10 December 1937 as does the 1991 Soviet list of dead.)

LOZYCHENKO, Aleksandr Gavriloevich, Maj., born 14 September 1910

From March to May 1937 he was a Zvena CO in the 40th IAE 83rd IAB Byelorussian Mil. Dist. An I-16 pilot, he had left for Spain on 15 May 1937 and returned to the USSR on 28 January 1938. He was a patrulla CO and later said to have been an Escuadrilla CO. Claimed two personal victories plus six in group. Awarded the Red Banner 28 October 1937 and the Order of Lenin on 2 March 1938. In February 1938 he became assistant CO for Flight Training in the 33rd IAP Byelorussian M.D. From February to October 1939 he attended VVS Tactical Flight School, after which he became the Flight Inspector for the 29th IAP 2nd Red Banner Air Army until October 1940. In October 1940 he transferred to the Far East where he became an Eskadril'ya CO in the 68th IAP. At the beginning of October 1941 he was made assistant CO of the 73rd ShAD, then in mid October 1941 became CO of the 610th IAP until July 1944. Later in 1945 he was the assistant CO of the 255th ShAD. He retired from the VVS 16 December 1955, and passed away 20 April 1985. (Berch, Pritsker, Abrosov, Kaminskii, *Pravda*)

LUCHIKHIN, V.I.

Aviational Engineer. (*MY*, Berch)

LUKOVNIKOV, Sergei Aleksandrovich, Lt., born 1912

Was a pilot in the 4th IAE 56th IAB Kiev Mil. Dist. In Spain he was an I-16 Pilot from 10 May to 26 October 1938, in the 2nd Moscas under RODIN/NEDELIN/SEMENKO. Fought his first air combat on 14 August in the Gandesa Region. In this battle he went nose-to-nose with a Fiat (flown by Jose Mesia Lesseps) and when the Fiat dove under his aircraft, his propeller cut the tail off the Fiat. The ensuing impact caused the I-16 to flip over and LUKOVNIKOV had all he could do to right the aircraft and bring it back to level flight. He was finally able to successfully land at the airfield. In Spain he had flown forty-four combat missions and fought in twenty-seven air battles and claimed two Fiats (one in a Taran or Ramming). Awarded the Red Banner 22 February 1939. Participated in WWII in the 909th IAP, and died in a crash on 6 January 1944. (Kaminskii, Semenov *Tov*., Abrosov, *Los Rusos, Pravda*)

LUK'YANOV, Sergei, born 1907

SB Bomber navigator, in Spain from 30 November 1937 to 30 June 1938. Awarded the Red Banner. (*Los Rusos*)

LUK'YANOV, Vasilii N., born 1916

Fitter from Aircraft Factory #1 assembling/repairing I-15 and SSS aircraft. In Spain October 1936 to 27 July 1937. Awarded the Red Star 2 January 1937. (*Los Rusos, Pravda*)

LYALIN, Sergei V., Capt., born 1895

In Spain from October 1936 until 3 June 1937. Said to have been the personal pilot to "Douglas." He flew a DC-2, says Carlos Ibañez in Icare 130. Goes on to say he was approximately 38-40 years old and that he transported Soviet flyers from one field to another. Awarded the Red Banner 2 January 1937. (*Icare 130, Los Rusos, Pravda*)

LYSENKO, Stepan T., born 1916

Codename "Zaleski," he was an I-15 technician in Spain from 14 January to 23 December 1937. Awarded the Red Star on 21 June 1937. (*Los Rusos, Pravda*)

MACHAIDZE, Vladimir T., born 1909

Observer/gunner on SSS from October 1936 to 7 April 1937. On 19 December 1936, during a nighttime training flight, his aircraft developed a problem and the pilot ZIMOVETS had to make a forced landing. Neither of them were injured in the landing. Awarded the Red Banner 2 January 1937. (Abrosov, *Los Rusos, Pravda*)

MACHIKHIN, Ivan Petpovich, born 1911

SB Radio/Gunner in Spain from 30 December 1937 to 18 May 1938. Awarded the Red Banner on 14 November 1938. (Semenov "*Parol*," *Los Rusos, Pravda*)

MAEV, Sergei I., born 1913

Mechanic, Served from October 1936 to 27 March 1937. Awarded the Red Star 2 January 1937. (*Pravda, Los Rusos*)

MAKARIN, Mikhail, Lt., born 1907

Pilot in Spain from 26 March to 10 June 1938. (Very possibly this is the same person as MAKAROV, M.V. SB pilot listed below) (*Los Rusos*)

MAKAROV, M. "Misha"

SB group Interpreter. (*Vmeste* 17)

MAKAROV, M.V.

SB Pilot, arrived April 1938. Awarded the Red Banner 11 November 1937. (Semenov "*Parol*," *Pravda*)

MAKARYCHEV, Vasilii Alekseevich Lt., born 1911

He was a pilot in the 12th IAE 111th IAB Leningrad Mil. Dist. An I-16 Pilot, he arrived in Spain on 31 May and was KIA on 25 July 1937, during the Brunete operations when his plane was shot down. (Kaminskii believes Peter Boddem shot him down.) He had been a member of PLESCHENKO's 2nd Esc. Awarded the Red Banner on 11 November 1937. (Berch, Pritsker, Shingarev, *Los Rusos* spell it MAKARECHEV, Kaminskii, *Pravda*)

MAKSIMENKOV, Simon Lavrovich, Sgt., born 1915

He had been a pilot in the 2nd IAE 56th IAB Kiev Mil. Dist. In Spain he was an I-16 Pilot in the 5th Moscas under GRITSEVITS. Arrived 10 June and returned home on 4 October 1938. On 9 August he crashed on landing at Valls, the plane had to be repaired. His plane CM 236 was shot down on 23 August; while pursuing a Fiat, his aircraft was hit by Republican AAA. He was able to bail out, but was injured. After release from the hospital he was sent back to the USSR. Awarded the Red Banner 22 February 1939, he had flown fifteen missions and fought in five air battles (twenty-five missions and seven air battles). During WWII he was CO of the 10th

IAP and was KIA on 5 June 1942 (some sources say 1944). (Semenov *Tov.*, airforce.ru/staff/who_is_who/index.htm, Abrosov, Kaminskii, *Pravda, Los Rusos* spell it MAKIMENKOV)

MAKSIMOV, Fedor Egorovich, Lt., born 1911
Served in the 11th IAE 111th IAB Leningrad Mil. Dist. An I-16 Pilot, went to Spain on 31 May 1937 and returned on 28 January 1938. Wounded on 16 July 1937, during an enemy bombing of his airfield. Flew 130 missions and shot down several enemy Aircraft in group. Awarded the Red Banner twice, on 3 November 1937 and 2 March 1938. Commanded the 2nd IAE 19th IAP of the 5th IAB during the Winter War against Finland. Awarded the Red Star on 4 July 1940. (Berch, Pritsker, Abrosov, Kaminskii, *Pravda, Los Rusos* spell it MAKIMOV)

MAKSIMOV, I.F.
Awarded the Order of Lenin on 22 October 1937. (Semenov "*Parol*," *Pravda*)

MALASHKEVICH, Timofei Vasil'evich, Maj., born 1908 (or 1903)
He had fought in the Russian Civil War in 1920-21, where he was a Platoon CO on the Western front. After the war he began service in the VVS and before going to Spain, he was a member of the first Surgical Dept. Staff for an Air Brigade in the Byelorussian Military District. In Spain he was an Aviation advisor to the SB crews and served from 14 December 1937 to 15 September 1938. Awarded the Red Banner. During WWII, he was chief-of-staff PVO (Air Defense) on the Eastern, Southern and later South Western fronts. In 1944 he was promoted to Major General. Passed away in 1959. (Semenov "*Parol*," *Los Rusos*, Voronkova p.84)

MALIKOV, Filipp M., born 1891
Head of the crew sent from Aircraft Factory #1 to assemble/repair I-15 and SSS aircraft. In Spain from 20 October 1936 to 7 April 1937. Awarded the Red Star 2 January 1937. (*Los Rusos, Pravda*)

MALIKOV, Nikifor E., born 1907
Mechanic, in Spain from October 1936 to 9 July 1937. Awarded the Red Star 2 January 1937. (*Pravda, Los Rusos*)

MARANCHOV, Boris
Salas in *Aeroplano* #8 says this was a pseudonym used by Boris TURCHANSKII, while in same issue, Abellan lists him as Commander of I-15s in the North in November 1936. See TURCHANSKII listing. (Salas, Laureau, Abellan)

MARICHEV, Petr P., born 1911
Technician on I-16 aircraft. Served from 14 January until 18 October 1937. Awarded the Red Star on 21 June 1937. (*Los Rusos, Pravda*)

MARKIANOV, Sergei Andreevich, Sr.Lt., born 1910
Pilot SB, arrived 30 May and returned on 15 November 1938. Awarded the Red Banner on 22 February 1939. (Berch, Semenov "*Parol*," *Los Rusos, Pravda*)

MARKIN, Aleksandr Andreevich, Sr.Lt., born 1908
Pilot SB in Spain from 30 December 1937 to 27 July 1938. His aircraft was part of the twenty SBs drawn from two Spanish and two Soviet Escuadrillas which attacked Salamanca on 28 January 1938. This raid experienced many problems; due to the distance, the bombers could not be escorted by I-16s. They were then required to fly at extremely high altitudes requiring the use of oxygen, which for some of the crews, ran out on the return leg. MARKIN's aircraft was hit by AAA in an area north of the River Ebro. He and fellow crewmembers SHUMILOV and SMERTIN were taken prisoner. Semenov says ordnance used on this raid were 500 kilo (1,100lb.) bombs. The Spanish Nationalists really whined about this attack. See listing for date in *Partes vol.1*. See also listing for MARTINOFF below. Later released in an exchange of pilots and arrived home on 27 July 1938. (Semenov "*Parol*," Berch)

MARKOSEENKO, Fedor Georgievich, born 1904
Engineer on Bombers, served in Spain from 10 October 1937 to 24 May 1938. Awarded the Red Star 22 February 1939. (*Pravda, Los Rusos* lists this person twice, once as MARKESEENKO)

MARTINOFF, Alexander Andrevitch
Captured pilot of SB, twenty-eight years old. This was actually MARKIN, A.A. (*Spain, mag.* 8/15/1938)

MARTINOV, Aleksandr I., born 1908
Aviation technician in Spain from October 1936 to 27 July 1937. Awarded the Red Star 2 January 1937. (*Los Rusos, Pravda*)

MARTYSHCHENKO, Nikita Ivanovich, Lt., born 1915
Before going to Spain he was a Zvena CO in the 57th IAE 142nd IAB Belorussian Mil. Dist. Commander of an I-16 patrulla in the 2nd Esc. de Moscas under RODIN in Spain. Arrived on 26 March and was KIA on 23 May 1938 in air combat with Fiat CR 32s in the Balaguer area. Awarded the Red Banner on 22 February 1939. (Semenov "*Parol*," Abrosov, *Los Rusos*, Kaminskii, *Pravda*)

MASHENETS, Mikhail I., born 1911
Parachute Instructor served from October 1936 to 27 March 1937. Awarded the Red Star 2 January 1937. (*Los Rusos, Pravda*)

MASLENNIKOV, Dmitri F., Capt., born 1900
Chief of Staff of the 62nd TBAE (Heavy Bomber Aviation Esc.) Kharkov Mil. Dist. Served from 30 December 1937 until 25 April 1938 as an Advisor. According to Abrosov, he was listed as irresponsible and illiterate, and sent home early because he was unable to do anything. But *Los Rusos* list as a SB Navigator. Said to have been awarded the Red Banner.

MASTEROV, Georgii Alekseevich, Capt., born 1908
Pilot in the 40th IAE 83rd IAB Byelorussian Mil. Dist. In Spain from 10 May 1937 until 28 January 1938, flew an I-15, in EREMENKO/SEROV's 1st Chato Esc. He downed two enemy aircraft including a CR 32 on 24 August 1937 in the region of Bujaraloz. Participated in the attack on Garrapinillos Airfield on 15 October 1937 Awarded the Order of Lenin on 2 March 1938, and Order of the Red Banner 3 November 1937. In WWII was CO of an Eskadril'ya in the 33rd IAP. (*Solidarity, Bajo la B.*, Shingarev, Abellan, Abrosov, Kaminskii, *Los Rusos, Pravda*)

MASTIUKOV, Sergei A.
Worker from Aircraft Factory #22 assembling/repairing SB aircraft. In Spain October 1936 to 8 March 1937. Awarded the Red Star 2 January 1937. (*Pravda, Los Rusos*)

MATSKO, Ivan C., born 1912
Technician on I-15 aircraft, served from 14 January to 28 December 1937. Awarded the Red Banner 21 June 1937. (*Los Rusos, Pravda*)

MATVEEV, Ivan Vasil'evich, NCO, born 1912
Radio/Gunner on SB from 14 December 1937 to 18 July 1938. Was a participant in the attack on the Cruiser Baleares 6 March 1938. Awarded the Red Banner on 14 November 1938. (Berch, Semenov "*Parol*," *Los Rusos, Pravda*)

MATVEEV, Mikhail Grigorovich, Sgt., born 1914
SB Pilot from 26 March to 3 September 1938. Awarded the Red Banner on 22 February 1939. (Berch, *Los Rusos, Pravda*)

MATVEEV, Stepan, born 1911
Duraluminum Specialist in Spain from 21 July to 10 November 1937. (*Los Rusos*)

MATVEEV, Vasilii Ivanovich, Sgt., born 1913
Sgt. Pilot in the 35th IAE 56th IAB Kiev Mil. Dist. In Spain he was an I-16 Fighter Pilot in the 5th Esc. Moscas from 20 July 1937 until 15 April 1938. On 26 November 1937, while landing at Caspe on the Aragón front, his aircraft Mosca CM 139 had a problem and overturned causing considerable damage, but MATVEEV walked away unhurt. Flew 120 missions and claimed one aircraft. In 1940 became CO of the 2nd IAE 69th IAP, and fought in WWII. Awarded the Red Banner twice, 2 March and 14 November 1938. (Gusev, Semenov "*Parol*," Abrosov, *Los Rusos*, Kaminskii, *Pravda*)

MATVIENKO, Andrei Grigor'evich, NCO, born 1913
Radio/gunner SB from 26 March to 13 August 1938. Was a crewmember in the aircraft flown by LIPASHOV. During a mission on 15 June he was able to fend off an attack on his aircraft by a lone Bf 109. Awarded the Red Banner 22 February 1939. (Berch, *Vmeste*, Abrosov, *Los Rusos, Pravda*)

MATYUNIN, Viktor Artem'evivh, born 1911
Zvena CO in the 34th IAE 56th IAB Kiev Mil. Dist. I-15 Pilot in Spain, among first group of volunteers, he shipped out on 20 October 1936 and returned to the USSR on 27

March 1937. While in Spain he used the codename Pedro. Had six aircraft to his credit; two (He 51) personal, three in pair plus one in group (on 5 February 1937 he claimed an He 59 in pair with E. KONDRAT near Malaga). Later fought in the Khalkhin-Gol with the 70th IAP where he flew fifteen combats missions and fought in seven air battles and claimed one Japanese aircraft. In December 1939 he became CO of the 32nd IAP. At the beginning of WWII he was in command of the 513th IAP. On 23 November 1941, while returning from a recon mission, his aircraft crashed and he was killed. Awarded the Order of the Red Banner twice, on 2 January and 17 July 1937. (Kaminskii, Berch, Zakharov, *Vmeste*, Pritsker, Lukes, Abrosov, *Pravda, Icare 130* spells it MATIOUNINE.)

MATYUSHKO, Konstantin Makarovich, NCO, born 1913
Radio/Gunner on SB from 30 May to 15 November 1938. Awarded the Red Banner on 22 February 1939. (Berch, *Los Rusos, Pravda*)

MAURICHEV, Ivan Mikhailovich, Lt., born 1907
Navigator SB, from 26 March to 3 September 1938. Awarded the Red Banner 22 February 1939. (Semenov "*Parol*," Berch, *Los Rusos, Pravda*)

MAYSTRUK, Mikhail I, Lt., born 1906
Pilot of SSS, in Spain from October 1936 to 8 March 1937. He and his gunner GORBATENKO, on their return after a night bombing mission on 22 January 1937 on the Madrid front, got lost. Their aircraft ran out of fuel and they made a forced landing on rough terrain; they were both injured in the crash. Awarded the Red Banner 2 January 1937. (Abrosov, *Pravda* and *Los Rusos* spell it MAISTRUK)

MAYTSKII, Petr V. Lt., born 1912
SB Navigator served from 16 June 1937 to 28 January 1938. Awarded the Red Banner twice, 11 November 1937 and 2 March 1938. (*Los Rusos, Pravda*)

MEDVEDEV, Aleksandr N., born 1906
Specialist from Aircraft Factory #1 assembling/repairing I-15 and SSS aircraft. In Spain from October 1936 to 2 July 1937. Awarded the Red Star 2 January 1937. (*Los Rusos* spell it MADVEDEV, *Pravda*)

MEDVEDEV, Dmitrii Petrovich
Radio/Gunner on the SB, arrived 26 March and returned in August 1938. Awarded the Red Banner 22 February 1939. (Berch, Semenov "*Parol*," *Pravda*)

MEDVEDEV, Sergei Georgievich
Awarded the Badge of Honor on 14 November 1938. (Semenov "*Parol*," *Pravda*)

MELIKHAN, Semen Konstantinovich, Lt., born 1912
Navigator SB arrived on 26 March and returned on 3 September 1938. Awarded the Red Banner 22 February 1939. (Berch, *Los Rusos, Pravda* spells it MELIKHON)

MELTESHINOV, Filipp S., born 1914
Technician on I-15 aircraft, served from 14 January to 3 September 1937. Awarded the Red Star on 27 June 1937. (*Los Rusos, Pravda*)

MEZHOV, Ivan Andreevich, Sr.Lt., born 1908
SB pilot, arrived 28 June and returned 15 November 1938, but *Los Rusos* lists as SB patrulla Navigator. Awarded the Red Banner 22 February 1939. (Semenov "*Parol*," *Los Rusos, Pravda*)

MIGRIN, Ivan, NCO, born 1913
Radio/Gunner SB in Spain from 30 May until 15 November 1938. (*Los Rusos*)

MIKHAILEVSKII, Aleksei F., Lt., born 1907
SB Navigator in Spain 16 June 1937 until 2 March 1938. Awarded the Red Banner 11 November 1937. (*Los Rusos, Pravda*)

MIKHAILOV
Jefe of a Patrulla of I-16s on Basque front July 1937 Var. Sp. MIJAILOV. This is either DEMIDOV or KUZNETSOV. (Tarazona, Laureau)

MIKHAILOV, Aleksandr B., born 1908
Mechanic in TARKHOV's group, arrived October 1936 and returned 8 May 1937. Awarded the Red Star 2 January 1937. (*Vmeste, Los Rusos, Pravda*)

MIKHAILOV, Vasilii Ivanovich, born 1915
Pilot in the 57th IAE 142nd IAB Belorussian Mil. Dist. He flew both the I-15 and I-16 in Spain. Served from 26 March until 18 August 1938. On 26 June, while trying to take off at Villar during an enemy attack, his aircraft was wreaked by an exploding bomb and he was injured. He had flown seventy missions and fought in fifteen air battles, and had one aircraft to his credit. Awarded the Red Banner on 22 February 1939. Fought in WWII, possibly with the 40th GuIAP. Said to have died in 1943. (Semenov "*Parol*," Abrosov, *Pravda, Los Rusos*, airaces.narod.ru says On 25 June 1938, while attacking a bomber, his aircraft was hit by fire from one of the bombers gunners, and he had to bail out. But there is no corroboration in Abrosov.)

MIKHAILOVSKII, Stepan I., born 1909

Mechanic in TARKHOV's group arrived Oct 1936 and returned 8 May 1937. Awarded the Red Star 2 January and Red Banner 27 June 1937. (*Solidarity, Vmeste, Los Rusos, Pravda*)

MIKHANOV, Grigori V., born 1905

Aviation technician, in Spain from October 1936 to 26 July 1937. Awarded the Red Star 2 January 1937. (*Los Rusos, Pravda*)

MIKHANOV, S.

Navigator in an SSS bomber Escaudrilla, flew with Finick. Undoubtedly a codename. (Finick)

MIKULOVICH, Andrei Stepanovich, Lt., born 1908

Born in Orsha, a city 100km from Smolensk. Attended the Stalingrad School for Pilots. Pilot in the 142nd IAB Belorussian Mil. Dist. In Spain was an I-16 Pilot in GUSEV's 6th Esc. from 20 August and was KIA on 12 October 1937 during an air battle with Fiats near Fuentes del Ebro while flying CM-150. Undoubtedly either killed out-right or badly wounded in the combat, as he did not attempt to recover from the dive says Gusev, who also said he died on 6 December while *Los Rusos* says 22 October 1937 as does the 1991 Soviet list of dead. Awarded the Red Banner 2 March 1938. (Gusev, Abrosov, *Los Rusos*, Kaminskii, *Pravda*)

MINAEV, Aleksandr Efimovich, Sr.Lt., born 1910

He was a Flight Inspector in the 117th IAE Moscow Mil. Dist. In Spain he was commander of the 3rd I-16 Escuadrilla, arrived on 13 June 1937. This Esc. was formed in June 1937 and was based at Barajas. He was shot down and killed on 15 July 1937 over Villanueva de la Cañada. Boris SMIRNOV was a Patrulla leader in this Escuadrilla along with IVANOV. VEREVKA then took over command of the Escuadrilla, and after VEREVKA's death SMIRNOV became CO. Laureau claims he was "Pablo" while SMIRNOV just calls him "Camarada Alejandro." Some list as having four aircraft to his credit. Awarded the Order of Lenin on 11 November 1937. Some sources say it was Garcia Morato who shot him down. (Tarazona, Lario, Smirnov, Vmeste, Pritsker, *Los Rusos* say first name was Aleksei and that he was a bomber pilot, Kaminskii, *Pravda*)

MINAEV, Aleksii Vasil'evich, Sr.Lt., born 1911

He was a Zvena CO in the 107th IAE 83rd IAB Belorussian Mil. Dist. In Spain he was an I-16 pilot, member of the Escuadrilla led by TARKHOV/KOLESNIKOV. Awarded the Red Banner twice, 2 January and 4 July 1937. Served from November 1936 to 27 March 1937. Listed as having three kills (two in pair and one in patrulla). After Spain, from May to September 1937, he was in the 107th IAE at Bryansk. Later was CO. of a Zvena and then a Detachment in the 20th IAE. In July 1938 he was the CO of the 40th IAP. From April 1939 to January 1941 he was CO. of the 71st SAP. During WWII, he commanded first the 282 IAP, then the 252 IAD and last from February 1943 until the end of the war he was CO of the 257 IAD. Died 5 November 1998. (Gusev, Laureau, Kaminskii, airaces.narod.ru, Abrosov, *Pravda*)

MINAEV, Vasilii K.B, 1911

Bomber Group Technician, in Spain October 1936 to 27 May 1937. Awarded the Red Star 2 January 1937. (*Los Rusos, Pravda*)

MIREK, Aleksandr

According to Shingarev, he was the radio/gunner on the SB flown by SENATOROV, which led UKHOV's Esc. North, but see GUMENNYI. (Shingarev)

MIROSHNICHENKO, Nikolai Ivanovich, Lt., born 1909
He was a Zvena CO in the 34 IAE 56th IAB Kiev Mil. Dist. I-15 pilot, departed for Spain on 20 October 1936. He was a Patrulla leader in RYCHAGOV's Escuadrilla. Rotated home on 7 April 1937. He had four enemy aircraft to his credit plus another three in pair. Lacalle says he was a Patrulla leader along with ZAKHAROV and SMEL'KOV. ZAKHAROV says he was shot down once and bailed out, but perhaps he is thinking of 5 November 1936 when during a battle with Fiats his landing gear was shot up and he crashed on landing. Awards were two Orders of the Red Banner on 2 January and 17 July 1937. Later commanded the 20th IAE, and then from March 1940 the 21st IAP Baltic Mil. Dist. Died May 1981. (Lacalle, *Icare 130*, Berch, Zakharov, *Vmeste*, Pritsker, Lukes, Kaminskii, Abrosov, *Pravda*)

MIROV
Air Force Commissar ? Questionable (Lacalle)

MISHCHENKO, Iosif Pavlovich, Sr.Lt., born 1910
Before Spain, was a pilot in the 34th IAE 56th IAB KVO (Kiev Mil. Dist.). Arrived in Spain on 13 June 1937 and returned 28 January 1938. He was an I-16 Pilot and had flown 160 missions and had two enemy aircraft to his credit. Awarded the Red Banner twice, 28 October 1937 and 2 March 1938 as a Captain. In 1939 he became a Major. During WWII, he was CO of the 170th IAP on the Western front, then later he was on the staff of the 74th ShAP on the same front. Passed away in 1957. (Abrosov, *Pravda*, airaces.narod.ru, Kaminskii)

MITROFANOV, Petr Aleksandrovich, Lt., born 1910
Pilot in the 109th IAE 36th IAB Kiev Mil. Dist. In Spain he flew an I-15 in RYCHAGOV's Esc, from 20 October and was KIA on 5 November 1936 in an air combat with Fiat CR 32s. He was the first Soviet fighter pilot killed in Spain. He is said to have bailed out over enemy territory. Posthumously awarded the Order of the Red Banner on 2 January 1937. (*Icare 130, MY*, Berch, Zakharov 24, *Vmeste*, Lukes, *Pravda*, Kaminskii)

MOISENKO, Ivan Feoktistovich, NCO, born 1912
Radio/gunner SB, arrived in Spain on 26 March and returned 5 August 1938. Awarded the Red Banner on 22 February 1939. (Semenov "*Parol*," Berch, *Pravda, Los Rusos* spell it MOISIAKO)

MOLODSHCHOV, Boris P., born 1913
Aviation Engineer with SB Bomb Group. In Spain October 1937 to 7 April 1938. Awarded the Red Star 2 January 1937. (*Pravda, Los Rusos* spell it MOLODSOV)

MOLOKANOV, Kriugin
"Miguel" Sq. CO RZs July 1937 says Logoluso, but the RZs were under Spanish control, not Soviet. Berch wondered if this was KRIGIN. Also the name MELOKANOV is listed in *Aeroplano* #18 pgs.4-10, Campañas de Marruecos y Pilots extranjeros, by J.L. de Meza (Logoluso, Berch)

MORGUNOV, Nikolai Nikiforovich
Navigator SB in Spain from 26 March until 5 August 1938. Awarded the Red Banner 22 February 1939. (Berch, Semenov "*Parol*," *Pravda*)

MOROZOV, Andrei Mikhailovich, Lt., born 1905
Was a Zvena CO in the 107th IAE 83rd IAB Belorussian Mil. Dist. In Spain he was an I-16 pilot in the Detachment led by KOLESNIKOV, and later on 15 November put in command of the same Detachment when KOLESNIKOV was ordered to take over the TARKHOV Esc. Arrived at end of October 1936, and returned home on 26 July 1937. Listed as having six aircraft to his credit (including five in patrulla). Awarded the Red Banner twice, 2 January and 17 July

1937. From April 1938 until May 1939 he was CO of the 5th IAP after which he became CO of the 61st IAB Baltic Fleet until August 1941. He had fought in the Winter War and was awarded the Order of Lenin on 21 April 1940. In WWII was CO of the 18th ShAP Black Sea Fleet in defense of Sevastopol. He died in the crash of a U-2 on 28 July 1942. (Pritsker, Rumyantsev "*Antonio*," Kaminskii, airaces,narod.ru, *Pravda*)

MOROZOV, Ivan Vasil'evich, Sr.Lt., born 1907
Pilot SB, in Spain from 30 December 1937 to 18 July 1938. Awarded the Red Banner 14 November 1938 and Red Star on 22 February 1939. Participated in the 7 February 1938 raid on Calamocha where his aircraft was shot up by attacking Bf 109s. During this battle, two Spanish and two Soviet crewed SBs were shot down (Laureau lists three Spanish flown SBs as downed), but MOROZOV was able to safely reach La Cenia airfield. He also formed part of the force that attacked the Nationalist Cruiser Baleares on 6 March 1938. LIPASHOV in *Vmeste* lists as Vasili and that his aircraft was shot down by a Bf 109, but no mention as to fate of the crew. (*Vmeste*, Semenov "*Parol*," Berch, Laureau Fr. Ed., *Los Rusos, Pravda*)

MOSEIKO, Anton Mikhailovich, Sr.Lt. Born 1910
Joined Red Army in 1929. Was a Detachment CO in the 108th IAE TOF (Pacific Fleet). In Spain he was an I-16 pilot, from 13 January to 14 June 1937. Listed as having downed one Fiat on 12 June 1937. He was KIA on 14 June 1937 along with one of his wingmen P. BUROV in air combat with Fiat CR 32s. Posthumously awarded the Red Banner 17 July 1937. Abrosov says he was possibly an Escuadrilla CO. *Los Rusos* list final date as 13 October 1937. (airaces,narod.ru, Abrosov, *Los Rusos*, Kaminskii)

MURAV'EV, Vasilii Andreevich, Lt., born 1903
SB Pilot, arrived 26 March and returned 5 August 1938. He was wounded when his aircraft was shot down by Bf 109s on 10 June 1938. Crewmembers were BELITSKII, Navigator, and PARAKHIN Radio/Gunner, who were also wounded, but all were able to bail out. Awarded the Red Banner on 22 February 1939. (Semenov "*Parol*," *Los Rusos, Pravda*, Abrosov)

MURZA, Ivan S., born 1909
Aviation Technician with the SB Bomb Group. Served from October 1936 to 27 March 1937. Awarded the Red Star 2 January 1937. (*Los Rusos, Pravda*)

NABORSHIKOV, Nikolai K., Lt., born 1913
SB Navigator, in Spain from May until 7 September 1937. Awarded the Red Banner 27 June 1937. (*Pravda, Los Rusos* spell it NAVORSHIKOV)

NADTOCHII, Ivan Ivanovich, Lt., born 1912
Navigator on SB, arrived 30 May and returned 15 November 1938. Awarded the Red Banner 22 February 1939. (Berch, Semenov "*Parol*," *Los Rusos, Pravda*)

NAGORNYI, Nikolai Nikiforovich, Maj., born 1901
Advisor to the Republic for Air Defense. In Spain from 25 December 1936 to 17 August 1937. Awarded the Order of Lenin on 17 July and the Red Banner 3 November 1937. He served during the Great patriotic War on the staffs of several PVO units. Retired as a General-Colonel. Passed away in 1985. (*Solidarity, KTO, Los Rusos, Pravda*)

NAKONECHNIKOV, Aleksandr Georgievich, Lt., born 16 Sept 1915
Joined the Army in 1933, and in 1935 graduated from Engel'ssuiu Mil. Pilots Aviation School. In 1936, he served with a BAB in the Kiev Mil. Dist. Volunteered for Spain, leaving the USSR on 30 May and returned 15 November 1938. He was a SB Pilot; on 31 August on a mission over the Ebro, his aircraft lost power on one of its engines and began to fall behind the formation and was attacked by Fiats. The Detachment commander KALACHIKOV noticed what was happening and slowed the formation down so that NAKONECHNIKOV could keep up, saving them from the Fiats. According to Semenov, on 21 September 1938 he crash-landed his damaged SB at the Valls fighter field.[1] Awarded the Red Banner on 22 February 1939. During WWII from June to August 1941 he was the CO of an Eskadril'ya in the 226th SBAP on the South Western front flying SU-2s, and then in 1942 was commander of the 78th Guards ShAP of the 2nd Guards ShAD. From September 1944 to May 1945, he was CO of the 11th GShAD of the 16th Air Army on the 1st Byelorussian Front. Participated in eighty-one air sorties. After the war was CO of the 76th ShAP Byelorussian Mil. Dist. Died 10 November 1946. Awards were H.S.U. 1 July 1944, Order of Lenin, three Orders of the Red Banner, Order of Suvorov 3rd Cl., Alek. Nevskii, GPW 1st Cl. (Berch, Semenov *Tov., Pravda, Geroi*, Abrosov, [1]Salas *Diario* indicates this could be BK-19 which landed that day at Reus.)

NALIETOV, Valentin, born 1916
Engineer from the Production Group (Aviation?), served from 2 April to 21 May 1938. (*Los Rusos*)

NARANCHOV

Howson says he was an I-15 pilot in Vizcaya. I think this is a typo of MARANCHOV (Howson 195)

NAYDENKO, Vasilii Mikhailovich, born 7 December 1915

Joined the Army in 1934, and attended the Odessa Military Flying School. Graduated in 1936. Said to have volunteered for Spanish duty and during his time there claimed three victories and six shared during twenty-seven aerial combats. In the summer of 1939, he fought against the Japanese at the Khalkhin-gol claiming five kills plus nineteen group credits. In the Winter War against Finland, he was a squadron commander in the 25th IAP. Here he claimed another four victories. In early 1941, he was assigned as a squadron commander in the 126 IAP, and it was with this unit that he began the GPW in June 1941. This unit was attached to the Moscow-PVO, and at first flew the MiG-3 and later the P-40 Tomahawk. The Regiment was later sent to the Stalingrad front with NAYDENKO as its commander. On 5 September 1942, after downing two Me 109s, his aircraft was shot down. NAYDENKO, badly wounded in both legs, had to bail out. He reportedly was strafed by two Fw 190s as he hung in his chute, but was not hit. Due to the wounds, one of his legs had to be amputated. Upon his recovery he led the 126th IAP to the end of the war. During the GPW, he claimed ten victories plus twenty-nine group credits, which brought his total to twenty-two victories and fifty-four group and shares. He retired from the military in 1953 with the rank of Polkovnik (Colonel). He died on 13 January 1969. Awards were: H.S.U. 21 April 1943, OL, ORB three times, ORS. Sources Seidl, Polak, Geroi Sov. Soiuza. *Note*: Polak and Seidl differ on his GPW score, I have used Seidl. Polak claims seventeen with thirteen of these as shares. Note: Neither Abrosov nor Kaminskii list as a fighter pilot in Spain.)

NAZZRENKO, Stepan V., born 1909

Technician, served from October 1936 to 7 April 1937. Awarded the Red Star 2 January 1937. (*Pravda, Los Rusos*)

NECHIPORENKO, Ivan Galaktionovich, Lt., born 1907

Navigator SB, served from October until 13 November 1936 when he was KIA. BIBIKOV pgs.17-18 says he was lost in action over Cordoba. According to Abrosov, he was the navigator on ROMANOV's SB when it was shot down by fighters on 13 November 1936 during an attack on Carabanchel Alto and Getafe. Awarded the Red Banner 2 Jan. 1937. (Vmeste, Abrosov, *Los Rusos*, *Pravda*, a list by M. Zhirohov lists date of birth as 1909)

NECHIPORENKO, Pantelei Trofimovich, Sr.Lt., born 1908

Navigator SB, departed for Spain on 30 May and returned to the USSR 15 November 1938. On 23 September, six SBs escorted by I-16s from the 2nd Esc. were attacked by Bf 109s. The SBs had problems with the ShKAS MGs on four of their aircraft. Several of the SBs were badly shot up and had to land at fighter bases. NECHIPORENKO was in one flown by SHARONOV (possibly BK-25) which landed at Reus. Awarded the Red Banner 22 February 1939. (Berch, Semenov "*Parol*," *Los Rusos*, Salas *Diario*, *Pravda*)

NEDELIN, Petr Ivanovich, Sr.Lt., born 1910

Before going to Spain, he was a Zvena CO at the 8th Odessa Pilots School in The Kiev Mil. Dist. Served in Spain from 10 June until 4 October 1938 and used the codename "Pedro." He first flew in the I-16 Escuadrilla under RODIN. When GRITSEVETS formed his Escuadrilla, he appointed him as second-in-command. Then in late July he became Commander of the 2nd Moscas which along with the 5th were under the control of GRITSEVETS. After an air battle on 26 August[1] he crashlanded[2] and as a result suffered injuries so severe as to render him no longer of service to Spain. His Escuadrilla was at that time taken over by KOROBKOV. He had flown forty-eight combat missions and fought in twenty air battles, had three aircraft to his credit. Awarded the Order of Lenin on 22 February 1939. In September 1939 he was assistant commander of the 49th IAP and fought in the Winter War against Finland. Awarded the Red Star 26 January 1940. In March 1940 became the CO of the 49th IAP. In the summer of 1941 during WWII, he was seriously injured in a crashlanding. Later he was in the PVO. Abrosov claims he died 11 August 1992, but Kaminskii and Aces site say died 11 June 1994. [1]Semenov says 21st. (Semenov *Tov.*, *Vmeste*, Kaminskii, *Pravda*, [2]according to Abrosov, In the evening of the 26th three aircraft from the 2nd Esc. were to take off on a patrol. On take-off an undercarriage cable snapped on NEDELIN's Mosca and he had to make a belly landing. The landing was so bad that his face struck the gun sight and he suffered severe trauma and never flew again in Spain. This was the second time he had had to make a forced landing; back on 27 July he had come

down due to engine failure about 10km. from his base. The aircraft was damaged and required repair but he was only slightly injured.)

NEFEDOV, D.I., born 1912
Escuadrilla Aviation Technician (SSS?). Served October 1936 to 2 July 1937. Awarded the Red Star 2 January 1937. (*Los Rusos, Pravda*)

NEGOREEV, Aleksandr Yakovlevich, Lt., born October 1911
Was a pilot in the 107th IAE 83rd IAB Byelorussian Mil. Dist. In Spain he was an I-16 pilot in TARKHOV'S Esc., and served from November 1936 to 23 January 1937. After the death of BOCHAROV on 14 November, NEGOREEV took over leadership of his Detachment. Listed as having one aircraft to his credit, an He 51, shot down on 9 December 1936. Awarded the Red Banner 2 January 1937. He returned to the USSR early due to health problems and died of tuberculosis on 5 April 1937. On 22 April 1937 he was posthumously awarded the rank of captain. (Rumyantsev "*Antonio*," Kaminskii, *Pravda*)

NESMENOV, Fedor Mikhailovich, Capt., born 1901
Was an Air Force Staff officer attached to the Estado Mayor Fuerza Aerea, served from 12 January 1938 and returned home on 7 February 1939. Awarded the Red Banner on 22 February 1939. (Abrosov, *Los Rusos, Pravda*, Semenov "*Parol*" spells it NESMELOV)

NESMEYANOV, Grigorii D., Capt., born 1914
In Spain from October 1936 until 8 May 1937. Commander of 3rd Escuadrilla de Kats of Grupo 12, in October 1936, but Abrosov says this Escuadrilla was dissolved early and all the crews were put into the first and second Escuadrillas. NESMEYANOV was sent to the 1st Esc., but after two combat flights he became the units supply officer. Awarded the Order of Lenin 2 January 1937. (Abrosov, *Los Rusos, Pravda*, but Laureau, Salas, Howson 277, *Bajo la B.*, Berch lists as Pavel Alekseevich)

NEVINNYI, Petr Danilovich, born 1906
Aviation Engineer on I-16s, attached to TARKHOV's Esc. Served from October 1936 to 27 August 1937. Awarded the Red Banner 4 July and the Red Star 2 January 1937. *Los Rusos* says name spelt NEVINEI and that he was the Aeronautical Engineer at Alcala. (*Vmeste* claims initial was A., Rumyatsev "*Antonio*," *Los Rusos, Pravda*)

NEZAMETDINOV, Sarvardin S., born 1906
Aviation technician in Spain from October 1936 to 27 May 1937. Awarded the Red Star 2 January 1937. (*Pravda, Los Rusos* spells it minus the D)

"NICHOLAI"
I believe this was N. MIROSHNICHENKO, who flew in the I-15 squadron with Baumler. (Baumler)

NIGAMATULIN, Said Sh., Lt., born 1907
SB Navigator in Spain from 16 June 1937 until 28 January 1938. Awarded the Red Banner 2 March 1938. (*Los Rusos, Pravda*)

NIKIFOROV, Arsenii Pavlovich "Noguin," NCO, born 5 May 1913
Pilot SB in Spain from 30 December 1937 to 21 July 1938. Participated in attack on the Nationalist Crusier Baleares 6 March 1938. Awarded the Red Banner on 14 November 1938. (Berch, Semenov "*Parol*," *Los Rusos, Pravda*)

NIKIFOROV, Grigorii Nikoforovich, Lt., born 1907
Pilot of an SSS Rasante arrived in November 1936. KIA according to CHERVYAKOV in *Vmeste* p.183. He was the pilot of SSS in which SHUKAEV was shot down on 4 December 1936. SHUKAEV says that they both survived the crash and that NIKIFOROV was shot and killed trying to escape capture. Awarded the Red Banner 2 January 1937. (*Vmeste, Los Rusos, Pravda*)

NIKIFOROV, Vasilii V., Lt., born 1905
Bomber (SSS?) pilot in Spain from October 1936 to 2 July 1937. Awarded the Red Banner 2 January 1937. (*Los Rusos, Pravda*)

NIKISHEV, Petr Fedorovich, Lt., born 1913
SB Pilot, arrived 26 March and returned on 3 September 1938. Awarded the Red Banner 22 February 1939. (Berch, Semenov "*Parol*," *Los Rusos, Pravda*)

NIKITIN, Nikolai Mikhailovich, Sgt., born 31 January 1912

Pilot in the 3rd IAE VVS KBF Red Banner Baltic Fleet. In Spain he was an I-16 pilot in DEVOTCHENKO's 2nd Esc. Served from 14 December 1937 to 10 June 1938. Flew 100 combat missions and fought in twenty-six air battles, one aircraft to his credit (Bf 109). Awarded the Red Banner 14 November 1938 and the Red Star on 22 February 1939. During the Russo-Finnish War he was commander of the 13th IAP VVS Red Banner Baltic Fleet. Awarded the Red Banner 21 April 1940. On 21 September 1941 during WWII, he was shot down in combat but able to bail out. On 29 June 1942 became CO of the 3rd GvIAP Baltic Fleet. Later from January to April 1944 he was CO of the 1st GvIAD Baltic Fleet, and then in May went back as CO of the 3rd GvIAP. Flew 500 missions and shot down five aircraft plus two in group. Stayed in the Naval VVS until he retired on 18 March 1962. Died 16 May 1992. (Semenov "*Parol*," Pritsker, Abrosov, *Los Rusos*, Kaminskii, *Pravda*)

NIKITIN, Nikolai Pavlovich

Pilot in the 107th IAE 83 IAB Byelorussian Mil. Dist. I-16 fighter pilot in Spain from November 1936 to 26 July 1937. One aircraft to credit on 18 February 1937. Awarded the Red Banner twice, 2 January and 4 July 1937. In the summer of 1941 he did not return from a mission on the South Western Front near Kiev. His remains were discovered in 2008. (Abrosov, *Los Rusos*, *Pravda*, Kaminskii)

NIKOLAENKO, Vasilii Fedorovich, Lt., born 1915

A pilot in the 41st (40th)[1] IAE 83rd IAB. An I-16 pilot, he went to Spain on 16 May and returned on 29 September 1937. He was a member of the 1st Moscas until he went to Santander on 2 July with UKHOV's Esc. Was wounded in air combat on August 1937 and returned home after release from the hospital. Awarded the Red Banner 28 October 1937. EVSEV'EV in Vmeste incorrectly says first name was Vladimir. After Spain he was commander of the 3rd IAE 16th IAP. In 1940 he was CO of an IAE in the 12th ZAP, then Flight inspector 9th SAP. From April 1941 to January 1942 he was CO of the 184th IAP after which he became CO of the 174th IAP until the end of the war. During WWII he had flown 317 missions and downed seven enemy aircraft. Remained in the VVS until retiring in 1956. Died in 1974. [1]Kaminskii lists as the 41st and Abrosov lists as 40th. (Kaminskii, Abrosov, Pritsker, *Vmeste, Los Rusos*, *Pravda*)

NITSAI, Vasilii Nikitovich, Sr.Lt., born 1908

Navigator SB, arrived 30 May and returned 4 October 1938. On 9 August the aircraft flown by YAKIMENKO crashlanded after being damaged by AAA near Balaguer. The pilot and gunner SHEVCHENKO were wounded, but in the landing NITSAI fractured both legs. This had been their 20th mission. Awarded the Red Banner on 22 February 1939. (Berch, Semenov "*Parol*," *Los Rusos, Pravda*, Abrosov)

NORETS, Fedor Efimovich

Head Engineer from Aircraft Factory #21 assembling I-16 aircraft. In Spain from October 1936 to 8 May 1937. Awarded the Red Star 2 January 1937. (*Pravda, Los Rusos*, but KRAVCHENKO in *Vmeste*, Rumyantsev "*Antonio*" say Engineer with the Tarkhov/Kolesnikov Escuadrilla.)

NOVAK, Vasilii V., born 1912

Chief engineer for fighter group from May to 29 September 1937. Awarded the Red Star 21 June 1937. Supposedly he and SOBOLEVSKII were given task of getting everything ready when the Night Fighter Detachment idea was conceived. (RSA, Lario 154, Shingarev, Logoluso, *Pravda, Los Rusos* list as Aviation Engineer for Aviacion de Asalto)

NOVIKOV, Aleksei M.

Aviation Technician served from October 1936 to 27 March 1937. Awarded the Red Star 2 January 1937. (*Los Rusos, Pravda*)

NOVIKOV, Anton V., born 1902

Engineer for Bomber (SSS) group. In Spain October1936 until June 1937. Awarded the Red Star 2 January 1937 and later a Red Banner on 17 July 1937. (*Los Rusos, Pravda*)

NOVIKOV, Ivan Vasil'evich, Lt.

SB Navigator in Spain from 28 June until 15 November 1938. Awarded the Red Banner on 22 February 1939. (*Los Rusos, Pravda*)

NOVIKOV, Petr Yakovlevich, NCO, born 1912

Los Rusos list in one area as radio/gunner in Spain 18 July to 13 October 1937, KIA over Fuentes del Ebro. Awarded the Red Banner on 2 March 1938. But in another area of same work, he is listed as armored personnel and KIA on 13 October 1937. (*Los Rusos, Pravda*)

OKOLELOV, Yakov Kharlampievich, born October 1906

Before Spain, he was a pilot in the 41st[1] IAE 83rd IAB Byelorussian Mil. Dist. An I-16 fighter pilot, he served in Spain from November 1936 to 27 March 1937. One Aircraft He 51 to credit, shot down on 6 December 1936. Awarded the Red Banner 2 January 1937. Later from May to December 1939, he was a Zvena CO and then a Eskadril'ya CO in the 47th IAP[2] and fought in the battle for Lake Khasan. Awarded 2nd Red Banner on 25 October 1938. In September 1940 was made CO of the 158th IAP and during WWII, commanded the 145th IAP, then the 518th IAP and at the end the war, the 91st IAP. Retired in 1946 and died on 31 March 1991. [1]Kaminskii lists as 41st but Abrosov lists as 40th. [2]Abrosov says 7th IAE (*Pravda, Los Rusos* gives start date as January, Kaminskii, Abrosov)

ONISHCHENKO, Mikhail Vasil'evich, born 1912

Originally a pilot in the 36th IAE 56th IAB Kiev Mil. Dist. An I-16 Pilot, he left for Spain 10 June and returned 26 October 1938. He flew in RODIN's 2nd Escuadrilla and later in GRITSEVETS Group. Awarded the Red Banner 22 February 1939. After his return, he wrote a report regarding the failure of the ShKAS machineguns on the I-16s. In WWII, he was deputy CO of the 28th IAP, and awarded the Red Banner 8 July 1941. Next was Commissar of the 436th IAP, then deputy CO of the 124th IAP. KIA 21 March 1943 during a combat mission on the Leningrad front. (Semenov *Tov.*, *Vmeste*, Abrosov, Kaminskii, *Pravda*)

OPROSHCHENKO, Fedor T., Lt., born 1907

Pilot in 1st Escuadrilla de Kats October 1936, says Laureau. But both *Bajo la B.* and *Los Rusos* say he joined the 1st Esc. on 3 January and returned home 8 May 1937. When his aircraft was shot up on 10 February 1937, they were forced to crashland near Motril and the crew destroyed the aircraft.[1] The navigator was SOKOLOV and gunner was ARAKCHEEV. Awarded the Red Banner on 27 June 1937. (G. y Rev 2, Laureau, *Bajo la B.*, Abrosov, *Los Rusos, Pravda.* [1]Apparently the aircraft was not destroyed and was recovered by the Nationalists and rebuilt. It had a white #1 on the tail fin.)

ORLOV, P.

I-16 Instructor in Spain. Very doubtful. (Salas)

ORZHANOV, Vasilii Matveevich, Sr.Lt., born 1910

I-16 fighter pilot, had been in the 40th IAE 83rd IAB Byelorussian Mil. Dist. Volunteered for Spain, arrived on 21 May and died in an accident 2 June 1937. While conducting a training flight, he was unable to pull out of a dive, most likely due to a wing problem. Awarded the Red Banner 11 November 1937. (Abrosov, *Los Rusos, Pravda*, Kaminskii)

OSADCHII, Aleksandr, born 1910

Aviation Technician, in Spain from October 1936 until 30 June 1937. Awarded the Red Star 2 January 1937. (*Los Rusos, Pravda*)

OSADCHII, Aleksandr Petrovich, Sr.Lt., born 29 May 1907

Ukrainian by birth. Joined the Army in 1929. Attended Flight School #2 in Borisoglebsk. From November 1934 to December 1936 was a Detachment CO in the 5th IAE 36th IAB, in December 1936 became CO of the 65th IAE Kiev Mil. Dist. Saw service in Spain from 10 January to 26 July 1937. Commander of an I-15 Escuadrilla (1st Chatos), then later in June was CO of Grupo 26 and the 3rd Esc. In Spain he used the nom de guerre Boris KAZAKOV. Flew Chato #38 and is said to have five enemy aircraft to his credit (one Do 17, two He 51s and two CR 32s). He was wounded during an air combat on 12 March 1937. Ajax Baumler was in his Esc. for a three month period and Frank Tinker for one month. Medals received for Spanish service were Order of Red Banner 27 June 1937 and Order of Lenin on 15 December 1938. From November 1937 to April 1938 he was CO of the 72nd IAE 56th IAB, then went to the 28th IAP which he commanded until March 1941. From March to May 1941 was CO of the 69th IAD. By December 1941 he was CO of the 64th IAD and from May to August 1942 commanded the 266th IAD. Then from August 1942 took over command of the 207th IAD, which in August 1943 became the 11th Guards IAD. He remained with this unit until the end of the war. Awarded title of H.S.U. on 27 June 1945. Other medals awarded for WWII service were Order of Lenin, Order of the Red Banner three times, Suvorov 2nd Class, Kutuzov 2nd Class plus others. *Geroi* says he died 3 March 1981, but Kaminskii says 2 May 1981 and that is also the date on his tombstone. (Morquillas, Berch, *Vmeste*, Zakharov, Lukes, *Geroi*, Abrosov, Kaminskii, *Pravda*)

OSIPENKO, Aleksandr Stepanovich, Sr.Lt., born 1 June 1910
Joined the Army in 1929. Attended Borisoglebsk Military Flying School, graduating in 1932. By the end of 1937 he was a Detachment CO in the 40th IAE 83rd IAB Byelorussian Mil. Dist. Came to Spain on 12 January 1938, as a Senior Lt. PTUKHIN decided to put him in the 1st Chatos under SIUSIUKALOV, where he was a Patrulla leader. Later he became Commander of the 1st Escuadrilla. Returned home on 28 June 1938. Laureau says he was before SIUSIUKALOV, but Semenov and Milany p.63 both say he took over Command of the Esc. from SIUSIUKALOV. Seidl says, "In eight months (?) combat he chalked up seventeen kills along with thirty-four (24?) more fractional credits to emerge as one of the outstanding pilots of the conflict." Whereas other sources list him as only having eight kills. He was awarded the H.S.U. on 22 February 1939 and the rank of Colonel, plus the Order of Red Banner on 14 November 1938. In 1940 he became deputy commander of the Moscow Air Defense (PVO), and by June 1941 had taken command of the 20th SAD with a rank of General Major. This unit fared well during the initial German strikes, losing only four of its 360 aircraft. In 1942 he was appointed commander of the PVO fighter forces. On 16 June 1944 he was made commander of the 8th IAK. After the war, he continued to serve with the PVO, retiring in 1959 as a General Lieutenant. Died 22 July 1991. Awards were H.S.U., Order of Lenin, Order of the Red Banner three times, Kutusov 1st and 2nd classes, Suvorov 2nd Class, GPW 1st Class, Order of the Red Star. (Laureau 232, Milany, Larios 152, Berch, *The Volunteer* December 1991, Semenov "*Parol,*" *Geroi*, Seidl, Abrosov, Kaminskii, *Pravda*)

OSIPOV, Aleksandr Aleksandrovich, Lt., born 1912
He was a Zvena CO in the 6th IAE of the 116th IAB Byelorussian Mil. Dist. An I-15 fighter pilot in Spain, he served from 30 December 1937 until 1 May 1938. He was CO of a patrulla in the 1st Chato Escuadrilla, his aircraft CA 007 was shot down on 17 January 1938 in an air battle with Fiat CR 32s, but he was able to bail out. Flew eighty combat missions and fought in sixteen air battles, claimed one Bf 109. Abellan says he landed a Chato in France at Cenne-Monestier on 11 March 1938 along with FERSKOV (see GORSHKOV). Massé p.101 correctly gives date as 10 March indicating FORSKOV's first name as Ivan, and lists OSIPOV as OZIPOFF. These two made their return flight to Spain on 16 March Awarded the Red Star 14 November 1938. During WWII, was CO of the 145th Eskadril'ya of the 75th IAD, and in 1945 was on the staff of the 593rd ShAP (IL-2s). Died 25 July 1976. (Laureau 111, Abellan, Abrosov, Massé, Kaminskii, *Pravda*)

OSTAPCHUK, Mikhail Kirillovich, Lt., born 1914
Navigator SB, arrived 28 April and left 3 September 1938. Awarded the Red Banner on 22 February 1939. (Semenov "*Parol,*" *Los Rusos, Pravda*)

OSTROVSKII, Mikhail I., Lt., born 1912
Pilot/navigator in the 7th LShAE (Light Assault Aviation Esc.). On Air Force Staff, in Spain October 1936 to 18 October 1937. Awarded the Red Banner 2 January 1937. (*Los Rusos* says Observer, Abrosov, *Pravda*)

OSTRYAKOV, Nikolai Alekseevich, Maj., born 17 May 1911
In 1932 he attended the GVF School for Naval pilots. In 1934 he was serving with the VMF (Navy). Went to Spain in December 1936, where he at first flew the SSS and then switched to the SB 1st Escuadrilla de Kats, where he later commanded the Sea Group. This was a detachment of SBs that patrolled over the east coast as far as Mallorca. He was one of the SB pilots involved in the bombing of Cadiz on 22 January 1937. Returned to the USSR on 29 September 1937. GUMENNYI in *Vmeste* says he was the pilot of the SB that bombed the German battle cruiser *Deutschland* at Ibiza, off the Spanish Mediterranean coast on 29 May 1937. Awarded the Red Banner 22 October 1937. Gagin

claims he flew 250 (!) sorties in Spain. In December 1937, he was appointed CO of the 40th BAP Black Sea Fleet. In April 1939 he was made CO of an AB in the Far East, where after only a month he was appointed as CO of the VVS Pacific Fleet. From December 1941 until his death on 24 April 1942 at age thirty-one, he was a Major-General Aviation Commander of the Black Sea Fleet. Killed in a Luftwaffe attack on the Fleet at Sevastopol. (see KOROBKOV, F.G. for more information.) Awarded the H.S.U. on 14 June 1942, also the Order of Lenin, two Order of the Red Banner and Order of the Red Star. (*Bajo la B.*, Salas, *Vmeste*, Boyd, *Pravda, Aviatsiya i Kosm. SSSR, Geroi*, Abrosov)

OZHEREDOV, Pavel Ivanovich, Capt., born 1911
I-16 pilot in the 40th IAE 83rd IAB Byelorussian Mil. Dist. He served in Spain from 31 May 1937 until 28 January 1938 as a Partulla CO in PLESHCHENKO's 2nd Esc. Flew 140 missions and claimed six aircraft personal and in group. Shot down and wounded in an air combat with Bf 109s in September 1937. Awarded the Order of Lenin on 2 March 1938 and the Red Banner twice, on 22 October 1937 and 2 March 1938. Fought in the Khalkin-Gol with the 31st IAP, later made deputy CO of the 21st IAP. During WWII, he was CO of 38th (later 21st Guards) IAP; he was killed in a crash on 19 March 1942. (Kaminskii, Pritsker says KIA in air battle October/November 1937, Abrosov, *Pravda*)

PAILOVICH
Aviation advisor at Bilbao, according to Alcofar p.94, see KOROBKOV, F.G. who used the codename PAVLOVICH. (Alcofar, Warheroes.ru)

PALACHEV, Georgii Afanas'evich, Capt., born 1898
Was Air Force Instructor in air group orientation at Air War Academy, then Chief of Staff 16th TBAB (Heavy Bomber AviaBrigade) Kharkov Mil. Dist. Served in Spain as Instructor in the Estado Mayor Fuerzas Aires from 14 January 1938 until 25 November 1938. Awarded the Red Banner on 22 February 1939. (Semenov "*Parol*," Berch, *Los Rusos, Pravda*)

PALOV, Fedor
CO. of replacement Esc. says Ibañez in *Icare 130*.

PAL'TSEV, Mikhail N., born 1913
Fitter from Aircraft Factory #21 assembling/repairing I-16 aircraft. In Spain from October 1936 to 8 May 1937. Awarded the Red Star 2 January 1937. (*Pravda, Los Rusos*)

PANCHENKO, Petr Andreevich
Gunner SB-2, arrived in Spain in June 1938. Awarded the Red Banner 22 February 1939. (Berch, Semenov "*Parol*," *Pravda*)

PANFILOV, Ivan Alekseevich, Lt., born 1911
A Zvena CO in the 142nd IAB Byelorussian Mil. Dist. In Spain he was a Patrulla CO of I-16s in the 6th Escuadrilla de Moscas under GUSEV. Served from 20 August 1937 until 28 February 1938. GUSEV says he was injured in a bad landing and after release from the hospital was sent home. He had flown sixty combat missions and claimed four enemy aircraft. Awarded the Red Banner on 2 March 1938. In WWII, he was CO of the 238th IAP. In April 1942 he was shot down and captured. Sent first to Hammelburg POW camp. Later in July 1944 he was sent to Mauthhausen Concentration Camp and was liberated by U.S. Army troops in April 1945. In 1979 he was living near Moscow. (Kaminskii, Semenov "*Parol*," Gusev 99 plus, Salas, Abrosov, *Pravda*)

PANIN, Pavel Alekseevich, born 1909
Said to have volunteered for Spanish duty, but there is no information on him in either Abrosov or Kaminskii nor on the airaces.narod.ru site. Flew in the Winter War against Finland. In the GPW, he was appointed commander of the 255 IAP of the Northern Fleet Air Arm in May 1942. During his 114 operations with this unit, he claimed thirteen victories. On 26 August 1943, he was KIA. Awards were H.S.U. (posthumously) on 22 January 1944, Order of Lenin, Order of the Red Banner 14 November 1938, and Order of the Red Star. (Seidl, Polak, *Pravda*, warheroes.ru)

PANIN, Petr M., born 1910
Fitter in crew from Aircraft Factory #22 assembling SB aircraft, in Spain October to 12 December 1936 Awarded the Red Star 2 January 1937. (*Los Rusos, Pravda*)

PANKRATOV, Vasilii A., born 1911
Mechanic in a patrulla, served from October 1936 to 26 July 1937. Awarded the Red Star 2 January 1937 (*Los Rusos, Pravda*)

PANOV, Alekseii Borisovich, Sr.Lt., born 1914

Born on 15 October 1914 in the Ukraine. After working as a joiner in the railway support workshop in Kanatop, in 1934 he enlisted in the army and began flight training. Graduated as a pilot in 1936. He became a Zvena CO in the 57th IAE 142nd IAB Byelorussian Mil. Dist. In 1938 he volunteered for service in Spain, arriving there on 26 March and returned 5 August 1938. He was a member of the 2nd Escuadrilla flying I-16s under the command of Fedor V. RODIN (and later commanded by GRITSEVETS). Saw action over the Aragon and Catalonian Fronts. During combat over the Ebro on 13 May 1938, he had to bellyland his badly damaged fighter at the airfield at Reus. PANOV was seriously wounded, but the aircraft while damaged with holes in the wings and fuselage and a hole through the No.1 cylinder head, was repairable. PANOV spent two months in a Spanish hospital before going home. He had flown ten combat missions and claimed one enemy aircraft. He was awarded the Red Banner on 22 February 1939. Upon his return to the Soviet Union, he attended the Zhukovskii Aviation Academy. Just before the start of WWII (22 June 1941), he was posted to the 185th IAP. During his time with this unit, he flew seventy sorties and participated in fifteen air combats, claiming six victories. In May 1942 PANOV took command of the 436th IAP which was flying Curtis Wright P-40s. Later in March 1943 this unit was renumbered as the 67th GIAP and in mid 1943 the 67th was re-equipped with P-39 Airacobras. In April 1943 the unit was awarded the Order of the Red Banner. In June 1943 the 67th was made a part of the 1st GIAD. During the period May 1942 to September 1944 this unit claimed 268 victories and had flown 4,250 sorties. In 1944 the 67th changed mounts again to the Yak-3. On 12 September 1944 while leading a fighter escort for Shturmoviks attacking near Warsaw, they encountered a large formation of Fw 190s. PANOV downed two in quick succession, his aircraft was then hit. He attempted a forced landing but on hitting the ground the aircraft burst into flames. Russian troops on the scene were unable to get him out of the burning machine. During the course of the war, he had claimed fourteen victories in 241 sorties with forty-one air combats. Awards were H.S.U. (posthumously on 23 February 1945), Order of Lenin, Order of the Red Banner four times, Aleksandr Nevskii, GPW 1st. Cl., Order of the Red Star. (Kaminskii, Semenov "*Parol*," Berch, *Vmeste*, Berch, *Geroi*, Seidl, Polak, *Pravda*)

PARAKHIN, Fedor Eliseevich NCO, born 1913

Radio/Gunner SB, He came 1 April and returned 13 August 1938. He was wounded in action, when his aircraft flown by MURAV'EV was shot down by Bf 109s on 10 June 1938. He and the other crewmembers were able to bail out. Awarded the Red Banner on 22 February 1939. (Berch, Semenov "*Parol*," *Los Rusos*, Abrosov, *Pravda*)

PARSHIK, Ivan Andreievich

Los Rusos list as an Aeronautical Engineer in charge of the use and maintenance of aircraft in the Groups. Served in Spain from May 1937 to December 1938. Participated in WWII. (*Los Rusos,* I believe they really mean PRACHIK, as their photo is of the same person)

PAVLOV, Dmitrii Fedorovich, Lt., born 1908

Pilot in the 107th IAE 83rd IAB Byelorussian Mil. Dist. An I-16 pilot, he went to Spain in November 1936. He was KIA when his aircraft was shot down in combat with Fiats on 17 November 1936, his Aircraft falling on Mount Garabitas. He had been flying in a Patrulla with LAKEEV and MINAEV from MOROZOV's detachment at the time. Posthumously awarded Order of the Red Banner 2 January 1937. (*Vmeste*, Rumyantsev "*Antonio*," Abrosov, Kaminskii, *Pravda*)

PAVLOV, Evgenii Dmitrievich, Maj., born 1906

Commander of the 33rd IAE Byelorussian Mil. Dist. Was in Spain from 10 January to 1 April (or 12 January to 31 March) 1938. Abrosov says he took over command of the I-15 group after STEPANOV and before KOTROV. Kaminskii on the other hand says CO of the I-16 Group. (*Los Rusos* list as CO of fighter Group and service date as 12 January to 31 March 1938.) During the course of WWII, commanded the 22nd IAP and then the 246th IAP and in January-February 1945, was on the Staff of the 234th IAD. Died on 18 April 1979. (Abrosov, *Los Rusos*, Kaminskii)

PAVLOV, Ivan Nikiforovich "Juan," Lt., born 1911

He was a pilot in the 2nd IAE 56th IAB Kiev Mil. Dist. In Spain he was an I-16 Pilot in the 2nd Moscas under NEDELIN, arrived on 10 June 1938. He was KIA 23[1] August 1938, while flying CM 206 on an escort mission with SBs. They were

jumped by a large group of Fiats; PAVLOV succeeded in downing two of the Fiats, but was himself then shot down.[2] Only the day before while landing after another escort mission, he had broken the left wing of another (?) Mosca. Also on 15 August returning from a mission he made a wheels up landing at Vendrell, damaging his Mosca. Posthumously awarded the Red Banner on 22 February 1939. ([1]Semenov *Tov.* gives date as the 25th as does the 1991 list of Soviet dead, *My* (1986), Abrosov, *Pravda*, Kaminskii says he was in the 5th Escuadrilla, [2]According to Abrosov his aircraft was badly damaged during air combat with 109s, while trying to make a forced landing he hit his head on the gun sight and was severely injured, dying three hours later.)

PAVLOVICH, General
See both KOROBKOV and PAILOVICH (Aizpuru).

PAVLYUK, Il'ya Afanas'evivh, Lt., born 1914 (Kaminskii lists as 20 June 1915)
Fighter pilot in the 120 IAE 95th IAB Transcaucasian Mil. Dist. He served in Spain from January to 26 July 1937. Possibly in the 1st Esc. de Chatos (Kaminskii says I-16s). Order of Red Banner 27 June 1937. From August 1937 until May 1938 was a detachment CO in the 120th IAE. Fought in the Khalkhin-Gol on the staff of the 56th IAP and was wounded in an air combat on 29 July 1939. Awarded the Red Banner for the second time on 17 November 1939. From September 1940 until June 1941 was CO of an Eskadril'ya in the 45th IAP. In June he became assistant CO of the 82nd IAP. At the start of WWII was on the Staff of the 12th Air Army. He was captured on 7 August 1941 and taken to Germany. He was liberated by the U.S. Army on 25 April 1945. Passed away on 28 November 1995. (*Bajo la B.*, Berch, Lukes, Abrosov, Kaminskii, *Pravda*)

"PEDRO"
Fighter pilot. Logoluso thinks is PETROV. (Lacalle)

PEKARSH, Viktor G.
Engineer from Aircraft Factory #22 assembling SB Aircraft. In Spain from October to 12 December 1936. Awarded the Red Banner 2 January 1937. (*Pravda, Los Rusos* spells it PEKARSK and say Engineer with the Estado Mayor F.A. from 7 May to 10 November 1937.)

PEREKHVATOV, Stepan Alekseevich, Lt., born 1908
Pilot SB, arrived 26 March and returned 3 September 1938. Awarded the Red Banner on 22 February 1939. (Berch, Semenov "*Parol*," *Los Rusos, Pravda*)

PESHETINKOV, Vasili (*Vmeste*)

PETIN, Pavel Sr.Lt. (Semenov "*Parol*")

PETRAKOV, Andrei N., Lt., born 1906
Bomber pilot, he served from October 1936 to 23 January 1937. Was sent home early due to illness. Awarded the Red Banner 2 January 1937. (*Los Rusos, Pravda*)

PETROCHENKO, Vasilii F., born 1908
Instructor in the repair of aircraft. In Spain October 1936 to 23 November 1937. Sent home due to illness. Awarded the Red Star 2 January 1937. (*Los Rusos, Pravda* lists as Aviation Technician.)

PETROV, Aleksei P., born 1907
BIBIKOV says was technician on SB's. Served from October to 12 December 1936, and was sent home due to illness. Awarded the Red Star 2 January 1937. (*Vmeste, Los Rusos, Pravda*)

PETROV, Georgii Kh., born 1912
Both *Pravda* and BIBIKOV in *Vmeste* indicate he was a technician on SBs. Served from October 1936 to 27 March 1937. Awarded the Red Star 2 January 1937. (*Vmeste, Los Rusos, Pravda*, but Demenchuk, Logoluso, Meroño, *MY*, Berch all say he was a pilot. But I think they are confusing him with Pavel PETROV listed below.)

PETROV, Ivan, born 1908
Aviation technician specialist in the assembly of synchronized weapons for fighter aircraft. Served from 2 April until 15 September 1938. (*Los Rusos*)

PETROV, Mikhail Sidorovich, Lt., born 1909
Pilot in the 34th IAE 56th IAB Kiev Mil. Dist. In Spain he flew the I-15 in EREMENKO's 1st Esc. from 13 May until 29 September 1937. Downed a CR 32 in July over El Escorial. He was badly wounded in an air combat over Brunete on 25 July where he claimed a second CR 32. After release from the hospital he returned home. Awards were two Orders of the Red Banner, 22 October 1937 and 2 March 1938. (Shingarev, Lukes, Abrosov, Kaminskii, *Pravda*)

PETROV, Pavel Petrovich, Sr.Lt., born 1907
SB Pilot in 2nd Escuadrilla Grupo 12. KIA during raid on Talavera 2 November 1936. Possibly downed by Mantelli. BIBIKOV says he was lost during attack on Cordoba, along with VLASOV and NECHIPORENKO, but he is mistaken as other crewmembers were VLASOV and TSIGULEV. Posthumously awarded the Red Banner 2 January 1937. Kotelnikov says KIA on 5 November

1936, while Los Rusos give date as 3 December and the 1991 list of Soviet dead gives 3 November (*Vmeste, Pravda*, Kotelnikov, Abrosov, *Los Rusos*)

PETRUKHIN, Nikolai Trofimovich, Lt., born 19 December 1907

A Zvena CO in the 118th IAE Moscow Mil. Dist. In Spain from October 1936 to 3 June 1937. He was a member of TURZHANSKII's I-15 Esc. in the North; he had two aircraft to his credit, one He 51 and a Ju 52. He was wounded in air combat on 4 January 1937 where he claimed a Ju 52. After his release from the hospital, he was sent home. Awarded Order of the Red Banner on 2 January and 4 July[1] 1937. Participated in the Russo Finnish Winter War with the VVS Baltic Fleet. Awarded the Red Banner 21 April 1940 and the Red Star on 7 February 1940. In June of 1940 he became the CO of the 10th SAB (Mixed Aviation Brigade) and continued as CO until February 1942 when he was appointed CO of the 61st SAB of the Red Banner Baltic Fleet. In July 1942 he was in command of a Special Air Group of the PGK Main Command Reserve. Two times he became CO of the 6th IAD Northern Fleet, first from July to September 1943 and then from June to December 1944. This unit supplied air cover for the Convoys coming to the Northern Ports. For his actions during WWII, he was awarded several medals including the Red Banner 23 October 1942. After the war he remained in the Navy and from December 1949 until June 1958 he was Air Defense Commander Pacific Fleet and Deputy CO of the Far Eastern Army Air Defense. In July 1958 became CO of Northern Army Air Defense. Passed away 16 September 1988. (Kaminskii, Abrosov, Lukes, *Pravda*, airaces.narod.ru, *Los Rusos* give 3 July as his end date. [1]Some sources say that he was awarded the Red Star on 4 July, but Pravda shows a Red Banner.)

PIGORIN, Anton

SB Pilot 1937. (Gringoire via Logoluso, but this is undoubtedly a codename)

PIL'SHCHIKOV, Konstantin A., born 1910

Mechanic on I-15 fighter aircraft, in Spain from 14 January to 18 October 1937. Awarded the Red Star 27 June 1937. (*Pravda, Los Rusos* spells name as PILSHIKOV)

PISAKOV, Stefan Tarosovich, Sr.Lt., born 1904

Joined the Army in 1926. In Spain he was an SB Navigator in the 1st Esc. 12th grupo, he served from October 1936 until 27 May 1937. Awarded the Red Banner 2 January 1937. Fought in the Russo-Finnish War in 1939-40. During WWII, in 1943, was on the staff of the 199th ShAD 4th ShAK 4th VVS Army on the Byelorussian front. The CO of the 199th was a fellow "Spaniard" Col. N.S. VINOGRADOV. Passed away 1992. (Voronkova, *Pravda, Los Rusos*, Logoluso, *Icare 130*)

PISAREV, Ivan V., born 1915

Worker in crew from Aircraft Factory #1 assembling/ repairing I-15 and SSS aircraft. In Spain October 1936 to 18 October 1937. Awarded the Red Star 2 January 1937. (*Los Rusos, Pravda*)

PISKALOV, Mikhail I., born 1913

Chief of crew from Aircraft Factory #22 assembling SB aircraft. Served from October to 12 December 1936. Awarded the Red Banner 2 January 1937. (*Pravda, Los Rusos* spell it PISKLOV)

PIVOVAROV, Konstantin L., born 1905

Aviation Technician on I-16 fighter aircraft. In Spain 14 January to 27 March 1937. Awarded the Red Star 17 July 1937. (*Los Rusos, Pravda*)

PLESHCHENKO, Grigorii Petrovich, Sr.Lt., born 1907

Before Spain he was a Detachment CO in the 12th IAE 111th IAB Leningrad Mil. Dist. Eleven Pilots had sailed from Leningrad to La Havre on the Soviet ship *Kooperatsiya*. Once there the group broke up into smaller groups to go to Spain. He along with MAKARICHEV, MAKSIMOV and SAFONOV, went to Lyon and then from there by airliner to Barcelona. He arrived 31 May 1937 and returned on 28 January 1938. In Spain he was CO. of the 2nd Escuadrilla de Moscas (in his memoirs on p.200 of Pritsker, he says that MINAEV got the second Esc. and he the third. But he is somehow mixed up, as it was just the other way around.) Some members of his Escuadrilla were, KIRILLOV, FEDULOV, KHOZYANOV, KOLOSOV, MAKARICHEV, MAKSIMOV, and SAFONOV. His Escuadrilla participated in the 15 October 1937 attack on Garrapinillos (Sanjuro) Airfield. In early November 1937 he was flying Mosca CM 102. During a briefing for an attack on the airfield at Granada, he requested

the use of an I-15, because it had four MGs. and carried four bombs; the request was said to have been granted. Flew more than 150 sorties and claimed two Bf 109s in pair with another pilot on 17 July 1937. Abellan claims he was shot down on 3 June 1937 during a battle with CR 32s and He 51s, and bailed out. Awarded the Order of Lenin 2 March 1938 and Red Banner on 22 October 1937. Fought in the Khalkhin-Gol with the 22nd IAP, claimed 1 Ki-27. During WWII, at first he commanded an IAP of the 201st IAD and then from August 1942 until September 1945 he commanded the 245th IAD (Abrosov says CO of the 244th AD). (Gusev 159, Laureau 241-2, Howson, *Bajo la B.*, Berch, Pritsker, Abrosov, Kaminskii, *Pravda*)

PLESHIVTSEV, Boris I., Sr.Lt., born 1909

CO of an SB patrulla, served from 16 June 1937 to 28 January 1938. Awarded the Red Banner twice, 3 November 1937 and 2 March 1938. (Shingarev, *Pravda, Los Rusos*)

PLETYUKHIN, Aleksandr Vladimirovich, Lt., born 1910

Pilot in the 5th IAE 36th IAB Kiev Mil. Dist. In Spain from 2 November 1936 to 27 May 1937. Was in TURZHANSKII's I-15 Esc. on the Basque front. Awarded Order of Red Banner twice, 2 January and 4 July 1937. Two aircraft personal plus two in group to his credit. In October 1939 he was CO of the 17th IAP, and in WWII he was CO of an Eskadril'ya of the 402nd IAP. KIA on 6 August 1941. (*Pravda*, Lukes, Abrosov, Kaminskii, *Los Rusos* wrongly list as bomber pilot)

PLYASOV, Sergei Kharitonovich, Maj., born 1913

Joined the Army in 1933. Pilot in the 107th IAE 83rd IAB Byelorussian Mil. Dist. In Spain he was an I-16 Pilot from 14 December 1937 to 10 June 1938. Initially put into GUSEV's 6th Esc., he later commanded a Patrulla in the 5th Esc. under SMOLYAKOV. Flew more than eighty missions twenty-five air combats and shot down two aircraft, including an S.81 on 6 February 1938. Awarded the Red Banner 14 November 1938 and the Red Star on 22 February 1939. In March 1939 he commanded an Eskadril'ya in the 36th IAP. From July to October 1941 he commanded the 84th IAP, renamed the 348th IAP in August 1941. Died on 4 March 1942. (Kaminskii, Gusev, Semenov "*Parol*," Abrosov, *Pravda*)

PLYGUNOV, Sergei Grigor'evich, Sr.Lt., born 1907

Detachment CO in the 61st IAE Byelorussian Mil. Dist. Served in Spain from 15 May to 23 December 1937. Kaminskii says was a patrulla CO, while Tarazona says PLYGUNOV led his group to the North, (See also SMIRNOV, Boris.) It would seem that Tarazona was mistaken. SMIRNOV led this I-16 escuadrilla of new Spanish pilots to the Asturias. Shingarev states that Arias said PLYGUNOV was an I-16 instructor, teaching the Spanish pilots frontal attack and firing at short distances at El Caramoli. YAMANOV in *Pritsker* says he traveled to Spain with PLYGUNOV in May 1937. In *Aeroplano* #12, they give his middle name as Gregorievich and also that his nom de guerre was "Antonio." Said to have flown 108 sorties and participated in nine air combats. Two aircraft to his credit, and he was awarded the Red Banner on 22 October 1937. Fought in the Russo Finnish War with the 149th IAP flying I-153s, claiming two enemy aircraft according to airaces/narod.ru. In the Spring of 1941 he was working as a Test Pilot. Died 1977 (Tarazona 46, Laureau 98, Shingarev, Berch, Pritsker, Sukhachev p.179-80, Abrosov, *Los Rusos* list as PLEGUNOV and say was bomber pilot, Kaminskii, *Pravda*)

PODGORNOV, Ivan M.

Chief of crew from Aircraft Factory #21 assembling/repairing I-16 aircraft. Served from October 1936 to 8 May 1937. Awarded the Red Star 2 January 1937. (*Los Rusos, Pravda*)

PODNISHEV, Nikolai, Lt., born 1908

Pilot in Spain from 26 March to 13 July 1938. (*Los Rusos*)

POLIKANOV, Viktor V., born 1916

Worker from Aircraft Factory #22 assembling/repairing SB aircraft. In Spain from October 1936 to 9 March 1937. Awarded the Red Star 2 January 1937. (*Los Rusos, Pravda*)

POLIVALOV, Mikhail M., Lt., born 1908

Pilot of SSS Rasante in STRELKOV's 2nd (1st) Escuadrilla. In Spain from October 1936 to 8 March 1937. KARPENKO was his navigator/gunner for a time. On 2 December 1936, during an attack on Illesca, his aircraft was damaged and he had to make a forced landing. Mistakenly thinking they were in enemy territory, they burned their aircraft. Awarded the Red Banner 2 January 1937. (*Pravda, G. y Rev 2, Vmeste*, Abrosov, *Los Rusos* spell it POLIVANOV)

POLUEKTOV, Aleksei D., born 1909
Aviation Technician, in Spain from October 1936 to 27 August 1937. Awarded the Red Star 2 January 1937. (*Los Rusos, Pravda*)

POLUSHKO, Fedor Ivanovich, Sr.Lt., born 1907
Served from 27 May until 10 November 1937. Was Patrulla leader in the 1st SB Escuadrilla under SENATOROV. He led the Moscas (B. SMIRNOV/F. Tarazona) to the North, landing at Gijon. Later in early September 1937 when the situation in Asturias deteriorated, he was sent to France where he picked up a Airspeed Envoy and helped to fly the remaining Soviets out to France. Awarded the Order of Lenin 28 October 1937, and the Red Banner on 2 March 1938. (*Vmeste, Los Rusos, Pravda*)

POLYAKOV, Ivan V., born 1913
Aviation Technician, served from October 1936 to 7 April 1937. Awarded the Red Star 2 January 1937. (*Los Rusos, Pravda*)

POLYAKOV, Pavel Vasil'evich, Lt., born 1910
Pilot in the 107th IAE 83rd IAB Byelorussian Mil. Dist. In Spain he was an I-16 pilot in TARKHOV/ KOLESNIKOV Esc. from November 1936 until 26 July 1937. On 27 December 1936 he was flying in MOROZOV's detachment escorting two Potez 540 bombers (Ñ and S) in an attack in the Teruel area. The bombers kept flying over the target very slowly several times, on the last pass they were attacked by Fiats. The Ñ was shot up, its left engine was on fire and had to crashland. He said two of the attacking fighters were shot down. He claimed a Fiat CR 32 in November 1936, a Savoia S.79 (!) on 7 November and later on the 22nd he shared a Ju 52 with KRAVCHENKO, and a Ju 86 in patrulla on 25 March 1937. Awarded the Red Banner twice, 2 January and 4 July 1937. After his return from Spain, he was appointed CO of the 142nd IAB Byelorussian Mil. Dist. During WWII was CO of the 35th IAP 298th IAD PVO. Passed away in 1998. (Pritsker, *Pravda*, Rumyantsev "*Antonio*," Kaminskii, Abrosov says he got one aircraft on 9 December 1936, airaces.narod.ru.)

POLYAKOV, Sergei Nikolaevich, Lt., born 1908
Pilot in the 40th IAE 83rd IAB Byelorussian Mil. Dist. Volunteered for Spanish duty and arrived in Spain 17 May 1937 and returned home on 28 January 1938. A member of PLESHCHENKO's 2nd Escuadrilla (I-16s), he was in the patrulla led by STARIKOV, A. together with OZHEREDOV, P. During his tour, he flew 150 sorties and claimed five victories. He was awarded the Order of the Red Banner twice, 28 October 1937 and 2 March 1938. Upon his return to the Soviet Union, he was promoted to Kapitan and put in command of an Eskadril'ya in the 7th IAP Leningrad Mil. Dist., which took part in the Winter War with Finland in 1939-40. A major in June 1941, he was commander of the 174th ShAP. This unit operated on the Leningrad front, and was later renamed the 15th Guards ShAP. On 23 December 1941 he was KIA while flying a Polikarpov U2 aircraft. Awards were H.S.U. and Order of Lenin (posthumously on 10 February 1943), and Order of the Red Star. (Kaminskii, Berch, Smirnov, Pritsker, Polak, *Geroi*, Abrosov)

POLYANSKII, Vladimir Ivanovich, Lt., born 1910
A Zvena CO in the 34th IAE 56th IAB Kiev Mil. Dist. In Spain he was an I-16 pilot and patrulla CO in the 1st Esc. from 31 May to 18 October 1937. Awarded the Red Banner 3 November 1937. In 1940 he was appointed CO of the 88th IAP. After the start of WWII, he claimed four aircraft and he was transferred to another Regiment in September 1941. In 1942 he was made a Major. (Kaminskii. Pritsker 145, *Pravda*, Abrosov)

POPANDOPULO, V.
SB Observer in November 1936. (*Bajo la B.*, Logoluso spells it PAPANDOPULO)

POPOV, Fedor V., born 1907
Fitter from Aircraft Factory #22 assembling SB aircraft. In Spain from October to 12 December 1936. Awarded the Red Star 2 January 1937. (*Los Rusos, Pravda*)

POPOV, Serafin, born 1912
Patrulla Mechanic, served from October 1936 to 7 April 1937. Awarded the Red Star. (*Los Rusos*)

POPOV, Vyacheslav Dmetrievich, NCO, born 4 March 1914
Before going to Spain he was a Sgt. Pilot in the 11th IAE 111 IAB Leningrad Mil. Dist. In Spain, he served from 20 August 1937 to 24 March 1938. He was a patrulla CO in EREMENKO's/SEROV's 1st Chato Esc. Flew sixty combat missions, and claimed three aircraft (two Fiat CR 32s personal and one S.79 in pair with SIUSIUKA' LOV on 4 November 1937). Wounded in air combat on 10 December 1937 during the air battle in which KOTYKHOV was shot down. On 10 February 1938 while testing his engine, he was injured and put in a hospital. After his release he returned home to the USSR. Awarded the Red Banner 14 November 1938. According to Kaminskii, he used the codename Grigorii and also Fernando Montanel. After his return home, from May to October 1938 he was a Zvena CO in the 7th IAP. In January 1939 he became Deputy Eskadril'ya CO in the 38th IAP and from 30 November 1939 until 13 March 1940 fought in the Russo-Finnish War. From April 1940 to December 1941 he was an Eskadril'ya CO in the 25th IAP at Baku. During WWII he served from 9 December 1941 until April 1942 as an Eskadril'ya CO and then as deputy CO of the 270th IAP on the Crimean front. He next took courses for commanders at the Air Force Acadamy until April 1943. He then worked as an Eskadril'ya CO and later in June 1943 as a deputy CO of the 179th IAP on the western front. Awarded many medals for his actions in the war, he retired on 10 November 1946 and passed away 1 January 1991. (Salas, *Bajo la B.*, Pritsker, Shingarev all list as Grigorii, Kaminskii, Abrosov, *Pravda*)

POPOV, Yakov A., born 1907
Bomber pilot (SSS?), in Spain from October 1936 to 2 July 1937. Awarded the Red Banner 2 January 1937. (*Los Rusos, Pravda*)

POPOVKIN, Yakov Parfenovich, NCO, born 1912
Radio/Gunner SB, arrived 26 March and returned on 18 August 1938. He was a crewmember on same aircraft as GUDOVICH. Awarded the Red Banner 22 February 1939. (Berch, *My (1986), Pravda*)

POSPELOV, Anatolii Pavlovich, NCO, born 1913
Radio /Gunner on SB, came 30 May and returned on 15 November 1938. Awarded the Red Banner on 22 February 1939. (Berch, Semenov "*Parol,*" *Los Rusos, Pravda*)

POTAPOV, Vasilii M., born 1914
Aviation technician, served from October 1936 to 27 August 1937. Awarded the Red Star 2 January 1937. (*Pravda, Los Rusos*, Kotelnikov who says was SB Tech and spells it POTAROV)

POVAROV, Dmitri, born 1910
Mechanic/technician on I-15 from 26 March to 15 September 1938. (*Bajo la B., Los Rusos*)

POZDNYAKOV
Commander of 3rd Escuadrilla SBs in April 1937 says Kotelnikov, but Abrosov says he was commander of a Zveno (Patrulla).

POZDNYSHEV, Nikolai Ivanovich, Lt., born 1908
Pilot in the 107th IAE 83rd IAB Byelorussian Mil. Dist. In Spain he was an I-16 Fighter pilot from 26 March until 13 July 1938. Flew nine combat missions and fought in one air battle where he was wounded. Sent to the hospital; after his release, he returned home. Abrosov says "early due to health problems." Fought in the Russo-Finnish War, awarded the Red Banner 21 May 1940. During WWII, was a member of the 145th IAP and became CO of an Eskadril'ya. Claimed one aircraft, an Fw 189 on 10 July 1941, but the next day he was shot down by an Me 109. Died and was buried at his airfield. Posthumously awarded Red Banner in 1941. (Abrosov, Kaminskii, *Pravda*)

PRACHIK, Ivan Andreevich, born 1903
Before going to Spain he was an Aviational Engineer in the 142nd IAB at Bobruisk Byelorussian Mil. Dist. where he was a specialist on the I-16. In his autobiography *Frontove Nebo,* he tells of problems with the new I-16s of the 142nd in December 1936 – January 1937, where the control knobs would break off due to the extreme cold, causing several crashes. He learned how to fly, his flight instructor was F. RODIN. Left for Spain on 30 December 1937 on the train, traveling through Poland, Germany, and finally reached Paris, where he met with people from the Soviet embassy. Next he went by train to Port-Bou in Spain. He also says that when he returned it was by bus from Port-Bou to Paris and then on to La Havre where he boarded a ship for home, arriving on 15 September 1938. When he arrived in Spain he met with F.K. ARZHENUKHIN, whom he says told him he was replacing B.P. ZAKHAREVSKII, who, he says had been in Spain for almost a year, saying he had arrived in the Fall of 1936. But a look at ZAKKHAREVSKII's service time, 14 June 1937 to 24 March 1938, and PRACHIK's time, 30 December 1937 to 15 September 1938, seems to contradict what he says. Other sources say he Succeeded REPIN, but service time is also questionable. He also mentions meeting up in late March 1938 with a new group of seventeen Soviet pilots led by RODIN, which had just arrived. They had come aboard the Soviet ship *Andrei Zhadanov* to La Havre and then by train to Spain. His assistant in repairing I-16 aircraft was BULYGIN. When telling of his departure from Spain, he says he had been there eighteen months (?). He participated in the fighting for Khalkhin-Gol, and later in 1940 he was appointed as Chief Engineer in the Far Eastern Mil. Dist., where he remainded until October 1942 when he then returned to Moscow and was put into the 269th IAD (which included the 254th, 287th, and the 45th IAP) and finished the war with it. Awarded the Order of Lenin on 14 November 1938. Passed away in 1984. (Semenov *Tov.*, Berch, *Vmeste, Los Rusos*, Prachik)

PRAVDA, Roman P., born 1905
Aviation Mechanic, in Spain from October 1936 to 9 July 1937. Awarded the Red Star 2 January 1937. (*Los Rusos, Pravda*)

PRESELVANSKY
Commissar General of the fighter pilots. (Lacalle, also see PREZHEVALSKII below)

PRESNUKHIN, Vyacheslav Konstantinovich, Lt., born 1911
Detachment CO in the 3rd IAE VVS KBF Red Banner Baltic Fleet. I-16 pilot in DEVOTCHENKO's 2nd Esc. from 14 December 1937 to 15 April 1938. Flew twenty-seven combat missions and fought in nine air battles. On 3 January 1938 his aircraft CM-103 collided with TROSHKIN (CM-019) on take off. He was injured when his face hit the gun sight, and was sent to hospital. After his release, they sent him home. It is believed that he died in Moscow in 1938. (Semenov "*Parol*," Pritsker, Abrosov, Kaminskii)

PREZHEVALSKII, Listed by Kondrat as the Escuadrilla Commissar (Kondrat)

PRIJMAK, Efim Ivanovich, Lt., born 1910
Navigator SB, arrived on 1 April and left on 3 September 1938. Awarded the Red Banner 22 February 1939. (Semenov "*Parol*," Berch, *Los Rusos, Pravda*)

PRIPISNYI, Nikolai T., born 1913
SB Aviation Technician, he served from October 1936 to 27 August 1937. Awarded the Red Star 2 January 1937. (*Pravda, Los Rusos* spell it PRIPISKOV)

PROCOPIEV
Estado Mayor del Aire under "Douglas." As below? (*Chantaje* 103)

PROKOFIEV, Gavriil Mikhailovich, Sr.Lt., born 7 April 1907

Before going into the Army, he worked in an automobile factory in Moscow. Joined the Soviet Army in 1929. In 1934 he graduated the Naval Navigators School at Yeisk, after which he served in VVS units in the Moscow Mil. Dist. Went to Spain in September 1936 as a Senior Lieutenant, nom de guerre "FELIX." Flew in the 1st Internacional Escuadrilla as an observer/gunner in a Br 19 flown by G.TUPIKOV. At the end of October 1936 he transfered to Albacete where the 1st Escuadrilla de Kats (SBs) was being formed under the command of E. SCHACHT. Serving as a Navigator on the SB, he took part in low level attacks on troop concentrations, airfields, fortifications, and other military targets. He flew reconnaissance missions over Toledo, Sevilla, Teruel, Merida, Casares, the Ports of Malaga and Ceuta and the town of Siguenza. Returned to the USSR on 8 May. 1937. Awarded the Order of the Red Banner on 2 January, and on 27 June 1937 he was given the title of Hero of the Soviet Union. In October 1937, he was sent to China where he commanded the first Soviet fighter squadron (I-16), together with a bomber squadron commanded by N.M. Kidalinskii.[1] This first group of Soviet VVS units in China were under the overall command of Pavel RYCHAGOV. During WWII, he taught advanced courses for navigation at Poltava and headed a senior officers air school. He was promoted to Major General of Aviation on 7 August 1943. He graduated the Air School of the Academy of the General Staff in 1949 and the Military History School of the Supreme Military Academy in 1951. Awards were the H.S.U., the Order of Lenin twice, the Order of the Red Banner twice, Order of the Red Star twice, GPW 1st Cl., and other decorations. After an illness in 1961, he was placed on reserve. He lived in Moscow, passing away on 14 June 1991. (Berch, *Vmeste, Pravda, Icare 130, Bajo la B., V Nebe Kitaya*, Slyusarev, *Geroi*) ([1]Note: while *'V Nebe Kitaya*" p.7 says October 1937, Slyusarev p.249 says 1 December at Nanking.)

PROKOPENKO, Georgii Nikolaevich, Lt., born 25 April 1914

Pilot in the 107th IAE 83rd IAB Byelorussian Mil. Dist. In 1938, volunteered for duty in Spain, where he flew an I-16 from 26 March to 22 September 1938 in the 5th Esc. Kaminskii says he served as an Escuadrilla CO for a period. Abrosov mentions that during a period when GLUSHENKOV was recovering from a wound and starting to put together a new escuadrilla, PROKOPENKO filled in for him. He flew seventy combat missions and fought in twelve air battles. Wounded in action on 13 June 1938 in a battle with Bf 109s, his aircraft was said to have forty-two bulletholes including three hits to the armored seat back. After being wounded, it seems he developed a "Messerfobia" or fear of the Messerschmitts. On the 20th, as he was leading the Esc. they saw 109s and he tried to avoid the battle, but his wingmen did not follow him and joining with the rest of the Esc. fought with the Messers. In September 1939, he took part in the Soviet occupation of eastern Poland. In June 1941 was a Kapitan in the 155th IAP (which later became the 3rd GuIAP, 235 IAD, 10th IAK) flying I-16s, and flying sorties on the Karelian, Volkhov, Leningrad and later the Stalingrad fronts. He was again wounded in an air battle on 10 July 1941, while downing a Me 109. In 1942 the regiment became the 3rd Guards IAP and PROKOPENKO was promoted to major. In June 1943, the regiment was flying on the Northern Caucasus front and PROKOPENKO had claimed his 10th personal victory. He had by this time flown 189 sorties and fought in forty-seven engagements. By the end of 1943 the regiment was fighting on the Southern front and he was appointed commander, with rank of Lt. Colonel. He claimed two more kills in early 1944 (some say fifteen total). He was KIA on 14 July 1944, when he was mistakenly shot down by a Soviet Pe-2. Awards were H.S.U. 8 September 1943, Order of Lenin, Order of the Red Banner (four times), Order of A. Nievskii, OPW 1st. Cl., and Order of the Red Star (twice). (Polak, Seidl, *Geroi V.2*, Abrosov both editions give date of H.S.U. as 28 September 1943. *Los Rusos* say date left Spain is 22 August, Kaminskii)

PROSHKIN, Nikolai Capt., born 1911

Escuadrilla flight instructor in Spain from 14 September 1938 until 14 April 1939 (?). (*Los Rusos*)

PROSKUROV, Ivan Iosifovich, Sr.Lt., born 18 February 1907
Ukrainen by birth, he worked in the foundry section of the "Engels" Factory. He attended the Workers School at Khar'kov, and then went to the Mechanical and Electrical Institute at Khar'kov. After completion of these courses in 1931, he joined the Soviet Army. In 1933 he was an instructor in the 2nd Eskadril'ya 23rd LBAB. From 1934 to January 1935, he was a Zvena CO in the 90th TBAE (Heavy Bomber Aviation Squadron). In January 1935 he was made a Detachment CO in the 89th TBAE at Monino (Moscow). In 1936, he graduated from a military school for flyers. For excellence in military and political studies, he was twice awarded the Order of the Red Star. With the rank of Senior Lieutenant he went to Spain in September 1936. He traveled by flying from Moscow to Berlin to Paris under the guise of a representative of a Moscow Automobile plant visiting the French auto company Renault. From Paris he then traveled to Toulouse in the south of France and then by plane to Spain. He was put into the 1st Internacional Escuadrilla based at Albacete, where at first he flew the Breguet Br 19. Then he began flying the Potez 540 Bombers and was made Patrulla CO. His three aircraft along with another Patrulla attacked the Nationalist aerodrome at Talavera on 27 October 1936. Here they claimed to have destroyed fifteen enemy planes. On 30 October three Potez under the leadership of a Spaniard, PROSKUROV and another Soviet volunteer, GORANOV, took off to attack enemy ground forces at Navacarnero. Approching the target, they were attacked by Fiat CR 32s of the 2nd Tercio Escuadrilla commanded by A. Mantelli. GORANOV's plane had the engines shot up and crashlanded between the front lines. PROSKUROV's aircraft was also damaged, but able to make it to Republican territory, coming down in a vineyard and was later recuperated. Shortly after this in November of that same year, he transferred to the new Soviet SB Grupo 12. He then commanded a detachment (six aircraft) that was attached to the Republican Fleet and based at San Javier Airfield. In early February 1937, he replaced E. SCHACHT as CO of the 1st Escuadrilla de Kats, Grupo 12 based at San Clemente. This Grupo was under the overall command of A. ZLATOTSVETOV or "Gold" as he was referred to. PROSKUROV took part in destroying a large shipment of military cargo, in the bombing of Sigenza, and in the destruction of enemy troop columns surrounding Madrid. He also participated in the attack on the German Battle Cruiser *Deutschland.* On 2 January 1937, he was awarded the Order of the Red Banner. Kotelnikov, says he replaced "Gold" on 23 April as CO of Grupo 12. He departed Spain on 14 June 1937. He was given title of Hero of the Soviet Union on 21 June 1937 and he was elected as a deputy of the Supreme Soviet that same year. On 4 June 1940 he was promoted to Lieutenant General of Aviation. At the beginning of the Great Patriotic War, he was the Assistant Commander of the VVS and commander of the VVS 7th Air Army. He was arrested on 27 June 1941 and shot on 28 October 1941, along with several other "Spaniards" such as SMUSHKEVICH. Awards were H.S.U., Order of Lenin, Order of the Red Banner, and Order of the Red Star twice. (Berch, *Bajo la B., MY 1 and 2*, Pritsker, Shukman, Boyd, *Vmeste*, Zil'manovich, Howson, Laureau, *Geroi*, Murphy, *Pravda*, Kotelnikov)

PRUNTOV, Ivan Matveevich, born 1902
Doctor/surgeon attached to the Air unit in Spain, 10 February 1938 to 25 January 1939. Codename Patrov. Awarded the Red Star on 22 February 1939. (Semenov "*Parol*," Berch, *Los Rusos, Pravda*)

PRUTSKOV, Fedor Maksimovich, Lt., born 1908
Pilot in the 40th IAE 83rd IAB Byelorussian Mil. Dist. In the first group of I-16 pilots sent, he arrived in Spain in November 1936 and returned to the USSR on 26 July 1937. Was a member of the enlarged I-16 Escuadrilla commanded by TARKHOV and later by KOLESNIKOV. Claimed one aircraft in patrulla (a Ju 86 on 25 March 1937). Awarded the Red Banner twice, on 2 January and 4 July 1937. On 5 November 1939 he was appointed commander of the 16th IAP PVO Moscow Mil. Dist. During WWII in 1942, he was part of the Fighter Aircraft Aviation Inspectors and was given the task of preparing the 434th IAP for

battle with its new Yak 1 fighters. During his period of leadership, the 434th IAP flew 880 sorties and shot down thirty-five enemy aircraft. PRUTSKOV himself flew twenty-eight, and claimed two enemy aircraft. On 1 November 1942 while flying to Leningrad, he had to crashland his MiG-3. He was badly injured and had to convalesce for some time. During the course of the war he claimed a total of five aircraft and was awarded the Order of Lenin on 28 October 1941 and the Red Banner on 4 March 1942. He died at the front on 5 August 1943. (Kaminskii, airaces.narod.ru, *Pravda, Vmeste*, Abrosov, *Los Rusos*)

PRYANISHNIKOV, Ivan Y.A., Sr.Lt., born 1908

Navigator in the 2nd Esc. de Kats, October 1936 to 9 July 1937. Awarded the Red Banner 2 January 1937. (*Pravda, Bajo la B., Vmeste, Los Rusos* give 27 September as end date)

PSHENICHNIKOV, Vasilii A., Sgt., born 1912

Radio/gunner SB from 14 December 1937 to 21 July 1938. Awarded the Red Banner 14 November 1938. (Berch, Semenov, *Los Rusos, Pravda*)

PTUKHIN, Evgenii Savvich, born 3 March 1902

Fought in the Russian Civil War. Graduated Military Aviation School in 1929, and until May 1934 was the CO and Commissar of the 15th IAE at Bryansk KVO. Then he became the CO of the 450th IAB at Smolensk. Next in July 1935 was appointed as CO of the 142nd IAB. He left for Spain on 15 May, arriving on 24 May 1937. Said to have taken over the Grupo from PUMPUR at the end of May 1937, when the latter was rotated home, but see FEDOSEEV. Later in early September 1937 he was made Soviet Commander of Republican Aviation replacing LOPATIN, with EREMENKO taking over as CO of the Fighter Air Group. (Semenov "*Parol*" p.30 says he took over from SMUSHKEVICH, but LOPATIN had taken over from "DOUGLAS" according to OSADCHII, PUZIEKIN and Abrosov. Boyd on other hand wrongly says he replaced KOPETS.) In Spain he used the codename "General Jose." Several times he would take part in air combats, claiming two aircraft – one Fiat CR 32 in patrulla on 4 June and one Bf 109 in pair with PETROVICH on 8 July 1937. Chantaje says he shot up a Ju 52 at night over the Aragon front, and that they were sure it went down (p.109), but I think this is wrong. He was wounded in an enemy attack on Alcala de Henares on 16 July 1937. Awarded the Order of Lenin on 22 October 1937 and the Red Banner on 2 March 1938, shortly after his return to USSR on 25 February 1938. After Spain he became Air Commander of the Leningrad District and as such fought in the Winter War against Finland. He was awarded the H.S.U. on 21 March 1940. Later he became Lt.Gen. VVS and Commander of the Special Kiev Military District. Arrested after the outbreak of war, with rank of General-Lt. Vasilevskii says he was arrested on 24 June 1941 and shot on 23 February 1942. Awards were H.S.U., Order of Lenin, Order of the Red Banner, and Order of the Red Star. (Pritsker, Salas, Gusev, Berch, RSA, Yakovlev, *Vmeste*, Abrosov, Shingarev, Rumyantsev "*Antonio*," Boyd, Sukhachev, *Geroi, Los Rusos* list as born 1900, Kaminskii, *Pravda*)

PUMPUR, Petr Ivanovich, born 25 April 1900[1]

Latvian by birth. During the Russian Civil War 1918-20, he attended various air technical schools and served on the Southeast, Western and Southern fronts. From 1922-24, he attended military schools at Borisoglebsk, Moscow and Serpukhov. He graduated in 1924 and served as a senior pilot, commanding a Zvena, then a detachment and finally a Eskadril'ya. In 1934 he became commander of the 403rd IAB, then the 83rd IAB Byelorussian Mil. Dist. In 1936, he graduated the Soviet Air Force Academy school of Operations in Moscow. He tested over thirty different types of aircraft, and was responsible for making numerous suggestions for modernizing the VVS. He went to Spain with the rank of Kombrig on 13 October 1936, where he used the nom de guerre "Colonel Julio." Commanded the fighter group until he returned home

on 11 May 1937, when it is said he was replaced a few days later by E. PTUKHIN, but see FEDOSEEV. Listed as having five aircraft to his credit. While in Spain, it is said that he contributed greatly to the organization of the Spanish Republican Air Force and to the aerial defense of Madrid. On 2 January 1937, he was awarded the Order of Lenin, and on 4 July 1937 he was given title of Hero of the Soviet Union. He later acted as Commander of the VVS on the Far Eastern front. D.A. Kudymov in *V Nebe Kitaya* pgs.119-122 says that PUMPUR help to set up his I-16 unit, the 9th Independent Fighter Squadron at Lanzhou China. In 1939, he directed test flights for the Aviation Industry and participated in the Russo-Finnish war. On 4 June 1940, he was promoted to General Lieutenant of Aviation. During 1940-41, he commanded the Moscow Military District and was elected as a Deputy of the Supreme Soviet. He was arrested on 31 May 1941 after a German Ju 52 had penetrated Soviet air space and flew to Moscow without having been noticed. Tried on 13 February 1942, and on 23 February he was shot. Awards were H.S.U., Order of Lenin twice and Order of the Red Banner. (*Solidarity*, Lacalle, RSA, Berch, Zakharov, Pritsker, *Vmeste*, Shukman, *Pravda*, Rumyantsev, "*Antonio*," *Geroi*, Kaminskii [1]Note, the Latvian National Encyclopedia lists his date of birth as 25 April 1905.)

PURTOV, Petr Andreevich, Sr.Lt., born 1906
He was a Zvena CO in the 5th IAE 36th IAB Kiev Mil. Dist. In Spain he was an I-15 Pilot in RYCHAGOV's Esc. He arrived on 20 October and was KIA over Madrid on 13 November 1936 in an air combat with Fiats. He is said to have shot one down before he was himself hit. DEMENCHUK in *Vmeste* says he was a Patrulla leader. He is listed as having one aircraft to his credit. Awarded the Order of the Red Banner posthumously on 2 January 1937. (*Pravda*, *MY*/Berch, Zakharov, *Icare 130* spells it POURTOV, *Vmeste*, Lukes, Kaminskii, Logoluso, *Los Rusos* give 13 December as date of death. Note! For some strange reason Abrosov who gives his initials as P.A. on p.28, later on p.341 gives his name as Aleksei Titovich, and the revised edition has not corrected it.)

PUSHKAREV, Fedor S., Lt., born 1908
SB pilot according to POLUSHKO in *Vmeste, Los Rusos* list as Pilot "Grupo Pedro," served from 31 May 1937 to 28 January 1938. Awarded the Red Banner twice, 3 November 1937 and 2 March 1938. (Shingarev, *Vmeste, Los Rusos, Pravda*)

PUTIVKO, Pavel Il'ich "Pasha," Lt., born 1911
I-16 pilot in the 40th IAE 83rd IAB Byelorussian Mil. Dist. In Spain he was a member of KOLESNIKOV's 1st I-16 Escuadrilla from October 1936 to 27 May 1937. He was badly wounded on 25 March 1937 during a Nationalist attack on Alcala de Henares. His aircraft was hit by fragments of an exploding bomb just as he was taking off and the plane was flipped over by the explosion of the bomb. The Esc. Engineer SUKHORUKOV was the first on the scene and helped to get him out. After leaving the hospital, he returned home. KRAVCHENKO in *Vmeste* p.45 says he along with CHERNYKH were Patrulla leaders in (TARKHOV-KOLESNIKOV) I-16 Esc., KTO lists him as being in the 1st Esc. I-16 December 1936 and that he rammed a fascist Aircraft. Flew approximately 150 missions in Spain, had three personal kills plus one in pair and one in group. Polak says on p.6 that PUTIVKO performed the first taran over Madrid. Awarded the Red Banner twice, 2 January and 17 July 1937. In 1938 he became CO of the 21st IAP and later in 1939 attended the Zhukovskii Flying School. After he finished the training course, he was appointed CO of the 31st IAP 8th ShAD. He was wounded sometime in late 1941 or early 1942 and went to the hospital. After his release he became deputy CO of the 10th Training Regiment. Died along with a Battalion CO on 9 July 1942, when he experienced a problem with his UT-2 Trainer and crashed in the village of Rudnia. (Kaminskii, *Vmeste*, Zakharov, Pritsker, Rumyantsev "*Antonio*," *Los Rusos, Pravda*)

PUZEIKIN, Vladimir Vasil'evich, Lt., born 1913
He was a Zvena CO in the 11th IAE 111th IAB Leningrad Mil. Dist. Began Spanish duty on 3 January 1937, shipping out with a group of Leningraders and returning on 7 September 1937. In the account of his experiences in Spain in Pritaker, he says he flew to Cartagena in a Lockheed with "Rosen" or "Rose-marie" (Rosmarin, an American flying for the Republic). He flew in OSADCHII's I-15 Escuadrilla in ZAKHAROV's patrulla. The American pilot Albert "Ajax" Baumler was also attached to this escuadrilla. (see also listing for VLADIMIR.) Switched to I-16s in April 1937 with KOLESNIKOV's Esc. after ZAKHAROV left Spain. Flew many missions and claimed two aircraft. Awarded the Red Banner twice, 27 June and 11 November 1937. Before the start of WWII he commanded the 2nd IAP and then became Flight Inspector of the 38th IAD.

In the fall of 1941 he was appointed CO of the 127th Warsaw Red Banner IAP. Awarded the Order of Lenin on 28 February 1942. Retired as a General Major, and passed away 3 September 1986. (RSA, Logoluso, Zakharov, Pritsker, *My* (1986), Abrosov, Kaminskii, *Pravda*, Baumler)

PYALISOV, Aleksandr P., Lt., born 1908
SB Radio/gunner in Spain from 15 June 1937 to 28 January 1938. Awarded the Red Banner twice, 28 October 1937 and 2 March 1938. (*Pravda, Los Rusos* spell it PIALISOV)

PYATIN, Pavel Epifanovich, Sr.Lt., born 1910
Before Spain he was a Zvena CO in the 57th IAE 142nd IAB Byelorussian Mil. Dist. I-16 Fighter pilot and patrulla CO in Spain from 28 April to 13 August 1938. Flew eighty missions and claimed two Fiats personal plus two Bf 109s in group. Awarded the Red Banner 22 February 1939. In 1940 he became deputy CO of the 31st IAP and then later CO of an Eskadril'ya in the 162nd IAP. Died in August 1941. (Abrosov, *Los Rusos* where it is spelled PIATIN, Kaminskii, *Pravda*)

"RAMON" Capt. (Sergei DENISOV)
I-16 detachment Commander at Guadalajara in 1937. (Tinker)

RATGAUZ, Leonid G., born 1903
Doctor attached to the Air Group. In Spain from 15 May 1937 to 4 April 1938. Awarded the Red Banner on 3 November 1937. Smirnov says he came to his airfield with a medical commission and caused problems regarding the pilots needing a long rest. (Gusev, Berch, *Los Rusos, Pravda*, Smirnov)

RAZHEV, Aleksandr M.
Worker from Aircraft Factory #21 assembling/repairing I-16 aircraft. In Spain from October 1936 to 8 May 1937. Awarded the Red Star 2 January 1937. (*Pravda, Los Rusos*)

REBROV, Nikolai K., born 1906
Worker from Aircraft Factory #22 assembling SB aircraft. In Spain from October to 12 December 1936. Awarded the Red Star 2 January 1937. (*Pravda, Los Rusos*)

REIZAREV, Aleksei
Los Rusos lists as Engineer with 1st Chatos. No dates given, but could well be RYTSAREV below. (*Los Rusos*)

REPIN, Aleksandr Konstantinovich
Aviation Engineer with the Air Group, in Spain from 21 May 1937 until 25 February 1938. He was replaced by PRACHIK (but see listing for PRACHIK). Awarded the Red Banner of Labor on 2 March 1938 and also the Red Star 3 November 1937. During WWII, he was head of Engineering-Technical Service under Novikov. (RSA, Shingarev, *Vmeste*, Semenov "*Parol*," Boyd, *Los Rusos, Pravda*)

REPNIKOV, Grigorii, NCO, born 1907
Los Rusos list as I-15 pilot KIA on 16 March 1937, saying "Murió en Guadalajara, su avion cayó envuelto en llamas." But a check of the records shows that only one I-15 pilot REUTOV was lost that day. Dates of service were 1 March to 16 March 1937. (*Los Rusos, Pravda* lists a REPNIKOV, G.S. as being awarded the Red Star on 2 January 1937, but unknown if with Air Group.)

RESHETNIAK, Evlampi, NCO, born 1913
Radio/Gunner SB, in Spain from 26 March to 3 September 1938. Awarded the Red Banner. (*Los Rusos*)

RESHETNIKOV, Vasilii Ivanovich, Lt., born 1912
Pilot SB, arrived in Spain 26 March and left 13 September 1938. Awarded the Red Banner 22 February 1939. (Semenov "*Parol*," *Pravda, Los Rusos* lists dates of service as 26 March to 13 March 1938 (?))

REUTOV, German Nikolaevich, Lt., born 1907
Pilot in the 120th IAE Transcaucas Mil. Dist. I-15 Fighter pilot, arrived 1 March and was KIA 16 March 1937 in combat with Fiat CR 32s. (Abrosov, airaces.narod.ru, Kaminskii)

RODIN, Andrei Khrisanfovich, NCO, born 1912
SB Radio/Gunner, departed for Spain on 28 June and returned on 4 October 1938. Awarded the Red Banner 22 February 1939. (Semenov "*Parol*," *Los Rusos, Pravda*)

RODIN, Fedor Vasil'evich, Maj., born 12 November 1902
Joined the Red Army in 1926. CO of the 57th IAE 142nd IAB Byelorussian Mil. Dist. In Spain from 26 March and returned to USSR on 4 October 1938. CO of the 2nd Escuadrilla de Moscas. Wounded in air combat in early June 1938 and went to hospital to recuperate. The original members of his Escuadrilla returned home in August, but RODIN remained to help the group. He had flown seventy combat missions and claimed three aircraft, one Bf 109 and two CR 32s. TUROV in *Vmeste* says, "We learned in particular about the terse fighting work of the two scanty groups of Soviet Volunteer Pilots under Commanders RODIN and GLUSHENKOV, which acting in conjunction with Spanish Escuadrillas every day endured severe and unequal battles." Awarded the Red Banner on 22 February 1939. In 1939 he was the CO of the 60th IAB Transcaucauas Mil. Dist. In September 1941 he was on the staff of the 187th IAP and in December became its CO. In 1942 he was made CO of the 22nd ZAP. Kaminskii gives date of death as 23 March 1994, but a web site on his life by his daughter lists the date of his passing as 17 October 1971. (*Vmeste* 242 and 264, Semenov "*Parol*," Semenov *Tov*. Abrosov, Kaminskii, airaces.narod.ru, *Pravda*, *Los Rusos* lists as born 1906 and that he left Spain 15 August 1938. (www.Kr-eho.info/index.php?name=News&op=article&sid=2697)

RODIONOV, Nikolai Ivanovich, NCO, born 1913
Radio/gunner SB, served from 30 May until 15 November 1938. Awarded the Red Banner 22 February 1939. (Berch, Semenov "*Parol*," *Los Rusos, Pravda*)

ROGOV, Vasilii M., born 1913
Los Rusos list as a Radio/Gunner in Spain from May until 7 September 1937. But I could only find this name in *Pravda* listed as a Technician, awarded the Red Banner 21 June 1937. (*Pravda, Los Rusos*)

ROMANOV, Aleksandr Georgievich, Lt., born 25 August 1912
Attended flying school before joining the Army in 1932. Graduated Military Pilot School in 1933. Was a pilot Inspector in the 35th IAE 56th IAB Kiev Mil. Dist. Volunteered for Spanish duty in 1938 and arrived in Spain on 26 March 1938. A fighter pilot with the rank of Lt, he was a member of 2nd Moscas under RODIN. During an air combat with seven Bf 109s on 7 June 1938, he claimed one. Killed on 21 June 1938 in an aircraft accident at Casinos Aerodrome, he crashed while testing the flaps on an I-16[1] (another bad wing problem?). Buried in Spain and was named H.S.U. on 14 November 1938. Claimed three aircraft, one Fiat, one Ju 52 and one Bf 109. Called an "Ace" by Tarazona. Haycraft lists as having five kills. Sirvent says he was in the 5th Esc., but I think he is confused with person listed below. (Tarazona, Salas, Ha 24, Semenov "*Parol*," Berch, Sirvent, *Geroi*, Abrosov, *Pravda*, Kaminskii claims he was an Escuadrilla CO, doubtful, *Los Rusos* list date of death as 2 June as does the 1991 list of Soviet dead. [1]Abrosov says he was testing the engine.)

ROMANOV, Iosif A., born 1913
Aviation mechanic, served in Spain from November 1936 to 27 August 1937. Awarded the Red Star 2 January 1937. (*Pravda, Los Rusos*)

ROMANOV, Matvei Dmitrievich, Capt., born 1908
Joined Red Army in1927. Before going to Spain he was a Captain in command of a Detachment in the 61st IAE Byelorussian Mil. Dist. Fighter pilot in Spain, he flew both the I-16 and I-15, serving from 14 June to 27 August 1937. Flew five combat missions, but he had

two nervous breakdowns and his health deteriorated, so he was sent home early. After Spain, he became a pilot instructor at a flying school. KIA during WWII, shot down on 4 April 1942 while flying a U-2. (Abrosov, Kaminskii, *Los Rusos*)

ROMANOV, Nikolai Alekdeevich, Sr.Lt., born 1908
Joined the Red Army in 1930. In 1936 was a Zvena CO at the 8th Odessa Air warfare school Kiev Mil. Dist. In Spain he served from 10 June to 5 September 1938. He was an I-16 Pilot in GRITSEVETS's 5th Moscas, he had also flown in GLUSHENKOV's escuadrilla before. He was in same patrulla as KHOTELEV and FILIPPCHENKO during Ebro fighting. Flew twelve missions and fought in three air combats, claimed two Bf 109s. During an air Battle on 19 July, he shot down a Bf 109, but was wounded and hospitalized. Following release from the hospital he returned to the USSR. Awarded the Red Banner twice, 14 November 1938 and 22 February 1939. During early WWII, he was commander of an IAP. On 18 October 1941 he failed to return from a mission. (Semenov *Tov.*, *Vmeste*, airaces.narod.ru, *Los Rusos*, Kaminskii, *Pravda*)

ROMANOV, Nikolai Nikolaevich, Lt., born 1915
Joined Red Army in 1934. Pilot in the 57th IAE 142nd IAB Byelorussian Mil. Dist. Served in Spain from 26 March until 18 May 1938. Refused to fly at the front, so sent home early. (Abrosov, airaces.narod.ru, *Los Rusos*)

ROMANOV, Sergei Petrovich, Lt., born 1908
SB pilot, lost in attack on Talavera on 13 November 1936, when his aircraft was brought down by AAA. He was twenty-three years old at the time. Awarded the Red Banner on 2 January 1937. (*Vmeste, Pravda*, Lukes, Abrosov, *Los Rusos*)

ROMASHEV, Llarion S., born 1908
Aviation Technician served from October 1936 to 3 June 1937. Awarded the Red Star 2 January 1937. (*Pravda, Los Rusos* spell it ROMASHOV)

ROSHCHIN, Ivan Vasil'evich, born 1909
SB navigator killed in collision 12 November 1936 between two SBs flown by FEDOROV and BAZHENOV. Awarded the Red Banner 2 January 1937. *Los Rusos* list as pilot. (Abrosov, *Los Rusos, Pravda*)

RUDAKOV, Aleksandr Vasil'evich, Lt., born 1910
Radio/gunner on SB, in Spain 14 December 1937 to 13 July 1938. Awarded the Red Banner 14 November 1938. (Semenov "*Parol*," Berch, *Los Rusos, Pravda*)

RUDENKO, Nikolai Ivanovich, Lt., born 1907
In Red Army in 1929. Before going to Spain, he was a Zvena CO in the 109th IAE 36th IAB Kiev Mil. Dist. An I-15 Fighter pilot, he departed for Spain on 20 August and flew in the 1st Esc. de Chatos. Died in an aircraft accident at Bujaraloz aerodrome on 9 September 1937. Awarded the Red Banner on 2 March 1938. (Berch, Abrosov, *Pravda*, airaces.narod.ru, Kaminskii, *Los Rusos* list date of death as 8 September)

RUSAK, Leonid Danilovich, Lt., born 1910
Joined the Red Army in 1931. Was CO of a Zvena in the 120th IAE Transcaucasian Mil. Dist. Served in Spain from 14 January to 27 August 1937. A fighter pilot and patrulla CO, he was a member of the 1st esc. Chatos. Injured on 14 June 1937, in a parachute jump from his shot-up I-15 aircraft during battle of Brunete. Returned home after release from the hospital. Awarded the Red Banner twice, 27 June 1937 and 2 March 1938. Participated in WWII, and passed away 6 June 1991. (Smirnov, Pritsker, Lukes, *Pravda*, airaces.narod.ru, *Los Rusos*, Kaminskii, *Icare 130* spells ROUSSAK)

RYABCHENKO, Tikor L., Capt., born 1900
Bomber pilot in Spain from October 1936 to 27 August 1937. Awarded the Red Banner 2 January 1937. (*Los Rusos, Pravda*)

RYABOV, Konstantin Aleksandrovich, born 1900.
Before going to Spain he had been on the Staff of the 107th IAE 83rd IAB Byelorussian Mil. Dist. In Spain from October 1936 until 2 July 1937, he was Chief of Staff of TARKHOV's Escuadrilla. *Pravda* 3 January 1937 says Commissar, and awarded the Red Banner 2 January 1937. At the start of WWII, he was the Battalion Commissar of the 4th ShAP. (Rumyanstev "*Antonio*," *Pravda*, Lukes, Abrosov, Kaminskii)

RYAZANOV, Andrei Matveevich, Lt., born 1906

Pilot in the 36th IAB Kiev Mil. Dist. An I-16 pilot, he served in Spain from 20 August 1937 until 15 April 1938. Flew 100 combat missions and had one Fiat to his credit. Awarded the Order of Lenin on 14 November 1938 and Red Banner 2 March 1938. After Spain he became the CO of an Eskadril'ya in the 43rd IAP Kiev Mil. Dist. From the start of WWII until June 1942 he was the CO of the 519th IAP and from 9 June to 5 July was CO of the 268 IAD. Then from July 1942 to July 1943 he was CO of the 282nd IAD and fought at Stalingrad. In February 1944 he was appointed CO of the 193rd IAD and died in a plane crash on 29 May 1944. (airaces.narod.ru, Semenov "*Parol*," *Los Rusos*, Gusev pgs.152, 239 where his first name is said to be Aleksandr, Berch, Kaminskii, *Pravda*)

RYAZANOV, Grigorii E., born 1901

Master of armaments from Aircraft Factory #1 assembling I-15 and SSS aircraft. Served from October 1936 to 7 April 1937. Awarded the Red Star 2 January 1937. (*Los Rusos, Pravda*)

RYBKIN, Leonid Grigor'evich, Lt., born 1912

Pilot in the 119th IAE 95th IAB Transcaucasian Mil. Dist. Served in Spain from 31 May until 18 October 1937. He was an I-15 Patrulla leader in EREMENKO's 1st. Esc. at El Soto. Whitey Dahl was member of his Patrulla. Later he was member of the Night fighter detachment, which was formed inside EREMENKO's Esc. in July 1937 along with YAKUSHIN. Aka: "Blanco." Kaminskii says he also flew the I-16. Claimed three aircraft, one personal and two in pair. Awarded the Order of Lenin on 2 March 1938 and Red Banner 28 October 1937. Fought in China, and was recalled in May 1938 to become Air Commander ODVA. Fought in the Russo-Finnish Winter War. Just before WWII he was Commander of the 34th IAP. Then from 26 November 1941 until 29 April 1942 he commanded the 148th IAD PVO and in 1943 was head of the 105th IAD-PVO. In July 1943 this was included into the 10th Rostovckii IAK PVO and in September 1944 he became CO of the 10th IAK. Awarded many medals for service during the war, passed away in October 1992. (Kaminskii, *Bajo la B.*, Gusev 69, Salas, Shingarev, Berch, Pritsker, Boyd, Lukes, *Pravda, Los Rusos* give the sevice dates as 31 July to 18 October 1937.)

RYBNIKOV, Vyacheslav I., born 1914

Engineer with the Air Group, from 14 January to 7 September 1937. Awarded Red Star 21 June 1937. Returned home due to illness. (*Pravda, Los Rusos* spell it RIBNIKOV)

RYCHAGOV, Pavel Vasil'evich, Sr.Lt., born 2 January 1911

Joined the Soviet Army in 1928. Finished Military Theory School VVS in Leningrad in 1930. Attended Borisoglebsk Flight School in 1931. He was commander of a Zvena in the 109th IAE 36th IAB Kiev Mil. Dist. before going to Spain and had been awarded the Order of Lenin on 25 May 1936. Volunteered for service in Spain in 1936. He was the commanding officer (Sr.Lt.) of an I-15 Escuadrilla from 20 October 1936 to 6 February 1937, nom de guerre "Pablo Palancar." He and his personnel traveled to Spain along with the unit's aircraft on the Soviet ship *Karl Lepin* in October 1936. Command of this unit was at the end of January 1937 turned over to A. OSADCHII. He flew eighty combat missions and is credited with shooting down six aircraft, five fighters and one bomber.[1] He was shot down on the afternoon of 15 November 1936 over Madrid while attacking a Ju 52. He was able to parachute on to the Castellana. Awarded the title of H.S.U. on 31 December 1936. In 1937-38, he was Commander of the Soviet Air Group in China. Awarded the Red Banner on 8 March 1938. In 1938, he commanded VVS and the allied Soviet Maritime Group Far East Front plus 1st Red Army. Participated in the Air and Ground operations against the Japanese at Lake Khasan in 1938, and then in the Russo-Finnish War 1939-40. In 1940, as a twenty-nine-year-old Lt.Gen. Rychagov was substituted for the 1st Deputy Chief VVS Soviet Army. Boyd says he replaced SMUSHKEVICH (due to failures by the Air Force in the war with Finland) in April 1940 as GU-VVS (Head of Directorate of the Soviet Air Force). In February 1941, he was Chief People's Commissar for Defense USSR. Voted in as a Deputy to the Supreme Soviet. Later according to Shukman, during the first days of the war, he had some angry words with Stalin. He was arrested on 24 June and later shot, along with his wife, on 28 October 1941. He was later rehabilitated on 23 July 1954. Awards were the Order of Lenin twice

Order of the Red Banner three times. (Berch, Koltsov 234, Lacalle, Gusev 91, *Pravda*, Andreev, RSA, Howson 193, Ha 24, Zakharov, *Vmeste*, Pritsker, Shukman 160-1, Rumyantsev "*Antonio*," Boyd. Lacalle says he left Spain around 15 December 1936 and then "JOSE" Ivan KOPETS took over command. But OSADCHII says RYCHAGOV was still CO. when he arrived in January. Boyd claims he was arrested before the German invasion. [1]Sliusarev in *Po Dorogam Kitaia* (Chudodeev Ed.) p.104 says RYCHAGOV downed twenty Fascist Aircraft in Spain (but fourteen were shared credits) also says he received a second Gold Star for his service in China, but I can only find one H.S.U.)

RYTSAREV, Aleksandr I., born 29 July 1910
Mechanic/technician on I-15s. In Spain from 14 January until 18 October 1937. Gagin says he was Sr. Technician for SEROV's Esc., while Shingarev says he was Chief of Staff for Grupo 26 Chatos. Awarded the Red Star 21 June 1937. (Meroño, *Bajo la B.*, Berch, Shingarev, Gagin, *Los Rusos*, Kaminskii, *Pravda*)

SADOVOI, Aleksei A., Lt., born 1907
Rasante SSS Pilot, served from October 1936 to 2 July 1937. Awarded the Red Banner twice, 2 January and 22 October 1937. (*Pravda, Los Rusos*, Logoluso, *Icare 130*)

SAFONOV, Nikolai Nikitovich, Lt., born 1913
He was a Zvena CO in the 12th IAE 111th IAB Leningrad Mil. Dist. As an I-16 pilot he arrived in Spain on 31 May 1937. There he was a patrulla CO in the 2nd Escuadrilla under PLESHCHENKO. He was KIA on 17 July 1937 during the Brunete operations. After helping to down two Bf 109s in pair with PLESHCHENKO, his aircraft was hit and caught fire. He was unable to bail out. The only I-16 brought down that day by the L.C. was by Hillmann of 2.J/88. Awarded the Red Banner twice, 17 July 1937 and 2 March 1938 (although both Abrosov and Kaminskii list these dates, I could not find them in the *Pravda* lists for those days. There is only a listing for N.P. SAFONOV on 2 March 1938). (Berch, Pritsker 202, Abrosov, Kaminskii, *Los Rusos* say he died when he bailed out over Navalcarnero)

SAFONOV, Petr Andreevich, Sr.Lt., born 1905
SB Navigator, arrived 28 June and left 15 November 1938. Awarded the Red Banner on 22 February 1939. (Semenov "*Parol*," *Pravda, Los Rusos* mistakenly give end date as 1939)

SAKHRANOV, Vasilii Titovich, Lt., born 10 March 1906
From 1934 he was a test pilot in the NII Moscow Mil. Dist. In Spain he was an I-15 pilot in TURZHANSKII's Esc. on the Basque front. Served from 1 November 1936 to 8 May 1937. Awarded the Order of Red Banner on 2 January 1937. After Spain, he was a test pilot at Factory #156 Moscow. In March 1941 he went to Factory #21 in Gorky, to test the LAGG-3, and when WWII began he was moved to Factory #1 Moscow to test fly the MiG-3 and Il-2 Sturmovik. On the night of 31 July after testing five Il-2 in very bad flying weather, the sixth one developed a problem and crashed, killing SAKHRANOV. (Kaminskii, *Pravda*, Lukes, Abrosov, *Los Rusos* spell name SAKHANOV)

SAKLAKOV, Aleksandr S., born 1907
Aviation Technician in Spain from October 1936 to 7 April 1937. Awarded the Red star 2 January 1937 and the Red Banner. (*Pravda, Los Rusos*)

SAL'NIKOV, Fedor Alekseevich, Maj., born 1902
Before Spain he had been CO of an IAE in the 56th IAB, then became CO of the 36th IAB Kiev Mil. Dist. In Spain from October 1936, he was put in charge of assembly, test flying planes and training Spaniards. Killed in an aviation accident on 21 January 1937, the starboard upper wing came off the I-15 SN 9958 he was test flying and the plane crashed into the ground. *Los Rusos* list as Fighter Group CO. Awarded the Red Banner 21 June 1937. (Abrosov, *Los Rusos*, Kaminskii, *Pravda*)

SAMSONOV, Fedor Aleksandrovich, Lt., born 1910
Pilot in the 107th IAE 83rd IAB Byelorussian Mil. Dist. He flew an I-16 and served in Spain from 26 March to 28 June 1938. On 18 May 1938 during an air combat his aircraft ran low on fuel and he crashed while making an emergency landing. He was injured and was taken to hospital, after his release he went home. Awarded the Red Banner on 22 February 1939. After Spain he was a senior pilot in the 49th IAP and participated in the Russo-Finnish War. KIA 8 December 1939 when his aircraft was shot down by a Finnish fighter. His resting place is unknown. (Kaminskii, Semenov "*Parol*," Abrosov, *Los Rusos, Pravda*)

SAMSONOV, Ivan Dmitrievich, Lt., born 1 February 1908
Pilot in the 5th IAE 36th IAB Kiev Mil. Dist. He served in Spain from 20 October 1936 until 29 September 1937. Initially he was in an I-15 Esc. and flew some combat missions. Later developed health problems and was relieved of flight duty. He was sent to Madrid where he acted as an observer in the Telefonica, advising of enemy air operations. Awarded the Order of the Red Banner 2 January 1937. After Spain, he became CO of an Eskadril'ya in the 164th IAP and just after WWII began he became an Eskadril'ya CO in the 177th IAP Moscow. Shot down two enemy aircraft, killed in an aircraft crash on 8 December 1941. (Kaminskii, *Pravda, Vmeste*, Lukes, *Icare 130*, Zakharov)

SAPOZHNIKOV, Samuil Grigorevich
Air Force Advisor in Spain from 12 January 1938 and returned home on 27 February 1939. Awarded the Red Banner 14 November 1938. (Semenov "*Parol*," Berch, *Pravda, Los Rusos* list as a Naval Lt.)

SAPRONOV, Mikhail Semenovich, born 1915
Before Spain he was a Zvena CO in the 4th IAE 56th IAB Kiev Mil. Dist. Arrived in Spain on 10 June 1938 and returned to the USSR on 4 October 1938. He was an I-16 Pilot in the 2nd Moscas under SEMENKO. He flew twelve combat missions and fought two air battles, claiming one Bf 109 on 14 August 1938 in pair with GRITSEVETS. In September he became ill and was sent home. Awarded the Red Banner on 22 February 1939. Partipated in WWII as a Flight Inspector in the Air Forces, in 1943 he became the senior inspector for the Central administrative board of combat training of frontline aircraft. In March 1943 he was at the Kuban as part of the 3rd IAK. After the war, he worked with polar aircraft. Retired with the rank of Colonel. As of 1976 he lived in Moscow. (Kaminskii, Semenov *Tov.*, Meroño, Vmeste, *Los Rusos, Pravda*, Abrosov lists middle nane as Stepanovich.)

SAVILOV, Vasilii F., Lt., born 1907
Observer with an SSS Esc., in Spain from October 1936 to 30 June 1937. Awarded the Red Banner 2 January 1937. (*Los Rusos, Pravda*)

SAVKIN, Viktor Sergeevich, Lt., born 1912
Pilot SB, arrived 30 May and returned 15 November 1938. Awarded the Red Banner on 22 February 1939. (Semenov "*Parol*," Berch, *Los Rusos, Pravda*)

SAZONOV, Petr V., Lt., born 1906
Pilot SSS, served from October 1936 to 2 July 1937. Awarded the Red Banner 2 January 1937. (*Los Rusos, Pravda*)

SBYTOV, G.A., Lt.
SB Navigator, in Spain from 14 June 1937 to 28 January 1938. Awarded the Red Banner twice, 3 November 1937 and 2 March 1938. (*Solidarity, Pravda*)

SCHACHT, Ernst Heinrich, Major, born 14 April 1904
Born in Basel, Switzerland, in 1904, he emigrated to the USSR in 1922. Joined the Army in 1923 and in 1924, graduated from Military Pilots School. From 1926 to December 1931, he was a Zvena CO in the 37th BAE 35th BAB in Central Asia. From December 1931 he was CO of a Special Purpose Escuadrilla based at Moscow's Central Airport. Later he attended the Air War Academy. Went to Spain as a bomber pilot with the 1st Escuadrilla Internacional in September 1936 and then transferred to the new 12th Grupo SBs becoming Commander of 1st Escuadrilla de Kats from October 1936 until he left 11 February 1937. From June 1937 he was the head of the High Flight School at Lipetsk. In April 1940 he became CO of the 167th Reserve Aviation Regiment at Ryazan, and in November 1940 became Deputy CO of the VVS School at Orel. Caught up in Stalin's purge of the Military, he was arrested on 30 May 1941 on charges of being a German spy and shot on 23 February 1942 (*Geroi* mistakenly says died in 1941). He had been awarded the title of H.S.U. on 31 December 1936. Shukman lists

his name as SHAKHT, says was thirty-seven-year-old Major General. Also says he was a German born in Bern Switzerland in 1904. Awards were HSU, Order of Lenin twice, Order of the Red Banner. (Semenov "*Parol*," Berch, RSA, Laureau, Salas, *Vmeste*, Pritsker, *Geroi*, Suvenirov, *Pravda*, Künzi, Boyd who mistakenly says was a "Fighter Ace"!)

SCHILOFF, Feodor Alexandrovich

Observer on SB-2, captured in 1938. Age thirty. See SHUMILOV. (*Spain magazine* 8/15/1938)

SCHMIDR, Vasili

Lt. Pilot SB in 1937. (Gringoire via Logoluso, codename?)

SEDOV

SB radio/gunner, October 1936 1st Esc. (*Bajo la B*)

SELIVERSTOV, A.A.

Photo in *Solidarnost* p.12, Semenov, but see SIL'VERSTOV, A.A.

SEMENENKO, Ivan D., born 1909

Was Head Engineer for the SB Group (according to Bibikov p.17 in *Vmeste*). Awarded the Red Star on 2 January 1937. *Los Rusos* list as Aviation Technician. In Spain from October 1936 to 13 August 1937. (*Vmeste, Pravda, Los Rusos*)

SEMENETS, Sidor Mefod'evich, Lt., born 1913

Navigator of SB patrulla, served from 14 December 1937 to 21 July 1938. Awarded the Red Banner on 14 November 1938. (Berch, Semenov "*Parol*," *Los Rusos, Pravda*)

SEMENKO, Viktor Mikhailovich, Lt., born 1912

Before Spain he was the assistant CO of the 4th IAE 56th IAB Kiev Mil. Dist. He arrived on 10 June 1938 along with thirty-three other fighter pilots. He was a patrulla leader in NEDELIN's 2nd Moscas during July 1938. Then took over command of the 2nd Escuadrilla, with GRITSEVETS as "Group" CO. at end of July after NEDELIN was injured. Returned home on 26 October 1938, after having flown sixty-five missions and fought in thirty air combats. Listed as having three aircraft to his credit. Awarded the Order of Lenin on 22 February 1939 and Order of Red Banner. Participated in WWII and in May 1943 he became the CO of the 896th IAP. Retired in 1967 and lived in Gatchina in the Leningrad region. (Kaminskii, Semenov *Tov*., Meroño, *Vmeste*, airaces.narod.ru, *Pravda*)

SEMENOV, Aleksandr. Fedorovich, Lt., born 7 April 1912

Entered the Army in 1933. Attended the Kharkov Military Air School. In 1936 he was a pilot in the 107th IAE 83rd IAB Byelorussian Mil. Dist. Volunteered for Spanish duty, shipping out on 14 December 1937 and returned on 15 August 1938. He served in GUSEV's 6th Mosca (I-16) Escuadrilla in PANFILOV's patrulla on the Teruel front. Injured on 11 January 1938[1] when his aircraft CM-153 lost a wheel on takeoff and crashed into the trees, flipped over destroying the Aircraft. After release from the Hospital he went home. At the time of his accident, Ivan DEVOTCHENKO was acting as temporary CO of the Fighter Group as GUSEV was in rehabilitation. In Spain he flew fifteen sorties and claimed one kill plus three shares. Awarded the Red Banner on 14 November 1938. During the Russo-Finnish Winter War, he commanded the 3rd IAE 7th IAP flying I-153s. Kapitan SEMENOV flew seventy-five sorties and fought in five air combats, claiming four kills. Awarded the Red Banner on 15 January 1940 and on 21 March 1940, he was awarded the H.S.U. Just after the German attack in June 1941, he was posted to the 122nd IAP flying MiG-3s. In September 1941 he joined the Staff of the 180th IAP commanded by his friend and ex-"Spaniard" Ivan KLUSOVICH. In the summer of 1942, as a major he served as CO of the 434th IAP (later 32nd Guards IAP), which was flying on the Stalingrad front. In February 1943 he left the 434th, and Seidl says he was put in charge of the "badly battered" 286th IAD, which he was finally able to get back in to shape. In February 1944 he went back to the 434th (now listed as the 32nd GIAP), but in May as a Lt. Colonel again left to be deputy CO. of the 3rd GIAD. Later in October he became CO. of the 322nd IAD on the 1st Ukrainian front and served in this Division until the end of the war. During the GPW, he had flown 240 sorties and participated in sixty-five air combats, claiming fifteen enemy aircraft plus twelve more as shared. Retired in 1970 as a Lt. General, he lived in Moscow and died on 13 February 1979. Awards were H.S.U., Order of Lenin (twice), Order of the Red Banner (four times), Order of Kutuzov 2nd. Cl., OPW 1st Cl., and Order of the Red Star. (Semenov "*Parol*," Gusev, polak, Seidl, *Geroi, Pravda*, Semenov, A.F., [1]while Russian sources list the 11th, Salas in Diario lists the 12th.)

SEMENOV, E.F., born 1910

Worker from Aircraft Factory #22 assembling SB aircraft. In Spain October to 12 December 1936. Awarded the Red Star 2 January 1937. (*Pravda, Los Rusos* list as Igor and give end date as 1937)

SEMENOV, Nikolai Vasil'evich, Sr.Lt., born 1906

Zvena CO in the 56th IAB Kiev Mil. Dist. I-16 Fighter pilot, he arrived 26 March and returned on 3 September 1938. Both Abrosov and Kaminskii say he was a patrulla CO and later an Escuadrilla CO, while *Los Rusos* say was CO of a Grupo Especial. Flew ninety missions and fought in eighteen air combats with seven aircraft to his credit. Awarded the Order of Lenin 22 February 1939. In June 1941 he was deputy CO of the 17th IAP, and from June 1944 until the end of the war he was CO of the 165th IAP. Died in 1947 in an airplane crash. (Gusev, Semenov "*Parol*," Abrosov, *Los Rusos*, Kaminskii, *Pravda*)

SEMENOV, Pavel Timoteevich, Lt., born 1910

He was a pilot in the 5th IAE 36th IAB Kiev Mil. Dist. In Spain he became a member of TURZHANSKII's I-15 escuadrilla in the Basque country from 1 November 1936 to 30 January 1937. He was sent home early due to illness. Awarded the Red Banner on 2 January 1937. After Spain he became CO of a detachment in the 31st IAE Kiev Mil. Dist. In 1939 was CO of an Eskadril'ya. (*Pravda*, Abrosov, Kaminskii)

SEMENOV, Stepan Ivanovich, Lt., born 1909

A Zvena CO in the 121st IAE 95th IAB Transcaucasian Mil. Dist. In Spain he was an I-15 Fighter Pilot from 14 January to 2 July 1937, he was CO of a patrulla. Shot down seven aircraft (six personal and one in group). Awarded the Red Banner 17 July 1937. (Semenov "*Parol*," Abrosov, *Los Rusos*, Kaminskii, *Pravda*)

SEMENYUK, Ul'van Zinov'evich, Lt., born 1909

Pilot in the 107th IAE 83rd IAB Byelorussian Mil. Dist. An I-16 Fighter pilot in Spain in TARKHOV's Escuadrilla from October 1936 to 27 August 1937. Awarded the Red Banner 2 January 1937. (*Pravda*, Kaminskii, Abrosov lists award as 21 January, but I think it's a typo.)

SENATOROV, Aleksandr Sergeevich, Sr.Lt., born 8 October 1912

Joined the Army in 1930, and in 1932 attended the 8th Odessa Military Aviation School. From September 1932 he was a pilot and then CO of a Bomber Detachment in the Byelorussian Mil. Dist. In Spain he was first a Escuadrilla CO, then became commander of Grupo 12, SBs. Served from 31 May 1937 until 15 January 1938, at which time Grupo 12 was disbanded. He was the pilot of the SB, which led the I-16s under UKHOV to the North, and Shingarev says he also led Tarazona's group to Santander (but see POLUSHKO who says he was the navigator on the SMIRNOV/Tarazona flight). Other crewmembers were DUSHKIN navigator and MIREK radio/gunner for the UKHOV trip, and supposedly DUSHKIN and IVANOV Radio/gunner for SMIRNOV trip. Listed as having flown 100 sorties in Spain. Awarded the H.S.U. on 14 March 1938. In May 1938 he became assistant CO VVS Forces for the Independent Red Banner Army Far East. In September of that year he became assistant CO for the 1st Independent Red Banner Army. In 1939, he attended the Genshtaba Military Academy. In June 1940 he was appointed CO of VVS Forces with the 1st Independent Red Banner Army. In July 1942 he became CO of the 9th Air Army Far East, then in September 1944 was named assistant CO for training with the 16th Air Army with General rank, remaining there until the end of the war. In 1948, he again attended the Genshtaba Academy. He retired in 1963 as a Gen.Lt. and passed away on 24 January 1993.[1] Besides the HSU, other awards were Order of Lenin twice, Order of Red Banner twice (once 22 October 1937 for Spain), Order of Bogdan Khmel'nitskii 1cl., Order of Suvorov 2nd Cl., GPW 1st. Cl. and Order of Red Star twice. (RSA, Laureau, Boyd, *Solidarity*, Lario, Howson, Smirnov, *Vmeste*, Pritsker, Shingarev, *Geroi, Pravda* [1]warheroes.ru lists his date of death as 29 December 1992.)

SENYUKHIN, Filipp, born 1909

Aviation Technician, served from October 1936 to 27 September 1937. Awarded the Red Star 2 January 1937. (*Pravda, Los Rusos* spell it SEMIUJIN)

SEREBRYAKOV, Nikolai Gavrilovich, Lt., born 21 May 1913

In 1932 he joined the Red Army and attended the 2nd Borisogleb Military Flyers School. After he graduated he was appointed as CO of a ShAE in the 253rd ShAB. Went to Spain on 30 December 1937 and returned 21 July 1938; he was an SB pilot and participated in the attack on the Spanish ship *Baleares* on 6 March 1938. Also had taken part in the 28 January raid on Salamanca. On the return flight from this attack, he and his navigator ABRAMOV became lost and wound up running out of fuel and having to ditch the Aircraft in the Mediterranean off Valencia. During a mission on 26 May his aircraft was hit by AAA fire, but he was able to bring it back for a landing. LIPASHOV in *Vmeste* says he was Commander of an Escuadrilla from March 1938 on, taking over from the departing STETISHIN (STECHISHIN). Awarded the Red Banner 14 November 1938. Fought in the Winter War against Finland with an Eskadril'ya of the 5th SBAP (Fast Bomber Regiment) of the 14th Army. This Regiment is listed as flying 567 sorties bombing targets in the enemy's rear. Awarded the H.S.U. on 7 May 1940. In WWII, in 1943 he was CO of the 58th Red Banner BAP. Retired in 1973 and passed away 3 July 1988. Awards were Order of Lenin twice, Order of Aleksandr Nevski, GPW 1st Cl. twice, Red Star three times (one for Spain 22 February 1939) and Order of the Red Banner of Labor. (Berch, Semenov *"Parol,"* *Vmeste, Pravda, Geroi, Los Rusos* list birth date as 1918 and also give rank as Major.)

SERENKO, Aleksandr Vasil'evich, Lt./ Capt., born 1912

Fighter pilot in the 34th IAE 56th IAB Kiev Mil. Dist. In Spain from 13 June 1937 to 28 January 1938 flying the I-16. He flew 130 sorties and claimed four aircraft (one personal plus three in group). Awarded the Order of Lenin on 2 March 1938 and the Red Banner 28 October 1937. After returning home he became CO of an IAE in the 28th IAP. From the fall of 1941 to June 1942 he was CO of the 4th IAP flying MiG-3s and Hurricanes. From 1943 to June 1944 he was CO of the 234th IAP with LaGG-3s and P-40s and from June 1944 until the end of the war he commanded the 162nd IAP flying Yak-9s. During WWII he claimed six aircraft and one spotter balloon. (Abrosov, *Los Rusos*, Kaminskii, *Pravda*)

SERKOV, Saveli A., Lt., born 1909

SB Radio/Gunner in Spain from October 1936 untl 8 May 1937. Member of 1st Esc. Grupo 12. Awarded the Order of the Red Banner on 2 January 1937. (*Bajo la B.*, Lukes/*Pravda, Los Rusos*)

SEROV, Anatolii Konstantinovich, Sr.Lt. "Rodrigo Mateo,"[1] born 20 March 1910

Joined the army in 1929. Attended Orenburg Military Air College, from which he graduated on 17 December 1931. From May 1936 he was a test pilot in the NII VVS Moscow. In Spain from 14 June 1937 until 21 January 1938, he was a Patrulla leader in EREMENKO's 1st Escuadrilla de Chatos. Became a member of the night fighter detachment, which was formed inside of EREMENKO's Esc., where he became the second man to score a night kill in Spain. This unit had been formed during the battle of Brunete under the command of KUZNETSOV until 18 July when the latter was rotated hom. SEROV then took over command of the detachment. On the night of 27 July 1937, he scored the second night kill of the war, when he shot down a Ju 52. In early September, he assumed command of the Escuadrilla from EREMENKO, when the latter was appointed as Commander of Grupo 26. The Escuadrilla was at this time based at Bujaraloz. Some members of the Esc. were STEPANOV, SIUSIUKA'LOV, EVTIKHOV, KOTYKHOV plus those added at Los Alcazares were POPOV, KUSTOV and GOROKHOV. On 18 October 1937 SEROV was appointed as Commander of Grupo 26 when EREMENKO was made Soviet Commander of Fighter Grupos (Escuadra 11). Returned home at the end of December 1937. Credited by R and R (p.32) with sixteen kills, but Bodrikhin and other Soviets credit him with eight plus seven in-group. Awarded the H.S.U. and Order of Lenin on 2 March 1938. On his return home, he was, at twenty-nine years of age, appointed as Head of the Air Force Inspectorate with the rank of Kombrig. He had been a test pilot before going to Spain, and was

killed in an accident on 11 May 1939 during a long-distance flight. Also killed in this accident was the wife of OSIPENKO says YAKUSHIN in *Aeroplano 7* p.86. Awards were H.S.U., Order of Lenin, and Order of the Red Banner twice, on 31 July and 22 October 1937. (Hidalgo de Cisneros, *Bajo la B.*, Salas, Laureau, RSA, *Aeroplano 7* p.83-88, Ha 24, Berch, *Vmeste,* Shingarev, Boyd, *Pravda*, Chalaya (1940 and 1958), Polak. [1]For more information on this controversy over Noms de Guerre, see listing for YAKUSHIN. Shingarev also says his name was Rodrigo Mateo, but Lukes gives wrong one.)

SEROV, Yakov Petrovich, NCO, born 1913

SB navigator killed in a collision on 12 November 1936 of two SBs flown by FEDOROV and BAZHENOV. *Los Rusos* incorrectly list as radio/gunner. Awarded the Red Banner 2 January 1937. (*Pravda*, Abrosov, *Los Rusos*)

SHABANOV, Efim, born 1891

Fitter in a workshop (aviation), in Spain from 30 December 1937 to 25 April 1938. (*Los Rusos*)

SHAKHURIN, Viktor I., born 1910

Engineer in an aircraft repair workshop, served from October 1936 to 27 March 1937. Awarded the Red Banner 2 January 1937. (*Pravda, Los Rusos*)

SHALYGANOV, Sergei Vasil'evich, Lt., born 1913

Before leaving for Spain, he was a pilot in the 119th IAE 95th IAB Transcaucasian Mil. Dist. Served in Spain from 31 May to 27 August 1937. Wounded at Brunete on 7 July 1937[1] while escorting a group of RZs attacking Quijorna. The four Soviet I-15 fighter pilots (others were SEROV, YAKUSHIN, and KARPOV) were attacked by a large group of Fiats. SHALYGANOV shot down a Fiat, but was hit and forced down behind his own lines. KARPOV was killed. Sent home after he left the hospital. Awarded the Red Banner 28 October 1937. Fought in the Russo-Finnish Winter War in 1939 as commissar in the 44th IAP 54th IAB, awarded the Red Banner on 7 April 1940. At the start of WWII he was still with the 44th IAP, but in December 1941 became Commissar of the 105th IAD. After the war in 1945-48 was CO of the 786th IAP Moscow Mil. Dist. (Salas, *Bajo la B*, Shingarev, Pritsker, Abrosov, *Pravda, Los Rusos*, Kaminskii, [1]Abellan says it happened on 12 July, as does Lukes.)

SHANTSEV, Fedor D., born 1913

Aviation Technician, in Spain from October 1936 to 27 August 1937. Awarded the Red Star 2 January 1937. (*Pravda, Los Rusos*)

SHARANOV, Andrei Rodionovich

Lt. General of Aviation according to *Los Rusos*. (But see SHARAPOV below.)

SHARAPOV, Andrei Rodionovich "Col. Lopez," born 1896

Air Staff advisor to the Sp. Republic Vice Minister for National Defense. But *Los Rusos* say Advisor Estado Mayor Fuerza Aire Grupo de Bombarderos. In Spain from 10 October 1937 until 27 February 1939. On 17 July he wrote a report about the constant breaking of wings on the I-16 during landings. Awarded the Red Banner 2 March 1938. (Abrosov, Semenov "*Parol,*" *Solidarity, Los Rusos, Pravda* lists as a Colonel.)

SHARONOV, Boris Stepanovich, Sr.Lt., born 1906

Pilot SB in Spain from 28 June to 15 November 1938, CO of a patrulla. On 23 September his Aircraft (poss. BK 25) was one of six SBs being escorted by I-16s from the 2nd Esc. They were attacked by Bf 109s from 3. J/88. The MGs jammed on four of the SBs and several of the bombers were badly shot-up, but none were lost. SHARONOV was able to land at Reus. On 10 October 1938, his aircraft was again badly shot-up, with all the crewmembers wounded. He brought the plane with its bomb load still intact, back to his airfield, but as he attempted to land, it crashed and caught fire. Fortunately the bombs did not explode. Awarded the Red Banner on 22 February 1939. (Abrosov, Semenov "*Parol,*" *Los Rusos, Pravda*)

SHAROV, Ivan Nikolaevich, Lt., born 1909

Before Spain, he was a Zvena CO in the 40th IAE 83rd IAB Byelorussian Mil. Dist. In Spain from October 1936 until 26 July 1937as an I-16 Fighter pilot in TARKHOV/ KOLESNIKOVs Escuadrilla. Awarded the Red Banner twice, 2 January and 4 July 1937. After Spain, as assistant

CO of the 15th IAP he fought in the Winter War from 27 February to March 1940. On 12 March he landed his fighter plane behind enemy lines to rescue a downed Soviet pilot Lt. Mikhail Dobrov from the 38th IAP. Awarded his third Red Banner on 22 February 1941. In November 1941 he was CO of the 137th ShAD, but later in May 1942 he was made assistant CO of the 136th ShAD. In October 1942 he became CO of the 238th IAD and then in August 1943 was appointed as assistant CO of the 286th IAD. Later in October 1943 he became assistant CO of the 234th IAD. KIA 26 June 1944 in air combat near Rogachev, Gomel Byelorussia. (Kaminskii, Abrosov, *Los Rusos, Pravda*, airaces.narod.ru claims he was given the HSU, no record found.)

SHAROV, Vasilii Vasil'evich, Lt., born 23 December 1909

Joined the Army in 1929. Attended the Orenburg Military Aviation School 1930-32. In December 1933 was a pilot in the 20th LShAE at Konotop, Khar'kov Mil. Dist. In April 1936 he was a senior pilot in the 28th SBAE at Ovruch, Kiev Mil. Dist. Volunteered for Spanish duty, and was one of the first Soviets to go there, arriving in September (October) and returning on 12 December 1936. Initially he was a pilot in the 1st Internacional Escuadrilla flying a Potez 540 says DEMENCHUK in *MY*. He then joined the newly formed Grupo 12 flying SBs. Following a mission on 25 November 1936, he crashlanded his aircraft. The SB was wreaked, but the crew were said to have been uninjured, but it is possible that SHAROV was hurt, as his tour of duty ended on 12 December. Awarded the Red Banner on 2 January 1937. Upon his return home, he became a Zvena CO and then a Detachment CO in the 22nd SBAE at Uman. Participated in the re-taking of the Western Ukraine in September-October 1939 (eastern Poland). Fought in the Winter War from 27 January to 12 March 1940 as commander of the 2nd SBAE of the 48th SBAP (Fast Bomber Aviation Regiment) of the 18th SBAB 7th Air Army. His rank at the time was Captain, and he flew forty-six bombing missions. Awarded the H.S.U. on 21 March 1940. In WWII, with rank of Major he failed to return from a mission on 2 August 1941. His aircraft had crashed near the village of Shepetova. Also awarded the Order of Lenin. (*MY*, Berch, *Vmeste, Pravda,* Abrosov, proza.ru/avtor/sholal

SHAULOV, Ivan Galaktionovich, Lt., born 1911

A Zvena CO in the 56th IAB Kiev Mil. Dist., He departed for Spain on 10 June 1938. He was an I-16 pilot in the 2nd Escuadrilla de Moscas. While landing after a combat mission on 13 August, he crashed but was uninjured. He was KIA on 5 September 1938, in air combat over the Ebro; after possibly downing a He 111, his aircraft CM-205 was hit. He tried to make it back to his airfield, but over Gandesa his plane exploded in the air. His remains were never found. (Semenov *Tov.* Abrosov, Salas Diario, *Los Rusos* give date as 6 September as does Kaminskii and the 1991 list of Soviet dead.)

SHAUTSOV, Fedor, born 1913

Aviation Technician, served from 14 January to 29 September 1937. Awarded the Red Banner and Red Star. (*Los Rusos*)

SHESTAKOV, Lev L'vovich, Lt., born 28 December 1915

Joined the army in 1934, and attended the Voroshilovgrad military Flying School. In 1935 after graduating, he served in the 2nd IAE. In the summer of 1937 he was a pilot in the 36th IAB Kiev Mil. Dist. Departed for Spain on 20 August 1937 and returned home on 25 April 1938. He was at first an I-16 Pilot in the 1st escuadrilla de Moscas. In mid October when the 1st escuadrilla was changed to Spanish command, he along with the other Soviets of the Escuadrilla, were transferred to the 5th Escuadrilla, under the command of DEVOTCHENKO. In August 1937, he had gone to the aid of Platon SMOLYAKOV, second-in-command of GUSEV' 6th Esc. when he had been attacked by three Fiats. During the ensuing battle SHESTAKOV's aircraft received ten hits, two of which struck the armored plating of his seat back and one which went through his leather pant leg. In the end he and SMOLYAKOV shared in the downing of one of the Fiats.[1] Again in December 1937, he went to the aid of a Spanish comrade who was being attacked by Messerschmitts. During his service in Spain, he flew 150 sorties and participated in ninety air combats, claiming eight kills

plus thirty-one group shares. For this he was awarded the Order of Lenin on 14 November 1938 and the Order of the Red Banner 2 March 1938. In September 1939 as a Captain, he joined the 69th IAP and later in August 1941 became its commander. Flying a Yak-1 he was shot down and wounded on 10 January 1943 after successfully downing a Bf 109 over Stalingrad. In late 1943 he became deputy CO. of the 6th GIAD, and then became CO. of the 19th GIAP, which was flying La-7s. On 13 March 1944 they attacked a large formation of enemy aircraft; he downed one Ju 87 and possibly a second before being himself shot down and killed. During his time in Spain and WWII, he was credited with twenty-nine kills plus forty-five shared kills. Awards were H.S.U. (10 February 1942), Order of Lenin (twice), Order of the Red Banner (twice), and GPW 1st Cl. (Michulec, R. *Stalinowskie Sokoly*, Lotnicz pub., Photo in *Solidarnost'* p.12, Kaminskii, Semenov "*Parol*," Berch, Shingarev, Bodrikhin, Polak, Seidl, *Los Rusos, Pravda*, [1]Gusev p.126, but the August date is not realistic.)

SHESTERNIKOV, Ivan I., born 1907

Aviation Technician served from 14 January to 29 September 1937. Awarded the Red Banner 3 November 1937 and the Red Star on 21 June 1937. (*Los Rusos, Pravda*)

SHEVCHENKO, Ivan I., born 1907

Aviation Technician in Spain from October 1936 to 26 July 1937. Awarded the Red Star 2 January 1937. (*Los Rusos, Pravda*)

SHEVCHENKO, Ivan Nikiforovich, NCO, born 1912

SB radio/gunner in Spain from 14 November 1937 to 21 July 1938. (*Los Rusos* has dates incorrect saying 14 November 1938 to 21 July 1939.) Awarded the Red Banner 14 November 1938. (Semenov "*Parol*," *Los Rusos, Pravda*)

SHEVCHENKO, Stepan Efimovich, born 1913

Radio/Gunner SB, arrived 30 May and left 4 October 1938. Before going to Spain he had been in the 114th ShAB at Gomel. A member of the crew on SB flown by YAKIMENKO, which on 9 August 1938 was hit by AAA fire during a mission. Both SHEVCHENKO and the pilot were wounded, and when YAKIMENKO crashlanded the aircraft the navigator NITSAI broke both his legs. Awarded the Red Banner 22 February 1939. (Abrosov, Voronkova, Berch, Semenov "*Parol*," *Los Rusos, Pravda*)

SHEVCHENKO, Vladimir Illarionovich, Sr.Lt., born 25 June 1908

Joined the Red Army in 1929. Attended the Borisoglebsk Military Aviation School in 1932. In Spain he served from 27 May 1937 until 20 January 1938. He was the Commander of an SB Patrulla, and flew over 100 combat sorties. Besides attacking the frontlines he also attacked enemy ships and ports. Since the bomber crews at the beginning had no experience of action over the sea, they had problems identifying the ships from one another. On one mission to Malaga to try and find the Nationalist Crusier *Canarias*, due to a faulty drawing of the ship they almost bombed a British warship, only pulling out at the last moment. Awarded the H.S.U on 14 March 1938 and Order of the Red Banner 28 October 1937. He fought in Khalkhin-Gol battles where he was the the CO of the 100th BAB and later in the Winter War against Finland where he commanded the 10th BAB. During WWII, he at first commanded the 37th Air Army on the Southwest Front until the Spring of 1942, Golubev, G. in *V Pare s Sotym* p.227 says he commanded the 216th IAD from May until October 1942. He then commanded the 1st Composite Air Corps (SAK) (this comprised the 288th IAD and 267th ShAD) from 23 October 1942, until 12 May 1944. From 8 July 1944 until the end of the war he commanding the 182nd ShAD. With rank of General Lt., he went into the reserves in 1946. Later he was arrested on charges of Anti-Soviet Activity. Died on 11 January 1972. Awards were H.S.U., Order of Lenin, Red Banner four times, Order of Suvorov 2nd Cl., Kutuzov 2nd Cl. and Red Star twice. (warheroes.ru., *Vmeste*, Shingarev, Boyd, *Geroi, Pravda*, Gagin, *Los Rusos*)

SHEVTSOV, Petr Fedorovich, Lt., born 25 July 1912

Joined the Red Army in 1930. Attended Okonchil Orenburg Military Flyers School in 1933. Was a pilot in the 107th IAE 83rd IAB Byelorussian Mil. Dist. He went to Spain in October 1936 and returned home on 13 August 1937. He was an I-16 Pilot in KOLESNIKOV's Esc., made Patrulla leader in April 1937 and later said to have been the Escuadrilla CO. Claimed four enemy aircraft (three personal and one in group). In Spain he is said to have flown one of the captured CR 32s and even used it to attack enemy aircraft and fire on ground troops. Awarded the H.S.U. on 22 October 1937. After return home he was made CO of the 66th IAB Byelorussian Mil. Dist. Fought in the Russo-Finnish War. During the period 1939-1940 he seems to have run into problems with the law due to drinking and fighting with the police. These problems caused his demotion several times to where he was just a flight instructor in the 7th IAD. With the outbreak of WWII, he was put in command of the 272nd IAP. Died 17 January 1944 in the crash of his La-5 fighter at the Dubrovka Airfield. Other awards were Order of Lenin, Red Banner twice (2 January and 4 July 1937), and GPW 1st Cl. Laureau/*Icare 130* spells CHVETSOV. (Kaminskii, Abrosov, Rumyantsev, Gusev, Berch, Laureau, *Vmeste*, Pritsker, *Geroi*, *Los Rusos, Pravda*)

SHILIN, Aleksii Andreevich, Lt., born 1912

Pilot in the 107th IAE 83rd IAB Byelorussian Mil. Dist. Arrived in Spain 26 March and died 11 April 1938. He had taken off from Celra Airfield on an escort mission; at about 3,000 meters a wing on his I-16 #102116 suddenly separated and the aircraft went into a spin, crashing to the earth. This was at first thought to have been caused by sabotage, but instead it was a defect in the aircraft. Abrosov lists that it was a "Strengthened" Type 10, there had been many problems with the 2nd batch of Type 5s delivered, but few with the Type 10s. (Semenov "*Parol,*" *My* (1986) pg. 294, Abrosov, *Los Rusos*, Kaminskii)

SHIMBALOV, Gavril P., Capt., born 1902

A pilot in Spain from 18 April until 18 October 1937. Awarded the Red Banner on 4 July 1937. (*Los Rusos, Pravda*)

SHIPITOV, Yakov Vasil'evich, Sr.Lt., born 1908

Detachment CO in the 36th IAE 56th IAB Kiev Mil. Dist. Arrived in Spain on 14 June 1937 and served until 28 January 1938. At first he was a patrulla CO, then CO of one of the I-16 escuardillas (possibly the 1st. until mid October). Flew 120 missions and fought in several air combats, one aircraft to his credit. Awarded the Order of Lenin on 2 March 1938 and the Red Banner 3 November 1937. Later from June 1938 until July 1941 he commanded the 43rd IAP. Nothing known after that. (Abrosov, Kaminskii, *Pravda, Los Rusos* spell it SHITIKOV and list as U-34?, possibly they mean Y-34 the supply ship.)

SHITOV, Grigorii, Lt., born 1905

Bomber Navigator, in Spain 15 March 1937 to 28 January 1938. Awarded the Red Banner twice. (*Los Rusos*)

SHKATOV, Nikolai, born 1914

I-15 Aviation Technician from 14 January to 23 December 1937. Awarded the Red Star 17 July 1937. (*Los Rusos, Pravda*)

SHKUDSKII, Il'ya Mareovich, NCO, born 1914

SB radio/gunner in Spain from 12 January until 21 July 1938. Awarded the Red Banner 14 November 1938. (Berch, Semenov "*Parol,*" *Pravda, Los Rusos* spell it SHUDSKI)

SHMAGLII, Aleksei Mikhailovich, born 1910

Was an Aero technician in the Escuadrilla commanded by RYCHAGOV. Served from October 1936 until 27 March 1937. Awarded the Red Star 2 January 1937. Listed in 1986 as a Colonel Engineer, Retired. But a second listing of him in *Los Rusos* give dates of service as as August 1936(?) to May 1937. (*Vmeste, Los Rusos, Pravda*)

SHMAKOV, Aleksandr, Sr.Lt., born 1907

Navigator SB, arrived 30 May and left 18 August 1938. (Berch, Semenov "*Parol,*" *Los Rusos*)

SHMEL'KOV, Nikolai Ivanovich, Lt., born 5 May 1912

Joined the Army in 1930. Attended Pilots School in Lugansk in 1932. Became a pilot, Zvena CO and then detachment CO in the 109th IAE 36th IAB Kiev Mil. Dist. He was in the first group of Soviet pilots sent to Spain. Serving from October 1936 to 23 January 1937. *Los Rusos* list end date as 23 March 1937, but also give date of birth as 1908. He was commander of an I-15 Detachment in 1936. Flew forty-nine sorties and shot down four enemy aircraft in aerial combat. He was also involved along with ZAKHAROV in the mistaken shooting down of the French Embassy Potez 540 F-A000 on 8 December 1936. During an air combat in January 1937, he suffered a head wound and was sent home. Awarded the title of H.S.U. on 31 December 1936. In 1938, he attended Higher Aviation KUKS. He commanded the 54th IAB Leningrad Mil. Dist. in the Russo/Finnish War 1939-40 and in June 1941 he was in command of the 145th IAP flying I-16s. In 1942 he graduated KUKS at the Air Force Academy. From 23 October 1942 until 22 July 1944 he was CO of the 297th IAD PVO (made up of the 938th and 939th IAPs) Trans Baikal Mil. Dist. From August 1944 until the end of the war he was deputy CO of the 234th IAD. After the war he was a Colonel in reserve. His total claims are all over the place; Seidl says thirteen aircraft in Spain, but *Geroi* says five and Matyas says six plus five shares. Decorations include the H.S.U., Order of Lenin, and Red Banner. Died on 24 March 1967. (Abrosov, Kaminskii, Lario, Lacalle, Berch, Pritsker, Zil'Manovich,*Vmeste*, Shingarev, Logoluso, *Icare 130*, Zakharov, Seidl, Polak, Matyas, *Los Rusos, Pravda*)

SHORIN, Aleksandr I., born 1912

Aviation technician in Spain from October 1936 until 29 September 1937. Awarded the Red Star 2 January 1937. (*Los Rusos, Pravda*)

SHRAMOV, G.N., born 1910

Aviation technician in Spain October 1936 to 27 July 1937. Awarded the Red Star 2 January 1937. (*Los Rusos, Pravda*)

SHUBIKOV, Arsenii Vasil'evich, born 5 May 1912

Pilot in the 3rd IAE VVS KBF (Red Banner Baltic Fleet). In Spain from 14 December 1937 to 10 June 1938. He was a member of ZHURAVLEV's Patrulla in DEVOTCHENKO's 2nd I-16 Esc. in December 1937 and remained as a patrulla CO later under RODIN. Flew 100 sorties and fought in twenty-five air battles, claimed seven aircraft (two personal CR 32s and five in group). Awarded the Red Banner 14 November 1938 and the Red Star on 22 February 1939. In 1939, he was appointed CO of an IAE in the 32nd IAP BSF (Black Sea Fleet). In 1940, the 32nd IAP created a special composite IAE of I-16 dive bombers with SHUBIKOV as CO and from June 1941 this unit the 2nd IAE was used to attack targets in Romania such as bridges, oil refineries and naval bases. KIA on 22 October 1941 during an air combat; his aircraft was hit and went down behind enemy lines. Kaminskii thinks it was a pilot from JG 77 who shot him down – Bergstrom p.226 lists the victor as Emil Omert of III./ JG 77. (Kaminskii, Semenov "*Parol*," Pritsker, Abrosov, *Pravda*, Bergstrom)

SHUBIN, Georgii Mikhailovich, Capt., born 1911

Pilot in 142nd IAB Byelorussian Mil. Dist. Called "Zora," in Spain from 20 August 1937 until 24 April 1938. Member of the 6th Moscas under command of GUSEV. Flew 100 sorties and fought in thirty air combats, he claimed two enemy aircraft (CR 32 and He 51) Awarded the Order of Lenin 14 November 1938 and the Red Banner on 2 March 1938. Gusev says he was the son of a miner, and had finished Voroshilograd Flight School in 1935. After Spain he is said to have served in the Odessa Mil. Dist. (Kaminskii, Semenov "*Parol*," Berch, Gusev, *Pravda, Los Rusos* spell it SHUBIKOV)

SHUGUROV, Il'ia Grigor'evich, Capt., born 1905

CO of the 4th IAE 56th IAB Kiev Mil. Dist. Departed for Spain on 10 June 1938, and served in the 5th Moscas, but according to Kaminskii, he was made an I-16 Escuadrilla CO. Flew six sorties and fought in two air battles.

KIA on he evening of 19 July 1938[1] in combat with Bf 109s in the Levante area. Buried at Utiel. Awarded the Red Banner 22 February 1939. (Abrosov, Kaminskii, *Vmeste, Pravda*, [1]Semenov *Tov*. Lists as the thirteenth as does the 1991 list of Soviet dead and also *Los Rusos* who spell it SHUGUNOV.)

SHUKAEV, Aleksandr Alekseevich, NCO, born 1911

Before going to Spain, he was in the 114th ShAB at Gomel. Served from October 1936 until 20 June 1937. He was a gunner/navigator in an SSS flown by NIKIFOROV, G.N. He was a member of the 3rd Esc. under command of TUPIKOV, in a Patrulla commanded by CHERVYAKOV. His aircraft was attacked and shot down by Fiats on December 4, 1936 over Torrijos Airfield during a bombing attack. In his memoir in *Vmeste*, he claims that before his aircraft was shot down, that the Fiats tried a head-on pass at them and that two of the Fiats were shot down. One he says by him. He said his plane was hit and that the engine seized. NIKIFOROV was able to crashland it in an olive grove and that both of them jumped out the aircraft uninjured. SHUKAEV was taken prisoner, but apparently NIKIFOROV was killed trying to get away. In prison, he used the name Aleksandr ALEKSANDROVICH. Released in June 1937 and returned home. Awarded the Red Banner on 2 January 1937. (*Vmeste, My, My 2, Pravda*, Voronkova, Meroño, *Los Rusos* list as a master armorer.)

SHUL'GIN, Vasilii I., born 1915

Air Electricial Technician, came to Spain with TARKHOV's Esc., served from October 1936 to 16 May 1937. Awarded the Red Star on 2 January 1937. (Semenov "*Parol*," Rumyantsev "*Antonio*," *Los Rusos, Pravda*)

SHUMILOV, Fedor Aleksandrovich, Lt., born 1908

Navigator of SB, served from 30 December 1937 to 27 July 1938. Was in the crew of the aircraft flown by MARKIN on the 28 January 1938 attack on Salamanca. On their return leg, the aircraft was downed by AAA. All three crewmembers were captured. See SCHILOFF. See also SMERTIN and MARKIN. (Semenov "*Parol*," Berch, *Los Rusos*)

SHUMILOV, Mikhail Stepanovich, born 1895

A.k.a. General Shilov left for Spain on 10 February 1938 and returned to the USSR on 12 May 1939. He was an advisor to Gen. Miaja. (Semenov "*Parol*," Berch, *Los Rusos*)

SHUSTOV, Pavel Nikiforovich, Maj., born 1902

CO of the 40th IAE 83rd IAB Byelorussian Mil. Dist. In Spain from 22 April to 22 October 1937. He was to have been the commander of the I-15 Grupo 26, but citing bad health he refused to fly at the front. Instead he was put in charge of new aircraft assembly and the training of Spanish pilots. It is said that he only flew at the front one time in a UTI-4 with the Pravda Correspondent Mikhail Koltsov as passenger. He was showing him the front and had a large escort of I-16s covering him. After Spain he was given the rank of Col. and was appointed head of the Aerial Combat Training Center. In 1940 he was a test pilot at Factory #292 building Yak-1s. During the war he was head of the airfield at Factory #1 building Il-2s. After the war he continued in the Aviation industry. Retired in 1950. (Abrosov, Kaminskii, *Los Rusos*)

SIDERENKO, Aleksandr T., born 1909

Aviation Armaments Technician in Spain from October 1936 to 2 July 1937. Awarded the Red Star 2 January 1937. (*Los Rusos, Pravda*)

SIDORENKO, Anton Ivanovich, Sr.Lt., born 1909

A Zvena CO in the 36th IAB Kiev Mil. Dist. He was in Spain from 20 August 1937 to 2 March 1938, as an I-15 Patrulla leader in SEROV's 1st Esc. He was wounded in the face by a AAA shell over the Madrid front while flying an I-16 on 13 September 1937. Kaminskii indicates that he was then moved to the 1st Esc. Chatos after his release from the hospital. Flew both the I-15 and I-16. Awarded Order of the Red Banner 2 March 1938, and Red Star 14 November 1938. Flew fifty missions and shot down two aircraft with the I-15. After Spain he was on the staff of the 29th IAP Moscow Mil. Dist. and in 1940 became CO of one of its IAEs. In 1941 he was commanding the 23rd IAP with the rank of Lt.Col. during the Winter War and first month of WWII. This unit is listed as having been disbanded on 15 July 1941. In August 1941 he was appointed as CO of the 66th ShAP and in October 1941 became CO of the 66th IAP. While coordinating actions to aid ground forces on 5 February 1942, he was killed in a bombing attack on his postion. (Abrosov, Kaminskii, airaces.narod.ru, Shingarev, Seidl, *Pravda, Los Rusos* lists as Aleksandr.)

SIGALIN, V.A.

Pilot (Meroño).

SILAEV, Mikhail G., born 1906

Aviation Technician from October 1936 to 30 June 1937. Awarded the Red Star 2 January 1937. (*Los Rusos, Pravda*)

SIL'VERSTOV, Anatolii Aleksandrovich, Sr.Lt., born 1910

Detachment CO in the 34th IAE 56th IAB Kiev Mil. Dist. In Spain from 20 August 1937 to 25 April 1938. He was first a patrulla CO, then later the commander of the 5th escuadrilla. Flew I-16 CM-111. Flew 140 sorties and fought in twenty-nine air combats, during one on 5 December 1937 his aircraft was badly shot-up but he was able to bring it back to the airfield. Had one aircraft to his credit. He was awarded the Red Banner twice, 2 March and 14 November 1938. During WWII, he was CO of the 249th IAD from July 1942 to May 1943 and then from August 1943 until October 1944 he was CO of the 295th IAD. There seems to be some problems with his last name; Abrosov and *Los Rusos* list as above, while Kaminskii lists it as SIL'VESTROV (SIL'VERSTOV) and Seidl lists the CO of the 295th IAD as SIL'VESTROV. (airaces.narod.ru, Abrosov, *Los Rusos, Pravda*)

"SILVESTRO"

Laureau says 3rd Escuadrilla I-16s, but R and R says Jefe I-15s. See above listing. (Laureau, R and R)

SIL'VESTROV, Petr Yakovlevich, Lt., born 1910

Pilot in the 30th IAE 142nd IAB Byelorussian Mil. Dist. Left for Spain on 20 August, and died in an aircraft crash at Cabeza del Buey Airfield on 19 September 1937. On takeoff his engine began to malfunction and he tried to turn back, but the plane went into a spin crashing to the earth. He had been an I-16 pilot in GUSEV's 6th escuadrilla, While Abrosov says he was awarded the Red Banner 14 November 1938, Kaminskii correctly lists date as 2 March 1938. (Gusev, Abrosov (p.143 for details of crash), Kaminskii, *Pravda, Los Rusos* say "Buried at Aerodrome of Cabeza de Buey, the 1991 list of Soviet dead gives 17 July as date of death, but he did not leave the USSR for Spain until 20 August so feel this is an error.)

SIMONENKO, Ivan

Aviational Engineer (Zil'manovich, Berch)

SIMONOV, Pavel F., Lt., born 1912

Pilot SSS served from October 1936 to 2 July 1937. Awarded the Red Banner 2 January 1937. (*Los Rusos, Pravda*)

SIMONYAN, Ruben M., Lt., born 1909

SB Navigator served from 14 June to 7 December 1937. Awarded the Red Banner 3 November 1937. (*Solidarnost* lists middle initial as I., Semenov "*Parol*," *Pravda, Los Rusos* list as leaving on 7 December 1938.)

SIRENKO, Arsenii L., Sr.Lt., born 1907

In Spain from October 1936 to 2 July 1937. Navigator/gunner on SSS Rasante flown by CHERVYAKOV. Awarded the Red Banner 2 January 1937. (*Vmeste, Pravda, Los Rusos*)

SIROCHENKO, Aleksandr Konstantinovich, Lt., born 1914

A Zvena CO in the 57th IAE 142nd IAB Byelorussian Mil. Dist. He served in Spain from 26 March until he was KIA on 13 June 1938 when his I-16 was shot down during an air battle with Bf 109s, crashing in enemy territory. Awarded the Red Banner on 22 February 1939. (Semenov "*Parol*," Abrosov, *Los Rusos*, Kaminskii)

SIUSIUKA'LOV, Nikita Timofeevich Lt., born 1905

Pilot in the 11th IAE 111th IAB Leningrad Mil. Dist. He departed for Spain on 20 August 1937 and returned home on 25 April 1938. He was a member of EREMENKO's and later SEROV's 1st Escuadrilla.[1] Kaminskii says his codename was Miguel Costeros. He and Korouz downed a Ju 52 on 24 August. He was a patrulla CO, then became commander of the 1st Chatos on 4 November 1937, after STEPANOV took over command of the 26th Grupo. On that day, while he was Flying Chato #CA-009, he and POPOV claimed an S-79 over the Mediterranean. His aircraft was then either hit or the engine developed a problem and caught fire and Nikita bailed out and landed in the water, where he was picked up by a Republican Motorboat. His and PLESHCHENKO's escuadrillas patrolled the Med. coast together at the end of December 1937, he was at that time flying CC-023. Later became commander of the 5th Moscas, from late February to April 1938. Flew ninety sorties and fought in thirty air combats and claimed 2 (Fiat CR 32s) personal and four aircraft in pair or group. Awarded the Order of Lenin on 14 November 1938 and Order of the Red Banner 2 March 1938. From September 1938 to March 1939 he was CO of the 7th IAP, then until January 1940 he was CO of the 38th IAP with which he fought in the Winter War against Finland. Awarded the Red Banner 4 July 1940. In February 1940 he was made CO of the 149th IAP and then later in 1941 became CO of the 43rd IAP 36 IAD kiev Mil. Dist. It was with this unit he fought against the Germans when the war began. He was KIA over Stalingrad on 4 August 1942. (Bodrikhin, Laureau, Milany 55, Meroño, Gusev, Berch, Pritsker, Shingarev, *Pravda*, Sirvent has information on him (?) pgs.18-19. Also says Patrulla leader was named ALEXIEV (?). [1]Kaminskii says he was CO of the 2nd Chatos, but this unit was under Spanish command. Shingarev mistakenly says (p.164) "Also participated in combat of 1 September during which HAYA is shot down.")

SKLYAROV, Viktor Dmitrievich, Lt., born 1910

Pilot in the 142nd IAB Byelorussian Mil. Dist. He volunteered for Spanish duty serving from 20 August to 30 December 1937. Flew an I-16 in GUSEV's 6th escuadrilla. Kaminskii says his codename was Victorio. In December 1937 he became a patrulla leader. KIA On 30 December 1937 in combat with Bf 109s over the Teruel area while flying CM-149.[1] He is said to have shot down a He 111 and a Bf 109 before his aircraft was hit. Bailed out, but his parachute failed to open. Listed as having seven personal plus nine in group victories. Awarded the Red Banner 2 March 1938. (Gusev, Berch, Polak, Abrosov, *Pravda, Los Rusos,* Kaminskii, [1]While Salas in Diario p.110, lists SKLYAROV as flying CM-009 and SUMAROV as flying CM-149, read also p.104 "A las 8:47 … el 009 fue derribado. A las 15:43 … fue derribado el 149. Now read Abrosov p.193, "In the morning…. Aleksandr SUMAROV was KIA." "In the evening … Viktor SKLYAROV died in combat." So this is why I believe CM-149 was SKLYAROV's aircraft.)

SKOROKHOD, Aleksandr F., Lt., born 1908

SB Navigator, in Spain from October 1936 to 27 May 1937. Awarded the Red Banner twice, 2 January and 17 July 1937. (*Bajo la B.*, Berch, Semenov "*Parol*," *Los Rusos, Pravda*)

SKOSEREV, Pavel Lt., born 1913

Los Rusos say bomber pilot. Served from 25 April until July 1937 when KIA. Awarded the Order of Lenin 2 March 1938, but I think they are confusing him with a tanker KIA on 25 July.)

SKOVORODNIKOV, Grigori Kuz'mich, born 1907

Pilot SB from October 1936 until 2 July 1937. Was a member of the 1st Escuadrilla SB under SCHACHT. Awarded the Red Banner on 2 January 1937. Later appointed Commander of an Escuadrilla according to GUMENNYI in *Vmeste.* (*Vmeste, Bajo la B.*, Lukes, *Los Rusos, Pravda*)

SKRYPCHENKO, Semen Semenovich, born 1911
Engineer in Bomber Escuadrilla from October 1936 until 27 March 1937. Awarded the Red Star on 2 January 1937 plus Red Banner on 22 February 1939. (*Los Rusos* spell it SKRIPCHENKO, *Pravda* misspelled it SKRYPNICHENKO 2 January, but correct spelling on 22 February)

SKUTOV, Zakhar Savel'evich, NCO, born 1912
SB Radio/Gunner, arrived 28 June 1938 and was KIA on 10 October 1938 when his SB was shot down by Bf 109s. The Navigator UTKIN and Pilot TRUBITSYN were able to bail out, but said that their repeated calls to SKUTOV went unanswered. Undoubtedly he was either dead or unconscious at the time. His aircraft crashed in enemy territory. SKUTOV was the last Soviet airman to die in Spain. (Semenov "*Parol*," Abrosov, Berch, *Los Rusos* list as 11 October)

SKVORTSOV, Sergei I., born 1908
Navigator, served from October 1936 to 26 July 1937. Awarded the Red Banner 2 January 1937. (*Los Rusos, Pravda*)

SLEPNEFF, Eugene Nicolaievich
Fighter pilot, Sgt. age twenty-six in 1938 when captured. Shingarev p.115 says SLEPNEV (SLEPNEFF) was nom de guerre of Evgenii STEPANOV. (Berch, *Spain Mag.* 8/15/1938 p.17)

SLESAREV, Gennadii A., Lt., born 1910
SB Radio/gunner arrived 16 June and returned home 10 November 1937. Awarded the Red Banner 11 November 1937. (*Pravda, Los Rusos*)

SMERTIN, Mikhail Ivanovich, Sgt., born 1912
Radio/gunner SB served from 14 December 1937 to 27 July 1938, captured when his aircraft returning to base from the 28 January raid on Salamanca was brought down by AAA in an area north of the River Ebro. Released in a prisoner swap. See SOKOLOWSKI. See also MARKIN and SHUMILOV. (Semenov "*Parol*," Berch, *Los Rusos*)

SMIRNOV
CO. I-15 Escuadrilla in October 1937 according to Sukhachev 190.

SMIRNOV, Boris Aleksandrovich, Lt., born 18 October 1910
Joined the Army in 1930, and attended the 7th Stalingrad Military Flyers School in 1933. Was Zvena CO in the 116th IAE Moscow Mil. Dist. Volunteered for duty in Spain, and according to both Abrosov and Kaminskii he began his Spanish service on 14 June 1937 and returned on 17 January 1938, but in his memoirs he says he arrived at Cartagena on 26 May on the *Aldecoa*, but that ship did not arrive in Spain until 21 June. Kaminskii says codename was Manuel Lopez Gorey. He was a member of Aleksandr MINAEV's 3rd Escuadrilla. Became commander of the 3rd Moscas on 26 July 1937 after the death of VEREVKA[1] who had taken over after MINAEV's death on 15 July. His second-in-command was Petr BUTRYM who then assumed command of the 3rd Esc. when SMIRNOV was temporarily transferred to the 4th (?) Moscas in August 1937. He flew to the North from the Central zone on 19 August 1937 leading a group of new Spanish pilots. While in the North he operated from La Albericia airfield in Santander. On 22 August, during an air combat, his aircraft along with three other I-16s were shot down. SMIRNOV was wounded in the crash. Upon his return from the North on 30 September, he went back to commanding the 3rd Esc. until he left Spain at the end of December 1937 and returned home in January 1938. Tarazoa mistakenly claims he used nom de guerre "Plygunov." EVSEV'EV in *Vmeste* mentions SMIRNOV arriving in Santander and states that with this new Escuadrilla they now had eighteen I-16s against 300 enemy aircraft. He flew more than 150 sorties, is listed as having six kills to his credit. Later flew in the Khalkhin-Gol as Inspector of Pilots for the 70th IAP. Claimed four kills there. Awarded the H.S.U. on 17 November 1939. During WWII, he was commander of the 288th IAD. Retired in 1946 as a General Major. Awarded the Order of Lenin twice

(2 March 1938 for Spain), Order of the Red Banner three times (28 October 1937 for Spain), Order of Suvorov 2nd Cl., Kutuzov 2nd Cl., Red Star, and GPW 1st Cl. Died on 17 May 1984. (Abrosov, Kaminskii, Smirnov, *Vmeste*, Rumyantsev *Geroi*, Laureau 242, Gusev 152, Howson 200, Chalaya, *Pravda, Los Rusos* list start date as 13 June. Shingarev, surprisingly has no mention of SMIRNOV on the Northern front nor even his participation in the attack on the (Sanjurjo) "Garrapinillos" airfield which is very strange. [1]Smirnov does not mention VEREVKA in his memoirs *Nebo Moei Molodosti*)

SMIRNOV, Ivan Fedorovich, Lt., born 1907

An SB Pilot, he arrived 30 December 1937 and returned 18 May 1938. His aircraft was one of two Soviet flown SBs (the other was SURZHIN's) downed by Bf 109s on 7 February 1938 during the Calamocha Operations. His Navigator BOLDYREV was killed. See listing for SURZHIN for details of this action. Awarded the Red Banner 14 November 1938. (Semenov "*Parol*," Smirnov, Berch, *Los Rusos, Pravda*)

SMIRNOV, Mikhail I., Lt., born 1907

Pilot SB, served from October 1936 to 27 May 1937. Awarded the Red Banner twice, 2 January and July 1937. (*Vmeste, Los Rusos, Pravda*)

SMIRNOV, Mikhail A., born 1907

Aviation Technician, served from October 1936 to 27 March 1937. Awarded the Red Star 2 January 1937. (*Los Rusos, Pravda*)

SMIRNOV, Viktor Sergeevich, Lt., born 1907

Pilot in the 107th IAE 83rd IAB Byelorussian Mil. Dist. In Spain he was an I-16 patrulla CO in 5th Esc., departed for Spain on 26 March and returned 13 August 1938. Flew ninety-eight sorties, had two CR 32s plus one aircraft in patrulla to his credit. Awarded the Red Banner 22 February 1939. Later fought in the Khalkhin-Gol as assistant commander of the 70th IAP, claimed four Japanese aircraft. Awarded two more Red Banners on 29 August and 17 November 1939. Was mentioned for the HSU, but no results. In WWII he was CO of the 3rd GIAP until January 1943, then transferred to the 235th IAD on the southern front. KIA in combat 4 August 1943, after failing to return from a mission. (Abrosov, Kaminskii, *Pravda, Los Rusos* list end date as 11 August)

SMOLEKOV

According to Laureau he was 3rd escuadrilla I-16 commander in January 1938. Used the name "Silvestro," but as noted under this name, R and R say he was commander of an I-15 unit. (Laureau p.242, R and R p.126. I believe they are confused with SMOLYAKOV of the 5th Moscas below.)

SMOLKIN, Vladimir A., born 1912

Parachute instructor in Spain from October 1936 to 2 July 1937. Awarded the Red Star 2 January 1937. (*Los Rusos, Pravda*)

SMOLYAKOV, Platon Efimovich, Lt., born 1912

Before Spain he was a Zvena CO in the 142nd IAB Byelorussian Mil. Dist. Patrulla CO in Gusev's, 6th Moscas or so-called "Gruppa Gusev." Began service on 20 August 1937 and returned home on 25 April 1938. Some members of the Esc. at the time were LISIN, PLIASOV, SEMENOV, SUKHORUCHENKO, SEMENOV and SUKHORYABOV. Airfield used at time was Sarrion, next went to La Señera field near Valencia, then to Villar del Arzobispo on the road from Valencia to Cruz de Moya in order to be closer to the battle zone (Teruel). He took over command of 5th Escuadrilla on 25 January 1938. After he was wounded in combat in late February, the 5th was then taken over by SIUSIUKA'LOV. Listed as having six kills plus twelve in group, he had flown ninety-eight sorties and fought in twenty-nine air combats. Awarded the Order of Lenin on 14 November 1938 and the Red Banner 2 March 1938. Fought in the Khalkhin-Gol as a unit commander in the 70th IAD. Claimed two Japanese aircraft. Served in WWII, he was CO of the 85th GIAP. Retired as a General Major. Died 28 May 1979. Arias claims he commanded the 2nd Esc., but he also says that DEVOTCHENKO "Pedro" was transferred to the 2nd in mid October 1937. DEVOTCHENKO became CO of the 2nd in mid February 1938 and remained as commander until he returned home in April 1938. (*Solidarnost'* p.12, Gusev 99+, Semenov "*Parol*," Abrosov, *Los Rusos*, Kaminskii, Arias, *Pravda*)

SMUSHKEVICH, Yakov Vladimirovich, born 1 April 1902

Joined the Red Army in 1918 and participated in the Russian Civil War. In 1931, he graduated Kachin Military Flyers School. Before going to Spain, he was Commander of the 201st LBAB (Light Bomber Aviation Brigade) Byelorussian Mil. Dist. In Spain codename was "Andre," but he used the name "General Douglas." Commander of VVS forces in Spain from October 1936 until 17 June 1937, he was a subordinate to General G.M. Shtern, the Chief Soviet Advisor to the Republican Government. Twice made H.S.U., first time was 21 June 1937. Based at Albacete during his tour of duty in Spain he was replaced by LOPATIN. Fought against the Japanese at the Khalkhin-Gol in Mongolia, where he was in command of the Soviet Air group. Awarded his second H.S.U. on 17 November 1939. Later Deputy Commander in GU-VVS Russia under Gen. Loktionov. Led VVS operations during the Winter War against Finland. In 1940, made General Lt. but was later relieved of his command due to the disastrous showing by the VVS. He was replaced by RYCHAGOV. After the German invasion, he was Arrested and on 28 October 1941 he was shot, along with several other "Spaniards" and RYCHAGOV's wife. His name was rehabilitated on 25 December 1954. Awards include two Orders of Lenin. Chantaje has a good chapter on him. Mistakenly says on p.116 that he also called himself "Montenegro" but in reality, this name was used by LOPATIN. Eherenburg p.499 says he was arrested and shot two weeks before the Nazis invasion! (*Chantaje*, Salas, Gusev 91, RSA, Berch, Eherenburg, Lario, *Lexikon*, Semenov "*Parol*," *Vmeste*, Pritsker, Shukman, Boyd, *Geroi*, Künzi, *Los Rusos* list date of birth as 1900)

SOBENIN, Fedor F., born 1910

Aviation Technician in Spain from October 1936 to 27 August 1937. Awarded the Red Star 2 January 1937. (*Pravda, Los Rusos*)

SOBOLEV, Nikolai Grigor'evich, Sr.Lt., born 1912

Pilot in the 35th IAE 56th IAB Kiev Mil. Dist. In Spain he was an I-15 pilot and flew in the 1st Escuadrilla from 31 May 1937 to 28 January 1938, first under command of EREMENKO. He was then made a Patrulla CO. Later in July 1937 he was appointed to the Night Fighter detachment under SEROV. Awarded Order of the Red Banner twice, on 3 November 1937 and 2 March 1938. Flew 150 sorties and claimed six aircraft (two personal and four in group). Lukes says had ten victories plus seven in group. In 1939 he was CO of an Eskadril'ya in the 2nd IAP Kiev Mil. Dist. In 1940 his Eskadril'ya became part of the 38th IAP and fought in the Winter War, where in one battle his group downed three Finnish fighters. He was awarded the Order of Lenin on 22 February 1941. During the early months of WWII he became CO of the 38th IAP; this unit was renamed in May 1942 as the 21st GuIAP. Later he became deputy CO of the 304th IAD (23 GuIAD). Here he flew a P-39N with "Krashnoyarskii Komsomolets" painted on it. This was for the group that raised the money for the plane. In WWII he flew 196 sorties and fought in seventy air battles claiming twelve aircraft personal and eight in group. Kaminskii says that he was discharged (fired) from the Air Force at the end of the war due to a conflict with the NKVD. As of 1986 he was living in Voronezh. (Kaminskii, Laureau, *Bajo la B.*, Pritsker, Shingarev, Abellan, *Pravda*)

SOBOLEVSKII, Oleg Vladimirovich "Kutiure," Maj., born 1899

Before Spain he was a Captain in the 111th IAB Leningrad Mil. Dist. Was an I-15 Staff officer in Spain from October 1936 to 28 October 1937. Los Rusos say he was an Instructor, and Shingarev, says that he and NOVAK were charged with the start up of the Night fighter detachment based at Alcala de Henares in July 1937. Boyd mistakenly claims that he led an SB Esc. and that his and another under SENATOROV went to the North escorted by two fighter Esc.s. Awarded the Red Banner and Red Star. Kaminskii says living near Moscow in 1966. (Laureau, Berch, Shingarev, Boyd, *Los Rusos*, Kaminskii)

SOBORNOV, Gennadii Aleksandrovich, Lt., born 1912

Fighter pilot in the 142nd IAB Byelorussian Mil. Dist. In Spain from 20 August 1937 to 25 April 1938, was a Patrulla CO in the 6th Moscas (I-16s) under GUSEV. Awarded the Red Banner twice, on 2 March and 14 November 1938. Flew 100 sorties and fought in twenty-eight air combats, had at least one aircraft to his credit. In August 1938 he was appointed CO of an Eskadril'ya in the 49th IAP. In June 1939 he was posted as an aide to the Commander of the Red Air Force. In early 1941 he attended the Zhukovskii Air Force Academy and when war broke out in June 1941, he was put into the 42nd IAP fighting on the Western front and shot down several enemy aircraft. In November 1942 his aircraft was shot down during combat with Me 109s. He was able to bailout, but was badly burned. From 1943 on he served in a training facility teaching combat flying. Died in 1962. (Kaminskii, Gusev, Abrosov, *Los Rusos*, Semenov "*Parol*," *Pravda, Solidanost*)

SOBORNYI, Nikolai P., born 1914

Aviation Technician, served from October 1936 to 27 March 1937. Awarded the Red Star 2 January 1937. (*Los Rusos, Pravda*)

SOKOLOV

Listed by POLUSHKO as an SB Pilot (*Vmeste*)

SOKOLOV, Aleksandr Dmitrievich, Lt., born 1907

A Zvena CO in the 107th IAE 83rd IAB Byelorussian Mil. Dist. In Spain from November 1936 to 27 March 1937, he was a pilot in TARKHOV's I-16 Esc. Awarded the Red Banner 2 January 1937. During WWII, was the commander of the 590th IAP. This unit later became the 590th ShAP (mixed) and in February 1943 was renamed the 43rd Guards ShAP. After the war he worked in Civil Aviation. As of 1969 he was living in Moscow. (*Vmeste*, Rumyantsev "*Antonio*," Abrosov, Kaminskii, *Pravda*)

SOKOLOV, Aleksandr N., born 1913

Aviation Technician from October 1936 to 7 April 1937. Awarded the Red Star 2 January 1937. (*Los Rusos, Pravda*)

SOKOLOV, Arsenii I., Lt., born 1912

Pilot, in Spain from 31 June until 28 December 1937. Awarded the Red Banner 28 October 1937. (*Los Rusos, Pravda*)

SOKOLOV, Grigorii M., born 1912

Mechanic in GUSEV's escuadrilla according to *Mir Aviatsii #2* 2001 p.20, but *Los Rusos* says served from October 1936 until 30 July 1937, so most likely the Gusev referred to is K. GUSEV with the SSS ground attack aircraft. Awarded the Red Star 2 January 1937. (*Pravda, Los Rusos*)

SOKOLOV, Ivan N., Lt., born 1908

Navigator on SB, 2nd Esc. He had arrived in October 1936 and flew in a Potez 540 in 1st Internacional Escuadrilla under Capt. Martin Luna. He later switched to the SB Grupo in November 1936. Returned home on 29 March 1937. Awarded the Red Banner twice, on 2 January and 17 July 1937. (*Pravda, Bajo la B.*, Demenchuk, Logoluso, *MY*/Berch, *Vmeste, Los Rusos*)

SOKOLOV, Ivan Vasil'evich, Lt., born 1911

Pilot in the 142nd IAB Byelorussian Mil. Dist. He was a member of GUSEV's 6th Esc. He had gone to Spain on 20 August 1937. On 18 January 1938 while flying CM 144 in combat, his aircraft was shot down by Bf 109s of 1./J88. He had tried to make it back to his field, but the aircraft crashed and he was killed. He was buried in the village of La Putela. He had fought in several air battles, and claimed three personal and seven in group. Awarded the Red Banner on 2 March 1938. Kaminskii says his codename was Vega. Polak claims he had three victories plus four shares, and mistakenly says that he was killed on 28 December 1937, but perhaps he confused him with either SKLYAROV or SUMAREV, both lost on 30 December 1937. (Semenov "*Parol*," Gusev 99, Polak, Abrosov, *Los Rusos*, Kaminskii, Salas *Caza Rusa*, *Pravda*)

SOKOLOV, Konstaintin A., born 1905

Engineer from Aircraft Factory #22 assembling SB aircraft. In Spain from October to 12 December 1936. Awarded the Red Banner 2 January 1937. (*Los Rusos, Pravda, MY*, Berch)

SOKOLOV, Mikhail Ivanovich, Lt., born 1914
Navigator SB, arrived 1 April and returned on 3 September 1938. Awarded the Red Banner 22 February 1939. (Berch, *Los Rusos, Pravda*)

SOKOLOV, Mikhail P., Lt., born 1908
Navigator SB, in Spain from 30 December 1936 to 29 September 1937. Awarded the Red Banner on 17 July 1937. (*Los Rusos, Pravda*)

SOKOLOV, Viktor Danilovich
Navigator SB, awarded the Red Banner 14 November 1938. (*Vmeste, Pravda*)

SOKOLOV, Viktor I., Lt., born 1907
SB bomber/navigator from 15 June to 23 December 1937. Awarded the Red Banner 14 March 1938. (*Pravda, Los Rusos* spell it SOKOLOVSKII)

SOKOLOWSKI, Michael Ivanovich
Gunner on SB, age thirty in 1938. This is the phony name used by SMERTIN when he was captured. (*Spain Mag.* 8/15/1938)

SOLDATENKO, Ignatii Semenovich, Lt., born 1910
Pilot in 2nd Escuadrilla SSS Rasantes, in Spain from October 1936 to 27 May 1937. While attacking enemy ground forces on 19 December 1936, the radiator on his aircraft was hit and he had to make a forced landing, but neither he nor his gunner/navigator ZHARSKII were injured. Later on 20 March 1937, his aircraft was shot down and ZHARSKII was killed, while he suffered severe burns. He returned home after his release from the hospital. Awarded the Red Banner twice, 2 January and 4 July 1937. Polak says, Graduated from military flying school in 1933, and subsequently served in Spain during the civil war as a volunteer, and incorrectly says he had nine victories (?) there, but was shot down and suffered burns. He returned to the USSR, where after recovery he was sent to the Air Academy. He graduated just before the German invasion of June 1941. From June 1942, he flew on the Southwest Front becoming CO of the 240th IAP during August, which he led in the battle of Stalingrad. This Regiment was to be one of the first to re-equip with La-5s. During the spring of 1943, the unit operated over Kharkov; on 14 April he was killed during an attack on the Regiment's airfield. Awards were Order of the Red Banner twice. (Pritsker, *Vmeste*, Polak, Abrosov, *Pravda*)

SOLENKO, Boris V., Sr.Lt., born 1904
Jefe de enlace y transmisiones Grupo de Aviacion, served from January to 29 September 1937. Awarded the Red Banner 17 July 1937. (*Los Rusos, Pravda*)

SOLOGUB, Dmitrii Fedorovich, NCO, born 1919 (?)
Radio/Gunner SB, arrived 26 April and returned 3 September 1938. Awarded the Red Banner 22 February 1939. (Berch, Semenov "*Parol*," *Pravda, Los Rusos* list start date as 26 August)

SOLOV'EV, Aleksandr, born 1914
Fitter at the Alcantarilla Factory, from 21 July to 10 November 1937. (*Los Rusos*)

SOLOV'EV, Petr Ivanovich, Lt., born 1914
Navigator SB, he departed on 26 March and returned 3 September 1938. Awarded the Red Banner 22 February 1939. (Semenov "*Parol*," Berch, *Los Rusos, Pravda*)

SOROKIN, Leontii Ivanovich, Lt., born 1911
A Zvena CO in the 2nd IAE Kiev Mil. Dist. In Spain from 3 January to 27 August 1937, he was an I-15 pilot in the 1st Escuadrilla de Chatos. Codename was "Leon." He was a member of the earlier escuadrilla and was later put in EREMENKO's Esc. as a Patrulla leader. Shingarev ,who lists him as Vladimir, says he flew his last mission along with KUZNETSOV on 18 July 1937 and then rotated home. Awarded the Order of Lenin 14 November 1938 and Red Banner 17 July 1937. In the Spring of 1938 he was CO of the 5th IAE 16th IAP and in 1940 was appointed CO of an Eskadril'ya in the 55th IAP Odessa Mil. Dist. When WWII began he was the Flight Inspector for the 20th IAD. On 12 June 1942 he was killed in the Rostov area. (Abrosov, Kaminskii, *Los Rusos, Pravda*, Shingarev, Laureau and RSA also list as Vladimir)

SOROKIN, Semen D., born 1910
Aviation Technician in Spain from October 1936 to 26 July 1937. Awarded the Red Star 2 January 1937. (*Los Rusos, Pravda*)

SOUKOF, Bernard
Escuadra España (White Russian?). Berch wonders if this could be spelled ZHUKOV. (Laureau, Berch, Thornberry)

STANPAKOV, Grigorii Ya., born 1907
SSS Pilot served from October 1936 to 27 May 1937. Awarded the Red Banner twice, 2 January and 4 July 1937. (Abrosov p.376, *Los Rusos, Pravda*)

STARIKOV, Aleksei Georgievich, Sr.Lt./Maj., born 1907
A Detachment CO in the 41st IAE 83rd IAB Byelorussian Mil. Dist. In Spain he was a pilot in PLESHCHENKO's 2nd Escuadrilla, arrived on 16 May 1937 and returned on 28 January 1938 (*Los Rusos* say first name was Aleksandr and his start date was 18 May.) He was later commander of the 5th escuadrilla I-16. Flew 170 sorties and had shot down two personal plus four in group. Awarded the Order of Lenin on 2 March 1938 and Red Banner 22 October 1937. After Spain he was CO of the 20th IAP and fought in the Winter War against Finland. In WWII while commanding the 20th IAP, he was awarded a second Order of Lenin in January 1942. He was killed in combat with Me 110s on 27 January 1942 over his airfield at Grabtsevo. (Kaminskii, Berch, Pritsker, *Los Rusos, Pravda*)

STARKOV, Vasilii Vasil'evich, Sr.Lt., born 1908
A Zvena CO in the 8th Odessa Military Pilots School in the Kiev Mil. Dist. He arrived in Spain on 10 June 1938. He was an I-16 Pilot, in the 2nd Moscas and became CO of a Patrulla. KIA on 27 September 1938 when during Aerial combat over the Ebro, another Republican fighter flown by P. GLUSHKOV came down on top of his aircraft. His plane CM-245 went down crashing. He had flown fifty-one sorties and participated in thirty-four air combats. Semenov says the 28th as does *Los Rusos* and the 1991 list of Soviet dead. Posthumously awarded the Red Banner on 22 February 1939. He was the last Soviet fighter pilot lost in Spain. (Semenov *Tov.*, *Vmeste*, Abrosov, Kaminskii, Salas, *Pravda*)

STARODUMOV, Georgii K., Lt., born 1908
SB Pilot, served in Spain from 15 June 1937 to 28 January 1938. During a mission on 13 November he had to abort and return to La Cenia when one of his engines failed. Awarded the Red Banner twice, 11 November 1937 and 2 March 1938. (*Solidarity, Los Rusos, Pravda*, Abrosov)

STAROVOITOV, Boris G., born 1907
Engineer on I-15s says OSADCHII in *Vmeste*, but *Los Rusos* says I-16. He was in Spain from October 1936 to 2 July 1937. Awarded the Red Banner 17 July and Red Star 2 January 1937. (*Vmeste, Los Rusos, Pravda*)

STASHKOV, Nikodim Ivanovich, Lt., born 1911
Fighter pilot in the 107th IAE 83rd IAB Byelorussian Mil. Dist. In Spain from 26 March to 28 June 1938. He experienced some problems with high altitudes and according to Kaminski, on one occasion is said to have passed out at 6,000m and only came to at 4,000m and then crashed on landing. So due to this and other problems he was sent home early. He had flown twenty sorties and fought in one air battle on 23 May 1938 and had three aircraft in group to his credit. On his return from Spain, he was transferred from fighters to attack aircraft. When WWII began he was a Captain in the 658th ShAP fighting on the North Western front. Died 6 February (some sources say 16 December) 1942. (Abrosov, Kaminskii, *Los Rusos*)

STECHISHIN, Andrei Romanovich, Sr.Lt., born 1906
SB Pilot in Spain from 14 December 1937 to 21 July 1938. LIPASHOV in *Vmeste* spells it STETISHIN, and says he was Commander. Also says when he arrived in Spain in March 1938 he met STETISHIN'S Escuadilla members at the airfield at Gerona as they were departing for the Soviet Union. Semenov "*parol*" says he commanded one of the two Soviet operated SB Escuadrillas (the other was Lt. LISOV) in Spain during late-1937/early-1938. Their base was the San Clemente Air Field. Before going to Spain, both he and LISOV had served in the Leningrad Military District, where they commanded Detachments (six aircraft) of bomber aircraft. These two Escs. had taken part in the Salamanca raid and also those on Seville and Valladolid. They also saw action in the Teruel and Alfambra battles. GUDOVICH in *My* (1986), says STECHISHIN was there at Gerona airfield in

March and April and that their two escuadrillas were transferred to the field at Lerida in late April. He also goes on to say that STECHISHIN was called "Comrade Andresu." Awarded the Red Banner twice, 14 November 1938 and 22 February 1939. (Semenov "*Parol*," Berch, *Vmeste, My* (1986), *Los Rusos, Pravda* in 22 February 1939 lists as STECHISHEV)

STENIN, Timofeii, born 1903

Engineer on Bombers, in Spain from 10 October 1937 to 3 September 1938. Awarded the Red Star 22 February 1939. (*Pravda, Los Rusos* spell as STIEPIN)

STEPANOV, Andrei Mikhailovich, Lt., born 1907

Fighter pilot in the 107th IAE 83rd IAB Byelorussian Mil. Dist. In Spain from 26 March to 13 August 1938. Flew both the I-15 and I-16 and had flown seventy-eight sorties and fought in seventeen air combats. Four aircraft (two Fiats and two 109s) plus nine in group to his credit. Awarded the Red Banner on 22 February 1939. As assistant CO of the 70th IAP he fought in the Khalkhin-Gol and was wounded. He had flown seventy-one missions and participated in thirteen air battles, claiming three Japanese aircraft. Awarded a second Red Banner on 29 August 1939. He was mentioned for the HSU, but no action taken. During WWII he was CO of the 24th IAP-PVO. He failed to return from a mission on 15 April 1942. (Kaminskii, Semenov "*Parol*," Abrosov, *Pravda*)

STEPANOV, Evgenii Nikolaevich, Lt., born 22 May 1911

Joined the Red Army in 1932. Attended the Borisoglebsk Military Flying School, graduating in 1933. A Zvena CO in the 12th IAE 111 IAB Leningrad Mil. Dist., he volunteered for Spanish service and served from 20 August 1937 to 27 July 1938. An I-15 pilot, he used the nom de guerre "Slepnev." Arrived in France on board the Soviet ship *Kooperatsii* along with DEVOTCHENKO and others. They then flew to Spain in an Air France Farman, arriving on 28 August 1937. Placed in the 1st escuadrilla under EREMENKO and later SEROV. Later, in August he become a Patrulla leader (with Dobias and Korouz, two Austrians flying for the Republic as wingmen). At the end of October he was made Escuadrilla Commander when SEROV became CO of Grupo 26 after the attack on Garapinillas. He downed an S-81 on the night of 25 October (he says two). Later towards end of November he downed a Do 17. Said to have flown Chato #6. He replaced SEROV as CO of Grupo 26 on 14 December 1937. On 5 January 1938, during a landing he flipped Chato #CA 046, but he was not injured. He was shot down and captured on 17 January 1938 while flying CA 028 (Abrosov lists 20th, but daily log again indicates the 17th) during the battle of Teruel. See also SLEPNEFF. Had flown eighty sorties and fought in sixteen air battles and shot down six aircraft personal and four in group. Kaminskii says he was exchanged for the L.C. pilot Otto Polenz. He left Spain in July 1938 and boarded a ship which went from France to Leningrad. Later fought in the Khalkhin-Gol as commander of an Eskadril'ya of the 22nd IAP. Flew 100 missions and claimed four personal kills plus one in group. Awarded the H.S.U. on 29 August 1939 plus the Mongolian Red Banner 18 August 1939. Took part in the Winter War against Finland with the 19th IAP. During WWII, he served in the Air Force Staff controlling the Air Defenses of Moscow. Died 5 September 1996. Awards were H.S.U., Order of Lenin, Order of the Red Banner twice (10 November 1937 for Spain), GPW 1st Cl., and Order of the Red Star twice. Lukes claims he had eight kills in Spain. (Gusev, Smirnov, *Bajo la B.*, Shingarev, Rumyantsev *Geroi*, *Aviation His.*, Polak, Lukes, Abrosov, Kaminskii, Salas *Caza Rusa*, Abrosov 2nd ed. wrongly gives date of death as 1994.)

STEPANOV, Nikolai F., born 1907

Was Chief Engineer Chatos says SUIAZIN in *MY*, in Spain from October 1936 to 2 July 1937. Awarded the Red Star 2 January 1937. (*Pravda, MY, Los Rusos* list as Aviation Technician)

STEPANOV, Nikolai I., born 1915

Worker from Aircraft Factory #22 assembling SB aircraft. In Spain from October to 12 December 1936. Awarded the Red Star 2 January 1937. (*Los Rusos, Pravda*)

STEPANOV, Sergei Ivanovich, born 1909

Armaments Technician (aviation?), served from 28 April to 28 October 1938. Awarded the Red Star 22 February 1939. (*Los Rusos, Pravda*)

STEPANYAN, Amenak A., born 1907

Aircraft armaments technician for I-16 fighters, served from 14 January to 18 October 1937. Awarded the Red Star on 27 June 1937. (*Los Rusos, Pravda*)

STOKLITSKI, Sergei I., born 1900

Engineer who performed the wing changes on the I-16 in Spain. He was there from 10 December 1936 to 13 August 1938. Awarded the Order of Lenin on 22 October 1937. (*Los Rusos, Pravda*, Abrosov, Tolmachev)

STOLYAROV, Pavel M., born 1909

Armaments Technician, in Spain from October 1936 to 30 June 1937. Awarded the Red Star 2 January 1937. (*Pravda, Los Rusos*)

STRAKHOV, Mikhail, Lt., born 1906

Navigator SB from 15 June to 27 August 1937. (*Los Rusos*)

STREKOPYTOV, Anatolii Vasil'evich, born 1902

Engineer (Aviation?) in Spain from 12 January 1938 to 22 January 1939. Awarded the Red Banner 22 February 1939. (*Pravda, Los Rusos* spell as STREKONETOV)

STRELKOV, Aleksandr Vasil'evich, Capt., born 1906

Before going to Spain, he was in the 114th ShAB Byelorussian Mil. Dist. at Gomel. In Spain he was CO. of the 2nd Escuadrilla[1] of Rasantes (SSS) from November 1936 to 28 April 1937. This unit was stationed at Santa Cruz da la Zarza. Awarded the Red Banner on 2 January 1937. Abrosov and *Los Rusos* list date of death as 28 April 1937 in an air crash during a training flight, saying "Durante un entrenamiento el avion se le cayeron las alas." According to Abrosov, during a training flight, both wings came off his aircraft while he was pulling out of a loop at 600m altitude. Ibañez in *Icare*, says he was killed in Spain as does list of Soviets lost in Spain in Salas *Guerra Aerea* p.393. *Icaro #96* pgs.5-6 says Aleksandr Ivanovich Strelkov, Died 6 June 1937, buried in Cementerio de Torre-Pacheco. (*Vmeste, Pravda, Icare*, Abrosov, *Los Rusos, Icaro*, [1]some sources such as Kotelnikov say he was CO of the 1st Esc.)

STUROV, Nestor K., Lt., born 1906

SB pilot in Spain from October 1936 to 23 January 1937. Returned home early due to illness. Awarded the Red Banner 2 January 1937. (Kotelnikov, *Los Rusos, Pravda*)

SUBBOTIN, Aleksei Nikolaevich, Lt., born 1907

CO of an SB patrulla, in Spain from 28 June to 15 November 1938. Awarded the Red Banner on 22 February 1939. (Semenov "*Parol*," *Pravda, Los Rusos* spell it with only one B.)

SUKACHEV, Fedor A., born 1909

I-15 Aviation technician, served from 14 January to 30 July 1937. Returned early due to illness. Awarded the Red Star 27 June 1937. (*Los Rusos, Pravda*)

SUKHANOV, Aleksandr Petrovich, Lt., born 1909

Fighter pilot in the 40th IAE 83rd IAB Byelorussian Mil. Dist. In Spain from 31 May to 13 October 1937. Awarded the Red Banner 3 November 1937. After Spain he was appointed as CO of an Eskadril'ya in the 16th IAP Moscow Mil. Dist. Later appointed as commissar to the 26th IAP and fought in the Winter War for which he was awarded the Red Banner on 7 April 1940. In WWII he was assistant CO of the 185th IAD; KIA on 27 December 1944 during an air combat over Latvia. (Abrosov, Kaminskii, *Los Rusos* lists as I-16 flight instructor and left on 17 October)

SUKHANOV, Aleksandr N., born 1907

CO of a bomber patrulla (SSS), in Spain October 1936 to 2 July 1937. Awarded the Red Banner twice, 2 January and 4 July 1937. (*Los Rusos, Pravda*)

SUKHORUCHENKO, Fedor Andreevich, Sr.Lt., born 1908

A Zvena CO in the 41st IAE 83rd IAB Byelorussian Mil. Dist. In Spain he was a member of the 6th Moscas and a patrulla CO from 14 December 1937 to 10 June 1938. Flew some eighty sorties and participated in twenty-four air combats Claiming two Bf 109s and one Fiat. Awarded the Red Banner twice, 14 November 1938 and 22 February 1939.[1] Later served in the 29th IAP Moscow Mil. Dist., and in 1939 he took over command of the 29th. Fought in the Winter War against Finland on the staff of the 80th SAP. On 24 March 1940 was made CO of an Eskadril'ya in the 145th IAP, then became assistant CO of this Regiment. Awarded third Red Banner 21 May 1940. (Semenov "*Parol*," Abrosov, Kaminskii, Los Rusos, Gusev p.191 (Czech Ed.) says name spelt SUKHORUKOV. [1]Both Abrosov and Kaminskii list as Red Banner 22 February 1939, but a search of this list could not find his name.)

SUKHORUKOV, Petr V., born 1906

Engineer in KOLESNIKOV's Escuadrilla from October 1936 to 7 April 1937. Awarded the Red Star on 2 January 1937. (Rumyantsev "*Antonio*," *Pravda, Los Rusos*)

SUKHORYABOV, Vladimir Vikent'evich, Lt., born 1910

A Zvena CO in the 107th IAE 83rd IAB Byelorussian Mil. Dist. GUSEV says he was in "our Escuadrilla (the 6th Moscas) from 14 December 1937 to 10 June 1938." Abrosov says CO of a Patrulla. Flew sixty sorties and fought in twenty air battles and claimed two Fiats. Awarded the Red Banner 14 November 1938. During WWII fom May 1942 to July 1943 he was CO of the 294th IAD and from August 1943 until the end of the war was CO of the 1st Guards IAD. (Kaminskii, Semenov "*Parol*," Gusev 191 (Czech ed.), Abrosov, *Los Rusos, Pravda*)

SUKHOV, Osman Kh., born 1907

I-15 Aviation Technician served from 14 January to 18 October 1937. Awarded the Red Star on 17 July 1937. (*Los Rusos, Pravda*)

SUMAREV, Aleksandr Mikhailovich, Lt., born 1913

Pilot in the 142nd IAB Byelorussian Mil. Dist. In Spain from 20 August 1937. KIA while flying CM-009[1] and not CM-149 on 30 December 1937 during an air combat in the Teruel area, with Bf 109s of the 1st Staffel. Kaminskii says Prestele got the kill. Posthumously awarded the Red Banner 2 March 1938. [1]See listing for SKLYAROV. (Abrosov, Kaminskii, Salas "*Diario*" *Los Rusos, Pravda*)

SUPRUN, Stepan Pavlovich, born August 2, 1907. Did not serve in Spain.

Soviet test pilot, flight instructor supposedly for Spanish pilots in USSR Aewarded H.S.U. 20 May 1940. Killed in combat on 4 July 1941. Flew the captured Bf 109 after it arrived in the USSR (for more on this and him, see Alexandrov and Petrov, "Messerschmitt Bf 109B-1" pgs.4-5 in *Skyways* #29 January 1994). (Berch, Tarazona, Yakovlev, *Lexikon, Vmeste*)

SURZHIN, Ivan Semenovich, Sr.Lt., born 1907

Pilot of an SB, in Spain from 15 December 1937 to 21 March 1938. He was flying one of the four SBs downed by Messerschmitts on 7 February 1938. During the attack on Calamocha, two Spanish SBs and two Soviet SBs were downed by the 109s. (See SMIRNOV, I.) SURZHIN's was attacked by a large group of 109s from both sides and the rear. The 109s kept pressing home the attack. Accoring to Semenov, "then hydraulic fluid began to stream from the opening for the landing gear and the gear began to come down causing the air speed of the bomber to fall. With the Navigator and radio/Gunner returning fire, the aircraft fell out of formation. The 109s came in again, continuing to fire at the striken SB. Finally they succeeded in hitting the fuel lines or tank and the aircraft burst into flames. The crew began to abandon the plane. When SURZHIN finally jumped, (he had a problem finding the ring for his chute and had to throw off his gloves) he saw the 109s coming in again so he free fell some distance before opening his chute. As it opened, he was jerked so hard that one of his flight boots came off. Even though he pretended to be dead, the 109s came down and made a firing pass at him which, he was able to avoid by pulling on the shroud lines and moving to the left. Shortly after landing, he encountered a Republican patrol. His face and hands were completely blistered from the fire in the Aircraft. He asked the Spaniards if they had found any other Soviet flyers, so they began to search. They found Ivan SMIRNOV with a broken foot and suffering from the cold. Next they found in a thicket of evergreens SMIRNOV's radio/gunner. He had a broken leg and had used strips from his chute to bandage it. SURZHIN continued looking for his crew LATYSHEV and GORELOV. He found LATYSHEV face down on the ground, he had been machine gunned as he fell. Next he came upon the charred wreckage of his aircraft. A short distance from the wreckage were some old stone buildings, at the entrance to one, there was a crowd of people. Looking in he saw GORELOV lying in a pile beneath a hole in the roof. All he could find was one burned up parachute strap and nothing else. He then realized that GORELOV's chute must have burned up when he jumped from the Aircraft and opened his chute too soon." The fate of BOLDYREV, the Navigator in SMIRNOV's aircraft, was the same as LATYSHEV, he had been machine-gunned while coming down in his chute. The three men were buried at Mora de Rubielos. Also according to Semenov "*Parol*," Viktor TROSHKIN was involved with this mission, which can only mean that DEVOTCHENKO's escuadrilla had been flying escort. Awarded the Red Banner 14 November 1938. (Semenov "*Parol*," Berch, *Los Rusos, Pravda*)

SUSLOV, Efim V., Lt., born 1908

SB Navigator in Spain 31 May 1937 until 28 January 1938. Awarded the Red Banner twice, 28 October 1937 and 2 March 1938. (*Vmeste, Solidarnost, Los Rusos, Pravda*)

SUVOROV, Vasilii Ivanovich, Maj., born 1905

Navigator SB, served from 14 December 1937 to 13 July 1938. He participated in the attack on the Nationalist Crusier Baleares, 6 March 1938. Before Spain, he had served in a Leningrad Bomber Eskadril'ya as Flag Officer Navigator. Awarded the Order of Lenin 22 February 1939 and Red Banner on 14 November 1938. (Berch, Semenov "*Parol*," Kotelnikov, *Los Rusos, Pravda*)

SUYAZIN, Vasilii Andreevich, Capt., born 1901

Before going to Spain he was on the staff of the 23rd TBAE (Heavy Bomber Aviation Escuadrilla) 107th TBAB (Heavy Bomber AviaBrigade) Moscow Mil. Dist. In Spain from October 1936 to 29 September 1937, on staff with the fighter group. Awarded the Red Banner on 2 January 1937. Fought in WWII, died in 1981. (*MY*/Berch, *Pravda*, Abrosov, Kaminskii)

SVERGUN, Il'ia Tikhonovich, Lt., born 1912

Pilot in the 4th IAE 56th IAB Kiev Mil. Dist. He was an I-16 Pilot in the 5th Moscas under GRITSEVETS/ KOROBKOV in August 1938. Arrived on 10 June and returned on 28 October 1938. Flew fifty-seven sorties and fought in thirty air combats and had two CR 32s to his credit. Awarded the Red Banner 22 February 1939, fought in WWII. Died in 1959. (Semenov *Tov.*, *Vmeste*, Abrosov, *Los Rusos*, Kaminskii, *Pravda*)

SVESHNIKOV, Boris Fedorovich "Col. Boris," born 1897

Col. Soviet A.F. Attaché in Spain from August 1936 to 22 April 1937. Awarded the Order of Lenin. During WWII, served as Chief of Staff of 7th Air Army. (Zil'manovich, Gusev p.18, *Bajo la B.*, Boyd, *Los Rusos*)

SVIRIDOV, Arkadii Konstantinovich, Lt., born 13 February 1911

In 1936 he was a pilot and later a Zvena CO in the 3rd IAE VVS Red Banner Baltic Fleet. Was an I-16 Pilot and patrulla CO in Spain from 14 December 1937 to 10 June 1938 in DEVOTCHENKO's/RODIN's 2nd Esc. Flew eighty sorties and participated in twenty air combats, had one aircraft to credit (Bf 109). Awarded the Red Banner 14 November 1938. After Spain he took Aviation Training Courses at the Lipetsk Military Aviation School. From September to November 1940 he was Inspector of pilot technique in the 6th IAP Pacific Fleet. After which until December 1942 he held the same postion with the 7th IAB. He then became assistant CO of the 12th IAP. In April 1944 he was posted as assistant CO of the 11th ShAD (Mixed) and fought on the Black Sea and then from July 1944 on the Baltic. From January 1945 until the end of the war he was the assistant CO of the 21st IAP Baltic Fleet. Awarded the Red Banner on 11 June 1945, plus several other medals. After the war he continued in Naval Aviation, retiring in 1958. Passed away 21 May 1989. (Kaminskii, Semenov "*Parol*," Pritsker, Abrosov, *Los Rusos, Pravda*)

SYKOV, Gavril, born 1908

Los Rusos says Aviation Technician in Spain from October 1936 to 27 August 1937. Awarded the Red Star. (But could not find him in *Pravda*) (*Los Rusos*)

SYTNIK, Valentin I, born 1908

Aviation Technician in Spain from October 1936 to 27 March 1938. BIBIKOV p.17 *Vmeste*, says he was an SB Technician. Awarded the Red Star 2 January 1937. (*Pravda, Vmeste, Los Rusos* spell it SETKIN)

TAKHTAROV, Boris Adil'gireevich, Lt., born 1910

After graduating Flying School in 1933, he first served in the North-Caucasus Mil. Dist. Then as a Lt. he flew with the 3rd IAE VVS KBF Red Banner Balitc Fleet. In Spain from 14 December 1937 to 15 April 1938, he was an I-16 Pilot in DEVOTCHENKO's 2nd Esc. He was wounded in the right leg and badly burned on 21 February 1938 when his aircraft (either CM-123 or 239) caught fire after being hit by Bf 109s and he had to take to his parachute. When he jumped his chute opened early, and on the way down the Germans tried to strafe him, but his comrades prevented them. He spent thirty-five days in the hospital and then returned home. He had flown thirty sorties and participated in ten air battles and had one Bf 109 to his credit. Awarded the Red Banner 14 November 1938. Other Baltic Fleet pilots (DENISOV, BAGROV, SHUBIKOV, NIKOTIN, BELOV, SVIRIDOV, TROSHKIN and PRESNUKIN) were in this same Escuadrilla in Spain. After his return home he joined the 13th IAP Baltic Fleet, he continued to serve in the 13th throughout the war flying in the Artic protecting the ships coming into Murmansk and Arkhangel. He continued to serve in the VVS after the war, and passed away in 1997. (airaces.narod.ru, Semenov "*Parol*," Pritsker, Abrosov, *Los Rusos*, Kaminskii, *Pravda*)

TALOV, Aleksandr Andreevich, Sr.Lt., born 1908

He arrived in November 1936 and was in the SSS Rasante Detachment under command of TUPIKOV, G.N. where he was the navigator/gunner on TUPIKOV's aircraft. Shot down during attack on Torrijos 6 December 1936, by AAA. He was killed trying to evade capture and TUPIKOV was captured. This mission had included four Patrullas of SSS aircraft, and was escorted by fifteen I-16 fighters. Posthumously awarded the Red Banner on 2 January 1937. (*Vmeste, My 2, Pravda, Los Rusos*)

TARASOV, Aleksandr Ignat'evich, Sr.Lt. Born 1909

A Zvena CO in the 41st IAE 83rd IAB Byelorussian Mil. Dist. He was an I-16 Fighter pilot, that arrived in Spain at the end of October 1936. A member of TARKHOV's enlarged Escuadrilla, he was a patrulla CO in the Detachment under KOLESNIKOV. He claimed one Ju 52 in mid/late November 1936 and is listed as having two personel plus four in group. He returned home on 27 March 1937. Howson says he commanded one of the first three escuadrillas, but he is confusing him with TARKHOV. Awarded the Order of the Red Banner twice, on 2 January and 17 July 1937. On his return to the USSR he was questioned by Alksnis, the Commander of the VVS, about different aspects of service in Spain. TARASOV told him that they only tried to attack the Ju 52 from the front, for if they attacked from the rear or side it would expose them to heavy MG fire. In 1937 he was appointed CO of the 50th IAE. He is last thought to have served in the Kharkov Mil. Dist. in 1939. (*Solidarity,* R and R 264, Howson 198, Ha 24, Rumyantsev "*Antonio,*" *Pravda,* Kaminskii.

TARBEEV, Evgenii I., Lt., born 1911

Radio/gunner served from 15 June 1937 until 28 January 1938. Awarded the Red Banner twice, 28 October 1937 and 2 March 1938. (*Los Rusos, Pravda, Solidarity* where it is spelt TORBEEV)

TARKHOV, Sergei Fedorovich, Capt. "Antonio," born 8 October 1909

In February 1936, he took command of the 107th IAE 83rd IAB Byelorussian Mil. Dist. at Briansk. In May 1936 this unit received the new I-16 fighter. He became one of the first to qualify in night flying. He and several other members of the 107th volunteered for duty in Spain. On 21 October they along with other volunteers

from the 40th and 41st IAEs boarded the ship *Kursk* in Sevastopol Crimea. The ship's Captain was Vitalii TSIL'KE. They sailed through the Black Sea, Bosporus and Dardanelles. Some of those onboard were LAKEEV, BOCHAROV, CHERNYKH, MINAEV, KOLESNIKOV, and RYABOV. Near Sardinia, they were tracked and photographed by Italian Aircraft. Off the coast of North Africa, the ship was met by several warships of the Republican Navy including the Crusiers *Libertad* and *Cervantes* which escorted them to Alicante.[1] He became commander of the enlarged (thirty-one aircraft) I-16 Escuadrilla which later became the 1st Mocsas. In a period of three days after their arrival, twelve aircraft had already been assembled. The group flew from Alicante on the 5th of November and landed at Albacete. There they met with Col. "Julio" PUMPUR. Later this same day the group flew over to Alcala de Henares, being led by PUMPUR and KOVALEVSKII. According to Rumyantsev, the group flew its first mission on the 6th,[2] attacking a formation of Junkers 52s attempting to bomb Madrid. As the twelve aircraft approched the bombers, they noticed a large formation of Fiats coming. Tarkhov ordered Senor Lt. BACHAROV, commander of the first detachment, to attack the fighters while he went after the bombers with the 2nd detachment. He attacked one of the Junkers, and after firing at it, it was seen to catch fire and then break in two, falling to the ground near Retiro Park. Ivan KRAVCHENKO also claimed a Junkers while P. KUZNETSOV claimed an He 51 and P. SHEVTSOV a Fiat. The other twelve aircraft, after being assembled, flew to a field near Guadalajara. These were led by Detachment Commander KOLESNIKOV. The main group included all services (ammo, fuel, technical support) remained at the Alcala base. On the 7th, Tarkhov claimed an He 51 and POLYAKOV got a Savoia. All told, the Escuadrilla claimed four bombers and two fighters for the 7th. He was shot down over Madrid on 13 November during an air battle. Tarkhov parachuted to the ground safely only to be attacked and shot by Milicianos thinking him a German. He died in the Palace Hotel which had been converted into a hospital on 23 November (this is the date and hospital information given by RSA and Koltsov). Salas lists him as dying on the 22nd at the Gomez Ulla Hosp. Laureau says he was shot down on the 10th and died on the 12th. He is listed as having 5+1 victories and was awarded the H.S.U. and Order of Lenin posthumously on 31 December 1936. Some members of his Esc. were KOLESNIKOV, DENISOV, LAKEEV, CHERNYKH, SHEVTSOV, KUZNETSOV, KRAVCHENKO, ZAMASHANSKII, BALANOV, PAVLOV, POLYAKOV, BOCHAROV, MOROZOV, KHOVANSKII, SOKALOV, NEGOREEV, MINAEV, TARASOV. (RSA, Koltsov, Laureau, Lacalle, *Pravda*, Salas, *Bajo La B*, *Icare 130* p.52, *Vmeste*, Pritsker, Rumyantsev "*Antonio*," Kaminskii, [1]Gonzalez Echegaray, R. *La Marina Mercante y el Traffico Maritimo en la Guerra Civil*, San Martin, Madrid 1977 says on p.277 that the *Kursk* arrived on 25 October at Cartagena. [2]This information on early I-16 operations is not really supported in Abrosov, *Los Rusos* claim he was born 1907.)

TCHURUPA, Capt.

Sec. of E.M. del Aire under Douglas (?). (*Chantaje* 104)

TEPLOV, Pavel Iosifovich, NCO, born 1907

Radio/Gunner on SB, from 30 December 1937 to 13 July 1938. He participated in the 7 February 1938 mission to Calamocha. According to Semenov, when his aircraft landed, more than forty bulletholes were counted. During the attack by 109s, a shell severed the pin coupling the machine gun to its mount. The weapon fell on the floor of the cockpit, smashing a lantern mounted there. TEPLOV's flight suit was torn apart by bullets, and he was later found to have nine skin burns from shells grazing him, but no wounds. Awarded the Red Banner 14 November 1938. (Semenov "*Parol*," Berch, *Pravda, Los Rusos* misspell name as TENLOV)

TERTYCHNYI, Nikolai Trofimovich, Lt., born 1913

Radio/gunner SB, came on 30 May and returned 15 November 1938. He along with two other SB gunners IL'IN and KOZHEMYAKO are said to have shot down the Bf 109 flown by J. Gamringer of 3. J/88 on 10 October when their formation was attacked. Awarded the Red Banner on 22 February 1939. (Semenov "*Parol*," Berch, *Los Rusos, Pravda*, Voronkova lists as a pilot/bombarder and mentions that during WWII, his aircraft was shot down in late 1942 and that he bailed out over enemy territory. He then encountered a group of partisans and joined with them until he could rejoin his air group.)

TIGROV, Col.

Commander SB 1937 (?). Possible codename. (Gringoire via Logoluso)

TIKHOMIROV, Aleksandr Mikhailovich, Lt., born 1906

Pilot SB arrived 15 June, was in SENATOROV's 1st Esc., shot down and KIA on 29 August 1937 over Villamayor by CR 32s. The claim for this aircraft was shared by G. Russin of the 19th Squadriglia and another pilot. Other members of the crew were FEOKTISTOV, navigator, and a Spanish gunner. *Los Rusos* list as Navigator and say "Derribado cayó envuelto en llamas. Enterrado en Sariñena." Awarded the Red Banner 28 October 1937. (Abrosov, *Los Rusos, Pravda*)

TIMOFEEV, Nikolai T., born 1895
Worker from Aircraft Factory #22 assembling SB aircraft. In Spain from October to 12 December 1936. Awarded the Red Star 2 January 1937. (*Los Rusos, Pravda*)

TIMOKHIN, Stepan Mikhailovich
Semenov *Tov.* says he was Commander at KIROVABAD in 1938. Awarded the Order of Lenin 22 February 1939. (*Pravda*)

TITOV, Vladimir Spiridonovich, Sr.Lt., born 1908
SB Navigator arrived 28 June and was KIA 24 August 1938. On a mission to bomb enemy troops near Gandesa, his aircraft was hit by a AAA shell. The crew bailed out, but the pilot VELICHENKO's parachute burned up and he fell to his death. TITOV landed in enemy territory and was MIA, the gunner RODIN was the only one to survive. (Semenov "*Parol*," Abrosov, *Los Rusos* list as Pilot and list date as the 25th .)

TKACHENKO, Mefodi E., born 1907
Mechanic in TARKHOV's I-16 Escuadrilla. Arrived in October 1936 and returned home on 8 May 1937. Awarded the Red Star 2 January 1937. (*Vmeste, Los Rusos* spell it TCHACHENKO, *Pravda*)

TKHOR, Grigorii Illarionovich, Sr.Lt., born 26 September 1903, died January 1943
An SB pilot, he arrived in September/October 1936, where he became a member of the 1st Internacional Escuadrilla under Capt. Martin Luna. Flew both Br 19s and Potez 540s. DEMENCHUK was a part of his crew at one time. He then in November switched to the newly formed 2nd Escuadrilla SB Grupo 12. Returned home on 2 July 1937. Flew 102 missions in Spain, according to S.V. Slyusarev in "Protecting China's Air Space" in *Soviet Volunteers in China 1925-1945*, Progress Pub. Moscow 1980. He bombed Burgos, Seville and Cadiz among other places. Awarded the Order of the Red Banner twice, on 2 January and 4 July 1937. In August 1938 he went to China with the Soviet Air Group. Awarded the Red Banner on 14 November 1938. In June 1941 with rank of Major-General, he was the replacement Commander of the 62nd BAD on the southwestern front and participated in the defense of Kiev. He was shot down and captured on 23 September 1941. He was executed in the German Flossenburg POW camp in January 1943. He was awarded the H.S.U. on 26 July 1991, forty-eight years after his death. Other awards were Order of Lenin 22 February 1939, and Red Banner three times. (*Solidarity*, Berch, Semenov "*Parol*," *Vmeste, MY*, Pritsker, *Pravda, C.L.V.B.P.F., Guerra y Rev. 2, Kto Byl Kto v Velikoi Otechestvennoi Voine 1941-1945*, Moskva 1995, *Los Rusos*)

TOROPCHENKO, Vladimir M., born 1911
Armaments specialist, served from October 1936 to 9 July 1937. Awarded the Red Star 2 January 1937. (*Los Rusos, Pravda*)

TRET'YAKOV, Anatolii Vasil'evich, Sr.Lt., born 1905
A Detachment CO in the 120th IAE Transcaucasian Mil. Dist. He was an I-15 Fighter pilot in Spain from 14 January to 26 July 1937. Awarded the Red Banner on 27 June 1937. After returning home, he was posted as CO of the 11th IAE, and in 1938 he became deputy CO of the 19th IAP 54th IAB and in 1939 fought in the Winter War with Finland. In October 1940 he became CO of the 19th IAP. During WWII he was appointed as CO of the 435th IAP flying La 5s. He was KIA in 1944. (Abrosov, Kaminskii, *Los Rusos, Pravda*)

TRETYAKOV, Nikolai N., born 1908
Mechanic/Technician on I-15s. *Los Rusos* claims he was Head Mechanic of an Escuadrilla. In Spain from 14 January to 18 October 1937. Awarded the Red Star on 4 July 1937. (*Bajo la B., Los Ruso, Pravda*)

TROSHKIN, Viktor Sergeevich, Lt., born 1911
Attended the Eiskuiu Naval Military Flyers School. After graduation, served in the 3rd IAE VVS KBF Red Banner Baltic Fleet Aviabrigade. In Spain, he was an I-16 Pilot in DEVOTCHENKO's 2nd Esc., arriving on 14 December 1937. He was KIA while flying CM-032 on the morning of 21 February 1938 in an air battle between twelve I-16s and Bf 109s from the 1st and 2nd Staffels. The German pilots claimed seven I-16s shot down, but in truth only three were lost. He was twenty-seven years old at the time. He had left for Spain in early December 1937 from Leningrad on the ship *Andrei Zhdanov* along with other pilots from the Baltic Fleet, V. BAGROV, B. TAKHTAROV, V. PRESNUKHIN, A.

SVIRIDOV, A. BELOV, A. SHUBIKOV, N. NIKITIN, and A. DENISOV. Also onboard were a whole group of SB personnel, pilots, navigators and radio/gunners. During the Teruel Ops., on 3 January 1938, he was flying CM-019 and PRESNUKHIN flying CM-103 crashed into one another while taxing for take off from Sagunto airfield following an alarm. Both aircraft were badly damaged. PRESNUKHIN was unhurt, but TROSHKIN suffered a head wound when he contacted the gun sighting tube. Awarded the Red Star Posthumously on 14 November 1938. (Semenov "*Parol*" says he was born in 1910, Pritsker, *Los Rusos*, Abrosov says it happened at La Cenia, Salas "*Diario*," Kaminskii, *Pravda*)

TRUBITSIN, Ivan Iosifovich, Sr.Lt., born 1908

An SB Pilot, he arrived on 28 June and returned home 25 November 1938. He was shot down by Bf 109s on 10 October, but was able to bail out. He was a member of the last Soviet SB Escuadrilla to serve in Spain. Shortly afterwards the Escuadrilla was withdrawn from service when the Republic sent all foreign volunteers home. Awarded the Red Banner 22 February 1939. (Semenov "*Parol*," Berch, Abrosov, *Los Rusos, Pravda*)

TRUSHIN, Ivan A., Sr.Lt., born 1906

Navigator SSS, he served from October 1936 to 19 June 1937. Awarded the Red Banner twice, 2 January and 21 June 1937. (*Los Rusos, Pravda*)

TRUSOV, Aleksei Sergeevich, Lt., born 1912

A Pilot in the 119th IAE 95th IAB Transcaucasian Mil. Dist. An I-16 Fighter pilot, he arrived in Spain on 31 May. On 6 July 1937, while his escuadrilla was escorting RZs on a bombing mission, they were attacked by Italian Fiat CR 32s. TRUSOV was shot down and crashed into the ground. Posthumously awarded the Red Banner 11 November 1937 (Abrosov, Kaminskii, *Los Rusos, Pravda*)

TSAPLIN, Dmitrii Capt., born 1910

An SB pilot, he served from 28 August to 3 September 1938. Awarded the Order of Lenin. (Is this really TSAR'KOV below? Dates of service given are very short – seven days!) (*Los Rusos*)

TSAR'KOV, Dmitrii Andrianovich

A Pilot SB, he came in April 1938. According to Semenov, both he and KRASNOGLAZOV were SB Escuadrilla commanders, replacing STECHISHIN and LISOV. He returned home September 1938. Awarded the Order of Lenin on 22 February 1939. (Berch, Semenov "*Parol*," *Pravda*)

TSCHERKASOFF, A.

Prisoner, used a phony name. See CHERKASOV/ CHERKAROFF. Laureau and Dahms, claim flew I-15 and spelt TSCHERKASSOV. Abellan claims it was spelt TCHARKASSOV, Alexis T. and flew an I-15 downed in battle with Fiats of the XXIII Grupo on 7 July 1937. (Hericourt, Laureau, Dahms, Abellan)

TSIGULEV, Nikolai Pavlovich, NCO, born 1913

Radio/gunner on SB, he was KIA along with PETROV and VLASOV when their SB was shot down over the San Bartalome area on 2 November 1936. They were on a mission to bomb Talavera. Awarded the Order of the Red Banner on 2 January 1937. (*Vmeste*, Abrosov, *Los Rusos* list last service date as 30 November)

TSYKOV, Prokofi Nikanorovich, Lt., born 1909

Navigator SB, he arrived 1 April and returned 3 September 1938. Awarded the Red Banner on 22 February 1939. (Berch, *Pravda*, Semenov "*Parol*," *Los Rusos* both of these last two spell it TSIKOV)

TUMAKOV, Petr A., born 1913

Aviation Technician in Spain from October 1936 to 26 July 1937. Awarded the Red Star 2 January 1937. (*Los Rusos, Pravda*)

TUPIKOV, Georgii Nikolaevich, Capt., born 10 (27) April 1907

Before going to Spain, he was in the 114th ShAB at Gomel. In Spain was in the 1st Internacional Escuadrilla de Bombardeos in September (October) 1936, flying Br 19s. He then transferred and became commander of the 3rd escuadrilla SSS Rasantes Grupo 15 in November 1936. On 6 December 1936, during an attack on the Torrijos airfield, his aircraft was shot down by AAA. He was wounded. His navigator/ gunner TALOV pulled him from the wrecked aircraft. Pursued and surrounded by enemy troops, he was captured and TALOV was shot and killed trying to evade capture. Laureau says shot down on 2 December and killed. While Salas says 2 December, he only mentions the gunner/observer as being killed. Nom de guerre was "Sedlachek." Repatriated on 20 June 1937, along with another member of his unit SHUKAEV, who says in *Vmeste* that his aircraft was also shot down during the same mission is apparently mistaken, as his

mission was to Navalmora de la Mata on 4 December, CHERVYAKOV in *Vmeste* says he took over command of the Detachment after TUPIKOV was downed but does not give the Escuadrilla number. SHUKAEV says TUPIKOV was a Detachment Commander with CHERVYAKOV, BOGACHEV and KOLBASOVSKII as Patrulla leaders, which would indicate that TUPIKOV was the Commander of an Escuadrilla. Awarded the Order of the Red Banner on 2 January 1937. Fought in the Russo-Finnish War in 1940, as CO of the 6th DBAP. During WWII, from August 1941 until March 1942, he served as CO of the 22nd BAD ADD. From March 1942 to May 1943 he was CO of the 52nd BAD ADD and from May 1945 he was CO of the 6th BAK ADD. After the war, in 1949 to 1950 he was Deputy CO of the 43rd BAK ADD and became its CO from September 1950 until February 1951. He then became Deputy CO of ADD from 1951 to 1953. In 1958 he became Colonel General, and passed away on 16 November 1961. (Howson 264, Berch, Laureau, *MY, MY 2*, Salas, *Bajo la B*, Meroño, *Vmeste* pgs.183 and 295-312, Pravda, Abrosov, *Los Rusos*, Voronkova)

TURCHIN, Ivan Ivanovich, Lt., born 1909

He was a Detachment CO in the 35th IAE 56th IAB Kiev Mil. Dist. An I-16 Pilot, he arrived in Spain on 26 March and was KIA on 23 May 1938 in an air battle with Fiat CR 32s in the Balaguer region. Awarded the Red Banner on 22 February 1939. (*Los Rusos* say last sevice date was 26 May as does the 1991 list. Semenov "*Parol*," Abrosov, *Los Rusos, Pravda*)

TUROV, Aleksandr Grigor'evich, Lt., born 1912, died 1983.

From November 1937 until April 1938 he had been a pilot in the 109th IAE[1] 56th IAB Kiev Mil. Dist. In Spain from 10 June to 4 October 1938, he was an I-16 Pilot in 2nd Moscas under SEMENKO. He was wounded on 15 August 1938,[2] while landing his plane it flipped over and crashed. TUROV says in *Vmeste* - Gorilovskii Ed. That was because his aircraft had been hit by AAA fire and he was wounded. He had flown five sorties and fought in four air battles. Awarded the Red Banner on 22 February 1939. From December 1938 until March 1940 he served as a senior aide in an Eskadril'ya of the 23rd IAP. Fought on the Russo Finnish War from January to March 1940 and and from March 1940 to July 1941 he was first Deputy CO, then CO of the 23rd. In July 1941 he became CO of the 43rd SAD on the Western front where he flew sixty-four sorties and participated in thirty-eight air combats, claiming four aircraft plus one in group. On 29 July 1941 he downed a Ju 88, but was then hit by MG fire from the stricken bomber. On landing his MiG-3 crashed and he suffered a broken arm and injured right leg. He was in the hospital from August to October 1941; after his release he was appointed CO of an Eskadril'ya in the 352nd IAP Central Asian Mil. Dist. serving there until April 1944. From April until the end of the war he was the Inspector for pilot technique with the 273rd IAD on the Byelorussian front. During this period he flew fifty-one sorties and fought in seven air battles gaining another two aircraft plus three in group. After the war he remained in the VVS until placed on the reserves on 11 April 1958. Died on 22 March 1983. (*Vmeste, Pravda*, Abrosov, *Los Rusos*. [1]Kaminskii lists as the 109th, but Abrosov lists as the 4th. [2]Kaminskii claims it happened on 20 August, while Semenov *Tov.* says wounded on the 21st.)

TURPIT'KO, Aleksei P., born 1907

Listed by KAL'CHENKO as a Technician in RYCHAGOV's Escuadrilla. In Spain from October 1936 to 7 April 1937. Awarded the Red Star 2 January 1937. (*Vmeste, Los Rusos, Pravda*)

TURZHANSKII, Boris Aleksandrovich, Col., born 26 February 1900

Joined the Soviet Army in 1918. Participated in the Russian Civil War. In 1921 completed the Egor'evskii Flight School, and in 1924 Zaraisk Superior Aviation School. In 1936 took courses at the Air Force Academy. In Spain, he commanded an I-15 Escuadrilla in the North from November 1936 until 11 February 1937. In mid October 1936, the Soviet Ship *A. Andreev* docked at Leningrad and took on a load of fifteen crated I-15s, and a contingent of eleven airmen., B.A. TURZHANSKII, P.A. ANTONETS, K.G. BARANCHUK, K.S. BENIKOVSKII, P.T. SEMENOV, P.A. GONCHAROV, A.I. KETOV, N.T. PETRUKHIN, A.V. PLETYUKHIN, V.T. SAKHANOV and S.G. BUKKIN. According to N. Chilingiri a member of the ship's crew writing in Pritsker, says, the ship set sail on 22 October, traveling through the Gulf of Finland, Baltic Sea, into the North Sea. Off the coast of France near Calais, on the 27th they encountered very heavy seas. TURZHANSKII was very worried

about it damaging his aircraft. The ship arrived at Santander on 1 November and at Bilbao on the night of 1-2 November where he and his men and aircraft were off loaded. Steer in *The Tree of Gernika* pgs.96-97 mentions this event, "The first weapons to be unloaded were twelve (really fifteen) single seat fighters, Russian biplane Boeings."[1] He also says "Russian pilots came with them, oldish men of thirty six and thereabouts." Awarded the H.S.U. on 31 December 1936, he is credited with six kills. Salas in *Mod. and His.* lists him as ALEKSANDROVICH, B. Later in *Guernica* pgs.62-63 Salas says fifteen I-15s were off loaded at Bilbao. He also says that on 4 January 1937 this Esc. downed a Ju 52 over Bilbao. Kaminskii says he had four He 51s to his credit. ADRIASHENKO, in the revised and enlarged 1986 edition of *MY,* gives the following information: "TURZHANSKII was a volunteer in the Red Air Force during the Russian civil war after which he attended Aviation school and proved to be an outstanding pilot, for which he received awards. He volunteered for duty in Spain in 1936, after graduating from the Air Force Academy. Arrived in the port of Bilbao on board a Soviet Steamship in November 1936. The appearance of this Escuadrilla was very much appreciated at the front. Fascist fighters and bombers incurred many losses from their attacks. With the curtailed bombings, the inhabitants of Bilbao and the troops at the front breathed with relief." He goes on to say, "That in its attacks on the numerically superior enemy forces, the flyers displayed extraordinary courage, but the main reason for their success was the ability of the commander to select the correct tactics. Ground attacks replaced patrols and aerial battles." He also quotes the Chief of Staff Francisco Ciutat de Miguel as saying this was a "Escuadrilla of heroes led by a Lion." During one of the air combats on 20 December 1936 TURZHANSKII's aircraft was hit and he was wounded. Though he fought to control the aircraft, it crashed in the mountains. It took two days for them to find him and take him to a hospital, where he had to undergo a serious Cranial operation. He lost sight in one eye and was told by the doctors that he would never fly again, but after his recuperation (in Russia), he began flying once again and later became a Test Pilot. ADRIASHENKO says that "he was in the very first of those serving in Spain to be awarded the H.S.U. and that it was Number 12." He also mentions that his name was used on Supersonic Missile Carriers produced during the 1970s. After TURZHANSKII's departure on 11 February 1937, command of the Escuadrilla passed first to BARANCHUK and later to Felipe del Rio. He also goes on to say that "the Escuadrilla was noticably depleated and that no replacment aircraft arrived." In March a group of Spanish pilots arrived in a transport aircraft. Whereas all others list number of aircraft delivered on November 1936 as between 12-15, ADRIASHENKO says twelve pilots and thirty aircraft were off loaded, which is incorrect. He saw service in WWII, and later as Chief Test Pilot at the Zhil Aviation factory works in Moscow. Among his awards are the Order of Lenin twice, Order of the Red Banner, Order of the Patriotic War 1st Cl., order of the Red Star and several others. He died on 14 June 1948. In 1968 the Town of Zaraisk erected an obelisk in the honor of TURZHANSKII and GIBELLI. (RSA, Morquillas in *A.G.*, R and R 264, Zil'Manovich, Salas in *M and H*, Howson 195, Ha 24, Pritsker, *Geroi, Pravda*, Boyd p.78 says he "was a Shturmovik Specialist," *MY*, Kaminskii, Abrosov, See also listing for MARANCHOV. [1]For more information on the arrival of this ship at Bilbao, where it was seen by men on a German ship, see Viñas *La Solidad de la Republica*, p.358)

TUTAEV, Nikolai Ivanovich, born 1908

SB Pilot, arrived on 28 June and returned on 15 November 1938. Awarded the Red Banner on 22 February 1939. (Semenov "*Parol*" p.201, *Los Rusos* list first name as Tarov)

TVERDOKHLEBOV, Yakov

Mechanic in first group under TARKHOV, October 1936. (*Vmeste*. Very possibly same as below.)

TVERDOKHVALOV, Akim P., born 1905

Aviation Technician from October 1936 to 7 April 1937. Awarded the Red Star 2 January 1937. (*Los Rusos, Pravda*)

TYAGUNOV, Aleksei Mikhailovich, Lt., born 1908

A Navigator on SB, arrived 26 March and returned 5 August 1938. On 2 May, during a raid on Zaragoza without fighter escort, his Aircraft was hit by AAA, and both he and the pilot ASAULOV were wounded. As their aircraft began to lag behind the rest of the formation, it was attacked by enemy fighters. The Escuadrilla Commander KRASNOGLAZOV ordered all the other SBs to close in and form a shield over the damaged aircraft, which caused the attacking fighters to break off their attack due to the heavy MG fire of all twelve aircraft. Later on 24 May,[1] at the close of their attack on enemy ground forces, his plane being flown by Patrulla

leader KORZINNIKOV was hit by AAA, and both TYAGUNOV and the pilot were wounded. The aircraft started to fall behind and then began to go down. The crew including the Gunner UDOVCHENKO were all able to bail out. Awarded the Red Banner 22 February 1939. (Semenov "*Parol*," Berch, *My (1986)* pgs.291-295, *Los Rusos*, [1]Abrosov p.233 indicates that it was on 23 May and their aircraft was only damaged and TYAGUNOV was slightly wounded.)

TYKIN, Yan A., born 1895
Base Air Defense, served from January to 28 August 1937. Awarded the Order of Lenin on 27 June 1937 and the Red Banner. (*Solidarity, Los Rusos, Pravda*)

UDOVICHENKO, Ivan Petrovich, NCO, born 1913
Radio/Gunner SB, he arrived 26 March and returned home 13 August 1938. He was a crewmember of the aircraft flown by KORZINNIKOV, which on 24 May was shot down by AAA. The crew were able to save themselves bailing out. Awarded the Red Banner 22 February 1939. (Semenov "*Parol*" gives middle name as Nesterovich, whereas *Pravda* lists as above, Berch, *My (1986), Los Rusos*)

UGROVATOV, Petr Vasilevich, Lt., born 1907
A Zvena CO in the 120th IAE Transcaucasian Mil. Dist. In Spain from 14 January to 7 April 1937, he was the CO of an I-15 patrulla. Shot down but able to bail out though badly burned on 18 February 1937. Kaminskii says he flew one combat sortie and participated in one air battle. Awarded the Red Banner on 27 June 1937. In November 1941 he was CO of the 169th IAP and later became the deputy CO of the 526th IAP on the South Western front. Died during the war. (Abrosov, Kaminskii, *Pravda, Guerra y Revolucion 2*, Logoluso, *Los Rusos* spell it UGRATOV)

UKHOV, Valentin Petrovich, Sr.Lt., born 1908
Before going to Spain he was a Detachment CO at the 8th Odessa Military Aviators School Kiev Mil. Dist. He arrived in Spain on 14 January 1937, and returned home on 13 September 1937 Served in the expanded I-16 group under KOLESNIKOV, and was Commander of the 1st Moscas from May 13 through June 1937. Then the Escuadrilla was turned over to LAKEEV and UKHOV took over command of a new Escuadrilla (4th) of I-16s, which went to Santander on 2 July 1937 (several sources incorrectly say 17 June). Tinker and Baumler were attached to his 1st Esc. and Tinker says he was still on the Madrid front up until 20 June! Turned command of this new Escuadrilla over to EVSEV'EV shortly after arriving at Santander. Shingarev says he went from Santander to the USSR, whereas Meroño claims, p.204, that he was the Commander of 2nd Moscas during the Battle of the Ebro? While Howson says he commanded the 5th escuadrilla after it was formed in mid July 1937 and Arias says he was Esc. CO on the Central front in August/September, but EVSEV'EV in Vmeste says, "At the beginning of July V. UKHOV had now served his appointed time in Spain and was recalled to the central front from which he departed for the homeland." Awarded the Order of Lenin 2 March 1938 and the Red Banner 17 July 1937, he had four aircraft to his credit. In March 1941 he was appointed CO of the 61st SAD. During WWII, in June 1941 he took command of the newly formed 210th IAD which later became the 3rd GIAD on 18 March 1943. From June 1944 he was CO of the 10th GIAD of the 8th Air Army fighting on the North Western front in Poland. Awarded a second Order of Lenin on 14 February 1943. After the war he was Assist. CO of the Taurian Mil. Dist. (VVS) and on 30 November 1950 he was arrested on charges of anti-Soviet activity and wreaking. He was sentenced on 2 September 1952 to ten years imprisonment based on only weak information. Finally after a new hearing in the Summer of 1953 he was released from prison and rehabilitated in 1954. He passed away 9 June 1957. (Meroño, Laureau, Tinker, Baumler, Salas, Howson, *Vmeste*, Shingarev, Geust, Arias, Smoldas, *Los Rusos*, Abrosov, Kaminskii, *Pravda*)

URUS, Voldemar G., Col., born 1896
Air Force Advisor. On his way to Spain 15 September 1936, he was arrested in Vienna on 25 September and sent back to the USSR. (Abrosov, *Los Rusos*)

USACHEV, Nikolai V., born 1913
Aviation Technician, 14 January to 18 October 1937. Awarded the Red Star 21 June 1937. (*Los Rusos, Pravda*)

USANIN, Ivan K., born 1912
Aviation Technician from October 1936 to 30 June 1937. Awarded the Red Star 2 January 1937. (*Los Rusos, Pravda*)

USATYJ, Fedor I., born 1904
Was head of the 5th School Political Dept. He was in Spanish service from 21 October 1937 to 13 August 1938. Commissar of the I-15 Escuadrillas – non-flying. Awarded the Red Banner 2 March 1938. (Abrosov, *Los Rusos, Pravda*, Gusev, Shingarev)

USTINOV, Anatoli I., born 1911
Parachute instructor, in Spain October 1936 to 29 September 1937. Awarded the Red Star 2 January 1937. (*Los Rusos, Pravda*)

UTKIN, Ivan Alekseevich, Sr.Lt., born 1908
SB Navigator, he arrived on 28 June and returned home on 25 November 1938. His SB was shot down on 10 October 1938, he bailed out along with the pilot TRUBITSYN, but the gunner SKUTOV died. Awarded the Red Banner 22 February 1939. (Semenov, Berch, Abrosov, *Los Rusos, Pravda*)

VALENTIK, D.
SB escuadrilla LISOV says Gagin p.60.

VALUEV, Ivan Ivanovich, Lt., born 1906
An SB Pilot, he came on 26 March and returned 18 August 1938. Flew aircraft crewed by GUDOVICH and POPOVKIN in KRASNOGLAZOV's Escuadrilla. Awarded the Red Banner 22 February 1939. (Semenov "Parol," Berch, *My (1986), Los Rusos, Pravda*)

VARAKSIN, Petr Ivanovich, Lt., born 1914
A Pilot in the 56th IAB Kiev Mil. Dist. He served in Spain from 26 March to 18 May 1938. According to Kaminskii, because of the problems with the wings and engines on the newly delivered I-16s, he along with several other pilots refused to fly them. He was sent back to the USSR. Later he was a Zvena CO in the 11th IAP, and on 14 May 1939 he was injured due to a failure of his I-16 near the airfield at Seima. During WWII, he was appointed as CO of an Eskadril'ya in the 122nd IAP. In early 1943 he was CO of an Eskadril'ya in the 20th IAP. He is said to have shot down six enemy Aircraft (three personal and three in group). According to Kaminskii, he was now afraid to fight with his Regiment and on 3 May 1943 during a training flight he deserted and flew to the Germans. He volunteered to fight with them and served on the aircraft of General Vlasov. At the end of the war he failed to return from a training flight. It is thought that he possibly was able to disappear using false documents. (Kaminskii, Abrosov)

VARANCHUK
CO. of an I-15 escuadrilla in 1936. (Salas in *Mod. and His.* in which he spells it with a W. See listing under BARANCHUK. Also in *Aeroplano #8*. See also Morquillas #25.)

VASILCHENKO, Nikolai Nikolaevich "Shura"
Military Attache in France (Gusev 103+, Berch, Shingarev)

VASIL'EV, Aleksei Nikolaevich, born 1904
Engineer on Armaments and bombs on SB from Factory 22 at Reus from 10 October 1937 to 15 September 1938. Awarded the Red Star 22 February 1939. (Kotelnikov, *Los Rusos, Pravda*)

VASIL'EV, Boris M., Sr.Lt., born 1910
Bomber (SSS?) navigator, in Spain from October 1936 to 2 July 1937. Awarded the Red Banner twice, 2 January and 4 July 1937. (*Los Rusos, Pravda*)

VATOV, Nikolai Ivanov
He went to Spain in September 1936, with the first batch of Soviets. Flew as a pilot of an SB in the 1st Esc. from October 1936 according to DEMENCHUK in *Vmeste* and Abrosov agrees. In Spain he used the nom de guerre "Shtefanov." He was KIA at Bujalance, near Cordoba (Andujar) on 3 January 1937 along with ZOTOV, V. the navigator plus an unmentioned Spanish gunner,

when their aircraft was attacked and shot down by Fiats. According to DEMENCHUK, in May 1931 VATOV was removed from the Bulgarian Army and prosecuted for illegal communist activities. The Central Committee of the Communist Party Bulgaria decided that he should go to the USSR. Therefore, he illegally emigrated from Bulgaria to the USSR using the name Pikar Ivanovich IVANOV. Awarded the Red Banner 2 January 1937 under this name. (*Bajo la B.* mistakenly says he was a navigator, *Vmeste* p.121, RSA, *Solidarity*, Berch, *Pravda*, Abrosov)

VECHNY, Petr P., Col.

Air Force advisor in Cataluña from 10 February 1938 to 27 February 1939. Awarded the Red Banner and Red Star. (Semenov "*Parol*," *Los Rusos* list date of birth as 1819 (!))

VELICHKO, Nikolai Alekseevich, Lt., born May 9, 1915.

An SB Pilot, he arrived 30 May 1938 and was KIA on 24 August. His aircraft on a mission near Gandesa was hit by AAA fire. *Los Rusos* says "Cayó en territorio enemigos." Abrosov p.264 says that he bailed out, but his chute burned up and he fell to his death. The Navigator TITOV fared no better; landing in enemy territory, he was never heard from again. Only the gunner RODIN survived. (Semenov "*Parol*," Berch, Abrosov, *Los Rusos* says born 1905 and list end date as the 25th.)

VELINKEVICH, Dmitri, born 1914

SB radio/gunner in Spain from 30 May until 18 August 1938. (*Los Rusos*)

VENGERSKII, Grigorii Sergeevich, Lt., born 1914

Before Spain he was a Zvena CO in the 4th IAE 56th IAB Kiev Mil. Dist. Became an I-16 patrulla CO in the 5th Moscas under GLUSHENKOV/GRITSEVETS. Arrived on 10 June and was KIA when shot down in a battle with Fiats and Bf 109s on 18 July 1938 in the Sagunto Valenca region. He had flown thirteen sorties and fought in three air combats. (Semenov *Tov.*, *Vmeste*, Abrosov, Kaminskii)

VEREVKA, Vasilii Ivanovich, Sr.Lt., born 1909

A Detachment CO in the 107th IAE 83rd IAB Byelorussian Mil. Dist. He arrived in Spain on 31 May 1937. At first he was a Patrulla Co, then given command of the 3rd I-16 Esc. after MINAEV was killed on 15 July. Later on 25 July he was KIA during an air combat. The Escuadrilla was then turned over to Boris SMIRNOV. Kaminskii says this is the only air combat he had fought in. Awarded the Order of Lenin 3 November 1937. (Pritsker p.200 and p.229, Abrosov p.127, Kaminskii, *Pravda*, a 1991 official list of Soviet dead gives date of death as 25 April 1937, but he did not arrive until 31 May.)

VERIGUIN, Sergei A., born 1911

Aviation Technician, served from October 1936 to 27 August 1937. Awarded the Red Star 2 January 1937. (*Los Rusos*, *Pravda*)

VIKHROV, Timofei Egorovich, born 19 August 1913

A Zvena CO in the 56th IAB. In Spain from 20 August 1937 to 15 April 1938. At first he was a patrulla CO, then from 23 February 1938 until the end of March 1938 he was Commander of the 2nd Moscas. Salas in *Diario* indicates that from 1 April to the middle of the month he was CO of the 5th Moscas, but I don't believe this is right since his mission ended on 15 April by which time he was back in the USSR. Flew 130 sorties and had four plus one aircraft to his credit. Awarded the Order of Lenin on 14 November 1938 and the Red Banner on 2 March 1938. After Spain he participated in the fighting at Lake Khasan and also at the Khalkhin-Gol, where he was an Eskadril'ya CO. Fought in five air battles claiming two Japanese Ki-27s. Awarded the Red Banner on 29 August 1939 and also the Mongolian Red Banner in 1939. In 1940 he was CO of the 129th IAP and in September 1941 he became CO of the 509th IAP. In February 1943 he was CO of the 4th Spare IAP, but in March of that year he was moved to the command of the 102nd IAP on the Stalingrad Front. From July 1943 to July 1944 he fought on the Western Front, fighting in thirty-six air combats and claiming sixteen enemy aircraft. Passed away in 1993. (Kaminskii, Semenov "*Parol*," Laureau, R and R, *Los Rusos*, *Pravda*)

VINETSKII, Yan B., born 1912
Aviation Technician in Spain October 1936 to 26 July 1937. Awarded the Red Star 2 January 1937. (*Los Rusos, Pravda*)

VINOGRADOV, Nikolai Sergeevich, Lt., born 1913
Before going to Spain he was a Zvena CO in the 12th IAE Leningrad Mil. Dist. Went to Spain on 2 January and returned on 13 August 1937. An I-16 pilot in KOLESNIKOV's Esc. he claimed four enemy aircraft (one personal and three in group). Awarded the Red Banner on 27 June 1937. After his return he became CO of the 19th IAP and fought in the Russo Finnish Winter War, for which he was awarded a second Red Banner on 7 April 1940. In October 1941 he commanded the 606th LBAP (Light Bomber Aviation Regiment). This was later renamed the 606th ShAP flying R 5s and then Il-2s. Next he was put in command of the 694th ShAP on the Stalingrad Front, where on 2 September 1942 he shot down two Me 109s. In 1943 he became CO of the 199th ShAD, then moved to CO of the 231st ShAD. From December 1944 to February 1945 was CO of the 5th Guards IAP and later became CO of the 1st Guards IAP. Died 5 September 1977. (Kaminskii, Pritsker, Abrosov, *Pravda*, Gagin mistakenly says UKHOV'S escuadrilla 5/1937 – 11/1937.)

VIZIREV, Ivan Yakovlevich, Capt., born 1903
An SB pilot, he arrived on 14 December 1937 and returned 21 March 1938. His SB was part the Escuadrilla that on 28 January 1938 bombed Salamanca. During this misson, the crew suffered from oxygen deficiency. (Berch, Semenov "*Parol,*" *Los Rusos*)

"VLADIMIR"
Flew in the I-15 escuadrilla with Baumler. I feel this was Vladimir PUZEIKIN as he was in the squadron. (Baumler)

VLADIMIROV
An SB radio/gunner November 1936, also flew in the Potez 540. According to PROKOFIEV, he was one of the Gunners on the Potez flown by PROSKUROV and was wounded on the 30th October mission. (*Bajo la B*)

VLADIMIROV, Filimon Vladimirovich, Lt., born 1908
A pilot in the 121st IAE 95th IAB Transcaucasian Mil. Dist. He was an I-15 fighter pilot and served in Spain from 14 January to 26 July 1937. Awarded the Red Banner on 17 July 1937 and also a Medal for Bravery on 14 November 1938. In 1941 he was assistant CO, then CO of a Regiment. From July to August 1943 he was CO of the 201st IAD, and then later became CO of the 324th IAD. Awarded the Red Banner 20 June 1942. KIA during an air combat on 2 February 1944. (Abrosov, Kaminskii, *Bajo la B., Pravda*)

VLASOV, Akim Fedorovich, Sr.Lt., born 1905
Navigator SB, he was KIA along with PETROV on 2 November 1936 over San Bartalome area. They had been on a mission along with three other SBs to bomb the airfield at Talavera. The aircraft was shot down by CR 32s. Awarded the Red Banner 2 January 1937. (*Vmeste*, Abrosov, *Pravda*)

VOCHEV
Major, Commander of Grupo 15 SSS in 1936. Logoluso says it's an alias for GUSEV. (Laureau, Alcofar, Howson 264)

VOLKOV, Ivan A., Lt., born 1911
Rasante (SSS) pilot, he arrived in October 1936. He and gunner/navigator AKULENKO were shot down on 2 December 1936 during attack on the airfield at Talavera de la Reina. Taken prisoner, he was later released on 11 May 1937. Awarded the Red Banner on 2 January 1937. (Mentioned by SHUKAEV in *Vmeste*, Lugoluso, *Los Rusos*, Abrosov, *Pravda*)

VOLKOV, Nikolai Ya., born 1908
Aviation technician, served from October 1936 to 9 September 1937. Awarded the Red Star on 2 January 1937. (*Los Rusos, Pravda*)

VOLKOV, Pavel G. Lt., born 1907
Aviation Technician from 14 January to 18 October 1937. Awarded the Red Star 21 June 1937. (*Los Rusos, Pravda*)

VOLKOV, Vladimir Stepanovich, Lt., born 1912
Pilot in the 4th IAE 56th IAB Kiev Mil. Dist. I-16 Pilot in Spain from 10 June to 26 October 1938 in the 2nd Moscas under NEDELIN/SEMENKO from July 1938. On 23 August in the early evening his Esc. was involved in a combat with Bf 109s. His aircraft was badly shot up and returning to the airfield, he had to land wheels up. In Spain he flew forty-eight sorties and fought in twenty-nine air battles, claiming two Fiat CR 32s. Awarded the Red Banner on 22 February 1939. Later he was on the staff of the 28th IAD and participated in the Russo Finnish War. In April 1940 he was assistant CO of the 88th IAP. He was KIA on 8 July 1941 during an attack on a German airfield, where he was shot down by AAA. (Kaminskii, Semenov *Tov.*, Abrosov, *Los Rusos, Pravda*)

VOLODIN, Ivan V., born 1907
Technician in aircraft workshops from 20 October 1936 to 7 April 1937. Awarded the Red Star 2 January 1937. (*Los Rusos, Pravda*)

VOLODIN, Vasili F., NCO, born 1911
Gunner on the Potez 54 and SB, he arrived in Spain September/October 1936 and returned on 23 January 1937. Awarded Red Banner on 2 January 1937. (Demenchuk in *MY* and in *Vmeste, Los Rusos, Pravda*)

VOLOSHCHENKO, Nikolai Andreevich, Lt., born 1909
Pilot in the 40th IAE 83rd IAB Byelorussian Mil. Dist. An I-16 pilot he arrived on 19 May and died in an aircraft accident on 4 November 1937. His aircraft CM-130 flipped on take off and he suffered a broken neck. Buried at Sabadell Airfield cemetery along with FINN. So said a note written on a wall at the field when the Soviets were stationed there in Spring 1938. He had gone to Spain with SMIRNOV. Used the codename "Nicolas." Awarded the Red Banner 3 November 1937. (Berch, Smirnov, Pritsker, Abrosov, Kaminskii, *Pravda*)

VOROB'EV, Anton P., Lt., born 1915
SB Bomber Navigator, in Spain from October 1936 to 23 January 1937. According to DEMENCHUK, he was GORANOV's navigator in November 1936 in Grupo 12. Returned home early due to illness. Awarded the Red Banner 2 January 1937. (*Los Rusos, Pravda*)

VOROB'EV, Mikhail Aleksandrovich, NCO, born 1913
Navigator SB in Spain from 28 June to 25 November 1938. Awarded the Red Banner 22 February 1939. (Semenov "*Parol,*" *Los Rusos, Pravda*)

VOROB'EV, Petr Nikiforovich, born 1908
Aircraft Mechanic, worked with PRACHIK on fighters. In Spain from 26 March to 25 November 1938. Awarded the Red Star on 22 February 1939. (Semenov "*Parol,*" Berch, *Los Rusos, Pravda*)

VOROB'EV, Vasilii Fedorovich, Sgt., born 1915
Pilot in the 56th IAB Kiev Mil. Dist. I-16 pilot, 2nd Moscas under NEDELIN. Arrived on 10 June and was KIA while flying CM-188 on 19 August 1938 during an air combat with Bf 109s. His aircraft was said to have exploded in the air after being shot up. He had flown twelve combat sorties and fought in seven air battles. Awarded the Red Banner 22 February 1939. (Abrosov, Kaminskii, Berch, Salas *Diario, Pravda*, Semenov *Tov.* lists 21st as date of death as does the 1991 listing of Soviet dead, while *Los Rusos* list date as 25 June.)

VORONIN, Ivan Ivanovich, Lt., born 1910
Was a pilot in the 40th IAE 83rd IAB Byelorussian Mil. Dist. An I-16 pilot he arrived on 17 May and returned 29 September 1937. He was wounded on 23 July during the Brunete operations. While trying to take off during an enemy attack on his field (Campo Real), his aircraft received a direct hit. Gagin says he was in PLESHCHENKO's 2nd escuadrilla. Awarded the Red Banner 22 October 1937. In July 1941 he was CO of an Eskadril'ya in the 26th IAP PVO. He is said to have shot down a Ju 88 on the 6th or 7th of August 1941. He is also said to have rammed an enemy aircraft in 1942. Died during the war. Was awarded the Red Banner on 4 March 1942. (Kaminskii, Berch, *Pravda, Los Rusos*, Gagin, Pritsker (lists as killed), Abrosov (typo on year wounded, states 1938, but all other dates are for 1937.)

VORONOV, Mikhail Vasil'evich, Lt., born 1907
Before going to Spain he was a pilot in the 109th IAE 36th IAB Kiev Mil. Dist. In Spain he was an I-15 Pilot in RYCHAGOV's enlarged escuadrilla, arrived 20 October 1936. Badly wounded in an air battle on 7 November 1936 with Fiat CR 32s; he tried to land his shot up plane, but it crashed. He died of wounds in the hospital on the 11th. Lukes says he died on the 7th while Abrosov says he was shot down on the 8th. Awarded the Red Banner on 2 January 1937. (*Icare 130,* Berch, Zakharov, *Vmeste, MY*, Abrosov, *Pravda, Los Rusos*, Lukes, Kaminskii)

VORONTSOV, Petr, Lt., born 1914
Pilot in Spain from 26 March until 18 May 1938. (*Los Rusos*)

VOROPAEV, Dmitrii Nikolaevich, Lt., born 1914
Before going to Spain he was a Zvena CO in the 57th IAE 142nd IAB Byelorussian Mil. Dist. An I-16 Fighter pilot, he arrived on 26 March 1938 and did not even have time to begin combat ops. He was wounded in a crash on 14 April while landing at Castellar in bad weather. His aircraft went into a bomb crater which had been covered with rain water and flipped over. He was badly injured. He was put into the hospital and finally returned home on 15 February 1939. Later, on May 11, 1940, he died as a result of a failed neurosurgical procedure. Awarded the Red Star on 22 February 1939. (Semenov "*Parol,*" Berch, Abrosov, *Los Rusos*, Kaminskii, *Pravda*)

VOROTN'EV, Nikolai E., Capt., born 1908
Aviation technician served from 11 November 1936 to 26 July 1937. Awarded the Red Star 2 January 1937. (*Los Rusos, Pravda*)

VYAZGIN, Nikolai A.
Worker from Aircraft Factory #21 assembling/ repairing I-16 aircraft, in Spain from October 1936 to 27 March 1937. Awarded the Red Star 2 January 1937. (*Pravda, Los Rusos*)

VYBORNOV, Grigorii E., born 1898
Worker from Aircraft Factory #22 assembling SB aircraft. In Spain October to 12 December 1936. Awarded the Red Star 2 January 1937. (*Pravda, Los Rusos*)

VYDRIN, Vasilii I., born 1912
Aviation technician on bombers, from October 1936 to 27 March 1937. Awarded the Red Star 2 January 1937. (*Los Rusos, Pravda*)

VZOROV, Vladimir Nikolaevich, born 1912
In Suzdal' Vladimirskii Oblasti. Claimed to have been a fighter pilot in the first group sent in October 1936, and that he along with AKULENKO were CHERNYKH's wingmen? Died 2002. Not on the *Pravda* awards list for 2 January 1937. (Airforce.ru, *Pravda*)

YAKIMENKO, Anton Dmitrievich, born 5 December 1913
While the two sources say he was in Spain, there is no mention of it in his biographies in *Geroi* or Rumyantsev. (Berch, Gusev, Rumyantsev?)

YAKIMENKO, Grigorii I., Sr.Lt., born 1905
Pilot SB, he arrived on 30 May and returned 22 September 1938. According to Semenov "*Parol*," on 9 August 1938 during a misson over the Ebro, in the vicinity of Zaragoza, the SB flown by YAKIMENKO was hit by a AAA shell and went down. No one saw exactly where it crashed, but two or three days later he and his navigator NITSAI were found in a hospital. The radio/gunner SHEVCHENKO was uninjured and returned to the group. But according to Abrosov, their aircraft was badly damaged by AAA and YAKIMENKO crashlanded it. SHEVCHENKO was wounded and NITSAI broke his legs. The aircraft was taken for repair. Awarded the Red Banner 22 February 1939. (Berch, Semenov "*Parol*," *Los Rusos, Pravda*, Abrosov)

YAKOVLEV, Pavel Grigorivich
Radio/gunner SB 1938. Awarded the Red Banner on 22 February 1939. (Berch, *Pravda*)

YAKOVLEV, Pavel Ya., NCO, born 1912
Radio/gunner SB, same person as above? In Spain from 14 December 1937 to 21 July 1938. Awarded the Red Banner. (Semenov "*Parol*," *Los Rusos*)

YAKUSHIN, Mikhail Nikolaevich, "Carlos Castejon," Capt., born 20 March 1910
Pilot in the 119th IAE 95th IAB Transcaucasian Mil. Dist. stationed at Baku. He arrived in Spain on 31 May 1937, and was a member of EREMENKO's 1st Escuadrilla, then became part of the Night Fighter detachment under SEROV. In *Aeroplano* #7, he says that "Mateo Rodrigo" was his nom de guerre, but Chalaya 1955 p.139 says this was the name given to SEROV as does Hidalgo de Cisneros, in his "*Cambio de Rumbo*" Bucarest 1964. Shingarev also supports this p.115 and p.122 as does a Spanish newspaper[1] saying that first night kill was by "Carlos Castejon." A member of the night fighter unit at Brunete, YAKUSHIN scored the first night kill, a Ju 52 on the night of 25-26 July 1937. In his memoirs in *Bajo la Bandera de la España Republicana,* he lists it as 26 June. For their actions in the Night Fighter unit, both he and SEROV received the Order of the Red Banner. Shingarev says, during an attack on Toledo on July 1st or 2nd, he downed a Fiat. In September he was in the Esc. now under STEPANOV's command. Returned home on 15 November 1937. He had flown 150 sorties and participated in twenty-five air battles, and had five plus one aircraft to his credit. Awarded the Red Banner twice, 31 July and 22 October 1937. He, SEROV and three other Spanish veterans gave a display of formation Aerobatics at the 1938 May Day Parade. Fought in China flying the I-15bis from June 1938 to early 1939; also fought in the Winter War. Awarded the Red Banner 5 July 1940. In July 1941 he was deputy CO of the 6th IAK PVO Moscow. After the death of Lt.Gen. G.P. Kravchenko on 24 February 1943, he took over commanded of the 215th IAD on the Volkhov front. This Division was part of the 8th IAK under command of A.S. OSIPENKO. After the war he continued to serve in the VVS and later participated in the Korean War as an advisor to the Chinese Air Force. Died 5 July 1999. (Salas, Laureau, RSA, *Bajo la B.*, Chalaya, *Aeroplano* #7, Berch, Zakharov, Pritsker, Shingarev, Boyd, *Pravda*, Abrosov, Kaminskii, [1]*Cronica de la Guerra Española, Tomo IV*, p.402, Polak lists five of his kills p.334, *Icaro 130* Julio 1999, Lukes lists wrong N. de G.)

YAKUSHIN, Vasilii Fedorovich, Capt., born 1907

Captain and CO of the 2nd IAE 56th IAB Kiev Mil. Dist. He arrived in Spain 10 June and was put into the 5th escuadrilla de Moscas (I-16). On 20 July 1938 his aircraft was badly shot up in an air combat with Bf 109s. He tried to make an emergency landing near Sagunto some 40km from his base, but crashed into a wall and was killed. He was said to have been buried near Sagunto. During this battle he is said to have been one of the wingmen for PROKOPENKO. Previously on 17 July while landing his aircraft crashed, but he was uninjured. He had only flown four combat sorties and participated in two air battles. Posthumously awarded the Red Banner on 22 February 1939. In his biographies by Abrosov, Kaminskii and *Los Rusos* they list him as CO of an I-16 escuadrilla, but at the time of his loss, the 2nd Esc. was commanded by RODIN and the 5th was under GLUSHENKOV, while GRITSEVETS and NEDELIN were in the process of taking over. So feel the information about him being a CO stems most likely, from his having been CO of the 2nd IAE before going to Spain. (Semenov *Tov.,Vmeste, Los Rusos*, Abrosov, Kaminskii, *Pravda, An* official list of Soviet dead from 1991, lists 22 July as date of death.)

YAMANOV, Valer'yan Aleksandrovich, Lt., born 1912

From 1935 he was a pilot in the 41st IAE 83rd IAB Byelorussian Mil. Dist. He departed for Spain on 16 May 1937, and after he arrived he was put into the 1st I-16 Escuadrilla. He says in Pritsker, that he went to Paris by train and then flew by plane to Barcelona. With him on the flight were KOMAROV, PLYGUNOV and NIKOLAENKO. Goes on to say that he arrived at Alcala de Henares by 15 May and that the Escuadrilla was commanded by KOLESNIKOV. But this is wrong as KOLESNIKOV died on 12 May in an accident. Also says LAKEEV took over the Esc., but that did not happen until the end of June 1937. Badly wounded during a Nationalist attack on his airfield on 23 July, he was sent to the hospital and underwent a serious operation. Returned home on 27 August 1937 and had further treatments in hospital there before finally being cured and able to return to his old unit at Bryansk. He had at least one aircraft to credit. Awarded the Red Banner on 22 October 1937. From June to September 1939 he was in the fighting at Khalkhin-Gol where first he was with the 22nd IAP and then became a Zvena leader in the 56th IAP and by the time the fighting was over he was assistant commander of the 56th, with four Japanese aircraft to his credit. Awarded a second Red Banner. During WWII from May 1943 he commanded the 160th IAP which was part of the 3rd GIAD 1 GIAK. On 14 April 1944 in recognition of their excellent performance the 160th was renamed the 137th GIAP. Retired from the VVS in 1959. (Berch, Pritsker, Abrosov, Kaminskii, *Pravda*, Rumyantsev (Ed.) *Na* ., Abrosov, *Los Rusos* list end date as 28 July.)

YAMARKEV, V.

Fighter pilot (very questionable). (Alcofar)

YANOVSKII, Vladimir A., Lt., born 1905

Bomber/navigator, he served from October 1936 to 30 June 1937. Awarded the Red Banner 2 January 1937. (*Pravda, Los Rusos* lists him a 2nd time as YAKOVSKI)

YARKOVOJ, Anastasii Nikiforovich, born 21 August 1914

In 1937 he was a pilot in the 57th IAE 142nd IAB Byelorussian Mil. Dist. An I-16 Pilot in Spain from 26 March to 3 September 1938, most likely in the 2nd esc. under RODIN and then NEDELIN. He flew eighty combat sorties and fought in sixteen air combats, with three plus one aircraft to his credit (all Fiats). Awarded the Order of Lenin 22 February 1939. From November 1938 to April 1939 he was the head of communications for an Eskadril'ya in the 35th IAP Byelorussian Mil. Dist. In June he was made assistant CO and later became CO of the 35th. When the war started in June 1941, the 35th IAP was fighting on the Transcaucasisan Front. From August 1942 until May 1943 he was CO of the 963rd IAP. Later he held positions in the 495th IAP and the 36th IAD. After the war he remained in the VVS, retiring in November 1957, and passed away on 29 May 1974. (Semenov "*Parol*," Gusev, Abrosov, *Pravda*, Kaminskii, airaces.narod.ru gives 3 October as date returned from Spain.)

YAROSHENKO, Yakov Semenovich, Sr.Lt., born 1909

Before going to Spain, he was a Detachment CO in the 6th IAE 116th IAB Byelorussian Mil. Dist. He is listed as arriving in Spain on 30 December 1937. His group of twenty-three fighter pilots had left from Leningrad on the 16th.

Now according to both Abrosov and Kaminskii, he was put in an I-16 Esc. Semenov "*Parol*" pgs.47-48 tells of him being shot down in combat on 20 January 1938, whereas according to Shingarev he was a member of ANTONOV's patrulla in SEROV's I-15 Escuadrilla.[1] Both Abrosov and airaces.ru list him as flying I-16s and Abrosov says he was possibly an escuadrilla CO while airaces.ru and Kaminskii say patrulla CO. This is not mentioned by Shingarev. While Semenov says he was KIA on 20 January 1938, as does Abrosov and Saiz, Shingarev, Kaminskii and airaces list the date as 7 January. He had only arrived in Spain on 30 December 1937. Shingarev pgs.297-298 state, "On 7 January YAROSHENKO with his wingman D. Petrovich at the end of a combat, saw J. Comas' aircraft being attacked by six Fiats. They went to his aid, and two of the Fiats came at YAROSHENKO. Petrovich then noticed that YAROSHENKO's plane was not reacting properly. He then saw a Fiat on the others tail, but it just continued flying in a straight line. Petrovich was able to make the Fiat leave, and as he flew alongside YAROSHENKO's aircraft, he saw that the other was slumped over, but raised his head slightly. He continued to fly towards the airfield, but when he tried to land the aircraft turned and the wing hit the ground and crashed. Petrovich landed and ran to the wreak, pulling YAROSHENKO out, but after a few minutes he died." He was buried in the village of Viver, on the Sagunto-Teruel Road. Awarded the Red Star 14 November 1938. It is also said that he had six personal and twelve in group victories. But since he was only in Spain a maximum of twenty days I believe this is extremely doubtful at best. (Semenov "*Parol*" pgs.47-48, Shingarev, Meroño, Lukes, Abrosov, Saiz, Kaminskii, *Pravda, Los Rusos* lists as Jefe Patrulla and give end date as 20 November 1938 in one place and 20 January 1938 in another. [1]SIUSIUKA'LOV was the CO of the 1st Chatos by the 19th.)

YASHIN, Semen Kuz'mich, Lt., born 1916

Was a pilot in the 57th IAE 142nd IAB Byelorussian Mil. Dist. In Spain he was a member of the 2nd I-16 escuadrilla under RODIN. Arrived on 26 March and was KIA when shot down in combat with Fiat CR 32s on 13 May 1938 near the airfield at Villar del Arzobispo. Posthumously awarded the Red Banner 22 February 1939. (Semenov "*Parol*" p.155, Abrosov, Kaminskii, *Pravda*, 1991 list of Soviet dead lists 12 May as date.)

YAS'KIN, Nikolai T., born 1912

Mechanic in Spain from October 1936 to 27 August 1937. Awarded the Red Star 2 January 1937. (*Pravda, Los Rusos*)

YUDIN, Ilya I.

Worker from Aircraft Factory #21 assembling/repairing I-16 aircraft. In Spain October 1936 to April 1937. Awarded the Red Star 2 January 1937. (*Pravda, Los Rusos*)

YUDIN, Nikolai Matveevich, NCO, born 1913

Radio/gunner SB, arrived 26 April to 3 September 1938. Awarded the Red Banner 22 February 1939. (Berch, Semenov, *Pravda, Los Rusos* which list as YURIN and have end date as 26 August)

YUKHANOV, Dmitri Petrovich, Maj., born 1909

CO of the 21st SBAE VRIO (Fast Bomber Aviation Esc. – Temporary Post) Byelorussian Mil. Dist. He was an SB pilot in Spanish service from 28 June 1938 and left Spain in late March 1939, returning to the USSR on 12 May 1939. According to Semenov "*Parol*," at the end of August YUKHANOV became an advisor to L. Mendiola, and he had transferred to the central zone. This may explain why he returned to the USSR so late. During WWII, he was the CO of the 1st. GvAD ADD – Long Range Aviation Division (on 1 May 1943 this became the 1st GvAK ADD). Kotelnikov and Semenov both say Commander of 2nd Esc. SBs. Awarded the Red Banner 22 February 1939. Died in 1947. (Berch, Semenov "*Parol*," *Los Rusos, Pravda*, Geust p.145)

YUMAEV, Vasilii Yu., born 1912

Armaments specialist, in Spain November 1936 to 27 March 1937. Awarded the Red Star 2 January 1937. (*Pravda, Los Rusos*)

YUSIMA, Maria Antonovna, born 1909

Translator with Air Group from 20 March 1937 until 21 July 1938. (Semenov, Berch, *Los Rusos*)

ZABELIN, Aleksei Fedorovich, Lt., born 1906

Pilot SB, in Spain from 14 February to 13 July 1938. He participated in the attack on the Baleares on 6 March 1938. Awarded the Red Banner 14 November 1938 plus Red Star 22 February 1939. Was living in Vitebsk in 1974. (Semenov "*Parol*," Berch, *Pravda*)

ZABIVOROT, Georgii A., Lt.

Aviation technician served from October 1936 to 29 September 1937. Awarded the Red Banner 22 October 1937. (*Pravda, Los Rusos* spells it ZABIBOROK)

ZABOLOTNYJ
Listed by Abrosov p.201, as an SB pilot.

ZAGORODNYUK, Aleksandr F., born 1914
Aviation technician in Spain from 14 January to 23 December 1937. Awarded the Red Star 17 July 1937. (*Pravda, Los Rusos* spells it ZAGODNIUK)

ZAIKIN, Michael Georgevich (real name Mikhail ZALKIN, see below)
Native of Kline, USSR. Age twenty-six, Capt. in VVS. Pilot of an SB, shot down and captured. Hericourt lists him as ZAIKINE. (*Spain mag.* 8/15/1938)

ZAITSEV, Aleksandr Andreevich, Sr.Lt., born 12 December 1911
From February 1934 he was a pilot in the 12th IAE Leningrad Mil. Dist. He arrived in Spain on 3 January 1937, and used the codename "Don Diego." He first flew I-15s in OSADCHI's Esc. then transferred to KOLESNIKOV's 1st Esc. Moscas when ZAKHAROV returned home. He then went to Santander with UKHOV. Returned home on 14 August 1937. Had gone to Spain along with PUZEIKIN, BELYAKOV, and VINOGRADOV. Listed as having eight kills (5+3) in Spain. Awarded the Order of Red Banner twice, 27 June and 3 November 1937. Later was a Detachment CO. and then CO. of 19th IAP. Fought in the Khalkhin-Gol from 11 May to 16 September 1939 during which he commanded the 70th IAP. Claimed six Japanese kills, in 118 sorties and twenty-nine air combats. Awarded the H.S.U. on 17 November 1939. Fought in the Russo-Finnish War with the 8th combined Air Army. During WWII, he was appointed CO of the 32nd IAP in 1942, then from 2 February 1944 until the end of the war he commanded the 431 IAP. Claimed one kill for a total of fifteen. Due to health problems he was put on reserves in 1952, and passed away 25 December 1965. Awards were H.S.U., Order of Lenin, Order of the Red Banner twice, Order of Suvorov 3rd Cl., Order of Aleksandr Nevskii, Order of the Red star twice. (Shingarev, Berch, Zakharov, *Vmeste*, Pritsker, Rumyantsev *Geroi*, Seidl, Abrosov, Kaminskii)

ZAITSEV, Ivan, NCO, born 1911
SB Radio/Gunner he served from 30 December 1937 to 31 March 1938. (*Los Rusos*)

ZAKHAREVSKII, Boris Pavlovich, born 1904
Engineer/technician on I-16s, but *Los Rusos* claim he was a bomber engineer. Served from 14 June 1937 to 24 March 1938. Awarded the Red Banner 2 March 1938. (Gusev 285, Berch, *Vmeste, Los Rusos, Pravda*)

ZAKHARIEV, Zakhari Simeonov, born 1904, died 29 April 1987
Bulgarian with the VVS. Inducted into the Bulgarian Army in 1923, he went through schooling and became a pilot. He was later dismissed from the military due to his pro-Communistic views. He emigrated to the USSR in 1931 and joined the VVS. When the war in Spain first began, he had been a Zvena commander in the GVF at Tambov. Volunteered for Spain, arriving there in late September 1936. He was put in the 1st Internacional Escuadrilla and served there September/October flying Br 19s and Potez 540s. Here, according to DEMENCHUK, he used the alias "Ekrem Khailil" and told people he was a Turk, but most knew him as Vulkan Semenovich GORANOV. After becoming thoroughly aquainted with the Potez, He flew his first mission in this type on 27 October 1936, attacking the enemy airfield at Talavera. They claim to have destroyed fifteen planes there, but the Italians based there say they were driven off by Fiats. He was flying Potez 540 "N" along with two other Potez on 30 October on a mission to attack enemy ground forces near Navalcarnero some 30km southwest of Madrid. His crew consisted of himself, three Spaniards (co-pilot, flight engineer and one gunner), two Russian gunners and a Ukrainian navigator. According to DEMENCHUK, the navigator, as they neared the target the Spanish flight commander who he names Sapillo changed course, causing them to fly parallel with the front lines. This allowed time for the enemy fighters to find and attack them. He goes on to say they were attacked by Heinkels, but in fact they were Fiat Cr 32s under command of A. Mantelli. During the ensuing battle two of the Potez were shot down.[1] On his, the two engines were shot up and stopped and both he and one of the gunners DESNITSKII were wounded. Struggling to reach Republican territory the aircraft had to make a wheels up landing in the middle of No Man's Land. The crew eventually got to safety and were sent to the hospital. The other Potez flown by

PROSKUROV was able to crashland in their territory. From what DEMENCHUK says, the third Potez was not attacked and the Spaniard was later charged with treason. In November 1936 he transferred to Grupo 12 SBs, where he was said to have flown twelve combat missions, but then his old wounds from 30 October caused him problems and he returned to the USSR. Awarded H.S.U. on 31 December 1936. Later he was a Col. General in the Bulgarian Republic, served from 1947 to 1954 and 1957 to 1959 as Commander of the VVS NRB (Bulgarian Air Force) and from 1954 to 1957 and 1965 to 1972 as deputy Minister of Defense for the NRB (Peoples Republic of Bulgaria). See also listing under GORANOV, name which he used while with the Soviets. (Berch, RSA, *MY*, Meroño, *Solidarity*, *Vmeste*, Demenchuk, [1]Bonomi in *Viva la Muerte*, Editorial Aeronautica, Rome 1941 says all three Potez aircraft were shot down.)

ZAKHAROV, Georgii Nefedovich, Lt., born 24 April 1908

Joined the Red Army in 1930. Attended the #7 Stalingrad Military Aviation School. He was a Zvena CO in the 109th IAE 36th IAB Kiev Mil. Dist. In Spain he served from 20 October 1936 to 7 April 1937. He was in the first large group of I-15 pilots sent, where he was a member of RYCHAGOV's Escuadrilla and commander of an I-15 Patrulla. Later he was second-in-command of the Escuadrilla, then under OSADCHII. Used the names "Enrique Lopez" and "Rodriguez Kromberg." Shot down six fascist aircraft plus four shares in Spain; also he was involved along with SHMELKOV in the 8 December 1936 erroneous shooting down of the French Civilian Potez 540 F-A000. Upon returning to the USSR, he was appointed Detachment CO of the 109th IAE. Fought in China from April to around October 1938 and claimed two more kills there. While testing a captured Mitsubishi A5M he crashed and broke his left arm and leg. In 1939 he was appointed as VVS commander of the Siberian Mil. Dist. From August 1940 he commanded the 43rd IAD Byelorussian Mil. Dist. In November 1941 he was relieved of his command, but in December 1942 he was appointed to the command of the 303rd IAD, which later included the French Volunteer Normandie-Nieman IAE. He was awarded the H.S.U. on 19 April 1945. Retired from the VVS in 1960. Died 6 January 1996. Awards were H.S.U., Order of Lenin twice, Order of the Red Banner four times (twice for Spain, 2 January 1937 and 17 July 1937 and one for China on 14 November 1938), Order of Kutuzov 2nd Cl., Order of Aleksandr Nevskii, Order of the Great Patriotic War 1st. Cl., Order of the Red Star twice. (Pritsker, *Solidarity*, Lacalle, Berch, Zakharov, *Vmeste*, *Geroi*, Seidl, Abrosov, *Pravda*, Kaminskii, SUIAZIN in *MY* claims he was the CO of an escuadrilla kept in reserve in early November 1936.)

ZALESSKII, Pavel Ya., born 1902

Ordnance Engineer on Bombers. In Spain from October 1936 to 27 May 1937. This is the man who converted many civil Aircraft into bombers and installed machine guns on civil types. Arrived in Spain with the first volunteers in October 1936. Awarded Order of the Red Star on 2 January and Red Banner 17 July 1937. (*Pravda, Los Rusos, Bajo la B.*, Berch, *Solidarity*, Gusev, *Chantaje* 84, *MY*, Pritsker - some of these list first name as Yakov, but *Pravda* lists as P. Ya.)

ZALKA, Andrei Mikhailovich "Andrash"

Died 1940; hanged. Related to Mate "Gen. Lukacs" Zalka. (Semenov "*Parol*")

ZALKIN, Mikhail Grigorevich, Lt., born 1911

SB pilot in Spain 31 May 1937. His SB was shot down on 12 July 1937 and he was captured. Released and returned home on 25 January 1939. See ZAIKIN above (Abrosov, *Los Rusos*)

ZAMASHANSKII, Filipp Karpovich, Lt., born 1909 d. 1937
Zvena CO in the 107th IAE 83rd IAB Byelorussian Mil. Dist. An I-16 patrulla leader in Spain from November 1936 until February 1937. KIA over the Jarama front on 18 February 1937. He was shot down in a large air battle by a Fiat CR 32, coming down and crashing in an Olive field. Abrosov says he was wounded and died trying to make an emergency landing. His body was recovered by Soviet Armored Personnel under Gen. Pavlov and buried in the cemetery of a small village. He had arrived in Spain at the end of October 1936 along with others in TARKHOV's enlarged I-16 escuadrilla. Awarded the Order of the Red Banner on 2 January 1937. (DEMENCHUK and KRAVCHENKO in *Vmeste*, Rumyantsev "*Antonio*," *Solidarity* 315, Abrosov, Kaminskii, *Pravda*)

ZAMOREZHCHENKO, Vasilii, Sr.Lt., born 1909
Pilot in Spain from 30 May to 3 September 1938. (*Los Rusos*)

ZAMOSKOVNYJ, Vladimir M., born 1912
Electrical Technician for Air Group. Served from April to 27 May 1937. Awarded the Red Star 21 June 1937. (*Pravda, Los Rusos* spell it ZAMOSHKOV)

ZANGIEV, Adam Khadzhi Muratovich, born 1911
Zvena CO in the 41st IAE 83rd IAB Byelorussian Mil. Dist. An I-16 Fighter pilot, in Spain from 14 June until 2 September 1937. Just after taking off on the 2nd he encountered a problem and while trying to return to the airfield he lost control of the aircraft and crashed and was killed. Posthumously awarded the Red Banner on 2 March 1938. Buried at Campo Real. (Abrosov, Kaminskii, *Los Rusos*)

ZAVARUKHIN, Pavel Filippovich, born 1913
Aviational Engineer, was in the 107th IAE 83rd Aviabrigade at Bryansk as a technician on I-16s in December 1935. In Spain from October 1936 to 29 September 1937, he was in TARKHOV's group of I-16 personnel sailing on the *Kursk*. Awarded the Red Star on 2 January 1937. Later served as commander of technicians on the northern front with UKHOV/ EVSEV'EV's Esc. Upon his return from Spain to the Soviet Union, he went to the 7th Stalingrad Military Flying School. After graduating he flew in the 34th IAP. Next he went to the 111th IAP flying I-153s, where he fought in the Khalkhin-Gol battles. During the Winter War, he commanded a Zvena of I-153s. KRAVCHENKO in *Vmeste* says his name was spelt ZAVORUKHIN and that he was an armaments engineer. Gagin on the other hand says his name was spelt ZAVARUKH. During WWII, he flew with the 744 IAP in 1942, and then in April 1943 went to the 72nd GIAP becoming its commander. Listed as having thirteen kills plus four shared. Polak lists awards as HSU in 1943 (but a search in *Geroi*, produced no results), Order of Lenin, Order of Red Banner six times, Order of A. Nievskii, and Order of the Red Star twice. (Berch, *Vmeste*, Pritsker, Gagin, Polak, *Pravda*, airaces.narod.ru, ainros.ru/osdg1/t5/zavarukhin_pf.pdf, *Los Rusos* lists as ZABARIJIN)

ZEITSOFF, Alessandrof Nicolavitch
Name noted in Baumler's log 1937. See ZAITSEV, Aleksandr Andreevich.

ZEKANOV, Ivan Lt., born 1903
CO of I-16 escuadrilla, in Spain 14 January to 26 July 1937. Awarded the Red Banner. According to *Los Rusos* (no back up in either Abrosov or Kaminskii).

ZELOV, Aleksandr Antipovich, Lt., born 1914
Navigator SB, arrived 30 May to 15 November 1938. Awarded the Red Banner 22 February 1939. (Berch, Semenov "*Parol*," *Los Rusos, Pravda*)

ZHARKOV, Vladimir A., born 1915
Worker from Aircraft Factory #1 assembling/repairing I-15 and SSS aircraft. In Spain from October 1936 to 18 October 1937. Awarded the Red Star 2 January 1937. (*Pravda*)

ZHARSKII, Petr. Matveevich, Lt., born 1913
Navigator/gunner in SSS Rasante flown by SOLDATENKO, which was shot down 20 March 1937 and ZHARSKII was killed. He had arrived in November 1936. During an attack in the Boadilla region on 19 December 1936, their plane had been hit by ground fire and crashlanded, Neither he nor the pilot SOLDATENKO were injured at that time. Awarded the Red Banner 2 January 1937. (*Vmeste, Pravda, Los Rusos* which list end date as 30 March)

ZHDANOV, Vasilii N.
(Lario 152, RSA, Boyd, Smoldas (They are most likely confused with D. ZHEDANOV below). *Los Rusos* lists a Vasilii Zhdanov as being in Spain, but in the Armored Unit.)

ZHEDANOV, Dmitrii Ignat'evich, Sr.Lt., born 1906
He was a Zvena CO in the 107th IAE 83rd IAB Byelorussian Mil. Dist. In Spain from November 1936, he was an I-16 patrulla CO. His Aircraft was hit during an air combat on 19 November in which the Moscas aided by RYCHAGOV's Chatos attacked a large formation of Ju 52s escorted by He 51s and CR 32s. The enemy force was said to have lost two Ju 52s and two He 51s. ZHEDANOV managed to get his stricken aircraft almost back to his field, but before he could land, it burst into flames and crashed and he was killed. Abrosov mentions that Corrado Ricci had claimed an I-16 in that combat. To his credit was a Ju 52 downed over the University City. Posthumously awarded the Red Banner on 2 January 1937. (*Vmeste*, Rumyantsev "*Antonio*," *Pravda*, Abrosov, Kaminskii, *Los Rusos* in a second listing misspelled name as ZHEGANOV and give date of death as 19 January 1936)

ZHERDEV, Evgenii Nikonorovich, Lt., born 1909
Navigator SB, he served from 30 December 1937 to 21 July 1938. Participated in the attack on the Baleares 6 March 1938. Awarded the Red Banner 14 November 1938. (Berch, Semenov "*Parol*," *Los Rusos, Pravda*)

ZHERDEV, Nikolai Prokof'evich, Capt., born 5 May 1911
Joined the Red Army in 1934. In December 1936, became a member of the 56th IAE at Bobruisk. In 1938 he was a Zvena CO in the 57th IAE 142nd IAB Byelorussian Mil. Dist. He served in Spain from 26 March to 3 September 1938, first as a pilot and later as a patrulla CO. He flew both the I-15 in the 1st Esc. and then the I-16 in the 2nd Esc. under RODIN. He had three aircraft to his credit, downed one Fiat on 13 July 1938 and then rammed another after running out of ammo. Abrosov claims the date was 18 July and that the Fiat he collided with was flown by G. Frattini who was killed. He had flown seventy combat sorties. Returned home in September 1938. Awarded the Order of Lenin on 22 February 1939 and given the rank of Captain. From 29 May to 16 September 1939 he fought in the battle of Khalkhin-Gol during part of which he was CO of the 70th IAP. Flew 105 combat sorties and participated in forty-six air battles. He had scored eleven personal kills and three in group. He was awarded the title H.S.U. on 17 November 1939 and the Mongolian order of the Red Banner on 10 August 1939. In WWII, was in the 821st IAP, fighting on the Southern and Caucasian fronts. KIA on 15 November 1942 while flying a U-2. Awards were H.S.U., Order of Lenin twice, Order of the Red Banner. (Semenov "*Parol*," Gusev 294, Berch, *Vmeste*, Rumyantsev *Geroi*, Seidl, Abrosov, Kaminskii, *Los Rusos, Pravda*)

ZHERULOV, Fedor D., born 1906
Worker from Aircraft Factory #1 assembing/repairing I-15 and SSS aircraft. Served from October 1936 to 27 May 1937. Awarded the Red Star 2 January 1937. (*Los Rusos, Pravda*)

ZHEZLICHEV, Pavel I.
Worker from Aircraft Factory #22 assembling/repairing SB aircraft. In Spain October 1936 to 8 March 1937. Awarded the Red Star 2 January 1937. (*Los Rusos, Pravda*)

ZHUCKOV, Timofei F., born 1908
Worker from Aircraft Factory #1 assembling/repairing I-15 and SSS aircraft, served from October 1936 to 7 April 1937. Awarded the Red Star 2 January 1937. (*Pravda, Los Rusos* lists as ZHUKOV)

ZHUKOV, Nikolai Andreevich, Capt., born 1909
Navigator on SB, he arrived on 14 December 1937 and returned on 13 July 1938. Awarded the Red Banner 14 November 1938. (Berch, Semenov "*Parol,*" *Los Rusos* which list as pilot.)

ZHUKOV, Vasilii Ivanovich, NCO, born 1913
Radio/gunner SB, arrived 30 May and returned 15 November 1938. Awarded the Red Banner 22 February 1939. (Berch, Semenov "*Parol,*" *Los Rusos, Pravda*)

ZHUNDA, Vladimir Yakovlevich, Lt., born 1910
Pilot in the 40th IAE 83rd IAB Byelorussian Mil. Dist. In Spain from 16 May to 29 September 1937. He had been a member of the 1st Escuadrilla de Moscas flying I-16s. On 2 July 1937 he went to Santander on the Northern Front with UKHOV in a newly formed Escuadrilla. Awarded the Red Banner 3 November 1937. In 1938 he was CO of the 4th IAE 16th IAP and in July 1940 he was the Commissar for the 44th IAD. On 28 July 1941 he was killed in a German attack on the airfield at Rotmistrovki. (*Vmeste*, Kaminskii, Abrosov, Shingarev, Berch, Pritsker, *Pravda, Los Rusos*)

ZHURAVLEV, Nikolai Ivanovich, Lt., born 2 December 1908
In Red Army since 1931 he was a pilot in the 11th IAE 111th IAB Leningrad Mil. Dist. Departed for Spain on 20 August 1937 and returned home 15 April 1938. An I-16 Patrulla leader and later second-in-command in DEVOTCHENKO's 2nd Esc. In a battle with Bf 109s on 10 March KOVENEV was shot down and ZHURAVLEV's plane was badly damaged. Flew some 100 combat sorties and had one aircraft (Bf 109) to his credit. Awarded the Order of Lenin on 14 November 1938 and the Red Banner 2 March 1938. In August 1938 he became CO of the 2nd IAE 25th IAP. Fought in the Winter War 1939-40, where he flew forty-one sorties and claimed five Finnish aircraft. From March to November 1940 he was assistant CO of the 45th IAP transcaucasian Mil. Dist., then he attended the VVS Military Academy. In April 1941 he was posted back to his prior postion with the 45th IAP. In October 1941 he was appointed the CO of the 481st IAP protecting the Baku oilfields. From August 1942 until the end of the war he held several positions with the 3rd Division office of Air Defense. Put on reserve on 28 August 1946, and passed away 3 May 1988. (Abrosov, Semenov *Tov*., Kaminskii, *Pravda*)

ZHURAVLEV, Nikolai Pavlovich, Lt., born 7 May 1916
Pilot in the 4th IAE 56th IAB Kiev Mil. Dist. He was in Spain from 10 June 1938 until 25 January 1939(?). An I-16 Pilot in the 2nd Moscas under NEDELIN in August 1938. Kaminskii says he used the codename "Manuel Roldan del Monte." He had two landing accidents, both times the aircraft was destroyed. The first was on 3 August (three I-16s CM 139, 165 and 176[1] were lost in landing crashes that day) he was uninjuried. But on the 5th of August, both Abrosov and Kaminskii say he crashed, but there is a passage in Kaminskii from a book by O. Savich (*Dva goda v Ispanii* – "Two Years in Spain") where ZHURAVLEV says his plane was shot up over the Ebro and he had to jump from a low height. Either way, this time he broke both legs and after release from the hospital he returned home. The aircraft he was flying at the time was CM 207. He had flown three combat sorties and fought in four air battles and had six aircraft to his credit (all in group). Awarded the Red Banner on 22 February 1939. Fought in the Winter War against Finland, he was awarded a second Red Banner on 26 January 1940. At the beginning of WWII he was deputy CO of an IAE, and 3 February 1942 he was shot down, but able to crashland behind enemy lines. He was rescued by another Soviet pilot who landed and picked him up. After leaving the hospital he was withdrawn from front line service. In 1943 he took classes at the Military Academy for Command. He graduated and was appointed as CO of the 105th GAP GVF (Guards Aviation Regiment Civil Air Fleet) flying Li-2 Transports and finished the war with that unit. After the war was over he worked in the Civil Air Fleet. Passed away 12 April 1961. (Semenov "*Parol,*" Pritsker, Abrosov, Kaminskii, *Pravda*, [1]Salas "*Diario,*" pg.27 lists three I-16s lost on the 3rd as CM 092, 165 and 176 all from the 5th Esc. but pg.216 lists CM 165 and 176 as from the 2nd, and also lists CM 139 as lost that day.)

ZIMOVETS, Petr P., Lt.
Pilot SSS, in Spain October 1936 to 27 May 1937. On 19 December 1936, while on a night training flight, he had to make a crashlanding. Neither he nor his navigator/gunner MACHAIDZE were injured. Awarded the Red Banner 2 January 1937. (Abrosov, *Los Rusos, Pravda*)

ZLATOTSVETOV, Avraam Efimovich "GOLD," Col., born 11 September 1900
Fought in the Russian civil war in the infantry; after the war in September 1922 he attended the Egorievskyi Theoretical School of the Red Air Fleet. In May 1925 he became a pilot in the 6th ORAO (Independent Reconnaissance Detachment) and in January 1926 he served as a senior pilot instructor at the 2nd military pilot school Moscow. From November 1930 until October 1935 he was the CO of the 43rd BAE BVO. In October 1935 he was appointed as CO of the 10th SBAE in the BVO. In Spain, he was the first Commander of Grupo 12 SBs serving in Spain from October 1936 to 13 September 1937. It has been reported erroneously in various publications that the name "GOLD" was used by GUSSAEV, I.A., commander of the 24th Grupo de Kats. but information supplied by Carlos Lazaro and others definitely shows that "GOLD" was the commander of the 12th Grupo. Thirty SBs arrived in October 1936, packed ten each on three Soviet Ships, the *Stari Bolshevik*, *KIM* and *Volgoles*. There were three escuadrillas of nine to ten aircraft each, under the command of ZLATOTSVETOV with KOTOV, P.A. as Chief of Staff. The SBs were the first of the Soviet aircraft to become operational, flying their first missions on 28 October. According to Abrosov p.89, when ARZHENUKHIN went to the Northern front, ZLATOTSEVETOV took over his task, and PROSKUROV took over command of the SB Grupo. Awarded the Order of the Red Banner on 2 January 1937. After Spain, he served until September 1941 in various capacities in VVS flying schools. In September 1941 he became VVS CO of the 38th Army on the Southwestern front. In July 1942 he was appointed as deputy CO of the 15th Air Army and then in November 1942 he became deputy CO of the 17th Air Army on the Southwestern front, where this unit fought at Stalingrad and Kursk. From 30 June to 24 August 1944 he was CO of the 1st Guards SAK on the 1st Ukrainian front. In September 1944 he again became deputy CO of the 17th Air Army fighting to liberate Yugoslavia and Hungary. After the war he served as deputy CO of the 16th Air Army. From June 1947 to April 1953 he headed several combat training staffs. Retired in April 1953 and died in Moscow 7 February 1970. Awards were Order of Lenin twice, Red Banner four times. Order of Suvorov 2nd class, Kutuzov 2nd class, and order of the Red Star. Laureau mistakenly lists his first name was Arkadi. (Salas, Laureau, *Solidarity*, Zil'manovich, Howson, *MY*, C. Lazaro, Berch, Boyd, *Pravda*, Abrosov, *Los Rusos* say "GOLD," http://voina.su/enc/people/)

ZOBOV, Nikolai A., Lt., born 1913
SB Pilot, served from 21 May to 28 December 1937. A member of OSTRYAKOV's Sea Group, on 26 July 1937 he and his crew ERGUNOV and BROVKIN were doing some bombing practice behind the lines, when they were attacked by Fiats and He 51s. He was able to get away, but had to crashland his SB. Later on 24 August 1937 his plane was mistakenly attacked by a Spanish flown I-15 and the gunner BROVKIN was killed. Awarded the Red Banner 3 November 1937. (Abrosov, Kotelnikov, *Pravda*, *Los Rusos* claim first name was Nikita)

ZORKI
Baumler lists him as Commander of I-15s, killed over Segovia on 2 June 1937. (Baumler, Laureau. See listing for ZOTSENKO below.)

ZOTOV, Dmitri V., born 1914
Electrician from Aircraft Factory #22 assembling SB aircraft. In Spain from October to 12 December 1936. Awarded the Red Star on 2 January 1937. (*Los Rusos, Pravda*)

ZOTOV, Polikarp I., Sr.Lt., born 1907
Bomber pilot, in Spain from October 1936 to 27 May 1937. Awarded the Red Banner twice, 2 January and 4 July 1937. (*Pravda, Los Rusos, Bajo la B.*, Lukes)

ZOTOV, Vladimir Nikiforovich, Lt., born 1907
Navigator on SB in 2nd Esc. arrived in November 1936. KIA, when shot down by a CR 32 on 3 January 1937 over Cordoba along with IVANOV/VATOV. Salas mistakenly lists as pilot of an SB in 2nd Escuadrilla in February 1937. Awarded the Order of the Red Banner 2 January 1937. (Salas, Meroño, Laureau, *Bajo la B.*, *Vmeste*, Lukes, *Pravda*, *Los Rusos* list date of death as 31 January)

ZOTSENKO, Vasilii Mikailovich, Capt., born 1906, died 1937
Before going to Spain he was a Detachment CO in the 121st IAE 95th IAB Transcaucasian Mil. Dist. Commander of an I-15 fighter Escuadrilla in Spain from 14 January 1937. His Escuadrilla was based at El Soto in May/June 1937. Shot down during a battle with Fiats and Heinkels, according to OSADCHII in *Vmeste* 177. This was Baumler's ZORKI who he said was downed on 2 June 1937 in the Segovia region. Tinker also mentions an I-15 CO. being shot down on that day in a big air battle with two squadrons of Fiats and Heinkels. Posthumously awarded the Red Banner 21 June 1937. (*Vmeste*, Baumler, Tinker, Abrosov, Kaminskii, *Pravda, Los Rusos* has two listing for him, first gives date of birth as 1911 while the second says "Jefe Grupo" and died 3 June.)

ZUBAREV, Ivan Ivanovich, Lt., born 25 October 1911
In 1937 he was a Zvena CO in the 36th IAE 56th IAB Kiev Mil. Dist. In Spain from 10 June to 12 October 1938, he was an I-16 pilot in the 2nd Moscas under NEDELIN. Flew eighteen combat sorties and fought in eight air battles and claimed three aircraft on 23 August 1938. Awarded the Red Banner on 22 February 1939. In September 1941 he was posted as assistant chief of Staff for Intelligence for the 210th BBAP (Short Range Bomber Regiment) until April 1942, then from April to August 1942 he served in the same position with the 6th Training Regiment and from August until the end of the war he occupied the same Intelligence position with the 229th IAD, fighting in Byelorussia and Prussia. Awarded the Red Star twice ,24 September 1943 and 24 May 1945. After the war he continued in the VVS. Passed away on 19 March 1980. (Semenov *Tov.*, Abrosov, Kaminskii, *Pravda*)

ZUBAREV, Sergei Pavlovich, born 1913
Pilot in the 5th IAE 36th IAB Kiev Mil. Dist. In Spain from 20 August 1937 until 25 April 1938, he was an I-16 pilot in the 5th Esc. Flew 100 combat sorties and participated in thirty air combats, one aircraft (Bf 109) to his credit. On 4 January 1938 he was wounded in combat. Returning to his field, at Villar he tried to land and overturned his aircraft CM 146. Awarded the Red Banner twice, on 2 March and 14 November 1938. On his return home he was appointed CO of an IAE in the 43rd IAP Kiev Mil. Dist. In WWII, he failed to return from a mission in the Kiev region on 10 July 1941. (Semenov "*Parol*," Abrosov, Pravda, *Los Rusos*, Kaminskii gives date of birth as 1914)

ZUBENKO, Fedor Nikifirovich, Lt., born 1912
He was a pilot in the 107th IAE 83rd IAB Byelorussian Mil. Dist. He was an I-16 pilot in Spain from 26 March to 10 June 1938. As soon as he arrived he began complaining that he was having health problems. He only flew seventeen hours training, and did not fly any combat missions. He crashlanded his fighter when the wheels failed to come down. He was returned early to the USSR. (Abrosov, Kaminskii, *Los Rusos, Pravda*)

ZUEV, Aleksandr E.
Worker from Aircraft Factory #21 assembling/ repairing I-16 aircraft. In Spain October 1936 to 8 May 1937. Awarded the Red Star 2 January 1937. (*Pravda, Los Rusos* lists as Head of the workshop)

ZVEREV, Nikolai Matveevich, Lt., born 1910
Pilot in the 109th IAE 36th IAB Kiev Mil. Dist. In Spain from 20 October 1936 until 13 June 1937. He was an I-15 pilot in RYCHAGOV's Esc. On 3 November 1936[1] while flying to a forward airfield, he along with KONDRAT'EV lost their orientation towards Alcala, and landed at a rebel airfield instead and were captured. On 12 March 1937 he is said to have been taken to Germany where they tried to recruit him to spy on Soviet aviation. In May 1937 he was exchanged for a German flyer and returned to the USSR, where he served in the 5th IAE 36th IAB Kiev Mil. Dist. Awarded the Order of the Red Banner 2 January 1937. (*Pravda, Vmeste*, Lukes, Abrosov, *Los Rusos* give end date as 13 May, [1]Kaminskii says it happened on 4 November)

ZVEREV, V.
Fighter pilot I-15 (Gusev 101, *Vmeste*)

ZYKANOV, Ivan Alekseevich, Lt., born 1903
Was a detachment CO in the 121st IAE 95th IAB Transcaucasian Mil. Dist. An I-15 Fighter pilot, in Spain from 14 January to 26 July 1937, he was a member of OSADCHIJ's Esc. Both Abrosov and Kaminskii claim he was an I-15 escuadrilla CO. Awarded the Red Banner on 27 June 1937. Upon return home, he was made CO of a Training IAE at the 2nd Military Pilots School. In 1941 he became CO of the 14th SAD. (Abrosov, Kaminskii, *Pravda*)

ZYUZIN, Viktor Vasil'evich, Lt. B.1907

A Zvena CO in the 56th IAB Keiv Mil. Dist. In Spain from 10 June to 23 September 1938. I-16 Pilot in 5th Moscas under GRITSEVETS. During a landing on 23 July his aircraft was damaged and had to be repaired. Later on 3 August his Mosca was completely destroyed in a landing accident. In the afternoon of 23 September 1938, while flying CM 237,[1] he was involved in a large air battle with Fiat CR 32s and he was KIA. (Semenov *Tov., Vmeste,* Abrosov, Kaminskii, Salas *Diario*, *Los Rusos* gives date of death as 9 September 1938, [1]Saiz lists his aircraft as CM 148)

APPENDICES

APPENDIX 1

Soviet Command of the Spanish Republican Air Force

Smushkevich – Lopatin – ptukhin – Arzhenukhin – Andreev

Overall Soviet Commanders of Fighter Groups
Pumpur – ptukhin – Eremenko – Pavlov – Kotrov

Command of I-16 Escuadrillas under Soviet control

– Bocharov – Denisov
1st Tarkhov – Denisov – Kolesnikov – Negoreev – Ukhov – Kolesnikov – Morozov

Lakeev – Shipitov or Shevtsov – October 1937 Spanish

2nd Pleshchenko – Devotchenko – Vikhrov – Lisin – Rodin – Nedelin – Semenko – Gritsevets – Spanish

3rd Minaev – Verevka – Smirnov – Butrym – Smirnov – Spanish

4th Ukhov – Evsev'ev – disbanded – Restarted Spanish (M. Zarauza)

5th Starikov – Devotchenko – Ivanov – Silverstov – Smolyakov – Siusiukalov – Bagrov – Glushenkov – Gritsevets – Korobkov – October 1938 Spanish

6th Gusev – Devotchenko – Gusev – April 1938 Spanish

7th Spanish

Commanders of Grupo 21
Kopets – Eremenko – Gusev – Devotchenko – Gusev – Glushenkov – Spanish

Command of Chato Escuadrillas under Soviet Control
1st Rychaqov – Osadchii – Eremenko – Serov – Antonov – Stepanov – Siusiukalov – Vikhrov – Kapustin – Osipenko – Spanish

2nd Kopets – ? – Spanish

3rd Zotsenko – Osadchii – Spanish

4th Spanish

North Basque Esc. Turzhanskii – Baranchuk – Spanish

APPENDIX 2

Illustrations

A group of Soviet SB pilots and navigators. (*Vmeste 1976*)

After their release from Franco's prison, left to right front: V.M. Kondrat'ev, G.N. Tupikov, N.M. Zverev; Rear: A.A. Shukaev, I.A. Volkov. (*Vmeste 1986*)

From left: F.A. Agaltsov, M. Fortus, F.K. Arzhenukhin, F.Z. Khimochko. (*Vmeste 1976*)

Bomber crews standing from right to left: Gunner S.I. Ivanov (first), Pilot G.K. Starodumov (Second), navigator V.M. Lavskii (third), navigator V.P. Baryshpol (fourth), navigator A.T. Ignatenko (fifth), Spaniard Matias (sixth), navigator P.I. Simonan (eighth). Sitting right to left Pilot P.P. Arkhangelskii (first), gunner E.I. Tarbeev (Second), pilot S.A. Doyar (third), navigator G.A. Sbytov (fifth), navigator Y.V. Suslov (sixth) in September 1937. (*Solidarnost'*)

A group of flyers, August 1937. From left to right: P. Smolyakov, V. Lopatin, "General Montenegro," at center is Ivan Eremenjo, then M. Kriguin and A. Gusev. (*M. Zhirohov*)

General Douglas Ya. Smushkevich on a visit to the frontlines. (*Archivo C. Ibañez*)

2nd Moscas, spring 1938. In the front row from left to right: V. Bobrov, N. Martyshchenko, G. Kogrushev, N. Koloskov, S. Yashin, F. Rodin, A. Sviridov, I. Turchin, and A. Romanov. In the second row left to right: V. Bagrov, A. Shubikov, M. Emel'yanenko, N. Zherdev, A. Panov, A. Sirochenko, N. Semenov, A. Yarkonoi, N. Nikitin and A. Lantukh. (*Semenov*)

I-16 pilots from Devotchenko's Escaudrilla. From the left: N.M. Nikitin, A.K. Sviridov, T.G. Vikhrov, V.V. Bagrov, and A.V. Shubikov. (*Semenov*)

I-15 fighter pilots from the first group that arrived in October 1936. In the front row from the left: N.I. Miroshnichenko, P.E. Agafonov, E.E. Erlykin, and G.N. Zakharov; second row N.I. Shmel'kov, A.V. Kovalevskii, P.V. Rychagov and K.I. Kovtun. (*Courtesy RIA Novosti*)

1st Chatos Spring 1938. Osipenko is at center rear with flight jacket with S. Evtikhov to his right. (*ADAR fondo general*)

Members of Devochenko's Escuadrilla. From left: F. Kovenev, G. Shubin, V. Bagrov, I. Devotchenko, N. Zhuravlev, S. Zubarev, V. Matveev, A. Sviridov, T. Vikhrov, G. Sobornov, N. Nikitin. (*Semenov*)

I-16 pilots N. Semenov on left and A. Sviridov, seated on right, with two Spaniards. (*Semenov*)

Left to right: K. Demenchuk, V. Zakhariev (Goranov) and P. Desnitskii on their return to the Soviet Union. (*Vmeste 1986*)

Teruel 1937, Standing from the left are: F. Kovenev, I. Sokolov, V. Lisin, A. Semenov, P. Smolyakov with a Spanish pilot kneeling. (*Gusev*)

Members of Gusev's 6th Moscas, Alcañiz Sept. 1937. From left to right, front row: I. Panfilov, V. Sklyarov, I. Sokolov, I. Bazarov looking over shoulders), E. Ptukhin (CO of VVS in Spain), P. Smolyakov, A. Gusev and V. Gorunov. In second row are: E. Sobornov, G. Shubin, M. Krigin (appears added later), A. Il'in, A. Milulovich and N. Ivanov. (*Gusev*)

Members of the first I-16 unit in Nov. 1936: from left are A. Tarasov CO, K. Dubkov, F. Zamashanskii, I. Lakeev and, A.V. Minaev. In second row: Mechanics I. Fomenko, G. Kon'kov, T. Krupenin, S. Mikhailovskii, unknown and unknown. (*Solidarnost'*)

From right to left are P. Smolyakov, L. Shestakov, G. Sobornov and A. Sil'verstov visiting the gravesite of Karl Marx in London on their return trip to the USSR. (*Solidarnost'*)

Fedor Rodin on the left with another Soviet pilot. (*Gagin*)

Yakov Smushkevich (Gen. Douglas). (*Archivo C. Ibañez*)

I-15 pilots on their arrival in October 1936. From the left: E. Kondrat, N. Mirshnichenko, G. Zakharov and L. Rusak. (*Courtesy ICARE*)

SSS airmen with a Spanish pilot center. At left is E. Chervyakov, and at right is A. Sadovoi. (*Courtesy ICARE*)

Members of Osipenko's 1st Chatos Escuadrilla at Sabanell Aerodrome in the spring of 1938. Standing fourth from the left is A. Osipenko. (*Archivos Juan Sayós via Clemente Ros*)

Two Soviet pilots of the 1st Chatos, spring 1938. (*Archivo Juan Sayós via Clemente Ros*)

Ivan Buryak on left standing in front of his aircraft with Lev Shestakov on the right. (*Courtesy S. Abrosov*)

Group of Soviet pilots of the 5th Esc. Moscas, spring 1938. L. Shestakov is first on the left. (*Archivo ADAR, fondo L. Shestakov*)

Four Soviet flyers. L. Shestakov is second from the right. (*Archivo ADAR, fondo L. Shestakov*)

Spring 1938. Soviet and Spanish pilots with their Escuadrilla mascot. (*Archivo ADAR, fondo L. Shestakov*)

Group of seven flyers captured during the war. They are from left to right: A. Markin, E. Stepanov, M. Zalkin, F. Shumalov, G. Khozyainov, A. Cherkasov, and M. Smertin. (*Author's collection*)

From the left: Spanish pilot Bastida, A. Zaitsev, and A. Osadchii. (*Lacalle*)

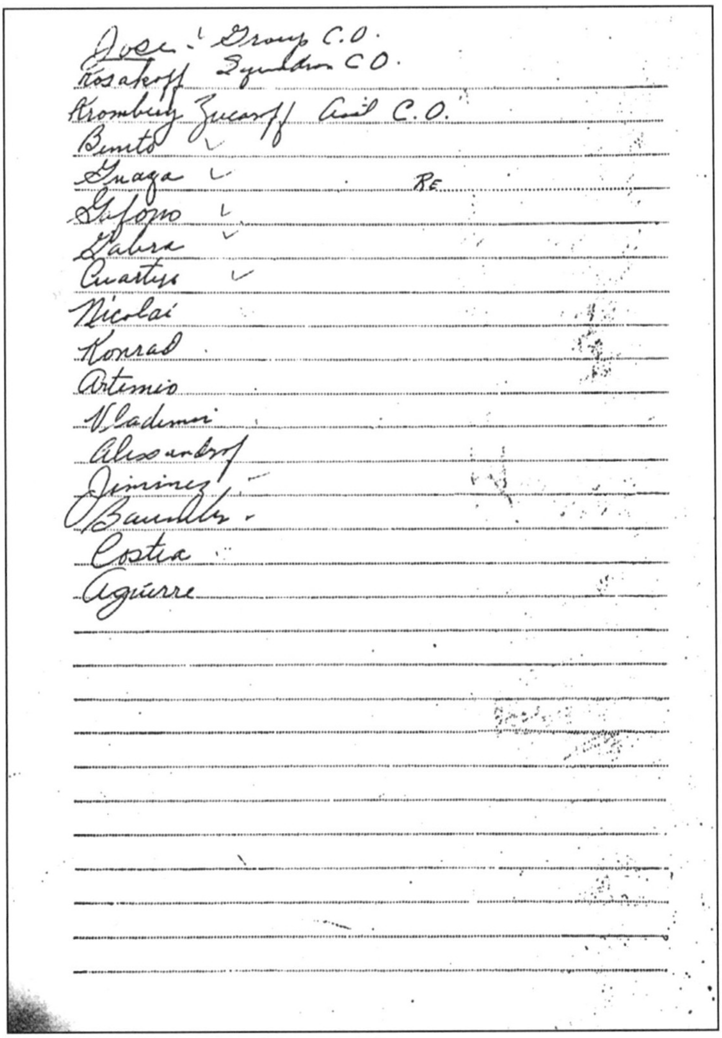

Page from Albert Baumler's flight log showing names of members of the Kazakov Escuadrilla.

APPENDIX 3

Soviet Supply Lines to the Spanish Republic

Sea Routes
(South)

Soviet Ports used on the Black Sea:

- Novorossiysk
- Feodosiya
- Sevastopol
- Odessa
- Kherson

Ships would load their cargos at these ports under strict secrecy and then proceed through the Bosporus and the Dardanelles. They then would stop at one of the small Greek islands and try to alter the ship's appearance. They would then sail through the straits between Greece and Crete into the Mediterranean. Then crossing between Sicily and Malta and turning east hugging the northern coast of Tunisia and Algeria, swinging up after Algiers to arrive at the Spanish Ports of Cartagena, Alicante and Denia. Later in mid-1938 with these Spanish ports basically blockaded, the Soviets would instead turn north after Algiers and proceed to the French port of Marseille and off load their cargos, which would then be put on ships of Spanish and other nationality registration and taken to Barcelona or Port Bou in Catalonia.

Sea Routes
(North)

From Murmansk ships went up around northern Norway, and following the Norwegian Coast sailed into the North Sea. Ships also left from Leningrad into the Gulf of Finland and then into the Baltic, sailing through the straits between Sweden and Denmark and into the Skagerrak, and then the North Sea where the two routes would converge to continue south, passing through the straits of Dover. At the beginning of the war, the ships continued south to the Spanish ports of Bilbao and Santander, but after the loss of the Northern front, the ships would use the French ports of Le Havre or Bordeaux. Ships coming from Polish ports used this same route.

Land Routes

Internal routes in the Soviet Union included a northern route from Moscow, Leningrad and other industrial centers to the port of Murmansk, or to Leningrad. Southern routes led from these centers to the Seaports on the Black Sea. Deliveries made to French ports, used land routes from those ports to the southern port of Marseille, then from Marseille by sea or overland south to Port Bou in Spain.

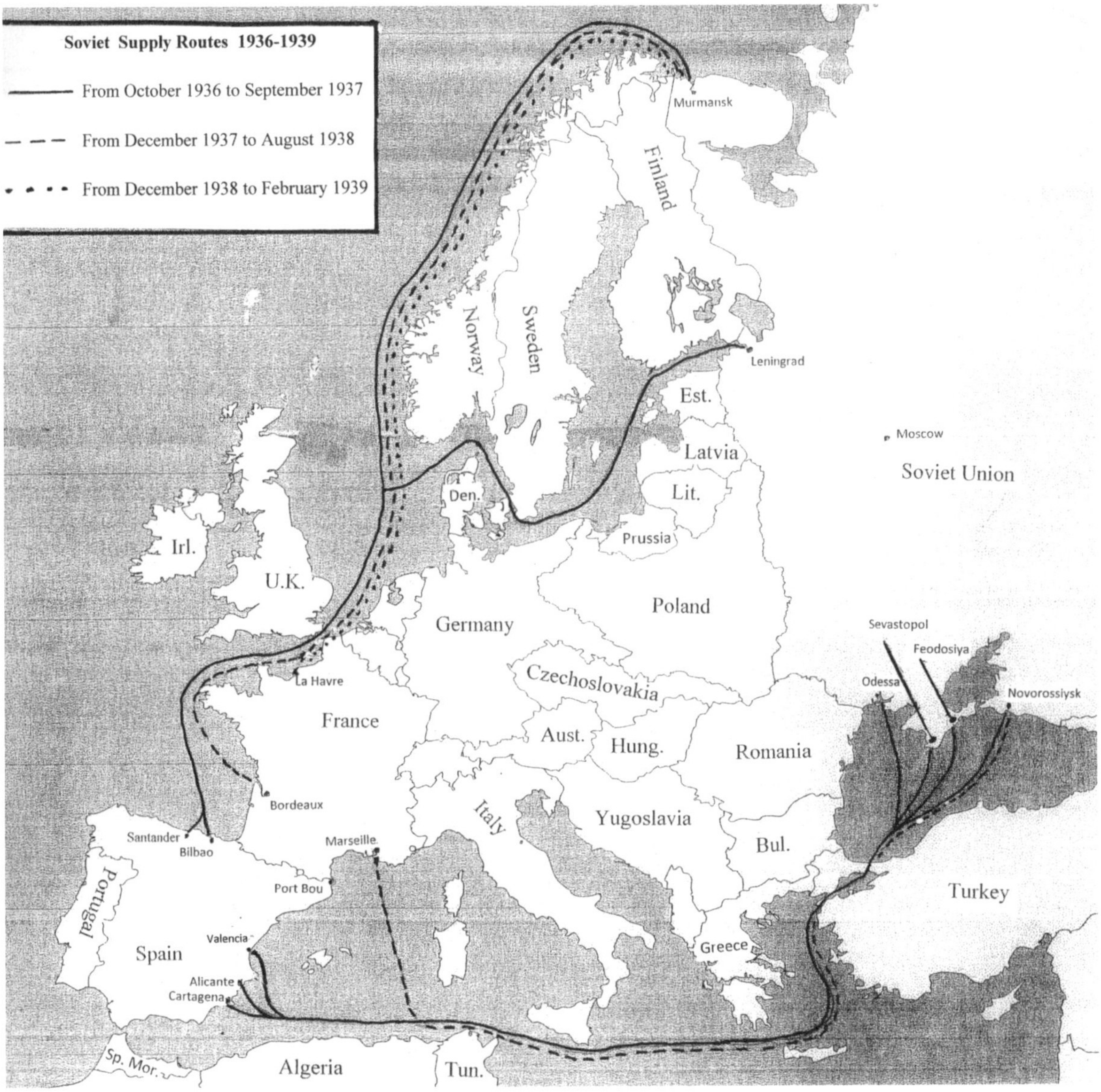

APPENDIX 4
Soviet Aircraft Types Used in Spain

TUPOLEV SB Fast Bomber

A twin-engine, mid-wing monoplane bomber of all metal construction, with retractable landing gear. Wingspan 20.33m, length 12.20m and height 4.39m. It was equipped with two M-100 engines, that were license built liquid-cooled Hispano-Suiza 12 Ybr rated at 730hp each. Top speed was 423Km/h with a cruising speed of 280km/h. Armament consisted originally of two DA 7.62mm machineguns, one in the nose and the other in the rear position. This was later changed to two ShKAS 7.62mm machineguns, with some of those delivered later having two ShKAS 7.62mm machineguns in the nose. A total of ninety-two SB bombers were delivered and put into service with the Republic.

An SB Bomber at Barajas at the end of the war, being examined by men from the Legion Condor. (*Archivo ADAR*)

Nose of a captured SB. (*AHEA*)

SB White 1 which was retrieved after being shot down and reassembled by the Nationalists in November 1936. (*Author's Collection*)

POLIKARPOV I-16

Low wing monoplane fighter of mixed metal and wood construction with retractable landing gear and fabric covered control surfaces. The first shipments were the Type 5 model that used the M-25 engine, a license built Wright Cyclone R-1820 F3 engine rated at 700hp. This model had a sliding canopy to make an enclosed cockpit. The next delivery was the Type 6 that used the M-25A engine and had a strengthened wing. Some of these were fitted with a different windscreen making it an open cockpit. Both of these models were equipped with two wing mounted ShKAS 7.62mm machineguns. In March 1938, the first of the new Type 10 models arrived. These also had an open cockpit and were equipped with the new M-25V 750hp engine plus two additional ShKAS 7.62mm machineguns mounted in the upper cowling firing through the propeller. The Types 5 and 6 had a wingspan of 9m a length of 5.9m and height of 2.56m. The Type 10 had a similar wingspan while the length was increased to 5.99m. In August 1938, the Type 10s of the 4th Escuadrilla were equipped with American made Wright Cyclone R-1820-F54 engines and an oxygen system. This allowed these I-16s to operate at higher altitudes in order to deal with the Bf 109s. The Spanish began production of the Type 10 but only managed to complete some four aircraft. During the course of the war 276 I-16s were sent from the USSR.

Two gun Polikarpov I-16 Type 5 coded CM-033. (*AHEA*)

Mechanics working on a Type 10 model with 4 ShKAS MGs. (*Archivio ADAR*)

POLIKARPOV I-15

Single-seat biplane fighter of mixed metal and wood construction. Wingspan was 9.75m, length 6.1m and height of 2.20m. The upper wing was made in two sections and attached to the fuselage in a gull fashion. The landing gear was fixed with a skid mounted in the tail. The engine was an M-25 license built Wright Cyclone R-1820-F3 producing 700hp. In fact some of the first aircraft received were equipped with Wright engines instead of the M-25. Armament consisted of four PV-1 7.62mm machineguns mounted in the fuselage with the barrels between the engine cylinders and firing through the propeller. During the war a total of 131 of this type were sent from the USSR. Additional aircraft of this type were built in Spain beginning in August 1937. The exact number built in Spain and put into service with the Escuadrillas is still in question, but the number ranges as high as 237.

I-15 Chato in flight in early 1937. (*IHCA*)

I-15 Chato with Hucks starter truck all ready to go. (*Archivo ADAR*)

I-15 of the 1st Chato Escuadrilla. This is the aircraft flown by I. Eremenko. (*Shingarev*)

One of the first I-15s delivered; this aircraft was captured by the Nationalists. (*AHEA*)

POLIKARPOV I-15bis

Single-seat biplane fighter made of mixed metal and wood construction, with a conventional upper wing. This was a modification of the I-15. The landing gear remained fixed but had spats fitted over the wheels. The engine was an M-25V rated at 750hp. Armament was four PV-1 7.62mm machineguns mounted in the fuselage firing through the propeller. Wingspan was 10.2m, length 6.27m and height was 2.20m. Only thirty of this type were delivered and assembled in January 1939, coming too late to see any combat service.

Two photos of the I-15bis aircraft after being assembled. In early February 1939, these were all flown to France to escape the approaching Nationalist forces. (*top photo Archivo ADAR, bottom photo U.S. National Archives*)

POLIKARPOV RZ

A two-seat biplane light bomber of mixed metal and wood construction. This was aircraft was a major modification of the earlier R-5. It was fitted with the M-34 a twelve cylinder liquid cooled engine producing 750hp. Wingspan was 15.5m, length 9.7m and height 3.6m. Maximum speed was 290km/h and cruising speed 250km/h. Armament was one PV-1 762mm machinegun mounted in the forward fuselage firing through the propeller and one ShKAS 7.62mm in the rear position mounted on a ring allowing it to turn and move up or down. Ninety-three of these aircraft were delivered from the USSR during the war. This type was only flown by Spanish crews.

Side view of the RZ flown by Jose Gomez Gomez. (*Author's collection*)

Rear view of a Polikarpov RZ. (*Archivo ADAR*)

POLIKARPOV I-16 UTI

This aircraft type was completely the same dimensions as the I-16 fighter, but made into a two-seat trainer. Four of these aircraft were supplied to Spain.

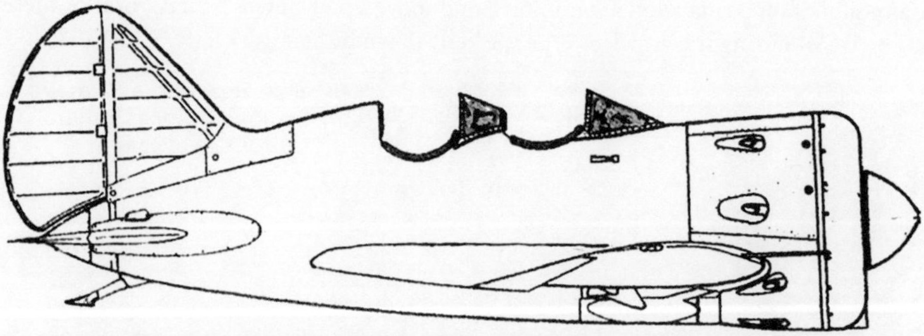

Drawing based upon M. Maslov drawing in "Istrebitel' I-16," Armada #2, p.57.

Polikarpov I-16 UTI. This particular machine is Russian and was captured by the Germans in the Soviet Union. (*Author's Collection*)

POLIKARPOV SSS

A two-seat biplane ground attack aircraft. Construction was mixed of metal and wood with fabric covering. Wingspan was 15.5m, length 10.56m and height of 3.62m. This was a modification of the R-5 model and there were several major changes. It was equipped with an M-17F liquid cooled twelve cylinder engine rated at 715hp. Giving it a maximum speed of 249km/h and cruising speed of 190km/h. The lower wing fairings were much larger and it had an internal bomb bay. Armament consisted of two ShKAS 7.62mm machine guns mounted in each of the lower wings plus one ShKAS 7.62mm mounted in the rear position on a type 8 ring that allowed it to be rotated almost 360 degrees and raised or lowered. Only thirty-one aircraft of this model were sent from the USSR, arriving in October 1936 and were formed into three Escuadrillas. Later in the summer of 1937 the remaining aircraft were stripped of their wings and guns then turned over to Spanish crews for use as night bombers.

Side view of the SSS in which the larger wing root fairings can be seen. The Moon and Bat emblem on the tail is ferom the night bomber Escuadrilla formed ater this type was turned over to the Spanish in the summer of 1937. (*U.S. National Archives*)

Front of an SSS showing the position of the ShKAS machine guns in the lower wings. (*Archivo ADAR*)

APPENDIX 5

Awards Given to Soviet Airmen in Spain

H.S.U. Gold Star, Hero of the Soviet Union. (*Author's collection*)

Order of Lenin. (*Author's collection*)

Order of the Red Banner. (*Author's collection*)

Order of the Red Star. (*Author's collection*)

Metal pesented to the Soviet veterans of the Spanish war in 1967. (*Author's collection*)

APPENDIX 6
Soviet Abbreviations Used in Text

AD	Aviation Division
AB	Aviation Brigade
AP	Aviation Regiment
AE	Aviation Squadron
ADD	Long Range Aviation
BAD	Bomber Aviation Division
BAP	Bomber Aviation Regiment
BBAR	Short Range Bomber Aviation Regiment
BVO	Byelorussian Military District
ChF	Black Sea Fleet
CO	Commander
DBA	Long Range Bomber Aviation
DBAP	Long Range Bomber Aviation Regiment
GAP	Guards Aviation Regiment
GBAP	Guards Bomber Aviation Regiment
GBF	Civil Air Fleet
GIAK (GuIAK)	Guards Fighter Aviation Corps
GIAP (GuIAP)	Guards Fighter Aviation Regiment
GShAD	Guards Ground Attack Aviation Division
GShAP	Guards Ground Attack Aviation Regiment
H.S.U.	Hero of the Soviet Union
IAB	Fighter Aviation Brigade
IAE	Fighter Aviation Squadron
IAK	Fighter Aviation Corps
IAP	Fighter Aviation Regiment
IAO	Fighter Aviation Detachment
KBF	Red Banner Baltic Fleet
Kombrig	Commander Brigade
Komdiv	Commander Division
Komesk	Commander Squadron
KVO	Kiev Military District
LBAP	Light Bomber Aviation Regiment
LBAE	Light Bomber Aviation Squadron
LIS	Test Flight Service
LShAE	Light Attack Aviation Squadron
MVO	Moscow Military District

NII	Scientific Research Institute
NKO	People's Commissariat of Defense
OAG	Independent Aviation Group
OMAG	Independent Naval Aviation Group
OIAE	Independent Fighter Aviation Squadron
OIAO	Independent Fighter Aviation Detachment
OKDVA	Independent Red Banner Far East Army
OShAE	Independent Attack Aviation Squadron
Otryad	Detachment, generally 6-9 Aircraft
PAD	Transit Aviation Division
PAP	Transit Aviation Regiment
PVO	Anti-Aircraft Defense
RAG	Reserve Air Group
RKKA	Workers and Peasants Red Army
SAB	Mixed Aviation Brigade
SAD	Mixed Aviation Division
SAP	Mixed Aviation Regiment
SBAP	Fast Bomber Aviation Regiment
SBAE	Fast Bomber Aviation
ShAD	Assault Aviation Division
ShAB	Assault Aviation Brigade
ShAE	Assault Aviation Squadron
Taran	A ramming attack, where the pilot crashes into the enemy aircraft
TBAB	Heavy Bomber Aviation Brigade
TBAE	Heavy Bomber Aviation Squadron
TOF	Pacific Fleet
VLTSh	High Altitude Tactical School
VMF	Navy
VVS/VMF	Naval Air Force
VVS	Air Force
Y + #	Voyage of Soviet Supply Ships
ZAB	Reserve Aviation Brigade
ZOVO	Western Special Military District
Zvena	Patrol, generally three aircraft

Spanish Words

Escuadrilla	Squardron
Patrulla	Patrol
Grupo	Group

BIBLIOGRAPHY AND SOURCES

ABELLAN, E., "Los Chatos en España," parte III, in *Aeroplano* #10, I.H.C.A., Madrid, 1992.

ABELLAN, E., *Los Cazas Sovieticos en la Guerra Aerea de España 1936/1939*, Ministerio de Defensa, Madrid, 1999, 220pp.

ABRAMSON, Paulina y Adelina Mosaico Roto, *Compañia Literario*, Madrid, 1994, 364pp.

ABROSOV, Sergei V., *Nebe Ispanii 1936-1939 gody*, Moscow, 2003, 432pp.

— Vozdushnaya Voina v Ispanii, Eksmo, Moscow, 2008, 605pp. 2nd Edition of the above work.

A.D.A.R. Alas Gloriosas issues Nos.0 de 15 Dic. 1978 to #36 Nov./Dec. 1984. Nos.3-4, 5-6, 10-11, 15-16, 21-22, 27-28, and 33-34 being double issues. Published by the Asociacion de Aviadores de la Republica, Barcelona, Spain.

A.D.A.R. (Madrid) Icaro, boletin de la ADAR Madrid, nos.1 enero 1987 – 109 Nov. 2012, plus Numero especial de Mayo 2007 dedicado a Natachas y Resantes.

A.D.A.R. (Barcelona) Magazine 2000, Veteranos de Aviacion, #0 Diciembre, 1999, 82pp.

airaces.narod.ru/spane/spane.htm Russian website on fighter pilots.

airforce.ru Russian Air Force website includes historical articles.

airforce.ru/staff/who_is_who/index.htm listing of various people in the Russian AF.

AIZPURU, M., *El Informe Brusiloff, La Guerra Civil de 1936 en el Frente Norte*, Alberdania, Irun, 2009, 331pp.

ALAS ALAS PLEGADAS, *Liga de Antiguos Aviadores de la Republica Española*, Editor Jose Falco, published in France Between 1960-2001, Nos. 1 (and 1bis) through 28 in one bound volume.

ALCOFAR, J.L. "SPANSKY," *Los Extranjeros que Lucharon en la Guerra Civil Española 1.*, Dopesa, Barcelona, 1973.

— *Los Asesores Sovieticos en la Guerra Civil Española*, Dopesa, Barcelona, 1971.

AMBA, A., *I Was Stalin's Bodyguard*, Frederick Muller Ltd., London, 1952.

ARIAS ARIAS, A., "Arde el Cielo," Edita: A. Delgado Romero, Madrid 1995

— *Ognennom Nebe*, Belarus', Minsk, 1988, 239pp.

ARILLA HERRERO, J.J., *Guerra Civil Aragón, La Aviación*, Editorial Delsan, Zaragoza, 2011, 310pp.

AVIATION HISTORY, Interview by Jon Guttman with Evgenii STEPANOV, 7/95.

BAJO La B., *Bajo La Bandera de la España Republicana-Recuerdan los Voluntarios Sovieticos participantes en la Guerra Nacional-Revolucionaria en España*, Editorial Progreso, Moscow, n.d.

BAUMLER, ALBERT J., Flight Logbook from Spain, xerox copy, Air & Space Museum, Washington D.C.

BERCH, Victor, *Berch*, Archivist of the ALBA.

BERGSTROM, C. and MIKHAILOV, A., *Black Cross, Red Star*, Vol.1, Pacifica Military History, Pacifica, 2000, 307pp.

BOCHKAREV, P. and PARYQIN, N., *Gody b Ognennom Nebe*, Voenizdat, Moscow, 1991.

BODRIKHIN, N., *Sovetskie Asy*, Tamp, Moscow 1998, 270pp.

— *Stalinskie Sokoly, Del'ta*, Moscow, 1997, 224pp.

BOTIN, M.S., *Toboj, Ispaniya, Voenizdat*, Moscow, 1976, 208pp.

BOYD, A., *The Soviet Air Force since 1918*, Stein & Day, N.Y., 1977.

CALVO Jung, C., Los *Ultimos Aviadores de la Republica, la Cuarta Expedicion a Kirovabad, Ollero y Ramos Editores, para La Fundacion Aena y El Minesterio de Defensa*, Madrid, 2010, 226pp.

CHALAYA, Z., *Anatolii SEROV*, Molodaya Gvagdiya, 1939 (1940), 253pp.

— LETCHIK SEROV, *Molodaya Gvagdiya*, Moscow, 1955, 216pp. New revised edition of the above work.

CHUDODEEV, IU. V., (Editor), *Po Dorogam Kitaia 1937-1945 Vospominania, Nauka*, Moscow, 1989, 368pp.

CONFORTI, O. GUADALAJARA, *Oiks-Tau Ediciones*, Barcelona, Spain, 1977.

DAHL, H., "'Whitey' Sky Fighting brought me a Death Sentence," in *True*, August 1940, xerox via R.S.A.

DAHMS, H.G., *La Guerra Española de 1936*, Ediciones Rialp, Madrid, 1966.

DEMENCHUK, K.T., "Ispaniya, Naval'karnero," in *Kryp'ya Rodiny* #10, 1988, pgs.8-9 in addition to his memoirs in *Vmeste* and *My*.

EHRENBURG, I., *Memoirs 1921-1941*, World Publishers, N.Y., 1964.

EMELYANOV, S.N., *In the Skies of Spain*, @ www.proza.ru/2007/04/17-271.

EMILIANI, A., *Italiani nell'Aviazione Republican Spagnola*, Edizione Aeronautiche Italiane, Firenze 1981.

— "Il 'Rata' Del Tenente Trevisan," in *Storia Militare*, Agosto, 2012, pgs. 48-54.

FERNANDEZ Sanchez, J., *Los Voluntarios de Vladimir Gorev*, Ediciones El Museo Universal, Madrid, 1990, 78pp.

FINICK, E., "Bombers Aloft," in *Tru,e* August 1939.

FLIEGER REVUE, Ausgabe, 3/229, 1972.

FORT, F.V., *Desti Bomb*, English trans. via T. Sarbaugh.

GAGIN, V.V., *Vozdushnaya Voina V Ispanii*, Voronnezhskii Al'manakh, Voronezh, 1998, 80pp.

— Revised 2nd edition of the above work published in 2001, 88pp.

GARRIGA, R., *la Legion Condor*, G. Del Toro, Editor, Madrid, 1975.

GEROI Geroi, *Sovetskogo Soiuza, Ministerstvo Oborony SSSR*, two volumes, Moscow, 1987-88.

GEUST, C., KESKINEN, K., STENMAN, K., *Red Stars*, AR-Kustannus Oy, Kangasala, 1993, 160pp.

GEUST, C., *Under the Red Star*, Airlife Pub. Inc., Shrewsbury, 1993.

GOLUBEV, G., "V Pare s Sotym", DOSSAF, Moscow, 1978, 254pp.

G. y REV. 2 and 3, *Guerra y Revolucion en España 1936-39*, Tomos 2 and 3 Editorial Progreso, Moscow, 1966 and 1971.

GUIU Lashers, J.M., *El Verano de los Halcones, Los Aerodromos Militares de Caspe (1936-1939)*, Centro de Estudios Comarcales del Bajo Aragon-Caspe, Caspe, 2008, 251pp.

GUSEV, A. I., *Hnevive Nebe Spanelske, Nase Vojsko*, Prague, 1979, Czech. translation of Gnevnoe Nabo Ispanii, Moscow, 1973.

— *Gnevnoe Nebo Ispanii*, Voenizdat, Moscow, 1973, 326pp.

HAYCRAFT, J.B., *Aircraft Losses during the Spanish Civil War 1936-1939*, Air Enterprise Publications, Newark, DE, 1991, Listed as Ha in this list.

HERICOURT, P., *Les Soviets et la France*, Editions Baudiniere, Paris, n.d. (1938?).

HIDALGO de CISNEROS, I., *Cambio de Rumbo*, tomo 2, Bucharest, 1964, Coleccion Ebro.

— *Meniaiu Kurs, Politicheskoi Literatury*, Moscow, 1967, 431pp. Russian language edition of the above work.

HOWSON, GERALD, *Aircraft of the Spanish Civil War 1936-1939*, Putnam, London, 1990.

— *Arms for Spain, the Untold Story of the Spanish Civil War*, John Murray, London, 1998, 354pp.

IBAÑEZ, Carlos, *Retrazos del Pasado*, 5pp. unpublished, via C. Lazaro.

ICARE 130, *La Guerre D'Espagne*, Vol. 2, Paris, 1990. Contains several articles on the arrival of the first Soviet air contingents.

KAMINSKII, O., *Ikh Nazyvali "Ispantsami"*, Druk, Odessa, 2008, 381pp.

KOLTSOV, M., *Diario de la Guerra de España*, Editions Ruedo Iberico, Paris, 1963. Translation of 1957 Russian edition.

KONDRAT, E., *Dostalsya Vek Nespokoinyi*, DOSAAF, Moscow, 1978, 208pp.

KOPENHAGEN, W., *Lexikon Sowjetluftfahrt*, Transpress VEB, Berlin, 1986.

KOTELNIKOV, V.R., *Skorostnoi, Skoropod'emnyi, Skorostrel'nyi*, Abiatsiya I Vremya #6 2001, pgs. 4 -13

KOWALSKY, D.L., *The Soviet Union and the Spanish Republic: Diplomatic, Military and Cultural Relations, 1936-1939*, Dissertation, University of Wisconsin-Madison, 2001, 521pp.

— *Stalin and the Spanish Civil War*, Columbia Univ. Press and Gutenberg, New York, 2004, 525pp. Printed edition of Gutenberg E-Book, this is an updated edition of earlier dissertation

KRIVITSKY, W.G., *In Stalin's Secret Service*, Harper & Brothers Pub., N.Y., 1939, 273pp.

— "Stalin's Hand in Spain," *Saturday Evening Post*, April 15, 1939, p.5-7+.

KTO BYL KTO V., *Velikoi Otechestvennoi Voine 1941-1945*, Respublika, Moscow, 1995.

KÜNZI, D., *C'était mon rêve, Ernst Schacht, un pilote Suisse avec les aviateurs sovietiques de la guerre d' Espagne*, DVD from SPM, Geneva, 2008, 74min.
LACALLE, A., *Mitos y Verdades*, Ediciones Oasis S.A., Mexico, D.F., 1973.
LARIO, J., *Habla un Aviador de la Republica*, G. del Toro Editor, Madrid, 1973.
LAUREAU, P., *L'Aviation Republicaine Espagnole*, Docavia, Edition Lariviere, Paris, 1978.
— *L'Aviation Sovietique en Espagne en 1936*. L'Echelon Precurseur in Icare #130, pp.32-39.
LAUREAU, P., CAPILLAS, S., PEREIRA, E., *La Aviacion Republicana Española*. Self published N.D., No place. This edition corrects many entries in the volume above.
LAZARO AVILA, C., *List of Russians in Grupo 12 and the Estado Major, using only Noms de Guerre*. Also lists monthly pay amounts. From files of Servicio Historico Militar.
LETECTOR KOSMONAUTICA, #23, 1971.
L'LOV, M., *Geroi Ognenny Let*, vol.6, Moskovskii Rabochii, 1983.
LOGOLUSO, A., "Aviabrigada 'X,'" three parts in *Storia Militare*, Nos.97, 98 and 99 (Oct-Dec. 2001).
LOS RUSOS en la Guerra de España, Fundacion Pablo Iglesias, Madrid, 2009, 308pp.
LUKES, P., "Polikarpov I-15," in *HPM* magazine Prague, Pt.1 #9, 1999, pp.8-12, Pt.2 #10 pp.18-23.
MARTINEZ, G., "Los Katiuskas," in *AEQ* 32, London, 1986.
MARTINEZ, J., *Chantaje a un Pueblo*, G. del Toro, Madrid, 1974.
MEROÑO, F., *En el Cielo de España*, Editorial Progreso, Moscow, 1979.
— *Aviadores Españoles en la Gran Guerra Patria*, Editoral Progreso, Moscow, 1986.
MILANY, J., *de Un Aviador de la Republica*, Editorial Nova Terra, Barcelona, 1971.
MIRANDA, J. and MERCADO, P., *World Aviation in Spain (The Civil War) 1936-1939, American and Soviet Airplanes*, Silex, Madrid, 1988, (Spanish edition 19).
MORQUILLAS, L., *Alas Gloriosas*, Nos.25 and 26, Barcelona.
MY, *My Internatsionalisty*, Moscow, Politizdat, 1975.
MY 2, Revised and expanded edition, Moscow 1986.
PARTES *Partes Oficiales de Guerra 1936-1939, Servicio Historico Militar*, two volumes, San Martin, Madrid, 1977.
PEDRIALI, F., *Guerra di Spagna e Aviazione Italiana, Aeronautica Militare Italiana Ufficio Storico*, Pub. Nuovo Studio Tecna, Roma, 1992.
POLAK, T., w/SHORES, C., *Stalin's Falcons: Aces of the Red Star*, Grub Street, London, 1999, 381pp.
PRACHIK, I.A., *Frontovoe Nebo*, Voenizdat, Moscow, 1984, 125pp.
PRAVDA, xerox copies of pages on awards for 2 January, 28 October, 3 November, 10 November and 11 November 1937 via P. LUKES, plus 31 December 1936, 21 June, 27 June, 4 July, 31 August, 22 October 1937, 22 February, 2 March, 14 March, 14 November 1938, 22 February 1939 from authors collection.
PRITSKER, D.P. and GUREVICH, A.M., *Leningradtsy v Ispanii*, Lenizdat, Leningrad 1989, 3rd edition, 412pp.
PRUTSAKOV, M. and LITVINENKO, V., *"Ispanets" c Kubani* (Ivan Eremenko), Aviatsiya i Vremya pt.1, 1/2000 pp.41-5, pt.2, 2/2000 pp.43-45.
RIES, K. and RING, H., *Legion Condor*, Verlag Dieter Hoffmann, Mainz, 1980, Listed as R & R. (U.S. edition Schiffer Publishing Ltd., 1992)
RSA Richard S. Allen, Aviation Historian.
RUMYANTSEV, N., *Geroi Khalkhin-Gola*, Voenizdat, Moscow, 1989, 384pp.
RUMYANTSEV, N., *Kapitan Antonio*, Privolzhskoe Knizhnoe, Saratov, 1979, 144pp.
— (Ed.) *Na Khalkhin-Gola*, Lenizdat, Leningrad, 1989, 253pp.
RYBALKIN, YURI, "Operatsiya 'X,' Sovetskaya Voennaya Pomosh, Respublikanskoi Ispanii 1936-1939," *Airo XX*, Moscow, 2000, 150pp.
— "Ayuda Militar Sovietica a la España Republicana, Cifras y Hechos," in *Ejercito*, Enero 1992, pp.44-50.
— "La Guerra Civil en España y las URSS en Visperas de la GM II," in *Ejercito*, Febrero, 1992, pp.90-96.
— *Stalin y España*, Marcial Pons, Madrid, 2008, 261pp. Spanish edition of "Operatsiya X."

SAIZ CIDONCHA, C., *Aviacion Republicana, Almena Ediciones*, Madrid, Tomo I, 2005, 415pp., Tomo II, 2006, 353pp., Tomo III, 2006, 351pp.

SALAS, J., *La Guerra de España desde el Aire*, 2nd edition, Editorial Ariel, Barcelona, 1972.

— *Modelismo & Historia* #1, "Chatos en España."

— *Aeroplano* #8, Comentarios al articulo "Los Chatos en España," Madrid, November 1990.

— "Los 'Natacha' en la Guerra Civil" Pt.1 in *Revista de Aeronautica y Astronautica* #458, Enero, 1979, pp.27-33.

— *Guernica*, Ediciones Rialp, S.A., Madrid, 1987.

— *Guerra Aerea 1936/39*, Tomo I y II, IHCA, Madrid, 1999, 429 y 364pp., Tomo III, Madrid, 2001, 310pp., Tomo IV, Madrid, 2003, 277pp,

— *Caza Rusa en España, segun su "Diario de Operaciones"* (Vol.1), Ministerio de Defensa, Madrid, 2007, 207pp.

— *Caza Rusa en España, segun su "Diario de Operaciones" Julio de 1938 a marzo de 1939*, (Vol.2) Ministerio de Defensa, Madrid, 2009, 253pp.

SALAS Larrazabal, J. y Madariaga Fernandez, R. de, *El Bimotor de Bombardeo Rapido Tupolev SB-2*, Minerterio de Defensa, Madrid, 2007, 255pp.

SANCHIS, M., *Alas Rojas sobre España*, Publicaciones Españoles, Madrid, 1956.

SAYOS, J., *Un Aviador de la Republica*, Craftair, Madrid, 1999, 229pp. A re-edition of the work listed under Milany, this time using the author's real name.

SCHROEDER, W., *Osterreichische Piloten im Spanischen Burgerkrieg*, in O.F.H. Nachrichten #4/90, Vienna, pp.4-8.

SEIDL, H., *Stalin's Eagles*, Schiffer Publishing Ltd, Atglen, PA, USA, 1998, 368pp.

SEMENOV, A.F., *Na Vzlete*, Voenizdat, Moscow, 1969, 215pp.

SEMENOV, G.K., *Parol' "Ispaniia,"* Khar'kov, "Prapor," 1976, 2nd edition. 336pp.

— *Tovarishch Sergio, Khar'kov, "Prapor,"* 1982, 2nd edition, 264pp.

— *Ispanskii Zakal, "Prapor," Khar'kov*, 1969, 198pp. Xerox via T. Sarbaugh

SHINGAREV, Sergei, *"Chatos" idut v ataku*, 2nd. edition Moscow, Moskovskii Rabochii, 1986, 287pp. (1971 edition 304pp.

SHUKMAN, H., (Ed.), *Stalin's Generals*, Grove Press, N.Y., 1993, 394pp.

SIRVENT CERRILLO, L. ESPAÑA, *La Guerra Aerea, los combates de un piloto de caza de la Republica*, self published, Madrid, 1993, 287pp.

SMIRNOV, BORIS, *Ispanskii Veter*, Sovetsnii Pisatel', Moscow, 1963.

— *Nebo Moei Molodosti*, Voenizdat, Moscow, 1990, 320pp. Xerox via Petr Lukes.

SMOLDAS, Z., *Ceskosloventsti Letci v Boji Proti Fasismu*, Nase Vijsko, Prague, 1987.

SNAJDR, MIROSLAV, *Soumrak Stihacich Dvouplosniku /1 Spanelsko 1936-1937*, Votobia, 1999, 335pp. */2 Spanelsko - severni bojiste 1937*, Fontana, 2005, 170pp.

SOKOLOV, V., *Krylbia u Nas Odni*, DOSAAF, Moscow, 1976, 158pp.

SOLIDARITY *International Solidarity with the Spanish Republic 1936-1939*, Progress Pub., Moscow, 1975.

SOLIDARNOST *Solidarnost' Narodov S Ispanskoi Respublikoi 1936-1939*, "Nauka," Moscow, 1972. Russian Edition of the above work, but has some spelling differences.

STEER, G.L., *The Tree of Gernika*, Hodder and Stoughton Ltd., London, 1938.

STUANI, C. and A., *Primo Gibelli*, Caravaggio, 1982.

SUKHACHEV, M.P., *Nebo Dlya Smel*ykh, Molodaya Gvapdiya, Moscow, 1979.

SUVENIROV, O.F., *Tragediya RKKA 1937-1938*, Terra, Moscow, 1998, 528pp.

TALON, V. *El Holocausto de Guernica*, Plaza & Janes, Barcelona, 1987, 326pp. + index.

TARAZONA, F., *Yo Fui Piloto de Caza Rojo*, Editorial San Martin, Madrid, 1974.

THORNBERRY, Robert S., *Andre Malraux et L'Espagne*, Librairie Droz, Geneve, 1977, 260pp.

TINKER, F.G., *Some Still Live*, Funk & Wagnalls, N.Y., 1938.

— *Flight Log from Spain*, xerox, Air & Space Museum, Washington, D.C.

TOLMACHEV, V.A., *Sovetskii Soiuz i Ispaniya: Opyt I Uroki Internatsional'noj Pomoshchi (1936-1939)*, Dissertatsiya, Leningrad, 1991, 284pp. Xerox via Gerald Howson.

U.S.S.R. *Aviatsiya i Kosmonavtika SSSR*, Ministerstva Obopony SSSR, Moscow, 1968, 599pp.

VARIOUS Authors, *Fighting side by side with Spanish patriots against fascism*, Novosti, Moscow, 1986, 76pp.

VARIOUS Authors, *V Nebe Kitaya 1937-1940*, Nauka, Moscow, 1980, 381pp.

VASILEVSKII, L., *Pages from a Hero's Biography*, Evgenii Savvich Ptukhin in Aviatsiia i Kosmonautika, September 1963, translation via RSA.

VMESTE s *Patriotami Ispanii, Politizdat Ukrainy*, Kiev, 1986, 334pp. Revised from an earlier edition. GORILOVSKOGO, L.L. (Editor).

— Earlier, shorter 1976 edition, same publication.

VODOP'YANOV, M.V., *Ural'ski Sokol*, Dosaaf, Moscow, 1964, via RSA.

VOLUNTEER, *The Organ of the Abraham Lincoln Brigade*, December 89, and May 90 issues.

VORONKOVA, I.IO., *Belarus' I Voina V Ispanii*, Belaruskaya Navuka, Minsk, 2009.

YAKOVLEV, A., *The Aim of a Lifetime*, Progress Pub., Moscow, 1972.

ZAKHAROV, G.N., *Povest' ob Istrebiteliakh*, DOSAAF, Moscow, 1977.

— Ya Istrebitel', (Voennye Memuary), Voenizdat, Moscow 1985 285pp

— "Des Chasseurs Sovietiques dans le Ciel D'Espagne," in *Icare* #130 pp.40-43.

ZIL'MANOVICH, D. IA., *Na Orbite Bol'shoi Zhizni.* IA.V. Smushkevich, Vilnius, "Mintis," 1971.

ZUGAZAGOITIA, J., *Guerra y Vicisitudes de los Españoles*, vol.2 Libreria Española, Paris, 1968.

September 1991 list of Soviet Volunteers killed in Spain, found at www.sgvavia.ru/forum/122-969-1 Memorialy Sobetskim Letchikam v Ispanii.